Scientific
Foundations
of Coaching

Russell R. Pate
University of South Carolina

Bruce McClenaghan
University of South Carolina

Robert Rotella
University of Virginia

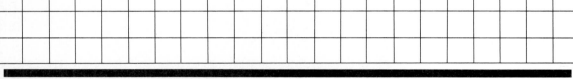

Scientific Foundations of Coaching

 **SAUNDERS COLLEGE PUBLISHING**   Philadelphia New York Chicago
San Francisco Montreal Toronto
London Sydney Tokyo Mexico City
Rio de Janeiro Madrid

Address orders to:
383 Madison Avenue
New York, NY 10017

Address editorial correspondence to:
West Washington Square
Philadelphia, PA 19105

Text Typeface: 10/12 Melior
Compositor: University Graphics, Inc.
Acquisitions Editor: John Butler
Project Editor: Diane Ramanauskas
Copyeditor: Kathleen McCullough
Managing Editor & Art Director: Richard L. Moore
Art/Design Assistant: Virginia A. Bollard
Text Design: William Boehm
Cover Design: William Boehm
Text Artwork: ANCO/Boston
Production Manager: Tim Frelick
Assistant Production Manager: Maureen Iannuzzi

Cover Credit: The coach is Carl M. Schnellenbach, of Ridley Senior
High School in Folsom, Pa. He was photographed while coaching his
wrestling team to his 250th career victory. This set a new record in
District I of the Pennsylvania Interscholastic Athletic Association.
Photography by Ken Kasper/Delaware County Daily Times.

Library of Congress Cataloging in Publication Data

Pate, Russell R.
    Scientific foundations of coaching.

    Includes bibliographies and index.

    1. Coaching (Athletics)   2. Sports—
Psychological aspects.   3. Sports—
Physiological aspects.
I. McClenaghan, Bruce A.   II. Rotella, Robert
J. III. Title.
GV711.P37   1984   796'.07'7   83-20117

ISBN 0-03-057961-9

Scientific Foundations of Coaching   ISBN 0-03-57961-9

3456   016   987654321

CBS COLLEGE PUBLISHING
Saunders College Publishing
Holt, Rinehart and Winston
The Dryden Press

**We dedicate this book
to our children:
Colin,
Johnna and Faris,
and
Casey Lauren**

Preface

This book is designed to present the scientific principles that constitute the basis for sound athletic coaching practices. The motivation to produce this volume began with the recognition of a strong worldwide trend toward implementation of certification programs for sports coaches. The American Alliance for Health, Physical Education, Recreation and Dance has published recommended guidelines for certification of coaches of school athletic teams. In recent years several states have adopted certification procedures for teachers who coach school sports. Numerous amateur sports organizations in the United States, Canada, and Europe have devised protocols for certifying coaches. In the United States, youth sports organizations have moved to upgrade the quality of the voluntary coaching services provided to young athletes. The certification criteria adopted or recommended by the various groups have, with consistency, indicated that coaches should demonstrate basic competencies in three scientific fields: sports psychology, biomechanics, and exercise physiology. These three applied sports sciences are the focus of this volume. It is our hope that the publication of this book will lend impetus to the trend toward improved academic preparation of sports coaches.

Our goal has been to produce a book that meets the needs of readers with diverse backgrounds and aims. We have assumed that the reader possesses some fundamental knowledge of biology and psychology. However, comprehension of the material in this book does not demand that the reader possess an extensive background in the basic sciences, human physiology, or psychology. We have attempted to produce a readable, understandable, practical summary of the key sports sciences. The only significant prerequisites needed to benefit from reading this book are possession of an interest in athletic coaching and/or sports performance, and an open, inquiring mind.

Many persons have been instrumental in the successful completion of this project. We are indebted to John Butler of Saunders College Publishing for his long-standing support of this publication. We express our appreciation to Dr. John Billing, University of North Carolina, Chapel Hill; Dr. Matthew Maetoza, Lock Haven State College; Dr. Thomas Meinhardt, Towson State University; and Dr. Dan Gould, Kansas State University, for their critical review of the manuscript. We thank June Lambert, Sandra Coppage, Jackie Boland, Arlene Robertson, and Nina Seaman for their conscientious clerical services in preparing the manuscript.

Finally, we wish to recognize the coaches who have impacted so importantly on our personal and professional development. For Robert Rotella: Frank Bizzarro of Rutland, VT; Jim Parmalee of Storrs, CT; Glen Thiel of Pennsylvania State University; and Nate Osur and Joseph Marrone of the University of Connecticut. For Bruce McClenaghan: Joel McKenzie, Tony Cera, Paul Kelley, and Jeff Holbert of Pompton Lakes, NJ; and Richard Walker and Dr. Michael Briglia of Glassboro State College. For Russell R. Pate: Vernon Cox of Springfield College; John Chew of Lockport, NY; and Robert Pate of Glastonbury, CT, who as both father and coach instilled in this author a love of sports and an appreciation for the joy of effort.

Russell R. Pate

Contents

Physiological Bases of Sports Performance

Credit: Photo courtesy of Linda Huber. From R. J. Sabock: *The Coach*, 2nd ed. Philadelphia. Saunders College Publishing, 1979.

The Scientific Approach to Coaching

1

Coaching is frequently perceived as one of the most glamorous and rewarding of all professions. Many coaches are deeply admired by their communities and sincerely respected by their athletes. Many coaches provide invaluable service to educational institutions and promote the healthy development of the young people whom they advise. Many coaches are true experts in human movement and perform throughout their careers as bona fide master teachers. Many coaches absolutely love their profession and would not exchange jobs with anyone. Many coaches constantly produce winning teams and champion athletes. Indeed, coaching can be an enormously enjoyable and rewarding occupation.

However, some persons who pursue a career in coaching find it to be neither enjoyable nor rewarding. Often, these individuals begin with an idealized image of coaching only to later become discouraged and disenchanted. The prospective coach must recognize that success does not await all who enter the coaching profession. As with any profession, coaching requires that the aspiring coach: (1) possess the basic interests and characteristics that are demanded by the profession, and (2) acquire the skills and knowledge that optimize the chances that success will be obtained. Failure is a likely result when a person enters the coaching profession without meeting these two criteria. This book deals primarily with the second of the aforementioned criteria. Its principle purpose is to provide the reader with an introduction to the three scientific disciplines that undergird sound athletic coaching practices. These three scientific fields are *sports psychology, biomechanics,* and *exercise physiology.*

In this first chapter, we shall define these scientific disciplines and describe how a working knowledge of the exercise sciences is employed by successful sport coaches.

The Knowledge Explosion in the Exercise Sciences

There may have been a time when the prospective coach needed no more than a desire to work with athletes and a fundamental knowledge of a specific sport. That time is long past. Today, successful coaches must possess an understanding of the scientific principles that explain and determine human athletic performance. In recent years, the scientific method has been applied to the study of sports in a major way. Thousands of scientists working in the field and in laboratories around the world have conducted studies designed to expand our knowledge of athletes and the factors that determine their performance levels.

The knowledge explosion in the exercise sciences has reached remarkable proportions. In the United States, many colleges and universities support research dedicated to the study of human movement. Many new research journals have been founded to accommodate the growing mass of research generated by legions of sport scientists. The content of books and journals directed to sports practitioners (e.g., coaches, trainers, sports medicine physicians) has become markedly more scientific than in the past. Perhaps most significantly, in recent years, the *practices* of many coaches have come to reflect the current state of knowledge in the exercise sciences.

As sports have become an increasingly important and visible part of American society, scientists from many scientific disciplines have utilized their talents to study athletes and athletic performance. To date, three basic sciences have spawned recognized subdisciplines directed to the study of sports. In the following paragraphs, we provide brief descriptions of these scientific fields.

Sports Psychology. Coaches have long recognized that mental attitudes can profoundly affect athletic performance. For many years, coaching books and journals have emphasized the need for coaches to instill in their athletes a proper mental outlook toward training and competition. However, only in recent years has the psychological aspect of athletic performance been subjected to serious scientific investigation. Psychology is that science that studies human behavior; sports psychology is a subdiscipline dedicated to the study of psychological phenomena in athletes and coaches. Specifically, sports psychologists attempt to describe the psychological characteristics of successful athletes and coaches and study the effects of various psychological treatments on the performance of athletes. Sports psychology is a relatively new field of investigation and consequently, to date, much of the study in this area has involved the application of accepted general principles of psychology to the behavior of athletes and coaches. However, sports psychology is rapidly developing its own respected body of knowledge. Sports psychologists have been particularly interested in the motivational phenomena that affect the performance of individual athletes and teams. Also, there has been considerable interest in the leadership characteristics of successful coaches and in the effects that stress can have on both coaches and athletes.

Biomechanics of Human Movement. Physics is the science that studies matter, energy, and motion. Biomechanics is a subdiscipline that involves the application of physics principles to the study of movement in living organisms. The interests of biomechanists are quite broad and, for example, include development of artificial limbs and organs. Sports biomechanics is concerned with the description of efficient, effective movement patterns in athletes. For example, biomechanists have used high-speed photography to study the movement patterns of successful baseball pitchers. The results of such studies provide information that can be used by coaches to perfect the techniques of their athletes. Also, biomechanists are interested in the forces that operate during performance of sports skills. Research of this sort has resulted in the development of vastly improved shoes for runners and joggers. These new shoes effectively absorb and distribute the forces that are transmitted to the leg during the contact phase of the running cycle. The application of computer technology in biomechanics promises to dramatically increase the volume of sport-related research in the coming years.

Exercise Physiology. Physiology is the study of the function of the human body. Exercise physiologists investigate the functions of the human body during exercise and observe how the body and bodily functions are altered by long-term exercise training. Exercise physiology is a well-established subdiscipline, having been a focus of research since early in the twentieth century. In recent years, the volume of exercise physiology research has mushroomed as a result of increased interest in the health benefits of regular exercise. Also, increased competitiveness in athletics has motivated exercise physiologists to explore new training methods and sports medicine procedures. Many exercise physiologists are interested in the metabolic systems that produce the energy needed to perform vigorous exercise. Others study the cardiovascular and muscular adaptations that result from various forms of exercise training. Still others observe how exercise performance is affected by various environmental conditions (e.g., heat, cold, high altitude) and by certain treatments and substances. Past exercise physiology research has done much to enhance the safety of athletes and has produced markedly improved training procedures. Future research in this field promises to provide a more precise knowledge of the physiological factors that affect performance in the many specific sporting activities.

The Scientific Approach to Coaching

Many established coaches would argue that successful coaching is as much an *art* as a *science*. This suggests that coaching demands creativity and individual interpretation of people and situations. The authors of this book agree totally with this contention—indeed, successful coaches must develop their own unique approach to coaching and must, through experience, develop a "sixth sense" that guides them in making some decisions. However, the artistic, creative aspect of coaching must rest upon a solid foundation of science. No level of creativity will produce success if coaching practices are scientifically unsound. The optimal coach is one who can be imaginative (yes, artistic) in the implementation of a scientifically based sports program.

The Scientific Method

Science is a branch of study involving observation and classification of facts. A goal of science is the establishment of general laws that can subsequently be utilized to predict the occurrence of natural phenomena. For example, the science of physics has established that a force called *gravity* causes a free-falling object to be accelerated toward the center of the earth at a predictable rate (32 feet per second). Using the law of gravity, we can predict with great certainty the time that will be required for an object, such as a baseball, to fall to the earth from a specified height.

Principles such as the law of gravity are identified through the use of a procedure called the *scientific method*. The components of the scientific method are presented in Table 1.1. The many scientific fields differ primarily in the topics that are studied and the procedures employed in collecting data (i.e., making observations). However, all reputable scientific investigations have one common characteristic and that is *objectivity*. Objectivity means that a study's observations and conclusions are not unduly affected by the personal beliefs of the individual investigator. True scientists always report their findings exactly as they were observed and never allow conclusions to be prejudiced by their own feelings. Objectivity is the major factor that differentiates science from opinion.

In coaching and other professions, it is common for successful individuals to be asked to explain the reasons for their success. The responses to such inquiries should be viewed

Table 1.1: Components of the Scientific Method

The scientific method employs an established set of procedures in solving problems. These procedures are as follows:

I. Statement of a Problem or Question

The first step in any scientific study is to pose a researchable question. This question should be stated clearly and concisely.

II. Advancement of a Logical Hypothesis

A researchable question may have several feasible answers. However, a study of the existing body of knowledge may suggest that one of the possible answers is more tenable than the others. A hypothesis is a statement of the investigator's belief regarding the most likely answer to a research question.

III. Testing of the Hypothesis

The essence of any scientific study is the selection of the methods to be used in testing the hypothesis. These methods should address the following:
A. *Identification of phenomena to be observed.* The human behaviors and traits and/or other variables to be observed should be identified.
B. *Methods of observation.* Measurement, observation and all data collection procedures should be described. All methods should be valid (i.e., accurate) and reliable (i.e., reproducible).
C. *Designation of subject pool.* The population from which subjects will be drawn and the methods for selection of subjects must be designated.
D. *Controlled observation.* Methods should be employed which minimize or eliminate the effects of extraneous influences.
E. *Data analysis.* Statistical or other procedures that will be used to analyze data should be selected.
F. *Decision making.* An answer to the research question should be selected on the basis of predefined criteria. The hypothesis will be accepted or rejected in accordance with these criteria.

with skepticism, since they are seldom based on objective, scientific study. For example, over the years many successful athletes have ingested vitamin supplements and have claimed that this has improved their performances. However, controlled scientific investigations have failed to reinforce this conclusion. It is undoubtedly true that some athletes have concur-rently ingested vitamin supplements and generated successful performances. But this does not imply a causative relationship between the two happenings. Thus, both coaches and athletes should maintain a healthy skepticism about claims that are advanced in the absence of truly scientific support.

Coaching and the Sports Sciences

In many fields of endeavor two types of persons work cooperatively to advance the quality of some service or product. These two occupational categories are the *scientists* and the *professionals*. A scientist is one who conducts investigations and advances the body of knowledge in one of the scientific disciplines (e.g., chemistry, physics, biology); a professional is one who delivers a service or produces a product and does so in a manner consistent with an established set of standards (e.g., law, medicine, teaching, engineering).

As suggested in the previous paragraphs, it seems important that coaches adopt a scientific attitude toward their occupation. However, this does not mean that coaches are expected to *be* scientists. In the sporting world, this is the task of exercise physiologists, biomechanists, sports psychologists, and others. These sports scientists are responsible for expanding and integrating the scientifically established body of knowledge related to athletes and athletic performance. It is also expected that these scientists will present and interpret their research findings to interested professionals in an understandable fashion.

A coach is a professional whose occupation is to assist athletes and athletic teams in the enhancement of sports performances. Since coaching is a profession, coaches are expected to provide their services in accordance with accepted professional standards. One critical professional standard dictates that services be provided in a manner consistent with *current* scientific knowledge of the field. Thus, it is essential that coaches be active consumers of the research generated by sports scientists. In order to optimize performances, guarantee safety, and promote well-being in athletes coaches must constantly update and modify their coaching practices. Such modification can occur only if coaches: (1) possess an understanding of established principles in each of the relevant scientific fields, and (2) regularly seek out new knowledge in the sports sciences. Coaches need not be scientists in the strictest sense, but to qualify as professionals, coaches must be active consumers and appliers of scientific information.

Characteristics of a Scientific Coach

Receptivity to New Ideas. A key characteristic of successful coaches is willingness to consider new ideas. As previously discussed, knowledge of the sports sciences is expanding rapidly. Therefore, coaches who close their minds to new information can expect their coaching practices to become antiquated within a very short period of time. Coaches who approach their work with a scientific orientation actively seek out new information and strive to modify their coaching practices in accordance with current knowledge. Contemporary coaches must avoid the adoption of a static, tradition-bound approach to their work. Those who unquestioningly accept traditional techniques and who reflexively reject new concepts are unlikely to succeed in coaching.

The Search for Magic Answers. Occasionally, in the world of science an investigator unexpectedly discovers a fact that rapidly revolutionizes a professional field. However, such occurrences are extremely rare. Far more typically, scientific knowledge is advanced through a gradual and logical series of observations and experiments. The vast majority of Nobel prizes awarded in the sciences have been won by persons whose work built significantly, yet logically, on the work of predecessors. There are very few truly revolutionary

discoveries in the sciences. Therefore, the scientific coach should be very skeptical of a claim that some new treatment or practice will "completely revolutionize" a particular athletic activity. This suggestion that coaches should be cautious and discerning in their evaluation of information is not inconsistent with the previous recommendation that they be receptive to new ideas. Coaches should be open to new information, but they should carefully evaluate such information before accepting it as fact. In particular, one should evaluate the credentials of a person who is making the claim and should assess the magnitude and quality of the research upon which the claim is based. Specifically, the coach can have considerable confidence in information that is presented by a reputable exercise scientist whose research findings are published in a recognized scientific journal. In contrast, one should be very cautious in interpreting information advanced by commercial organizations that fail to provide truly scientific support for their claims. Remember, there probably are no magic answers to the problems that confront athletes and coaches. If a new idea sounds too good to be true, it may be just that!

Evaluation of New Techniques. Although the volume of research in the sports sciences has expanded greatly in recent years, exercise scientists will never answer the innumerable, sports-specific questions that arise in coaching. For example, a high school tennis coach, having observed that several successful tennis professionals employ a two-handed backhand stroke, might logically wonder whether or not that approach is optimal for all or most players. In seeking an answer to this question an appropriate first step would be to determine if any controlled, scientific research has been done on this topic. One might find such research data by consulting respected teaching professionals, by scanning the tennis magazines for references to such research, or by directly searching the related scientific journals. Frequently, such a search will be fruitless because the question involved is so specific that no scientist has ever directly studied the issue.

In the absence of a definitive research-based solution to such a situation, the coach may be left to evaluate the new technique himself or herself. While it is usually impractical for the coach to conduct a rigorous scientific study, the scientific method should be used in analyzing and solving (at least tentatively) day-to-day coaching problems. For example, a first step would be to answer the following question: Is the new idea consistent with accepted fundamental principles in the related scientific fields? To continue with the example of the tennis backhand stroke, the coach would ask: Is the two-handed stroke consistent with the accepted principles of motor skill learning and biomechanics? If the answer to this question is "no," then the concept may not warrant further attention. However, if this question is answered affirmatively, additional consideration is appropriate. It should be emphasized at this point that the aforementioned question could be answered only by the coach who possesses a fundamental understanding of the exercise sciences.

If we assume that the two-handed backhand stroke is apparently sound biomechanically and could be learned by young tennis players, the next step would be to experiment. The coach might randomly assign several team members to learn and utilize the two-handed stroke (note: It would seem wise to conduct such an experiment in the off-season). During the experimental period the coach would systematically observe the players in an attempt to answer previously designated questions such as: Can the players master the new technique within a reasonable period of time?, How effective is the stroke in terms of accuracy and power?, Does learning the new stroke have any positive or adverse effects on other aspects of the player's game?, Are the effects of the new stroke consistent among all players or is the stroke best suited to certain types of players? In making these observations and in drawing any

conclusions the coach should endeavor to be as objective as possible. Based on the conclusions of this "study," our hypothetical coach would decide whether or not to recommend the use of the two-handed backhand stroke to some, all, or none of his or her players.

This approach to solving realistic coaching problems does not constitute "research," in the strict sense of the term, and will never generate scientifically respected knowledge. Certainly, the "study" described contains many flaws in research design (e.g., no control group, small number of subjects, no rigidly applied data collection procedures). However, such a process is based on the scientific method and is an acceptable, useful way for the coach to answer some practical questions. Certainly, such a procedure is preferable to adopting practices on the basis of tradition or totally unsubstantiated recommendations.

A Day in the Life of a Scientific Coaching Staff

Coaches may occasionally be called upon to utilize the scientific method to produce new information. However, a far more common practice of successful coaches is the use of previously established scientific information in the design and execution of coaching practices. In this section, we endeavor to demonstrate, through hypothetical examples, how we feel coaches should employ scientific information in their day-to-day activities. In the following passages we present fictional, yet realistic, examples of how the coaching staff of a large high school might use scientific information in the execution of its professional duties.

Monday, 6:30 a.m.

Swim coach Jim Finn welcomes his team to the first of its two daily training sessions. As the athletes arrive at the pool to begin their pre-training stretching routine, Coach Finn systematically observes and chats briefly with as many of the swimmers as possible. He notes that one of his most promising sophomores, a talented female free-styler, does not look well this morning. She appears pale and her eyes are slightly bloodshot. Coach Finn inquires as to how she is feeling and learns that she has contracted a head cold. Remembering that the risk of "staleness" is high in swimmers and recognizing that a heavy training session could excessively stress this athlete, the coach instructs her to complete a light warm-up and to take the rest of the day off from training.

Tuesday, 3:30 p.m.

Karen Fleet, women's track coach, is approached by one of her middle distance runners. The athlete has been experiencing pain in the knee area and today reports that the pain has become so severe as to prevent her from running normally. Coach Fleet examines the athlete and asks her to describe specifically where the pain is located and the circumstances under which the pain occurs. She then calls the team physician and, using her knowledge of functional anatomy, explains that her athlete is experiencing chronic pain in the tendon of the rectus femoris muscle (quadriceps muscle group) at its insertion into the patella (knee cap). The pain, she reports, is quite severe when the knee joint is extended against resistance. The physician recommends that the athlete rest for two days, perform moderate static stretching of the quadriceps muscle group, and then resume training at a reduced level. The coach relays this advice to the athlete. Also, recognizing that fast running involves forceful eccentric contractions of the quadriceps muscle group, Coach Fleet directs the athlete to avoid sprint running and jumping for at least the next week.

Wednesday, 4:00 p.m.

Women's field hockey coach Denise Southworth's team is loaded with talent but is pres-

ently bogged down in a three-game losing streak. The team members are discouraged and are losing confidence in themselves quickly. Coach decides it is time to do something special to get the team moving in a positive direction. After seating the team in a circle, she reminds them they are developing a negative outlook and are beginning to doubt themselves. Each player is asked to state two very positive characteristics of their team. Her plan is intended to get the players to focus on the team's positive aspects. When this session ends a half hour later, a more positive and enthusiastic attitude begins to emerge. Coach Southworth then surprises her team with a 15-minute highlight film in which she has captured the team's best plays from their previous games. Her intent is to show them what they are capable of doing and to get them to think of themselves as successfully executing in competition rather than worrying about playing poorly and "blowing" good opportunities.

Thursday, 3:00 p.m.

Golf coach Tom Green meets a promising sophomore prospect at the driving cage. The coach's primary goal on this day is to begin determining whether or not this athlete should switch to driving clubs that have longer shafts than those that he used the previous season. Coach Green is somewhat uncertain because, although the athlete has grown 2 to 3 inches in height during the past year, he does not appear to have gained a proportional amount of weight or muscular strength. The coach knows that, in biomechanical terms, a longer club will be beneficial since velocity of the club head will be greater at a particular angular velocity. However, if the athlete is not strong enough to control the longer club, accuracy and even club velocity could suffer. To solve this dilemma, the coach has decided to instruct the athlete to experiment for several days with a longer driver while he carefully observes the mechanical aspects of the swing as well as the accuracy and distance of the shots. During this initial practice, the coach focuses his attention entirely on the fundamental mechanical aspects of the swing. After five or six practices the coach plans to evaluate club speed by filming the athlete while he swings both the longer and shorter clubs.

Friday, 10:00 a.m.

Head football coach Joe Conlon, whose principal occupation is teaching history, uses his free period to plan his team's off-season training program for the next two weeks. Recognizing that success in football depends largely on high levels of anaerobic power, Coach Conlon designs a program that emphasizes development of muscular strength. However, in surveying the team's statistics from the previous season, he has noted that his team was outscored by opponents 2–1 in the fourth quarter. In response, the coach elects to place greater emphasis on development of cardiorespiratory endurance and, thus, each athlete's training program includes at least 20 to 25 minutes of continuous running on three days per week.

Friday, 7:15 p.m.

Basketball coach Dean Knight is preparing to enter the locker room prior to the school's big rivalry game against its cross-city opponent. The game will determine the league as well as the city championship. Coach has noticed all week that his players are anxious and really "up" for the game. He feels his team is capable of winning if they play their best and if he coaches his best. But he also knows there are some doubts in his players' minds. They remember that they have been beaten by the opponent the last five times they have played. Coach also realizes he has a team consisting mainly of sophomores and juniors.

Coach Knight decides he must enter the locker room projecting a very positive attitude. He must demonstrate his complete confidence in his team. He realizes that he must prevent his already aroused and anxious team from getting "too high" or "psyched-out." Coach decides to remain calm and simply emphasize key fundamentals and strategies that his team will execute during the game. He knows his players care deeply, and that they are taking the game seriously. They know they have a tough challenge ahead of them. He does not need to remind them of how skilled the opponent is or how important the game will be. Coach intends to get their minds on the task and to avoid worry or fear of possible negative outcomes. He knows the players, like himself, are somewhat frustrated over recent losses to this team and must allow this to help rather than hinder motivation and concentration. Coach Knight decides to end his talk with one final thought, which he has emphasized daily in practice, "Concentrate, be patient, and execute like you have been doing every day in practice and in your other games. This is what we have been preparing for—now let's go enjoy reaping the rewards of our preparation."

Purposes and Contents of This Book

This book is designed to provide the reader with an introduction to the three scientific disciplines that relate most directly to athletic coaching: sports psychology, biomechanics, and exercise physiology. A totally comprehensive discussion of each of these exercise sciences is beyond the scope of this text. Rather, the intent is to present information that falls in two main categories. First, in each scientific area we shall provide background material that forms the foundation upon which human athletic performance is based. Second, we shall address scientific topics that have direct applicability to the coaching situation. It is our strong belief that successful coaching depends on a mastery of both types of information.

The initial section of the book is dedicated to sports psychology. In this section, we present current information regarding the factors that affect motivation of athletes and athletic teams. Also, we shall discuss the leadership characteristics that contribute to successful coaching. Athletic competition is implicitly stressful and, therefore, successful athletic performance and successful coaching careers depend on the ability to deal effectively with stress. Consequently, we shall dedicate one chapter to the effects of stress on sports performances and another chapter to the methods by which coaches can cope with the stress associated with their profession.

The book's second section focuses on the biomechanics of human movement and is intended to promote an understanding of the anatomical, mechanical, and developmental factors that affect human performance. We shall describe the anatomy of the skeletal and muscular systems of the human body and will summarize the laws of physics that determine the nature of human movement. The processes of growth and development profoundly affect athletic ability and, therfore, we dedicate a chapter to physical changes associated with aging. In addition, we provide a discussion of the methods that coaches can use to critically and systematically assess the mechanical aspects of an athlete's performance.

Exercise physiology is addressed in the final section of the book. This section begins with summaries of the fundamental concepts of muscle and cardiorespiratory exercise physiology. Emphasis is given to the metabolic processes that provide the energy needed to support vigorous exercise. Next, individual chapters are dedicated to the nutritional and environmental factors that affect athletic performance. Finally, a series of three chapters apply the principles of exercise physiology to the process of conditioning athletes for optimal athletic performance.

No textbook can realistically hope to provide the reader with all the important information about a topic as broad as "sports science." However, an introductory book, such as this one, can expose a reader to new areas of knowledge, can refocus a reader's image of a professional field, and can stimulate a reader to seek more information. The authors of this book hope that the reader will come to share their fascination with the scientific foundations of sports performance. Only by continuously seeking out new scientific information can the reader hope to build a successful coaching career and to extend that career into the twenty-first century.

Recommended Readings

Burke, E.J., (Ed.) *Toward an Understanding of Human Performance.* 2nd ed. Ithaca, New York: Mouvement Publications, 1980.

Fisher, A.C. *Psychology of Sport.* Palo Alto, California: Mayfield Publishing Co., 1976.

Fox, E.L., and Mathews, D.K. *The Physiological Basis of Physical Education and Athletics.* 3rd ed. Philadelphia: Saunders College Publishing, 1981.

Hay, J.G. *The Biomechanics of Sports Techniques.* 2nd ed. Englewood Cliffs, New Jersey: Prentice-Hall, Inc., 1978.

Sabock, R.J. *The Coach.* 2nd ed. Philadelphia: Saunders College Publishing, 1979.

Thomas, J.R. *Youth Sports Guide for Coaches and Parents.* Washington, D.C., AAHPER Publications, 1977.

Thomas, V. *Sport and Science.* Boston: Little, Brown and Company, 1970.

Credit: University of Virginia Sports Information.

Leadership in Coaching: On Becoming a Great Leader

2

Imagine a team of athletes without any one person directing and coordinating their efforts. With no overall direction a team may have great difficulty in coordinating activity and may become conflict riddled and demoralized. In the absence of a leader, there may be little agreement on goal orientation or on how goals can be best attained. Clearly, leadership is vital to the effective functioning of a team. The purposes of this chapter are to discuss the various styles of leadership that are frequently employed by coaches and to recommend certain leadership techniques that can contribute to successful coaching.

Fundamentals of Leadership
A Definition of Leadership

Most people have a general notion of what is meant by the term "leadership." Historically, a number of different definitions have been popular in the scientific literature. Consider for a moment the way in which you use the term "leadership." Think, for example, of a classmate or friend who seems to be a leader.

You may think of leadership in terms of an *individual's characteristics*. For years it was assumed that leaders were born with innate traits that made them successful leaders. Supposedly, innate traits such as physical stature, energy levels, tone of voice, and other personality traits such as intelligence, aggressiveness, dominance, and dependability predisposed individuals to become leaders. Inherent in this view was the assumption that people possessing these characteristics would always be leaders and others would be followers.

An alternate view defines leadership in functional terms. You may think of a leader as a person who performs *certain functions*. For example, leaders can be seen as individuals who can effectively organize, control, and direct the work of others. These responsibilities have been labeled "formal leadership functions" in classic management theories.

Another definition of leadership, based upon human relations theories, involves the *individual's relationship with a group*. In this view, leaders are individuals who are sympathetic to the personal problems of followers, who support subordinates emotionally, and who listen to and allow followers to have a voice in the decision-making process.

Finally, a leader may be thought of as *an individual who possesses the highest level of skill for the task at hand*. The basic premise of this contemporary view is that leadership is situationally specific. A leader in one situation is not necessarily an effective leader in another situation. An individual who is an effective leader in one situation must be flexible in order to be effective in other situations. Success in coaching one sport or at one school or level may not guarantee success in another sport, at another school, or at another level.

Each of these views emphasize a different aspect of leadership. Yet, all of them include one common element: a leader is *someone who exerts more influence than the other members of the group*. Indeed, this is the definition that has been used most frequently in scientific literature.

Leadership Styles

One does not need to observe too many coaches to realize that there are various leadership styles that are successful. Some leaders appear to be cold and indifferent, while others are warm and caring. Some allow their subordinates autonomy; others supervise very closely. The list of factors is endless; but in the present context, emphasis will be placed on two aspects of leadership style: (1) authoritarian versus democratic leadership styles and (2) people-centered versus task-centered styles.

Authoritarian Versus Democratic Leadership Styles. For many years researchers have attempted to determine whether a democratic or an authoritarian style of leadership is more effective. Typically, authoritarian coaches: (1)

use authority to control others, (2) issue orders to others in the group, (3) try to have things done according to their beliefs, (4) act in an impersonal manner, (5) punish members who disobey or deviate, (6) decide upon the division of labor, (7) determine how work should be done, and (8) judge the soundness of ideas. Democratic coaches, on the other hand, generally (1) act in a friendly, personal manner, (2) allow the group as a whole to plan, (3) allow group members to interact with one another without permission, (4) accept suggestions, and (5) talk only a little more than the average group members. Figure 2.1 provides a graphic comparison of the authoritarian and democratic styles of leadership.

In studying leadership styles one should realize that a leader does not have to exist at one extreme or the other. A particular leadership style may be used to varying degrees in different situations. Many coaches display combinations of authoritarian and democratic styles. There are distinct reasons for displaying either leadership style and there are advantages and disadvantages to either style.

Many coaches lead in an authoritarian manner because: (1) they perceive their role as authoritarian, (2) they are persons who have high needs for control of others and have gravitated to sports to fulfill their needs, (3) stressful leadership situations that arise in most sports call for control of the participants by the coach, and (4) certain athletes seek authoritarian behavior from their coaches, so coaches act to meet the athletes' expectations. Thus, it is understandable that authoritarian leadership is very common in athletics.

Available research indicates that the authoritarian leadership style is advantageous in certain circumstances. This research indicates that an authoritarian style may be preferred when speed and action are urgently needed. Likewise, with larger groups involved with complex tasks that are perceived as important, authoritarian styles of leadership may be particularly advantageous. An authoritarian style may also allow time to be used more effectively and may

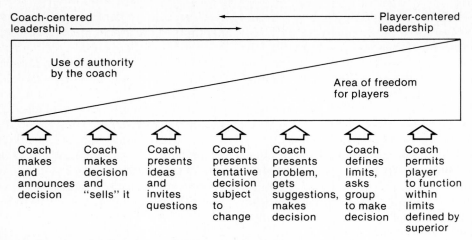

Figure 2.1 Tannenbaum and Schmidt's model of leadership behavior. (From Robert Tannenbaum and Warren H. Schmidt: How to choose a leadership pattern. *Harvard Business Review,* May–June 1973. Copyright 1973 by the President and Fellows of Harvard College, all rights reserved.)

allow insecure athletes to feel more secure and protected in a stressful situation.

There are, however, some marked weaknesses in the authoritarian style. In general, more work is produced, but it is of less quality than that produced by democratic leaders. Team members tend to display less satisfaction and lower morale.

Democratic leaders also have reasons for leading in their preferred style. They believe that: (1) each individual exists as a social being, (2) each individual functions as a whole, complete person, not as a series of parts, (3) each individual has goals, purposes, and values that motivate behavior, and (4) a democratic style will lead to increased cohesiveness and member satisfaction. Coaches who utilize a democratic style typically believe that their style will most efficiently allow for the educational development of their athletes. Great importance is attached to independent thinking and the carry-over value of sports. It is implied that interpersonal interactions and communication are keys to success in sports as well as in later life.

The democratic style also has its weaknesses. In the short run, it may not be the most effective way to utilize time. This may be crucial to coaches who have only two weeks to prepare a team for the first contest. As compared with authoritarian leadership, democratic leadership may lead to lower levels of aggression, a trait that may be important in some sports. Finally, a democratic style may be ineffective when quick decisions must be made and accepted.

In summary, it is clear that there are advantages and disadvantages to either leadership style. Most successful leaders in sports do not exist totally at one extreme or the other. They utilize the advantages of both styles when it is best for accomplishing the task and for promoting team morale and development. This means that successful coaches may adopt an authoritarian leadership style during practice sessions and during competition, particularly closely contested competitions. They may, however, be very democratic and humanistic before or after scheduled practice sessions, in the off-season, or during relaxing breaks during practice sessions. Successful coaches adopt a flexible leadership style that will allow them to fufill various coaching roles.

People-Centered Versus Task-Oriented Leadership Styles. The second aspect of leadership that must be understood pertains to whether successful leaders are people-centered or task-oriented (see Figure 2.2). The people-centered coaches place primary emphasis on fulfilling the personal needs of their athletes. In contrast, task-oriented coaches tend to focus more exclusively on winning competitions.

A number of research studies indicate that the preferred leadership style is dependent upon the particular situation in question. One clear way in which situations differ is in the degree to which they are favorable to the leader. It has been suggested that three characteristics of group situations determine how favorable it is to leadership: (1) *the leader's personal relationship with the group* (the extent to which the leader is liked and respected), (2) *the task structure* (the extent to which the work roles of the group members are spelled out in detail), and (3) *the leader's legitimate power* (the extent to which the leader has access to rewards and punishments for the members of his group).

Although there is a need for more study, the bulk of research suggests that the task-oriented approach is preferred whenever the situation is very favorable or very unfavorable to the leader. If the leader initially has the support of the group, the task is clear, and the leader has a lot of power the group may prefer a task-oriented leader. Similarly, in situations that are extremely unfavorable to leadership, such as one in which the leader has a bad relationship with the other members of the group, the task is vague, and the leader has little official power, a task-oriented leader would also be more effective. In the latter case, the situation is so bad the leader would have to be primarily concerned about the task in order to get anything done.

However, if the situation is moderately favorable, a person-centered leader would be more effective than the task-oriented leader. For example, in a situation in which the leader's relationship with his subordinates is relatively poor, the task is structured, and the leader's power position is strong, a person-centered leader would try to develop better relationships with subordinates. Given this situation, a task-oriented leader would be less effective because he/she would tend to overlook relationship building.

Therefore, it appears that both task-oriented and people-centered leaders can be effective, provided they are placed in the right situation. People-centered leaders would do best in a situation of medium difficulty. Task-oriented leaders would do best in either very difficult or very easy assignments.

Prior to concluding this discussion, it must be mentioned that some researchers argue that maximal effectiveness in leadership is attained only when leaders are highly concerned about both tasks and people. It is possible to focus on both.

Certainly, sports contain many of the features considered favorable to leaders. It appears that the ideal would be for coaches to be task-oriented with a special emphasis on being person-centered in situations in which it is possible to interact with their athletes.

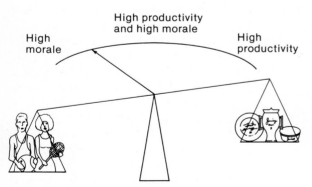

High productivity and high morale

High morale

High productivity

Figure 2.2 Balancing concern for players and concern for winning. (Adapted for P.M. Williams and D.J. Wassenaar: *Leadership*, San Jose: California. Lansford Publishing Co., 1975. Reprinted with permission of the publisher.)

In general, leaders who are too player-oriented place too much emphasis on human relations, which does not necessarily lead to high morale or team success. Coaches who are too task-oriented fail to manage interpersonal conflicts and as a result their teams suffer. Often, they turn players off owing to their over-emphasis on winning. Effective coaches learn to strike a balance between being task-oriented or player-oriented. Their leadership style fluctuates as it must for effectiveness rather than because it is their preferred orientation. They are flexible and their leadership style fluctuates as it must to be effective. The best coaches are not locked into a single leadership style.

Can Coaches Be Too Athlete-Oriented?

It is indeed possible to become so concerned with meeting all of the needs of athletes that coaches can completely lose sight of team goals. Coaches need to find a way to meet individual needs while still accomplishing the predetermined team goal. This is a most important challenge for coaches. It is a major reason that sports have been so strongly valued by our society as a training ground for achievement in adult life.

Coaches, particularly at the higher levels, who meet only *interpersonal needs* at the expense of team tasks are as ineffectual as ruthless coaches who meet only task needs. Frequently, coaches who focus excessively on athlete needs have *an extreme need to be needed*. They may be responding primarily to their need to be needed and may overlook the athlete's needs. Such coaches are self-centered and narrow-minded power hungry individuals who lead with a strong authoritarian style owing to their need for power.

It is noteworthy that coaches who are dominated by the need to be needed often believe that power hungry coaches are narrow-minded and selfish. Power-seeking coaches view coaches who need to be needed as weak and ineffective. Both groups somehow fail to rec-

ognize that the needs that they leave unfulfilled are important. One type believes that powerful leadership from above is the only way to coach. The other believes that interpersonal needs and player-coach rapport is the secret to coaching success. *Great coaches recognize that success in coaching demands the fulfillment of both of these needs.*

Coaches who are dominated by the need to be needed may have perceptual blind spots. These coaches fail to recognize that, despite its humane qualities, their way is not realistic for effective team performance. Too often, coaches with this tendency develop a dependency on their athletes that is great for meeting the coach's needs but leaves athletes without the ability to function independently. Athletes coached in this way may fail to grow or adjust to life without their coach or when they must play for very different coaches. With this possible result, one must admit that there are serious weaknesses in coaches dominated by the need to be needed.

Communication for Leaders

Many of the greatest coaches in sports possess a tremendous ability to build a close bond between leader and followers. Some have suggested that this bond is a result of a trait labeled "charisma." It has been argued that it is charisma that allows coaches to convince their athletes that they can overcome any obstacle.

Coaches who achieve success through the charismatic nature of their personalities all have one characteristic in common. They all lead from *within* the framework of the team rather than from *above*. They communicate with their athletes and with their assistant coaches. They believe that communication is crucial to team success.

Increase Awareness

A first step in improving communication is to increase self-awareness. Growth will not occur in the absence of sensitivity to strengths and weaknesses related to communication skills. To help in this process coaches should attempt to answer, as honestly as possible, the following questions.

1. How would you feel about playing for a coach who led exactly as you do?
2. What are your five major strengths and five major weaknesses as a coach?
3. What have you done to improve your ability to communicate with your athletes or other coaches within the last two months?
4. What were your major complaints of coaches for whom you played? Did you ever complain or find your coach making decisions that were irrational or intolerable? If you find that in many ways you have imitated this coach, have you improved upon the strategies that upset you when you were an athlete? Or do you have a new insight into the reason that your coach behaved the way he/she did? If so, have you attempted to explain this perspective to your athletes so they will understand rather than be frustrated?
5. When an athlete comes to you with a suggestion concerning some aspect of your coaching style, do you begin defending yourself before really listening to and accurately evaluating the athlete's suggestions?
6. What is the biggest challenge facing you as a coach?
7. What do athletes get out of playing for you?
8. Have you asked any of your athletes if they agree with your response to question number 7?
9. Can you think of anything more important than your continuing to improve the coaches and athletes on your team?

Coaches desirous of maximal success must learn to understand themselves more fully. There is a fine line between coaches having so much confidence in themselves that they place all the blame for failure or team dissension on the players and coaches having so little confidence in themselves that they take all the blame themselves and begin second-guessing their ability to coach successfully.

Coaches should consider their motives whenever any important decision is made. Will the decision be made solely for the purpose of protecting the coaches and their egos? Will it be made to avoid the potential embarrassment associated with changing a well established leadership style? Will it be made in order to ensure that all players will like the coach? Or will the decision be made because it is in the best interest of all members of the team—including players and coaches?

Making coaching decisions in the latter manner will improve effectiveness. If a coach takes only personal needs and concerns into account, effectiveness will not be maximized. A comfortable blending of the needs of athletes and coaches will lead to the optimal motivation and performance of the team.

Communication Demands Trust

Optimal communication between the team and the coach cannot occur without complete trust. In this context, *trust is a perception by athletes that their coach would never do anything that was not in their best interest.* Trust is not something that is given automatically. It must be *earned* by a coach's behavior. In the ideal situation trust becomes a two-way street with coaches and athletes having complete trust in each other.

Great coaches realize that trust does not mean that there will always be agreement with decisions that they make. But when their decisions are made, the best interests of the athletes and their goals are considered first and foremost. Great coaches constantly ask themselves: "Is this decision in the best interest of the athletes?" "Will the athletes perceive this decision as being in their best interest?" "If not, why not?" "How can I help them to understand that it is in their *long-term best interest* despite their inability to see it as such at the present time?" "Should I be trusted?" "Do my athletes all behave as though they trust me?" "How can I continue to be trusted?" "Am I always honest with my players and am I always there to help when they need me?"

The majority of athletes behave up to the level to which they are trusted or act down to the level to which they are distrusted. There will of course be exceptions. Coaches must have confidence in their ability to develop trust and should respond with understanding and increased trust when their trust is violated. *If repeated violations occur it may be necessary to sit down with individual athletes and discuss the importance of trust and the potential consequences of repeated violations of trust.* Coaches must realize that many athletes have had an abundance of past experiences with coaches and others that have not reinforced the development of trust.

A certain level of maturity is needed for coaches to be capable of fostering trust. Without maturity coaches can easily allow their leadership style to become overly influenced by their ego. All coaches have ego involvement. This in itself is not debilitating, but when ego needs cause coaches to reach mainly for satisfaction of their own personal needs above the needs of athletes, outstanding leadership cannot occur. Great coaches recognize the natural human tendency to respond in an emotional rather than a rational manner. Great coaches constantly attempt to maintain control over ego needs and in so doing develop trust in their athletes. Great coaches know that this approach will lead to increased satisfaction of the ego needs of all concerned, including coaches.

Often, coaches assume that there is a conflict between: (1) developing trust and controlling the ego, and (2) being tough and disciplined. This assumption is incorrect. Great coaches usually have disciplined teams with clear and well-defined roles, rules, and responsibilities. But great coaches communicate a feeling of trust and respect by *avoiding the desire to always be right.* Rather than becoming egocentric in their decisions, they believe that it is all right to reverse or modify a decision when the available evidence indicates that the original deci-

sion was not correct. Coaches who are lacking in confidence often feel that reversing a decision would result in a lack of respect or a blow to their ego. They respond emotionally by defending themselves rather than doing what is necessary for the good of the team and *the coach.*

It must be mentioned that we are not recommending flighty or unstable coaching decisions. Such behavior could certainly lead to a lack of respect and questioned leadership. Much advance thought must be put into decisions. But if coaches know that a decision has been made that could work against team success, they must be willing to admit the error and correct it. This attitude will develop trust and enhance team effectiveness.

Listening: An Important Aspect of Communication

Communication is a two-way process. It includes speaking to and listening to others. Too often, coaches appear to think that they are always supposed to do the speaking and athletes should always do the listening. *Great coaches learn when and how to speak to and listen to their athletes.*

Communicating with athletes should be a regular part of any coach's responsibility. It should *not* occur only when athletes are in trouble or have done something wrong. When this is the case it is likely that little real communication will occur. When coaches lead by *episode,* the athlete in question often responds emotionally and resists the coach's efforts to communicate. The athlete may resent the coach's comments and either let them go in one ear and out the other, or seek revenge upon the coach at some later point in time.

A crucial time for fostering coach-player communication is a couple of weeks after the completion of the regular season. The two-week time period immediately following the last game of the season may be used for two purposes: (1) a rest and evaluation period for the coach, and (2) a meeting with graduating seniors. Seniors should be thanked for their dedication, and support for their future plans should be offered. An invitation to stop by and visit in the future should be extended.

Returning athletes should be allowed to relax during the two-week period. If meetings are scheduled sooner than this, many athletes will not yet be interested in getting ready for the next year. This may not be quite so true for winning teams or highly motivated athletes. The coach should schedule a 15-minute to half hour meeting with each of the future players and discuss their: (1) thoughts on the past seasons, (2) plans for the future season, and (3) improvement plans for the off-season.

This meeting is an ideal time to find out if the coach and athletes have similar views about athlete strengths and weaknesses and strategies for remedying them. It is also an ideal time to ask individual athletes for honest feedback about the way in which the coach utilized each athlete on the team. Coaches must seek out feedback that will help them coach each athlete in a more effective manner. Coaches should attempt to get each athlete to leave the meeting with enthusiasm for the next season and an agreed upon off-season physical and psychological training program. If athletes have developed poor habits or flaws, this is a perfect time to begin remedying them.

A personalized and ethusiastic follow-up letter a couple of months before the start of the season is also beneficial. Another individual meeting with each athlete should again occur just prior to the start of the season. Progress and improvement should be discussed along with roles and goals for athletes and the team. This will be discussed in more detail in Chapters 3 and 4.

Preseason practice should begin with a team meeting. During this meeting coaches should emphasize that both player-coach and player-player rapport will be crucial. It should be emphasized that coaches will try to understand athletes and respond to their needs. Athletes should be encouraged to try and do the same with both coaches and teammates. Athletes need to realize that narrow-minded thinking on their part can lead to cliques and team dissension. Athletes should be encouraged to prevent such self-centered rather than team-oriented interactions from occurring. The same exercises provided in Appendix A for helping coaches develop perceptual alternatives can be reworded slightly and used with athletes. These exercises can greatly facilitate the development of cohesiveness within a team.

Active Listening

When coaches and athletes are interacting, athletes often telegraph needs and sources of motivation. Active listening requires that coaches examine every statement of substance made by each athlete. When engaged in an emotionally charged discussion it is best to not disagree, argue, or try to convince athletes that they are wrong and the coach is correct. Rather, one must recognize that such a strategy will either end the conversation or cause it to become more emotionally charged and less productive. Instead, the coach should rephrase the athlete's comment and give it back to the athlete in an understanding and empathetic tone of voice. This simple strategy, if not made too obvious, will allow the athlete to get rid of the passion. Once the emotion is removed effective communication and progress can begin.

There are several ways in which coaches can learn to improve their listening skills (it's a good idea to teach athletes how to listen also). The first step is to realize that there are several obstacles to effective, active listening. The most typical problems occur when coaches: (1) concentrate mainly on what they want to say next when athletes are speaking, (2) allow certain statements made by athletes to trigger distractions so that the rest of what the athletes have to say goes unheard, (3) interrupt athletes' statements before they finish talking, (4) feel that they are threatened by the athletes' comments and begin to prepare a defense rather than continue to listen, (5) nod their heads in the wrong places at the wrong times or otherwise show signs of merely pretending to be interested in athletes' statements, (6) "listening" to athletes because they feel they must rather than from a true desire to understand.

Coaches must remember that their main responsibility is to motivate each athlete to reach his/her fullest potential. Coaches who listen effectively are capable of effective communication. Coaches must learn to *listen for ideas rather than just words*. If an athlete says something important or stimulating that is best not forgotten, the coach should make a written note and return immediately to listening. This will keep coaches from the distraction of trying to remember the important point, will allow listening to occur, and will permit the important point to be discussed later in the conversation. As coaches become more successful at active listening, communication will improve. With time, coaches will gain in confidence with the result being increased relaxation and improved listening skill.

The Psychology of Perception
Perception: A Key to Successful Coaching

Sports psychologists have become increasingly aware of the fact that perceptions have a profound influence on coaching behaviors. As a result of studying perception they have also recognized that two coaches do not necessarily perceive a particular situation in a similar manner; therefore, two coaches may respond quite differently to the same situation.

Cited in Box 2.1 is an example of two coaches perceiving a similar situation in very different ways. As a result of their perceptions they responded to the situation very differently. The first coach decided that *control* was not possible. New ideas and training strategies were not even attempted because the coach believed that nothing could help. The coach felt

Box 2.1 The Power of Perception

A few years ago a sports psychologist was studying coaching behaviors in a high school where the basketball team had been losing for several years. The school and the community had little interest in the team. Even the school and athletic administrators displayed a lack of interest in the program. The coach had little confidence and was quite discouraged. To the coach it was obvious that the school just was not basketball oriented. The coach often stated openly in the local paper that there was little talent on the team and the chances for a successful season were quite grim.

The coaches and assistants spent most of their out-of-season practice time bemoaning the lack of talent with which they had to work. The players spent most of their time complaining to their teammates and families that the coaches were lousy, lacked enthusiasm, and seemed interested only in yelling at them when they erred. The most frequently heard feedback was, "When are you going to learn how to shoot, dribble, block out, or play defense?" The possibilities for improvement were indeed grim. Losing had become an accepted tradition.

Finally, at the end of the second year the coaching staff resigned. A new coach was hired. The coach was well aware of the past history of the basketball program but viewed the situation as an exciting challenge. The coach felt that building a winner in such an environment would say something powerful about the role of the coach. The coach had been in other situations in which winning came easily. The new job was a new and different opportunity. From the first moment that the coach was hired emphasis was placed on the fact that there would be a new and positive attitude toward building a successful basketball program. The coach frequently stated in public that there was plenty of talent in the community, but it would have to become excited about playing basketball. Fundamentals would be taught and weaknesses would be eliminated. An out-of-season conditioning program was developed and players were given the opportunity to play in a summer league. They were taught how to mentally prepare for the upcoming season and to think like winners no matter how many excuses they had for thinking like losers. As preseason practice began and players made mistakes, they were told that they had erred, but then were taught how to perform more effectively. When players wanted to stay after practice for extra help the new coach was willing. Soon, the players were excited about basketball, their families began supporting the coach, young kids began to like playing basketball, and youth teams were formed. The first year the team finished one game over .500. The following years the team continued to improve. Basketball is now an important and successful sport in that community.

helpless and incapable of influencing the situation. The second coach believed that the situation could be changed and that enthusiastic leadership along with the best and most up-to-date training strategies could be implemented. This coach felt that these techniques would give the team an edge over schools who did not use them.

Coaches must constantly be aware of their perceptions. They must understand themselves and be sure that they are responding to their athletes in a *self-enhancing* rather than a *self-defeating* manner.

Encouragement: Developing Perceptual Alternatives

All great coaches have mastered the science and the art of motivating people through the process of encouragement. Since the early writings of the well-known psychologists, Alfred Adler and Robert White, it has been recognized that *growth does not occur without encouragement*. It is the first step in any change process. Therefore, encouragement is a significant process that all coaches must understand and master so that they may effectively use it to their advantage.

It is unlikely that anyone in the coaching profession has the luxury of working only with "turned-on" and excited athletes. To the contrary, most coaches have many athletes who are "turned-off" and quite lacking in enthusiasm. To be as successful as possible coaches must be able to excite these athletes. Coaches also must be able to continue to stimulate enthusiasm in those athletes who are already excited and to encourage those athletes who begin at a neutral point.

Coaches who are encouraging leaders have learned the importance of developing perceptual alternatives. The term suggests that *perceptual alternatives* refer to the many different ways of viewing and interpreting the same situation. The more ways coaches have available to them for observing athlete behavior the greater the likelihood that coaches will understand all of their athletes and be capable of encouragement rather than discouragement (see Appendix A for activities for developing perceptual alternatives).

Coaches who have a narrow perspective believe that the attitudes and behaviors that they view as appropriate are the only choices available or acceptable. As a result they either force all athletes to accept their way of thinking or they end up discouraging many athletes. Few coaches are in situations in which they can afford to have this occur.

The view that coaches must develop perceptual alternatives does not mean that coaches must give up principles and behaviors that they feel are crucial to team success. It does suggest that these views should be regularly questioned to ensure that they are valid. It may be appropriate to tell athletes that there are some coaching behaviors that you will demand be followed by all (e.g., start practice on time, run on and off field, complete attention when coach is speaking, and so forth). But there should be other practices about which the coach will remain open-minded.

As coaches learn to develop perceptual alternatives they must understand the differences between: (1) athletes asking and/or expecting the coach to be flexible and encouraging, and (2) athletes taking advantage of the situation so that they can justify being lazy or irresponsible. There are athletes who sometimes even unknowingly fail to fully develop their potential if their coach is *too* understanding. Great coaches learn to realize *when to bend* to meet athletes' needs and *when the athlete needs to bend* to the coach's wishes in order to perform optimally. The openness that these coaches display causes their athletes to model their behavior and be more receptive to change themselves.

It is sad to see coaches who never improve. These coaches have become rigid and closed to new and perhaps better ideas. Often, they have lost their enthusiasm and desire to give their time and energy to their players. But when this type of inflexible behavior is seen in young coaches with little or no experience, it is truly depressing.

Coaches who function in this manner and athletes who play for them will not reach their potential. *Often, these coaches feel threatened and attempt to protect themselves by defending their beliefs no matter how illogical they may be.* These coaches have stagnated at an early age. They have denied themselves the opportunity to grow and improve. Such growth can happen only by questioning beliefs and values.

Open-minded coaches who constantly strive to improve throughout their careers may still respond in old, stereotypical ways in certain situations. But they do so because they have studied other responses and decided the old way was the better way. They were not, however, afraid to risk finding out that their old way may have been wrong. It is this view that allows open-minded coaches to eliminate their weaknesses and maximize their strengths so that they can become great leaders.

Most developing coaches need to work at developing perceptual alternatives. It is far easier for coaches to view the world from a self-oriented perspective and spend great amounts of energy convincing themselves and others that their view is correct. Scientists studying perception often marvel at the tendency of athletes to see most problems as stemming from poor coaching. A few years later the same athletes become coaches and view the same problems as being caused by athlete-centered problems such as low ability or poor attitude. *Great coaches remember how they and other athletes viewed the sports world when they were players and use this knowledge to coach in a more effective manner.*

Great coaches realize early that different athletes may view the same coach from very different perspectives. Likewise, two coaches may view the same athlete in vastly different ways. One coach may focus on only the positive qualities, while another may focus only on the negative qualities of a particular athlete.

Most coaches find it much easier to encourage athletes who share their beliefs, values, and behaviors. It is easier and more natural to focus on the positive qualities in these athletes. As a result athletes who share these beliefs, values, and behaviors feel comfortable and confident playing for these coaches. In turn, coaches respond by encouraging these athletes who, in turn, gain more confidence and improve more and more. These athletes like and respect their coaches for helping them to develop. Soon, a very positive and complimentary cycle is initiated, which is beneficial to both coaches and athletes. *They encourage and support each other.*

But just the opposite interaction typically occurs when coaches focus mainly on the negative qualities of athletes who have very different beliefs, values, and behaviors. Typically, unless they are gifted, these athletes get far more negative feedback from their coaches. Such athletes begin to feel uncomfortable and lose confidence. Coaches often respond by further discouraging these athletes by emphasizing their shortcomings on a daily basis. Confidence diminishes rapidly. Soon, athletes finding themselves in such a situation start to defend their athletic abilities by: (1) placing blame on their coaches, which may cause these athletes to respond in an even more negative manner to their coaches; or (2) trying hard to show their coaches that they have athletic ability and a "good attitude." Oftentimes, athletes who choose the latter alternative "tie themselves into knots" and end up further justifying their coaches' original impressions.

Coaches must face the fact that it is difficult to be an encouraging leader when attention is focused primarily on the negative qualities in certain athletes. Coaches can improve their coaching skills to a great extent by focusing on the positive qualities of their athletes. It will then be much easier for them to communicate in a positive and encouraging fashion with their athletes.

It has been well documented that a *self-fulfilling prophecy* occurs when coaches focus on the positive aspects of their athletes. Coaches tend to give a greater *quality* and *quantity* of feedback to athletes viewed in this positive perspective. These athletes tend to be viewed by their coaches as being talented and capable of improvement. With time, such athletes come to view themselves in a similar manner. As a result of their enhanced self-perception these athletes develop increased motivation, improve continuously, eventually attain success, and become extremely coachable. They become their coaches' dream rather than their nightmare.

Great coaches recognize the importance of encouragement and use it to their advantage with as many athletes as possible within their team. Only coaches who have developed perceptual alternatives will be capable of behaving in this manner.

Power and the Coach

Whether coaches desire it or not, they are in positions that wield great power. Power has been defined as the probability that one actor within a social relationship will be in a position to carry out his/her own will despite resistance (Weber 1963). Some people actively seek out a career in coaching because of the power it affords them. Many others enter coaching for status, the joy of helping athletes, the need to help athletes improve, the continual thrill of competition, or prestige, or perhaps for recognition, achievement, and social approval.

Coaches must learn to view their power as a responsibility that is not to be taken lightly. Successful coaches learn to blend a concern for winning with an interest in their athletes. The most successful coaches, even in society's most pressure-filled sport of professional football have recognized the importance of this blend. Don Shula of the Miami Dolphins and Chuck Noll of the Pittsburgh Steelers have often expressed the opinion that if coaches develop their athletes to their fullest potential, winning will be a natural by-product. Many coaches have found out the hard way that their overconcern with winning will not necessarily lead to winning if the athletes' needs and development are overlooked.

In the present and future sports world coaches who use their power to satisfy only their own needs will not survive long in the coaching profession. Coaching power increases with team success. Success, with few exceptions, tends to occur when attention is given to player needs. When coaches are successful they gain more power and more flexibility. They can be more innovative without being subject to criticism. They will have a greater freedom of job choice from level of play to location of team. Success also provides coaches the opportunity to go into almost any situation and have the team believe that success will soon follow.

Summary

Leadership is a crucial ingredient in team success. Without it a team will be lost. Leadership has been defined in many ways. All the definitions possess one common element: a leader is a person who exerts more influence than the other members of a group.

Differing leadership styles are discussed. Critical analyses of authoritarian versus democratic styles and people-centered versus task-oriented styles are provided. Successful coaches are able to employ leadership styles that best suit their own personalities and that are most appropriate for the situation.

Coaching in today's world is not an easy task. In fact, coaching is a demanding and ever-changing profession. Successful coaches remain receptive to new information and yet are able to recognize when traditional approaches are most appropriate.

Effective leaders are perceptive and, as a result, respond to their athletes in a self-enhancing rather than a self-defeating manner. Their perceptiveness allows these coaches to appropriately utilize their power.

Successful leaders master the art and science of communicating with their athletes and assistant coaches. They earn the trust of their athletes through the skill of active listening. Encouragement is a most crucial component of their coaching strategies. Successful coaches manage to establish a balance between task-orientation and athlete-orientation, and this balance allows them to become consistent winners.

References

Tannebaum, R., and Schmidt, W.H. How to choose a leadership pattern. In *Behavioral Issues in Management*. Edited by H.C. Jain and R.N. Kanungo. Toronto: McGraw-Hill-Ryerson, 1977.

Recommended Readings

Adler, A. *The Practice and Theory of Individual Psychology*. London: Routeledge and K. Paul, 1971.

Burns, J.M. *Leadership*. New York: Harper & Row, 1978.

Dinkmeyer, D., and Dreikurs, R. *Encouraging Children to Learn: The Encouragement Process*. Englewood Cliffs, New Jersey: Prentice-Hall, Inc., 1963.

Fisher, A.C. *Psychology of Sport*. Palo Alto, California: Mayfield Publishing Co., 1976.

Neal, P.E., and Tutko, T.A. *Coaching Girls and Women: Psychological Perspectives*. Boston: Allyn and Bacon, Inc., 1975.

Sabock, R. *The Coach*. Philadelphia: W.B. Saunders Co., 1973.

Sage, G. Machiavellianism among college and high school coaches. In *Sport and American Society*. Reading, Massachusetts: Addison-Wesley Publishing Co., Inc., 1974.

Singer, R.N. *Myths and Truths in Sports Psychology*. New York: Harper & Row, 1975.

Smoll, F.L., and Smith, R.E. Techniques for improving self-awareness of youth sport coaches. *Journal of Physical Education and Recreation*, 51:2, 1980.

Weber. *Basic Concepts in Sociology*. New York: The Citadel Press, 1963.

Appendix A
Activities for Developing Perceptual Alternatives

Exercise 1

Think for a moment of two different athletes on your team. One you really enjoy coaching and one you find difficult to coach because he/she tries your patience. Write down five to seven qualities or characteristics that accurately describe them—first the athlete that you enjoy coaching and then the one you dislike coaching. If you do not coach, do the same for two teammates, two coaches, two friends, or two athletes who play for a team that you follow closely.

Athlete You Enjoy Coaching	Athlete You Dislike Coaching
1.	1.
2.	2.
3.	3.
4.	4.
5.	5.
6.	6.
7.	7.

Now look carefully at the lists you have developed. Did you tend to see positive qualities in one athlete and negative qualities in the other? It is quite possible that you have been focusing mainly on negative qualities in the athlete you don't enjoy coaching. Chances are that if you are seeing only negative qualities in the athlete, you have not been very encouraging to this athlete. It is probably reflected in how often you smile, respond enthusiastically, and provide confidence-provoking statements to this athlete. Most likely, you are discouraging this athlete. Try to focus on some positive qualities in this person and express it in your interactions with him/her. Continue to do so and watch what happens to the communication between the two of you and to the athlete's performance.

Exercise 2

Constantly look for other ways in which you have possibly helped to discourage athletes. See if you can do something different that can encourage them. Decide that you will make at least one encouraging comment to an athlete you have tended to discourage each day for the next two weeks and study the response you get.

Exercise 3

Identify a player on your team to whom you do not tend to give very much feedback. Perhaps it is a bottomline player. Maybe it is even a regular. Try to determine if there is a good reason for this athlete to get a reduced quantity and quality of feedback from you, the coach. If not, commit yourself to change.

Exercise 4

Imagine that you are one of the best players on the team that you coach. Now, from that athlete's perspective, write a paragraph describing what you see, think, and feel about the coach.

Exercise 5

Imagine that you are one of the poorest players on the team that you coach. Now, from that athlete's perspective, write a paragraph describing what you see, think, and feel about the coach.

Exercise 6

Some time in the near future take an opportunity to sit down individually with the athletes you described in exercises 4 and 5 and ask them the questions you responded to in questions 4 and 5. Were your responses similar? Were you afraid to find out? Are you willing to realize that you may not view yourself the same way that your players view you?

Exercise 7

Begin to develop perceptual alternatives. Try to recall the last time that you had a disagreement with one of your athletes or assistant coaches. Remember their position on the issue. Put yourself in that person's position, including their experiences and knowledge, which may be quite different from yours. Try to recall when you were in that person's position. Try to understand the other person's perspective. You are developing perceptual alternatives if you are beginning to understand the other person's point of view. You need not agree with it, but if you can understand their different perspec-

tives, you perhaps will be patient enough to be a more encouraging coach.

Adapted from Dinkmeyer, D., and Dreikurs, R. *Encouraging Children to Learn: The Encouragement Process*, Englewood Cliffs, New Jersey: Prentice-Hall, Inc., 1963.

Credit: University of South Carolina Sports Information.

Motivating the Individual Athlete

3

Not all athletes are equally motivated by the same strategies. In today's sports world coaches must recognize and respond appropriately to the motivational needs of all athletes. To do so effectively, a framework for motivation must be developed. This chapter provides guidelines that can be used by coaches to establish a motivational framework that will optimize their athletes' performances.

A Framework for Individualized Motivation

Coaches should strive to develop in athletes motivation that will become *long-term* and *self-directing*. All athletes will not, despite the best efforts, become self-directed. But coaches should at least strive for this goal. Coaches' jobs are much like that of parents—to meet their athletes' needs of dependence and yet strive to prepare them for eventual independence. Independence and self-direction in athletes are often difficult for coaches to accept. Many coaches prefer to have athletes depend upon them. Teaching athletes to be capable of functioning without coaches' help is sometimes an uncomfortable thought, but it should be the goal.

Jumbo Elliott, noted track coach at Villanova, long ago recognized this point. Don Paige, one of Jumbo's famous runners, has stated, "The great thing about Jumbo is that he knows there are things he doesn't know, that coaching personality may contribute to the fact that so many of Elliott's athletes continue to perform well once they are out of school." Another of Coach Elliott's star runners has stated, "A lot of coaches want to be your Guru. But by the end of your sophomore or junior year Jumbo expects you to be able to coach yourself. And you can. European and communist coaches can't believe that people like Eamonn Coghlan and I actually coach ourselves." [Telander 1980]

It is the athletes, not the coaches who must compete, cope, adjust, and perform. Certainly, coaches can intervene during breaks in play and during practice, but in the off-season and during play athletes must be capable of self-motivation and direction.

Each athlete's success or failure at self-direction will be significantly based upon the coach's wisdom and ability to teach self-motivation. John Wooden, the famous basketball coach at the University of California at Los Angeles, emphasized this point several years ago. The sports psychologist Cal Botterill (1980, p. 262) recently paraphrased Wooden's thoughts when he stated, "It is important to remember that the preparation of an athlete is complete when the coach is no longer needed."

Unfortunately, every coach does not have a team filled with athletes as intelligent or self-directed as Don Paige or the athletes at UCLA. Many coaches work with younger athletes who are too lacking in knowledge or experience to be able to completely motivate themselves. Some athletes expect their coaches to motivate them. Others expect their coaches to teach them how to self-direct themselves. Still others play sports mainly for social reasons and really do not love playing. What then are coaches to do?

Teaching Self-Motivation

Long-term motivation is ideal when it evolves naturally from the athlete's own desire to optimize performance. Coaching would be a much easier occupation if all athletes were self-directing. But as long as sports remain popular many talented athletes who lack self-direction will need help in attaining their potential.

Coaches must decide if it is worth both their time and the team's time to try to motivate each and every athlete. In the preseason, coaches may decide that certain athletes are not worth the effort required and thus eliminate them during try-outs. But once a team is chosen, coaches must attempt to enhance the perfor-

mance of each athlete. Certain talented athletes, despite their coaches' best efforts, may never become totally self-directing. These athletes may require more of a coach's energy, at least until they become more self-motivated.

Self-motivation is particularly important during off-season practice when athletes must practice without coaches directly controlling their efforts. This also has far-reaching implications for the carry-over of sports participation into adult life.

Teaching Self-Responsibility

Athletes vary in their tendency to assume self-responsibility for their motivation in sports. Some athletes lack motivation and, quite simply, do not try hard enough. Others try so hard that they actually work against themselves. Many athletes need to have their level of motivation modified. Some of these athletes are highly receptive to change, but others initially resist even minor adjustments. Coaches must help all athletes attain motivational *balance*.

Many athletes do not believe that they can control their destiny in sports, and are said to manifest an "external locus of control." Other athletes believe that they are in total control of their success in sports ("internal locus of control"). Certainly, there are situations over which athletes do not have control, but they do or can control many sports situations. Athletes must learn to identify situations accurately and learn when they can and cannot affect their environment. As athletes realize they can influence their own success they will be more willing to accept self-responsibility. Unfortunately, the skill of perceiving the world in a manner that will lead to maximum effectiveness and self-control is not a skill that is automatically learned by all athletes. Rather, it is a skill that must be taught to athletes by their coaches. To accomplish this successfully coaches must understand the perceptual differences between athletes that have *learned effectiveness* and those that have *learned helplessness* (Rotella 1979; Seligman 1975).

Learned Helplessness

Many athletes who fail to self-direct their own behavior perceive the sports world in a way that leads them to believe that they have little or no control over their success. In their view, it does not matter if they try hard because they believe they lack the talent to be successful. When athletes perceive themselves to be *helpless* they perceive their success as being due to a *lucky day, easy opponent,* or *lack of challenge.* As a result of this perception they seldom, if ever, reward themselves for hard work and persistent efforts. An exaggerated and extended state of learned helplessness can lead to anxiety and/or depression in athletes.

Learned helplessness, even when less severe, can produce three deficiencies in the behavior of athletes. First of all, it can produce a decrease in the motivation to initiate self-directed actions. Second, it can retard the development of the ability of athletes to perceive and believe that their competitive performances are successful, even when in reality they are successful. As a result, athletes who perceive themselves to be helpless fail to gain confidence even when potentially confidence-enhancing situations present themselves. Third, helplessness can disturb the emotional balance of athletes with the resulting consequences of anxiety and depression, which can interfere with learning, performance, and self-motivation. In this state of mind athletes are usually so lost in their own thoughts that they are hindered in their ability to concentrate on sources of information that might be helpful.

With *repeated failure* or *perceived* repeated failure helplessness often tends to generalize from one situation to another. Feelings of helplessness may generalize to other sports, aspects of one sport, or nonsport-related activities. All athletes should learn through their sports ex-

periences that with persistent efforts appropriately, directed success can be attained. Feelings of helplessness should not be bred through sports.

Causes of Helplessness. Helplessness is a learned state of mind. Thus, it can also be unlearned.

Typically, helplessness is caused by: (1) frequent experiences in situations in which athletes really could not control outcomes, (2) merely being told by significant others that they have no control over their improvement or performance (only applies if information is believed), (3) a tendency toward an external personality orientation (those who believe that most of the important things in their lives are outside of their personal control), and (4) early sports experiences in which an individual athlete or an entire team loses continuously and by large margins.

In the latter case, individual failure is more likely to lead to helplessness than is team failure. It has been quite well documented that many team athletes attribute team failure to the poor play of others. They believe, absolutely, that failure occurred in spite of their own superior play (Roberts 1977). In some situations, an entire team may save face and confidence by blaming failure on their coaches, and continue to believe that the team members are highly talented.

Even though repeated failure can have serious motivational consequences, occasional losing may be quite useful. It may "immunize" athletes from feelings of helplessness by showing them that losing can be overcome by persistent practice or increased intensity, which will lead to enhanced perception of control.

Coaches must realize that even constant failure does not necessarily lead to a learned helplessness state if coaches are *enthusiastic, optimistic,* and provide a *plan for improvement.* When athletes encounter failure, their response to it is determined largely by the attitudes of their coaches. If coaches begin to perceive their coaching situations as being out of control and hopeless, their athletes and entire programs are in jeopardy. Team performance and motivation will suffer if coaches' perceptions of control falter. Thus, when failures occur coaches must accept responsibility for aiding their athletes in avoidance of learned helplessness.

Helping Athletes Handle Helplessness. There are several strategies for aiding athletes who suffer from feelings of helplessness. Three of the more specific strategies will be presented. The first approach is to provide helpless athletes with situations in which they can experience control. The experiences need not be dramatic. For example, an athlete might be given playing time early in a game, a chance to start, practice with the first team, or competition against an opponent over which there is a good chance for success. *The key is to help athletes develop the belief that events are under their control.* Psychologists call this technique *immunization by a contrary expectancy.*

A second useful strategy is labeled *immunization by discriminative control.* The idea is to eliminate the tendency to generalize feelings of helplessness. Coaches must teach their athletes to limit their perceptions of uncontrollable failure to a particular situation, a particular time and place, and a particular set of conditions. Through this strategy coaches can prepare athletes to perceive that they can have control in future situations against the same or similar opponents. This strategy may also include teaching athletes to attribute failure to factors other than ability (e.g., overtired, caught us on a bad night, didn't work hard enough, team hasn't peaked yet). Blaming failure in any of these ways can lead to perceptions of control in future situations.

A third important strategic technique relates to the *significance of two situations.* Learned helplessness tends to generalize from important to less important events. It does not move in the opposite direction. So anything coaches can do to downplay the importance of failure can be quite valuable in helping athletes to avoid feelings of helplessness.

Many coaches with good intentions try to help athletes who experience helplessness with *sympathy.* Initially, sympathy may be useful. But sympathy may also exacerbate feelings of incompetence. Such a response may cause coaches to intentionally or unintentionally lower athletes' expectations. Sympathy may also stand in the way of learning and improvement and may lead athletes to expect too much help. As a result, responsibility may be taken away from athletes. It is best to *empathize* and explain to athletes how the coach, or another athlete, overcame an equivalent problem and went on to attain success.

The Beginning of Helplessness in Athletes. Coaches are indeed challenged by athletes who perceive themselves to be lacking in control over their success in sports. But it is a vitally important challenge. Perhaps the sports experience is more significant to athletes struggling with feelings of helplessness than to others. Some of the most pleasurable moments in coaching come from helping such athletes "get themselves together."

Coaches must realize that athletes' inclinations toward helplessness often have roots in childhood. Young athletes are likely to feel helpless in new situations when they have experiences (particularly sports experiences) in which little mastery is combined with a lack of control.

Young athletes need to build up early experiences with control over their success. Athletes must be taught early that they can cope with and overcome skill weaknesses, failures, frustrations, and anxiety. Overcoming such obstacles through increased efforts can lead to a sense of increased effectiveness. The more frequently athletes are given the opportunity to *confront* and *overcome* challenging obstacles the more likely they will develop feelings of dignity, power, worth, and pride (Seligman 1975).

Owing to the developmental and motivational values gained by overcoming obstacles, *too much success* can also, ironically, lead to perceptions of helplessness. If failure has never been experienced teams or individuals confronted with failure for the first time may have little or no idea how to overcome it. Athletes may need to fail occasionally in order to learn how to manage and respond to failure. But, of course, if given the choice, motivation would be more likely enhanced by success than by constant failure. However, as will soon be pointed out, the effect is quite different in some athletes who have made a career out of overcoming seemingly insurmountable obstacles. *Obstacles or failure actually excite these athletes and enhance their motivation.* One challenge for coaches is to teach their athletes how to think in a style similar to those athletes who have learned effectiveness in order to enhance their motivation.

Learned Effectiveness

Coaches who wish to get the most out of all their athletes must know how to teach them to think like winners. Athletes must learn how to think and act in a manner that will eventually lead to success. Recent developments in sports psychology have provided a clearer understanding of how this learning process can occur. Coaches must teach their athletes to *model* the thinking patterns and behaviors of effective individuals.

Athletes must be taught that there is much more to attaining success in sports than having talent, although talent certainly helps. But athletes' perceptions of their talents and the effectiveness of their approach to maximizing their potential may be more crucial. Athletes who *make themselves* successful are not always the most gifted physically. Often, there are many obstacles that can prevent athletes from becoming successful. But in many athletes their mental approach to sports allows them to find suc-

cess. These athletes believe that they can control their own success or failure in sports. They accept personal responsibility.

Bob Cousy and Phil Ford could easily have decided that they were too short to become great pro basketball stars. Chris Evert could have decided that she was too slow to become a great tennis player. Carlton Fisk could have become frustrated with his lengthy stay in the minor leagues and never allowed himself to become a top baseball catcher in the American League. Fred Belitnicoff could have considered himself too slow to become a great receiver in the National Football League. Calvin Peete and Arthur Ashe could have decided that black athletes could not make it in professional golf or tennis, respectively. Nancy Lieberman could have believed that a woman couldn't develop great skill in basketball. Phil Mahr, the 1980 Olympic medal winner in skiing, could have decided that there was no way he could return in a year's time from a terribly debilitating ankle injury. Carole Johnson was a finalist in the 1979 National Collegiate Gymnastic Championships (including a performance on the uneven bars, despite the loss of her right arm from the elbow down). She could have easily used her "handicap" as an excuse for failure or not trying. Instead, she failed to perceive herself as even having a handicap. She, like others, simply had an obstacle that needed to be overcome. These examples are taken from the ranks of the well-known athletes. But thousands of similar examples are available anywhere that sports are played.

There is a consistent trait in athletes who manage to cope with the difficulties and challenges inherent in sports. *These athletes always find a way to perceive events in a way that increases their motivation.* They find a solution to the obstacles in their way and continue to work toward attaining their goals.

A motivational approach to sports that has tremendous practical application is *learned effectiveness.* This technique is based on the theory that there is a way to perceive and react to sports situations so as to maximize athletes' effectiveness. Athletes who have learned effectiveness read their minds and bodies in a rational and realistic manner and, thus, allow themselves to attain their potential.

Rather than viewing a novel or ambiguous competitive situation with the view: "I can't do that," or "I doubt that I can do it," an athlete who has learned effectiveness approaches the situation with the perception that "I can do it." Such athletes have to be convinced otherwise before they will believe that they cannot succeed.

Athletes who have learned effectiveness realize the importance of *patience* and *persistence*. They persist even in the face of repeated failure. They respond to failure by reevaluating their practice strategies in a realistic manner, reformulating their practice plans and then increasing the intensity of their efforts.

When frustrations arise and improvement is slow, athletes with learned effectiveness *actively seek out events* in their environment that *justify their continued efforts*. They talk to other athletes and read about other athletes who have gone through similar experiences and have had their continued efforts rewarded. These athletes take great *pride* in the difficulty of the task that they are attempting to accomplish. They appreciate and value their own ability, no matter how meager it may be. Weaknesses are viewed as *exciting challenges* that must be overcome. Effective athletes find a way, through new knowledge or new strategies, to overcome their weaknesses. Less effective athletes believe that it is not fair when other athletes have more physical talent. The result is frustration and a justifiable excuse for failure. Effective athletes focus on the fact that they are more dedicated and have more self-discipline than more talented athletes.

Athletes who have learned effectiveness develop a great deal of pride in their mental and physical strengths. They give credit to their abilities and their efforts and this leads to in-

creased motivation. They are willing to occasionally give up responsibility for failure when doing so will increase their motivation.

Athletes who have been involved in sports for many years will have formed many practice and performance habits. Athletes may be unaware of many of these habits and may have no logical explanation for why the habits developed. Some such habits may work against athletes and prevent them from performing up to their potential. Some habits may cause certain athletes to feel incompetent and unable to control their success or failure in sports.

Athletes who desire success in sports must be aware of their motivational inclinations. Differences in motivational tendencies frequently separate learned effective athletes from others in the world of sports. Surely there are exceptions. A small percentage of highly talented athletes will find success in sports despite motivational weaknesses. But even these athletes will not come close to performing at their peak performance level.

If coaches find certain athletes on their team thinking that it is unfair that another athlete with a "bad attitude" is playing more than they are, take notice. They are probably beginning to question the fairness of sports, their competence in a particular sport, or the purpose of their efforts. Such thoughts may indicate that motivational pitfalls are developing. Coaches have a responsibility to help their athletes learn to read these thoughts and feelings and use them in a self-productive rather than a self-defeating way. But awareness of pitfalls is only the first step. Once athletes recognize pitfalls they must know how to correct them.

Athletes who have learned effectiveness purposely seek out a sport in which they will have a realistic chance of becoming successful. They search for a sport in which intense and persistent efforts will be rewarded. They are not interested in sports that are lacking in challenge any more than they are interested in sports in which success would be totally impossible no matter how hard they tried. Athletes who carefully select their sports tend to optimize their performance because they find it much easier to persevere in their efforts. Think how much more difficult it is for athletes to persevere when they do not believe they have any chance of being successful or when they regularly doubt their chances.

Likewise, athletes who are learned effectives fully believe that they will eventually obtain success. When they fail, they treat their failures as momentary failures. They read their failures and use them as valuable sources of information to help them guide their future practice sessions. As a result, they approach practice sessions following failure with enthusiasm over the likelihood of improvement for the future.

Well in advance of competition, learned effective athletes prepare by thinking much more frequently about their weaknesses than their strengths. *But they think about their weaknesses in a positive manner.* They plan practice time to eliminate the weaknesses identified and to maintain their strengths so that they can perform better in the future. Their practices are designed to eliminate past mistakes. They do not dwell on feeling incompetent or embarrassed about past errors or failures. Rather, they feel competent and proud and practice diligently to do something about improving.

Maximizers also *read* their *anxieties* to help themselves guide their practices. They attempt to recall when they felt anxious during previous competitions. Then they try to anticipate when and where they might feel anxious in future competitions. Once they are increasingly aware of these anxieties they implement a plan for eliminating them.

Athletes cannot avoid thinking of past weaknesses and anxieties or upcoming challenges and threats. Thoughts of future challenges make even effective athletes somewhat anxious about what might happen if they are not prepared. But such anxiety and worry should be only momentary and should not be debilitating. Anxiety and worry should be used to help prepare for upcoming challenges.

Most coaches encounter players whose major problem is that they dwell on their weaknesses. Coaches and athletes must recognize that it is one thing to work on weaknesses in practice and something very different to do so during a competitive performance. Athletes must have confidence in their skills or they will not be ready to perform optimally when it is time to compete.

Too often, athletes who fail to maximize their potential accept blame for their failures, but do not allow themselves to take credit for their successes. As a result, they may fail to develop pride in their improvements. Such athletes often underestimate the value of their success when they are making consistent progress and attaining goals that they once thought were unreachable. Instead of feeling good about themselves and proud of their accomplishments, they suddenly decide that the tasks were simple and not so difficult after all. The result is a wasted opportunity to increase feelings of competence and excitement about the value of persistent and intense efforts.

Athletes cannot develop to their potential if they fail to take advantage of motivational and confidence-enhancing opportunities. Coaches must teach athletes to believe that their successes are due to their athletic competence and their efforts to succeed. Failures must be viewed as valuable learning experiences that can be useful to future success. Occasionally, it may even be beneficial to attribute failure to sources outside of their control, such as a bad day, tiredness, good luck by their opponent, or their own bad luck. Using these excuses too frequently, however, will work against continued future improvement. So coaches should teach athletes to use excuses only when they are beneficial and realistic.

Coaches should teach their athletes how to move in a forward, growth-oriented direction. One useful technique is to encourage athletes to observe other athletes who are or are becoming successful. Athletes should actively look for examples in which effort has been important to success. Such models can serve as stimulants for continued motivation. One should not emphasize exceptional athletes who became successful with relative ease. Examples like these can become excuses for giving up. Rather, coaches should help athletes to honestly determine if others are more talented than they are. If others are more talented, then the athletes should learn to take pride in the self-discipline that will allow them to work harder than others. Athletes can develop a greater strategic understanding of their sport than others. They can gain a mastery of the mental aspects of the sport, and become intelligent athletes. Athletes can be taught to make up for potential disadvantages by utilizing other elements that are important to success in sports.

The Impact of Time Orientation on Athletic Motivation

Time orientation refers to an athletes' inclination to think mainly in the present, past, or future time perspective. All athletes must learn how to adjust their time orientation so that it can work to their advantage. Coaches and athletes must read their present and past weaknesses and anxieties when designing training and practice sessions. But they must also antic-ipate future challenges for which they will have to be prepared.

There are two very popular and useful time-orientation strategies. One approach is to think positive and enjoyable thoughts related to *future* success in sports. The resulting emotions will positively enhance motivation. A second technique is for athletes to think of all of the other athletes that they will have to compete against in the near or *distant* future if their wished for goals are to be reached. Athletes should think about opponents who have defeated them in the past. Thoughts of success over these opponents or, if necessary, the possibility of being beaten by them can convince athletes to practice with intensity. An important part of success in sports requires that athletes develop the self-discipline to have quality workouts for a sustained time period. The use of thoughts related to *fear of future failure* are often helpful for enhancing self-discipline in practice or training; but such thoughts are debilitating if they occur during a competition or if they become the primary source of motivation.

Often, athletes who fail to improve worry too much about failure in the past or future. The potential feelings of incompetence, shame, and embarrassment that result may prevent athletes

Table 3.1: Useful Time Orientations

Past Time Orientation	Present Time Orientation	Future Time Orientation
Should Be Used:	**Should Be Used:**	**Should Be Used:**
To analyze past success or failure	During competition	To prepare for future competition
When discouraged—think of past successes	When lost in worry	When feeling discouraged—think of future successes
To enhance motivation by thinking of past successes or failures	During actual practice	When feeling lazy—think of future opponents and challenges
		To enhance motivation by thinking of future successes or failures

from acting to avoid future failures. Commonly, when such athletes are preparing for future competition they simply avoid their weaker skills and focus on their strengths. Other times, athletes fail to advance beyond the "worry" stage. Either response can be detrimental to self-improvement.

The preceding paragraphs indicate that the fear of failure is not necessarily detrimental to the progress of athletes. However, athletes may start to believe that they are incompetent when the fear of failure controls their thought processes. WATCH OUT! Such athletes may be on the verge of giving up or giving themselves an excuse for failure. They may soon begin to assume that there is no sense in practicing.

Time orientation has a very significant impact upon sports success. Athletes have a tendency to think in either a past, present, or future time orientation. Each time orientation has particular strengths and weaknesses. Athletes must be taught by their coaches how to utilize each particular time orientation to its fullest advantage. Table 3.1 provides some suggestions regarding the use of time orientations by athletes.

Goal Setting

Coaches have a responsibility to teach their athletes how to develop a mental approach that will increase their chances for success. A positive and effective mental approach does not automatically result from involvement in athletics. Such an approach must be taught to all athletes.

Self-Image Psychology

Self-image is one's conception of oneself. This image is not formed or changed overnight. In the case of athletes, self-images are based upon past experiences in and out of sports, including all of the athletes' past successes and failures. Since failures may outnumber successes, it is imperative that athletes learn how

to appropriately respond to their failures. Far too frequently athletes respond to failure by thinking negatively and imagining themselves failing to attain their goals.

Thinking in this manner can be extremely limiting. Athletes who picture themselves as being defeated have taken the first step toward guaranteeing failure and disappointment.

The first step to attaining goals is to develop self-thoughts and self-images that are consistent with the goals that are sought.

Most athletes err in the direction of underestimating themselves. As long as athletes remain realistic they are far better off to imagine themselves attaining their goals. Error in the direction of overestimation of abilities is far less self-defeating than is underestimation, particularly during competition.

The Science of Cybernetics

Cybernetics is the science that compares the functions of the human nervous system to those of computer-controlled machines. Cybernetic research has helped psychologists to realize that man's brain and nervous system represent an advanced goal-striving mechanism. Coaches desiring to get the most out of their athletes must strive to understand the basics of cybernetics (Wiener 1961; Smith 1981; Brown 1977).

Depending upon how people program their built-in guidance system (i.e., the brain) it can be utilized as a mechanism for either success or failure. The body will tend to respond in a way that is consistent with the brain's input. Athletes who continuously provide negative input develop a *failure-oriented* system. Those who continuously provide positive input develop a *success-oriented system.* In essence, the human system can be viewed as a goal-striving mechanism that operates in a manner consistent with the way it is programmed.

Whenever athletes have sports experiences they create new neural pathways in the gray matter of their brains. Repetition of experiences strengthens these pathways. The pathways are stored in a fashion similar to the manner in which data are stored on magnetic tapes in computers. As a result, these stored pathways can be utilized whenever athletes remember a past experience.

For athletes whose past experiences have been highly successful the frequent recall of success experiences is highly beneficial. Such recall programs their system quite naturally for success. However, this process must be utilized very differently for athletes who have had an abundance of failure experiences. These athletes must consciously work to replay their success experiences and to forget their negative experiences. Continuous replaying of positive experiences will strengthen them to the point that they become dominant and automatic. Since athletes are by their very nature goal-striving, they must learn to program themselves for success rather than failure.

Fortunately, because the brain of human beings is so highly developed, it is almost totally under the athletes' control. The brain does not even need actual success experiences in order to be programmed for success. All that is required is to regularly imagine success. The nervous system is unable to differentiate between real and imagined experiences. Consequently, coaches should teach their athletes how to operate their goal-striving systems effectively through planned goal setting and the use of vivid imagination.

Preparing for Goal Setting

Most athletes go through a process that is quite consistent as they make decisions about approaching or avoiding goals. This process must be understood prior to outlining a goal-setting program.

When athletes are initially placed in a situation involving an achievement task (sport), they attempt to determine their chances of success (or failure) and whether or not the task is worth striving to attain. This self-analysis involves asking: (1) whether or not the necessary talent is available, (2) how much effort and persistence will be required, (3) how much luck will be involved in success or failure, and (4) how difficult is the task. Factors such as quality of opponents; and quality, cost, and availability of instruction, equipment, practice facilities, and practice partners are often considered.

This very conscious evaluation of the task leads to an estimation or prediction of personal chances for success or failure. It is here that both expectancies for success and failure as well as the hope of success and the fear of failure are initiated for a specific task.

If an athlete decides to pursue a task, then goal-directed behavior is initiated. The athlete formulates plans for attaining success and avoiding failure and then begins carrying out the plan.

Next, athletes must compete in the achievement situation (competition). With each performance opportunity athletes reevaluate their plans and their progress. A realistic self and task appraisal is gradually formulated. Athletes must learn to believe in themselves and in the effectiveness of their plans while remaining flexible enough to make adjustments.

These decisions are based upon a self-evaluation of *why* success or failure occurred. Was success or failure due to: (1) ability or a lack of the necessary ability, (2) investment or lack of investment of the necessary effort, (3) being lucky or unlucky (or at least perceiving that success or failure was due to good or bad fortune), or (4) the difficulty of the task?

This reevaluation process, which follows goal-directed behavior and performance, leads to feelings of pride or shame and expectancies of future success or failure at future tasks that are similar.

The importance of self-perception in this process cannot be overemphasized. Athletes must be taught how to positively attack their weaknesses in practice so that they can think positively about them during competition. This process is crucial to the goal-setting process.

Teaching Athletes How to Set Goals

Today, success in sports must include effective goal setting. This is the first step in attaining athletic potential. Setting goals fulfills at least four important functions. First, it prepares athletes mentally and emotionally to act out their commitments. Second, goals elicit an expression of confidence. Third, goals create a positive self-image, one in which athletes see themselves in control of improvement and performance. Fourth, goals provide a focus for future efforts.

Goal setting should emphasize a process of striving for goals that are *challenging, yet attainable.* Coaches must teach their athletes that it is the process of attaining the goals, rather than winning or losing, that is most important in sports. Even successful coaches at the highest levels, like Vince Lombardi, former coach of the Green Bay Packers, have emphasized this point.

> "Winning isn't everything, it's the only thing. I wish the hell I'd never said the damn thing. I meant the effort.... I meant having a goal.... I sure as hell didn't mean for people to crush human values and morality." [Michener 1976, p. 432]

Goals must be realistic. But it is not always easy to determine whether a goal is realistic or impossible. For this purpose, goals should include both long-term and short-term goals. As short-term goals are accomplished athletes move closer to the attainment of the long-term goals. If only long-term goals are set, goal setting may induce tension and frustration. Athletes need intermediate successes to build confidence and persistence.

Coaches must help their athletes in the goal-setting process (see Table 3.2). Together coaches and athletes may draw up a master list

Table 3.2: Setting Goals and Attaining Them

There are at least six steps that are crucial to the goal-setting process:

Step 1: Know Yourself

How good an athlete are you?
How good would you like to be?
Why in the past have you not progressed as you would like?
Are you self-disciplined?
Do you concentrate when you practice?
Are you willing to take responsibility for your achievement or would you rather blame others or bad luck for your failure?

Step 2: Skills Required for My Sport

What are the skills required for success in your sport?
Do you understand the strategies and rules in your sport?
Do you understand the mental aspects of your sport?
Do you know which muscle groups are utilized in your sport and how to develop them?
Do you know which muscle groups must be relaxed to consistently perform effectively?
Do you have enough flexibility to perform up to your potential?

Step 3: Self-Evaluation

What are your greatest strengths as an athlete in your sport?
What are your greatest weaknesses in your sport?
Do you know how to go about improving each of them?
How much time are you willing to put into your practicing?
Do you tend to practice only the moves you enjoy?
Are you practicing perfectly to ensure success or are you just putting in time?
Do you tend to practice your strengths or the skills in which you are already good with very little time allotted to improve your weaknesses?
Is the amount of time you spend on each skill related not only to what needs the most improvement, but also the skills that mean the most to success in your sport?

Step 4: Define Your Goals

Define your goals. Be sure that your goals are challenging but realistic. Be certain that if you put the time and effort planned into them that you will attain them. Once you attain them you will automatically raise your level of aspiration and raise your goals.

Step 5: Plan

Plan how you will meet your goals.
How much time do you have to attain your long-term goals?
How can you best use the resources at your disposal in the time you have to learn?

Table 3.2: Setting Goals and Attaining Them (*cont.*)

What will your plan of attack be for attaining each of your
  subgoals?
How much will you attain each day, week, month, year?

Step 6: Evaluate Your Progress

Evaluate your progress.
Are you programming effectively?
Is your improvement on schedule?

of all the skills required for reaching the desired goals (physical skills, conditioning, mental skills, and so forth). The list should be very specific and should include practice suggestions for improvement in each area.

Next, athletes should detail in sequential order their current skills from the weakest to the strongest. When this list has been completed, a specific amount of time must be allocated daily for practicing individual areas of weakness. As each athlete's weakest skill is improved, time is spent on the next weakest skill. Coaches should also make certain that athletes know what their strongest skills are and spend sufficient time maximizing these strengths.

Imagine the Accomplishment of Goals

One way to program the system for success is to constantly remind oneself of the desired goals and to imagine accomplishing them. Athletes should spend five to ten minutes per day imagining themselves accomplishing their goals.

The strategy of closing one's eyes and imagining successful completion of goals is called *mastery rehearsal*. Psychologists are uncertain as to whether or not actual visual pictures in the mind are necessary. It may be just as useful to simply think about the attainment of goals even if a visual image does not appear. Either way, the system needs to be stimulated by success experiences on a regular basis. Structured mental practice on the part of each athlete is the best way to accomplish this task. It should, however, be constantly combined with confidence-enhancing statements by coaches reminding team members that success will occur (see Appendix B).

Special Motivational Considerations

Coaches must work with many types of athletes. Athletes vary from having little or no talent to being very gifted, and from being very motivated to being totally lacking in motivation. Modern science provides information that can aid the coach in developing motivational programs that are appropriate for each of the various types of athletes.

Coaching Overachievers: Dedicated Hustlers Who May Try Too Hard and Care Too Much

Every coach works with some young athletes who are totally dedicated to their sport. The most highly valued dream of such athletes is to "make it" in their chosen sport. Their energy is unlimited. During the season they are the first to practice and the last to leave. They quite willingly spend endless hours practicing alone while others may be loafing. These individuals, termed overachievers, view these potentially lonely hours as opportunities to get ahead of others and to prove their dedication. Their self-discipline is unmatched.

Overachievement is a motivational term used to describe extremely highly motivated athletes. The term does not necessarily refer to the amount of success that an athlete experiences. However, it does suggest that athletes who are overachievers need to be shown how to find balance in their motivational approach to sports. Despite good intentions, overachieving athletes may encounter problems that coaches have described as: "tying themselves up in knots," "trying too hard," "caring too much," or being "good practice players." Many aspects of the overachievement tendency can be beneficial to the attainment of athletic potential. But when motivation gets *out of control* and athletes become perfectionists, problems soon follow.

Available research (Burns 1980; Ogilvie and Tutko 1968; Rotella 1979) suggests that in their early years overachievers manifest learned effectiveness, a positive trait in athletes. But, as these athletes engage in sports in which their talents are lacking or are not appreciated, the tendency to deny their limitations may develop.

This very tendency may for years constitute a means of survival. Indeed, an athlete's early sports experiences may consistently reward this attitude. However, as these athletes progress to higher levels of sports, problems usually begin. Despite frequent discouragement, they fall back on the very strategy that got them to their present level: they refuse to accept their limitations. As a result, their goals may become unrealistic in relation to their true abilities. They fail to accept their limitations and to play within themselves. They try to do things that they are not capable of doing. At this point, overachievers may become difficult to coach. If the coach disagrees with their thinking, overachievers tend to protect themselves by questioning the coach's judgment. Such athletes may actively seek out friends who will agree with their viewpoint. Unfortunately, this tends to reinforce their own thinking and prevents them from accepting their coaches' advice. If the coach happens to be incompetent this may be a useful way to think. But in general, the blinders that allow overachievers to get to a certain level in sports have a deleterious impact that may keep them from getting any farther.

Overachievers typically have advanced in sport by believing absolutely that intense and persistent efforts to improve themselves would be rewarded. But unfortunately, they eventually find that this is not always the case, particularly at the higher levels of competition. Overachievers may try harder and have a great

attitude, but in high-level athletics these virtues are not valued unless combined with performance results. More talented players often reap the rewards of sports despite poor attitudes.

Frequently, athletes who are overachievers become frustrated during the course of their careers if they do not receive rewards for their efforts. They often feel cheated and begin to feel sorry for themselves. For the first time in their lives, they view the sports world as being unfair. They begin to experience jealousy or envy of more successful teammates, especially those who are highly talented but lack dedication and commitment to team success.

Work, Work, and More Work. Overachieving athletes tend to believe that hard work will and should always solve their problems. They seldom realize that a different training strategy or taking an occasional rest from sports will be productive. As competition nears, overachievers typically increase rather than decrease their efforts. As a result, they are often tired and lacking in competitive hunger on the day of an important competition.

Observation suggests that overachievement problems are common in all sports. But sports such as distance running and swimming, in which persistent efforts often are rewarded, may be heavily populated with and especially attractive to overachievers.

Some coaches have found ways of helping athletes cope with overachievement problems. The following description of the track coaching genius of the late Jumbo Elliott at Villanova University provides an example.

"The thing I remember most about Jumbo's practices is that they were a lot of fun," says Fred Dwyer (one of his ex-athletes), who as a rival coach is still one of Elliott's good friends. "Jumbo used to stutter a little and in practice I'd be on my way to a 60-second lap in the mile and he'd want me to slow down or sprint, and he'd call out 'Si—si—si. . . .' I'd stop and say, 'Si—si—si, what?'

And then he'd chase me around the track. You need light moments like that, because running itself requires so much discipline."

Elliott has always understood the need for occasional levity, in life as well as running. One of his catch phrases is "stop and smell the roses." He once advised the intense Marty Liquori to spend twenty minutes a day smiling into a mirror. [Telander 1980, p. 74]

This approach is an excellent start. But it is far from enough for most overachieving athletes. The problem is not restricted to sports. Athletes who tend to be overachievers often strive for high achievement in everything they do, from the athletic field to the classroom. Such athletes become so concerned with success that the urge controls them. They are no longer in control of their strivings. Working hard becomes their passion. Even when they attain success they devalue it or fail to enjoy it. This inclination appears to be related to the tendency to deny limitations and to protect an image of themselves that may be inaccurate.

Overachievers often refuse to accept compliments and tend to deny the quality of their performances. Their hope is that others will perceive them as very special athletes if they discount a very impressive win.

Many overachievers use their performance as a measure of their true self-worth. They are seldom, if ever, happy with their performance or themselves. Coaches must help athletes realize that they can be respected and successful persons even when their sports performances are unsuccessful.

Always Thinking Ahead. The thoughts of overachievers tend to be very future oriented. They often motivate themselves by continually thinking about the days ahead when their efforts will pay off. Often, these future-oriented thoughts interfere with concentration during competition. This is particularly true when they are losing in competition. Their tendency is to begin thinking ahead and analyzing their performance before the contest ends. This inclination certainly hinders attention and performance.

These future-oriented behavior patterns help explain how overachieving athletes over-practice and thus become overtired. So future oriented is their thinking that they fail to read their bodies and minds in the present. The signal that a rest is needed is sent, but overachievers tend to overlook or misinterpret this warning.

Despite the negative aspects of overachieving, there are many advantages to such tendencies. The future orientation of overachievers helps them continue to be motivated even when faced with persistent failure. If they can direct their efforts toward realistic goals, they can become very successful in sports and in life. But athletes with a tendency toward overachievement must overcome their urge for perfection. They must learn to relax and get their minds off their athletic goals. Failure to do so can result in "burn-out" and a loss of motivation before goal attainment. An enthusiastic but evenly paced approach to success in sports is vitally important.

Overachievers must develop a realistic and controlled approach to their efforts. This means that coaches must teach athletes how to have fun while they work hard at improving their skills. It also suggests that such athletes must learn to develop a sort of *positive fatalism* to help them recognize that perfection in sports is never realized. Perhaps this is what makes sports so attractive to athletes and coaches. No one ever totally masters a sport.

Coaches can help overachievers avoid unnecessary frustrations by giving them sound guidance concerning future sports participation. Coaches are in a very influential position and they must be careful not to shatter dreams that are attainable. Yet, coaches must give accurate and honest advice so that impossible goals are not established. For example, sometimes high school athletes are well-advised to attend smaller colleges where they can play certain sports despite their lack of quickness, size, or other uncontrollable abilities. At times, athletes may even need to be advised to pursue other sports or to channel their energies into nonathletic activities.

It is well worth a coach's time to help overachieving athletes with their motivational inclinations. Such assistance can help these athletes become happier and more successful. In Table 3.3 we present some suggestions that should prove helpful in counseling overachieving athletes.

Table 3.3: Keys to Counseling Overachievers

Coaches should help overachieving athletes to:
1. Conduct a realistic self-appraisal
2. Assume a realistic and valued role on the team
3. Learn to accept themselves for what they are and who they are while still striving for improvement
4. Accept limitations and play within themselves
5. Accept the fact that human beings will never attain perfection
6. Accept failure as a natural part of sports that can be useful to athletic development
7. Recognize that envy and jealousy are emotions that are counterproductive to sports, life success, and happiness
8. When frustrated or discouraged, compare themselves to those who are less talented or fortunate (handicapped, retarded, less talented athletes)
9. Learn that breaks or rest may be as important to sports success as hard work
10. Learn to set priorities for goals and values
11. Make certain to enjoy success, teammates, friends, and coaches
12. Recognize that true friends will value athletes for who they are, rather than for how they perform
13. Allow self-pride to motivate but not retard improvement
14. Be confident in themselves, but be accepting and open to the views of others
15. Do the best possible and to avoid feeling guilty if perfection is not attained
16. Be patient, to give improvements time to come, and to make certain that improvements are not ignored
17. Realize that backing off, viewing oneself honestly, and trying to change in accordance with the ideas on this list will help them to perform to their maximum potential

Motivating Underachieving Athletes

Underachieving athletes, like overachievers, fail to reach their potential because of motivational tendencies that are ineffective. But the thinking and behavioral patterns of the underachiever are very different from those of the overachiever.

Underachieving athletes often are quite talented, particularly at an early age. These athletes may perform quite well despite their motivational deficiency. Coaches typically describe these athletes as being "lazy" or "not caring enough." Coaches usually recognize that despite playing below their ability level these individuals may help the team win. Coaches are usually concerned about: (1) how to help these athletes, (2) how the attitude of these individuals will influence the attitude of other team members, (3) whether or not these athletes are worth keeping on the team, and (4) how to communicate to these athletes that they must continue to improve if they wish to succeed.

Development of the Underachieving Athlete. Today's sports world tends to reward the outcomes of achievement rather than the process involved in striving for success. Few rewards are given to athletes who practice diligently but fail to achieve success. Clearly, this can be discouraging to athletes who fail to win. But it also works *against* many early-maturing, gifted athletes who are successful early in their careers.

Because of the reward systems that are prevalent in most of our youth sports programs many athletes develop a highly ineffective process for attaining their potential. Athletes who are talented at an early age are usually victorious at a wide variety of sports activities. Often, in their first experiences with new sports activities they perform much better than their peers who may have been playing or practicing the sport for an extended time period. In some ways, these experiences work to the advantage of early-maturing athletes. It certainly is great for their confidence and gives them much enthusiasm for sports. But in the motivational domain these seemingly positive sports experiences can be disadvantageous.

Often, talented athletes form a perception that sports success is due only to an abundance of talent. They begin to believe that effort and persistence seldom make a difference in success or failure. If effort is a key ingredient in success, why do they win without even practicing a sport? Why do they defeat peers who invest much more effort in improvement?

Frequently, of course, early success in sports results from an advanced state of growth and development. But the advantages of early maturity may work to athletes' disadvantage. The early maturers or highly talented youths may think that they: (1) "have it made," (2) do not need to keep improving, and (3) have a great future no matter what happens. They tend to develop a behavior pattern that is typical of someone who is lazy and lackadaisical. In reality, they are simply behaving in a manner consistent with their experiences in sports. Laziness is the resulting behavior.

Early-maturing or highly talented young athletes have a special need for educated and caring coaches. Without the guidance of such leaders the potential problems confronting these individuals will be further compounded by other factors. First, such athletes do not always develop the *emotion of pride* as fully as other athletes. The pride they do have is associated with their competence rather than the pride that comes from wanting something and then working hard to attain it. It is not surprising that the most successful athletes have talent *and* learn early in life from their parents, coaches, or others to develop pride in both competence and persistent effort.

A second factor that often works to the disadvantage of early-maturing athletes is *time perspective*. They often become very present oriented. They live for the moment and concentrate well during competition. To compete well athletes must be able to concentrate in the present. But this very strength works to their disadvantage when it is time to plan practice strategies and to accurately assess their performance weaknesses.

Skilled coaches can help talented athletes avoid the tendency to focus only on the present. Often, this tendency is most debilitating in the out-of-season time period. This is a time period when athletes should strive to eliminate weaknesses and build upon strengths. Because many underachievers do not naturally tend to think of past errors or of future opponents they may function poorly when left to train alone.

A typical case of an underachieving athlete serves as an excellent example of this problem:

A 17-year-old athlete named Chris K. was referred to a sports psychologist by his coach. The coach described the young athlete as "one of the most talented athletes in his sport in the country." As a 10-, 11-, and 12-year-old this athlete had won all of the national age-group championships. At the time of his first visit to the psychologist the athlete was viewed by the head coach and several assistant coaches as being lazy, lacking in dedication, constantly breaking school policies, and regularly failing to prepare his equipment for competition. His training during the off-season was sparse. But on return to practice, Chris would regularly outperform others in training and conditioning drills despite being out of shape and failing to continue to improve his conditioning.

On several occasions during the previous year the athlete had been invited "out on the town" by peers on the night prior to major competitions. Chris usually chose to go with them. Often, he returned well after midnight and somewhat intoxicated. He would then show up for competition unprepared, both mentally and physically. His skills and his performances were going nowhere. For the first time in his life he was not winning all of the time. Athletes he used to beat easily were defeating him. He felt he was losing his ability. He was losing his confidence. His coaches and his parents were growing weary of trying to deal with the problems he caused. His teachers were also growing increasingly impatient with his lack of effort in the classroom.

As Chris lost confidence in himself he more frequently turned to others who would sympathize with him and give him support. The chances of his continuing in his sport and becoming a national-caliber athlete were quite low. Chris had begun to believe that he just did not "have it." He did not believe there was anything he could do, so maybe he should quit. His coaches were losing patience and were at the breaking point.

This scenerio is witnessed far too often in the contemporary world of sports. Many early-maturing and talented athletes fail to maximize their potential. Often, they are not mentally ready when they begin to experience failure. They frequently perceive failure as being caused by inadequate ability, since this is what experience has always taught them. As a result, they feel that they can do little or nothing to change a losing situation. They begin to feel incompetent and, thus, decrease rather than increase their efforts.

Helping Underachievers. Fortunately, underachievement is not an irreversible problem. It is an ineffective tendency that can very definitely be improved or totally eliminated. Many underachievers, unlike the majority of overachievers, will get many second and third chances because they have lots of talent. Sometimes, one meaningful experience turns them around.

To be a success in sports athletes must have a realistic approach to planning for success. Underachieving athletes cannot allow themselves to be fooled into believing that success in sports is due only to natural abilities that they cannot affect. On the other hand, athletes must

be taught by their coaches that there are situations in sports in which the most intense and persistent efforts in the world will not result in success if the goals are unrealistic.

Early-maturing and talented underachievers must be taught to *compare themselves to athletes whose talent is equal to or better than their own*. Their goal-setting plans and practice sessions must be designed with these considerations in mind. Their goal must be detailed and should be in writing.

To be successful at this task, coaches must teach underachieving athletes the importance of a *future time orientation* during pregame preparation. At the same time, these athletes should continue to utilize their present time orientation during competition. They must learn to appreciate meticulous precompetition preparation and must come to accept personal responsibility for their performances. This process often involves helping athletes realize that their sloppy practice strategies of the past will not suffice. At higher levels of competition preparation strategies become increasingly important.

Clearly, the understandings just described will not develop overnight. Changes should not be presented in a threatening manner. Patience and understanding will be required. But the importance of change must be emphasized.

Purposeless Underachievers. A second type of underachieving athletes, purposeless underachievers, are also frequently encountered by sports psychologists. These athletes are not necessarily highly talented, but they do fail to perform up to their fullest potential. They desire to become successful in sports and often believe that they are slowly progressing. But on closer observation, their view is quite unrealistic and inaccurate. They have no understanding of the process of achievement. Most of their practice time is spent "playing." They often have a great deal of enthusiasm, but there is little purpose to their practice.

These athletes tend to be present oriented. They concentrate well when they practice. But they do not carefully analyze past errors or anticipate future challenges. Little or no planning is done prior to practicing. Likewise, little or no analysis follows practice or competitive situations. To a well-trained eye this practice is aimless and progress is very slow. Following is an example of a purposeless underachiever:

The athlete, a 14-year-old named Laura, came to a sports psychologist for help because she was concerned that she was not progressing rapidly or consistently enough in her sport despite playing several hours each day. When questioned about her practice partners, she responded that she practiced with anyone she could find, usually athletes younger and less skilled than herself. She also confided that she had no regular physical and psychological training programs. Her practice sessions were always unstructured with no particular starting point. Practice usually ended when she or her partner grew tired. No attempt at developing a prepractice plan was ever considered.

Later, Laura was quite surprised to hear from the psychologist that other athletes had highly structured and organized practice sessions during the off-season. She had never given much thought to doing drills or working on her weaknesses despite the fact that she did so during her in-season practices when her coach structured the sessions.

In general, underachieving athletes like Laura can make rapid progress. Most of their past ineffectiveness is due to ignorance of how to practice effectively. Enthusiasm, which is usually present to begin with, increases markedly when they find an intelligent and rational explanation for their lack of improvement. Many of the athletes who manifest this underachieving tendency enjoy planning practices and analyzing their workouts. They often make dramatic improvements in- and out-of-season and impress their coaches and teammates. A well-developed goal-setting program is extremely helpful for such athletes.

Success in sports does not come from having quality practice only when athletes feel like it, or are "in the mood." Athletes who desire success in sports must understand that self-discipline and direction are required. Few athletes can achieve high levels of success without a knowledgeable and caring coach.

Coaching Gifted Athletes

Some athletes are indeed gifted. They possess skills and abilities that set them apart from the rest.

With barely more than three minutes remaining in the half, David Thompson gathered in a pass, and as he turned toward the basket, he squared off face-to-face with Michael Cooper. Thompson took Cooper left across the lane, and Cooper stayed with him stride for stride. When Thompson went up for his shot, Cooper went right up with him. For a long moment the two hovered there, Thompson's body full extended and Cooper right in his eyes. "When David got to the top of his jump, Cooper leveled off with him, and then David did something that only David can do—he started up again," says Denver Coach, Donnie Walsh, accepting on faith Thompson's seeming defiance of physical laws. "Cooper was as high as he was going to get, and when David started to rise again, Cooper got this puzzled look on his face, like he couldn't believe it. You could look at his eyes and see that he was finished for the night . . . that game, that one play was as close as the NBA is ever likely to come to an ascension." [Newman 1980, p. 36]

Most coaches will have at least one opportunity to work with an athlete who is exceptional. There is little doubt that such athletes are special and, consequently, special coaching strategies are required in order to help such athletes attain their potential. Coaches must be able to provide for the special needs of gifted athletes without having teammates feel that they are being treated unfairly.

Motivational coaching strategies that are designed for athletes of average ability may not suffice. Coaches must understand that gifted athletes may have very different needs and perceptions than they themselves had when they were athletes.

Coaches need to make a realistic appraisal of the potential of gifted athletes. Very different developmental plans may be necessary for high school athletes with the potential to succeed at the major university, Olympic, or professional level from athletes who probably cannot progress beyond high school participation.

Even talented athletes need quality coaching. If mutual respect and rapport are established, coaches may effectively aid special athletes in reaching their potential. However, if respect and rapport are lacking, coaches often withdraw and leave special athletes alone. In this situation, talented athletes often fail to develop as they might.

If the latter situation applies a coach may help talented athletes by bringing in a well-known expert (higher level coach, athlete, or other). Doing so may serve two functions: (1) it may show athletes that the coach does care about their welfare, and (2) provide reinforcement for what the coach has been recommending.

This initial step should be combined with earnest attempts to convince talented athletes that their skills provide them with access to very special opportunities. If this is not done gifted athletes are likely to perceive their gifts as a constant source of pressure.

While the pressure of being talented should not be overemphasized, it should not be ignored either. Many coaches find it difficult to view talent as a source of stress. But special talent and special confidence do not necessarily come together. Marques Johnson, perennial National Basketball Association All-Star, states:

> "You know, maybe one of the reasons I put on such a stoic front is because I've always had secret doubts about myself. I've always had a tendency to downplay my talents. I would always go into a situation thinking I wasn't as good, maybe as I really was—in high school, in college. Coming out of college, even though I'd been Player of the Year, I still had doubts. I heard people say that I might not be good enough. I thought, 'Can I really play with these guys?' Then I got to my first pro training camp. One hour. No more doubts. No more doubts at all." [Papanek 1980, p. 48]

Bring Them Along Slowly. It is easy to expect gifted athletes to put it all together quickly. But this does not always happen. When gifted athletes struggle, some coaches start to overcoach. Certainly, gifted athletes must be taught and developed, but often, the way to do so is to sit back, observe, and learn from watching them. Foge Fazio, University of Pittsburg's defensive coordinator for football, says the following about coaching talented players: "The main thing we try to do is not to overcoach them, because they are so doggone good" (Looney 1980, p. 60). Coach Jumbo Elliott said it a little differently: "If you have a runner as naturally gifted as, say, that hurdler, Renaldo Nehemiah, the way you coach is to not foul him up" (Telander 1980, p. 73). Talented athletes may not need as much feedback as other athletes during practice sessions. At times it is best to leave them alone.

At other times, extra time and attention are needed to provide drills designed to develop their special skills. Such drills may be totally inappropriate to other team members. Coach Terry Holland and his staff at the University of Virginia found that their All-American center, Ralph Sampson, had special needs despite his exquisite talents. As a freshman, Ralph could not play with his back to the basket and did not have a hook shot. His skills were more suitable for a guard than a center. In his freshman year the news media criticized Holland for letting Sampson play so far from the basket. But they did not realize that he lacked confidence in his ability to play with his back to the basket. Early in his freshman season the coaches did not want to force Sampson to do something that might cause him to lose confidence in himself or the coaching staff. So they let him play in the manner to which he was accustomed in the preseason and in the first half of the season while working on his weaknesses every day in practice. Each day plenty of feedback was provided that emphasized that Ralph had a good inside game and a great hook shot. This continued until Sampson finally said, "Coach, why don't I try playing low with my back to the basket and use my new moves?" He was ready. He felt good about himself and the coaches. Perhaps most importantly he was receptive to beginning to work on a new skill.

Motivational Hazards of Gifted Athletes. Gifted athletes are often faced with special problems and coaches must be aware of these potential hazards. Members of the opposite sex will often go to great lengths to distract gifted athletes from training. Peers may do almost anything to earn their "friendship," but they might not be true friends. Gifted athletes must learn to sort out peers who wish to use them for their own advantage from those who will help them reach their potential and find happiness.

Even classroom teachers sometimes put pressure on gifted athletes. Teachers may expect talented athletes to be great at everything they do. But many talented athletes are only average in the classroom. Teachers should expect a "good attitude" in the classroom, but recognize that they may not get special results from such athletes.

Teachers often feel uncomfortable around gifted athletes. From the moment they see their class roster, they realize that these students are different. Like others, teachers are excited about knowing these athletes and are particularly interested in their thoughts and ideas. They may be easily offended if athletes do not enjoy their subject matter. It is not unusual for gifted athletes to feel uncomfortable in the classroom. They may "hide in the corner" in an effort to be inconspicuous.

As a result of these early pressures, gifted athletes may experience the "fear of success." The fear of success often has been considered an unconscious fear. But most gifted athletes are very aware that their success causes them to fear that being anything short of the best will be judged a failure. Gifted athletes must learn to be their own judge. They must learn to block out the opinions of persons who are not in a position to be helpful. At the same time, these athletes must continue to strive for improvement and to learn from their coaches.

Talented athletes must be taught to initiate social contacts with teammates and friends. It is easy for others to feel that gifted athletes do not need their friendship. But the gifted, perhaps more than others, do need friends. They always will. So they must develop close friendships and strive to keep them even as they become "superstars." It will be their responsibility to initiate and maintain relationships. It is too easy for others to be intimidated by star athletes' successes and gradually allow friendships to deteriorate. But balance is still needed. Gifted athletes must care about the thoughts and feelings of others without letting them control their performance. When this happens a disaster can result.

The pressures to keep improving and performing never subside. Once the challenge of fulfillment is accepted the pressure is constant. Proving oneself never ends. Talented athletes simply advance to a higher level of performance and the proving starts all over again (see Table 3.4).

"Gene Banks (Duke University All-American) is unlike any player I ever had

Table 3.4: Common Problems Faced by Gifted Athletes

1. Performing at maximum ability with humility
2. Trying not to alienate other teammates
3. Continuing to push self toward valued long-term goals
4. Failing to recognize the team as more important than personal success
5. Keeping motivated in practice against less skilled players
6. Allowing fans to dictate expectations
7. Managing the jealousy of teammates
8. Realizing whether "friends" like you for what you are or for who you are
9. Coping with media attention
10. Becoming confident without becoming overconfident and lazy
11. Feeling that team success rests upon your shoulders
12. Being special and yet trying to be average off the field
13. Understanding what it's like to be average in ability
14. Constant pressure to be a role model
15. Preparing to advance to the next level of sports

or ever will have," said West Philadelphia High School coach, Joe Goldenberg. "It was not all peaches and cream between him and I. But from the time he laced up his sneakers, he was out to show he was the best. He had to prove it every day. He'd try to intimidate everyone, even in practice." [Smith 1981, p. 21]

To keep gifted athletes motivated they must be challenged. It is natural for them to get bored and develop sloppy habits when they are not. Unfortunately, the hazard here is that they are so good that they can "get away" with fundamental errors that will later haunt them.

It is usually helpful to bring in older or more skilled athletes to practice against these individuals. Sessions in which they are challenged will keep gifted athletes interested and motivated. It will show them why they need to keep improving. Lacrosse, soccer, and hockey players can benefit from practicing against better goalies or more experienced defensive or offensive players. Baseball and softball players can

practice hitting against advance pitchers. Tennis players can practice against "big league" servers.

Many high school coaches use themselves or graduated players who have continued playing as opponents to provide a challenge for gifted athletes. All-star games can provide this same function.

Some Do Not Recognize Their Talents. One of the most damaging of all of the motivational hazards faced by gifted athletes is failure to recognize their talent. Oftentimes, gifted athletes come by their skills so easily that they fail to appreciate them.

Skills that others sacrifice for and still fail to attain are taken for granted by the gifted, in some cases. Talented athletes must be shown that theirs is a wonderful gift. They must be helped to realize that they will probably never find another endeavor that will reward their efforts as much as the one in which they are gifted.

The Ultimate: Giftedness with Learned Effectiveness. Giftedness is a relative concept. At one level an athlete is considered gifted. At the next level the same athlete may be considered average. Typically, giftedness in sports is reserved for those athletes who have great physical skills. But it is possible to possess average physical skills with gifted mental skills such as those described earlier under "Learned Effectiveness."

Certainly, average athletes who learn that the only way they can play is to hustle all the time, practice with twice as much intensity, do the little things, never miss practice, and be great team players are gifted. They have the special gifts of perserverance and self-discipline.

It must be remembered that perserverance and self-discipline also are skills that only a few possess. When an athlete has the rare combination of physical and psychological giftedness, a truly exceptional athlete emerges. Pro basketball player Mike Newlin appears to be such a player. Much can be learned from listening to his thoughts on getting the most out of one's potential.

"Criticism doesn't bother Mike," says Cindy Linscomb, his girl-friend, who lives in Houston, "because he has never played for a harsher critic than himself." One of Newlin's teammates, Jan van Breda Kolff, says that "Mike treats it like a compliment when someone points out a deficiency. He listens very carefully and then goes right to work correcting the fault."

Newlin is totally dedicated to the game. "Guys get to be pros," he says, "and they think they don't have to practice hard anymore. That's a big mistake." With that, he looks into his omnipresent notebook for a quote he has copied: "Genius is perseverance in disguise." He offers it without comment, but there's no doubt that's how he views himself. [Looney 1981, pp. 28–31]

Coaching Athletes with Average Motivation

The majority of athletes have an average amount of motivation. In many ways it is easy and enjoyable to work with such athletes. They tend to do what their coaches ask without question. They show up for practice and work hard during practice time but do nothing extra. Such athletes seldom do anything that is creative. Analysis is not a natural tendency for these athletes and structured, out-of-practice work on skills or conditioning is unheard of for them.

Athletes with average motivation do not get the most out of their talents without the right coach. This is not to say that such athletes should be viewed in a negative light. The decision whether to maximize or waste one's talents is a value judgment. It is possible that most athletes with average motivation are happy and secure and should not be changed.

But in the world of organized athletics achievement is emphasized. Certainly, a major function of sports participation is to teach athletes the process of achievement. Therefore, it appears important that athletes realize that their motivational tendencies may be preventing them from discovering the limits of their potential. They must understand how to change if they so desire.

Athletes with average motivation should understand the perspectives of their teammates. Coaches should teach these athletes about the process of learned effectiveness. Coaches must emphasize that it is the process of achievement that is so important and useful. It is one of the main values gained in sports. The process may not make them superstars, but it will help these athletes to understand themselves and get the most out of their abilities and efforts.

Coaching Athletes with a "Bad Attitude"

Even great coaches encounter athletes described as having "bad attitudes." They are in many ways similar to the underachiever. But athletes with "bad attitudes" have problems that are more temporary in nature. Nonsport problems usually preoccupy the minds of such athletes and these problems interfere with concentration on sports. As a result, athletes with "bad attitudes" may approach practice sessions or competitive situations with little commitment or receptiveness to coaching feedback.

Discover the Origin of the "Bad Attitude." The first step in helping athletes with "bad attitudes" requires coaches to discover the cause of the problem. Clearly, previously established trust and respect are helpful at this point in time. There are several basic guidelines that can be useful.

1. Communicate with the athlete rather than attempt to ignore the problem and hope that it goes away.
2. Discover whether or not the athlete is aware that there is a problem. If the initial answer is "no," read the athlete's face to

help you determine if there really is a problem. If you feel there is, keep talking.

3. Encourage the athlete to relax and tell you the truth about the problem.
4. Direct the discussion to the wants and needs of the athlete.
5. Identify when, where, and why the problem first occurred.
6. Identify feelings, thoughts, and behaviors associated with the problem.
7. Encourage the athlete to explain what needs are not being met and discuss how they can be met or how to cope with not having them met.
8. Is the "bad attitude" caused by something that happened in practice, the game, or at home? There is always a source for the "bad attitude."
9. Ask the athlete how the coach can help and aid the athlete in realizing that the attitude is presenting a roadblock to attaining the desired positive results of sports participation.
10. Check to see if there is a conflict between the value system of the coach and the athlete or certain teammates and the athlete.
11. Encourage the athlete to look beyond the immediate problem and focus attention on positives.
12. Schedule future meetings and make some agreements on how the athlete will be treated until the problem is totally resolved.

Discourage Half-way Efforts. When working with athletes with "bad attitudes" coaches must discourage half-way efforts. On the other hand, they must avoid initially taking the "shape-up or ship-out attitude." Explain to such athletes that eventually, if change does not occur, they may have to be dismissed from the team. Be certain, however, that they realize that they are needed and wanted. Taking a stronger stand in initial meetings with athletes with "bad attitudes" is probably taking an unnecessary gamble. Coaches must keep in mind that attitude problems suggest that athletes are somewhat

confused as to whether or not continued participation is worth the effort.

Athletes must know that their coaches are willing to help. A grace period can be given. But in the meantime, a 100% effort will be expected during practice or competition. It may be useful to have athletes with "bad attitudes" stay away if they are not ready to go all out (Kauss 1980). This approach, however, may cause problems with other athletes on the team. They must understand the problem and accept their coaches' strategy. If athletes with "bad attitudes" have faked problems or skipped practices in the past teammates may be quite lacking in understanding. Coaches finding themselves in such situations must carefully analyze the merits of helping such athletes and the effects this will have on the team. Such decisions aren't necessarily easy, particularly when athletes with "bad attitudes" are star players. Decisions must be based upon long-term influences rather than immediate effects alone.

Pull from Ahead Rather than Push from Behind. There is probably nothing more frustrating to coaches than athletes who lack enthusiasm for attaining their potential. It is natural to respond emotionally. But emotional responses will not solve the "head" problems these athletes are experiencing. It is best to remain calm and, if possible, to start out *gently* describing the situation as a problem that coaches, athletes, and team members all share (Kauss 1980).

Screaming at and upsetting athletes with "bad attitudes" will only add to the problem. Remember that such athletes are already despondent and coaching responses that add to this feeling will decrease rather than facilitate communication and positive change.

Coaches must attempt to direct these athletes' thoughts in a new direction. Coaches may openly discuss a time when they had a "bad attitude" and provide insight into how they solved the problem. Such athletes might be asked to discuss the positive benefits of sports participation versus the negatives. A frank discussion of teammate attitudes is often warranted. Discussions should initially be positive, emphasizing the caring and concern that teammates and coaches have for these athletes. But it must also be stated that caring and patience are not necessarily everlasting. Patience may be minimal for seniors and maximal for freshman or athletes who have not historically had "attitude problems."

The Coach as a Positive Influence Agent. Coaches can help athletes with "bad attitudes" by being positive models. Words alone will not get the job done. Athletes are too sharp. They will see right through coaches who try to lead with words alone.

Teams do tend to take on the personality of their coaches. But most coaches only wish to admit and accept this point when they are successful. Research is incomplete on this tendency, but if teams have an *abundance* of "attitude problems" it is most likely due to the fact that: (1) athletes are imitating coaches who have "bad attitudes" themselves, (2) athletes do not respect their coaches and are, therefore, not imitating them, or (3) athletes have not yet been under the coaches' influence long enough for him/her to have had a behavioral impact on them.

Coaches often encounter overachieving athletes whose motivation gets out of control and goes beyond an effective level. Such athletes become perfectionists and refuse to accept their limitations. Several strategies are available for counseling athletes with overachieving tendencies.

Also, coaches should learn to effectively motivate underachieving athletes who may be quite talented. Modifying the motivational tendencies of these athletes should be a gradual process. But detailed help in structuring a goal-setting program is crucial to their future development.

Special techniques are required to properly motivate gifted athletes, average athletes, and athletes with a "bad attitude." Understanding the special needs of athletes and their impact upon individual motivation is important to coaching success. Effective management of individual motivation is the groundwork for developing athletes who are willing to sacrifice and work hard for the benefit of the team.

This chapter has not attempted to explain all the variables that affect motivation. Emphasis has been placed on especially important motivational issues. Coaches must recognize that there are many other factors that will influence individual motivation.

Summary

Every athlete is unique. It takes a knowledgeable and sensitive coach to respond to the motivational needs of all the athletes on a team. The goal should be to develop long-term and self-directing motivation. Behavioral tendencies of athletes vary from "learned helplessness," in which there is a perceived lack of self-control, to "learned effectiveness," in which there is a realistic perception of self-control. Coaches can benefit their athletes by developing in them this latter approach to motivation. It combines a productive utilization of present, past, and future time orientations.

References

Botterill, C. Psychology of coaching. In *Psychology in Sports: Methods and Applications.* Edited by R.H. Suinn. Minneapolis, Minnesota: Burgess Publishing Co., 1980.

Brown, B.B. *Stress and the Art of Biofeedback.* New York: Harper & Row, 1977.

Burns, D.D. The perfectionist's script for self-defeat. *Psychology Today,* (Nov.): 34–52, 1980.

Kauss, D.R. *Peak Performance: Mental Game Plans for Maximizing Your Athletic Potential.* Englewood Cliffs, New Jersey: Prentice-Hall, Inc., 1980.

Looney, D. When it comes to grit. *Sports Illustrated,* (Dec.): 60–63, 1980.

Looney, D. Genius is perseverance in disguise. *Sports Illustrated*, (Mar. 30): 28–32, 1981.

Michener, J. *Sports in America*. New York: Random House, 1976.

Newman, B. Flying high once more. *Sports Illustrated*, (Nov.): 36–41, 1980.

Ogilvie, B.C., and Tutko, T.A. *Problem Athletes and How to Handle Them*. London: Pelham Books, Ltd., 1968.

Papanek, J. At the top of the profession. *Sports Illustrated*, (Dec.): 40–49, 1980.

Rotella, R.J. Counseling motivational problems of athletes. *Sports Psychology Conference Proceedings*. Charlottesville: University of Virginia, Department of Health and Physical Education, 1979.

Seligman, M.E.P. *Helplessness: On Depression, Development and Death*. San Francisco: W.H. Freeman and Co., 1975.

Smith, G. Tinkerbell and Sivert heir. *Inside Sports*, (Feb. 28): 21–27, 1981.

Telander, R. Nobody's bigger than Jumbo. *Sports Illustrated*, (Mar. 10): 64–75, 1980.

Wiener, B. *Theories of Motivation*. Chicago: Markham, 1972.

Recommended Readings

Botterill, C. Psychology of coaching. In *Psychology in Sports: Methods and Applications*. Edited by R.H. Suinn. Minneapolis, Minnesota: Burgess Publishing Co., 1980.

Burns, D.D. The perfectionist's script for self-defeat. *Psychology Today*, (Nov.): 34–52, 1980.

Kauss, D.R. *Peak performance, Mental Game Plans for Maximizing Your Athletic Potential*. Englewood Cliffs, New Jersey: Prentice-Hall, Inc., 1980.

Ogilvie, B.C., and Tutko, T.A. *Problem Athletes and How to Handle Them*. London: Pelham Books, 1968.

Roberts, G.C. Children in competition: Assignment of responsibility for winning and losing. In *Proceedings of the NCPEAM/NAPECW National Conference, 1977*. Edited by L.I. Giduilas and M.E. Kneer. Chicago: Office of Publication Services, University of Illinois at Chicago Circle, 1977.

Seligman, M.E.P. *Helplessness: On Depression, Development and Death*. San Francisco: W.H. Freeman and Co., 1975.

Appendix B
Mastery Rehearsal

Mastery rehearsal can be best understood as athletes imagining themselves performing *perfectly* and without stress and anxiety. Through mastery rehearsal athletes can facilitate the development of correct response patterns in the brain. By learning how to recall these response patterns when performing during competition, athletes will be better able to maximize their performance potential.

Mastery and Tapes

One method of practicing mastery rehearsal is through the use of tapes (typically cassette tapes). Mastery tapes are produced by athletes for the purpose of providing a relaxing and anxiety-reducing method of mental preparation for competition.

Mastery tapes consist of scripts produced by athletes that describe their performance under perfect conditions. Their performances are completed in a nonstressful environment and situation.

Making a Mastery Tape

Athletes can start to make their mastery tape after they have carefully identified their personal "perfect performance." This thought process in itself can facilitate performance, since it helps athletes develop self-awareness of all aspects involved during their competition. Also, this thought process may help athletes *focus their attention* on what they should be concentrating on during performance. In this manner, the thought process develops self-coaching and self-management strategies that are important in helping athletes develop a sense of self-control.

After athletes have considered what their "perfect performance" involves, it is a good idea for them to talk with their coaches about their thoughts and ideas regarding their "perfect performance." This is important because athletes must be sure that their "perfect performance" is realistic relative to their abilities and past experiences in competition. While mastery rehearsal is visualized perfect performance, it is the *striving* for this perfect performance by athletes that must be emphasized. Remember, athletes are attempting to program their minds and bodies to perform effortlessly and flawlessly while at the same time realizing that they may never achieve a "perfect performance."

Once athletes have progressed to the point at which they understand what their mastery rehearsal tape should include, they can begin to write a script. A script is a written version of their "perfect performance" from which their tape will be made. After athletes have written their scripts, it is again a good idea to have other athletes or coaches review them.

There are several points to consider when writing a script. Athletes should attempt to dramatically describe how their body *feels* during all aspects of performance. For example, how does the body feel as a skier waits in the starting gate, or how do the leg muscles feel as the skier races down the slope? Furthermore, athletes should include other sensory information such as how objects look, the vividness or dullness of colors, and what they hear as they perform. The more athletes can include body feelings and sensations in their tapes the more realistic and the more useful they become.

A good way to start a tape is to describe the environment or environmental conditions in which the performance will take place. By describing the environment and its unique conditions, athletes "set the stage" for their performance.

To help facilitate realism on mastery tapes, athletes should use technical terms that apply to their performance. Athletes should focus their attention on terminology that is meaningful for them. This focusing of attention will help promote concentration on the right things as athletes listen to their tapes over and over during mastery rehearsal.

Another way to make tapes realistic is to have athletes make their performances exactly the same length as the time they have decided is their "perfect performance." For example, if athletes have decided that the time for their perfect race is 60 seconds, then the race on the tape should last for 60 seconds. However, some athletes may mentally visualize their performance in slow motion; in which case, they need not be concerned about the length of time their race takes on the tape. But athletes should be sure that they focus on their race on a time they are attempting to accomplish. The tape should include all prerace preparation—not just the 60 second race.

Many athletes may want to use introductory or background music on their mastery tapes. This is a good idea as long as athletes feel that the music enhances confidence and concentration. Besides music, the type of voice used on the tape must be considered. Some athletes may choose to use a very soft, mellow voice, while other athletes may prefer a loud, boisterous voice. Either extreme is useful, as long as athletes demonstrate an *emotional involvement* in what they are saying on the tape. This emotional involvement through music and voice will elicit mental images that will lead to enhanced confidence and performance.

The most important aspect of making a "good" tape is to realize that every athlete is an individual and will perceive situations differently. When athletes describe how they feel about or look at something, their descriptions may vary greatly. On the other hand, there are certain sensory feelings or concentration cues that all athletes should include in their tapes.

Coaches should be certain that both individual differences and team commonalities are considered.

An Example of a Mastery Script

As I wake up this morning, feelings of excitement fill my head. It is a good feeling, as if I were about to do something special. Today is the first Giant Slolam Race of the year. For me to succeed today I will have to break into the Top 10. This is a big race for me, but I am not nervous because I have prepared both physically and mentally for this race throughout the entire training and racing season. I have worked hard for this race and I know I will succeed. Everything seems to be going right for me this morning. Even when I ran I could feel my muscles energize with every stride. I feel that I am ready to succeed. Today when I get to the lounge my equipment is ready, especially my skis. Last night I tuned them so they would be clean and fast on the hard packed snow. I also waxed and scraped my skis so they would move fast over the snow. I get my bib at the race registration. I am running 38th, which is pretty far back, but it doesn't bother me because I know I will move up on my first run. I will succeed. I feel confident about breaking into the Top 10. I get to the top of the course for my race inspection. As I look over the course I try to pick up the key points. I feel the course is fast and that is how I like it. Subconsciously, I know the other racers will have to ski fast today to beat me, because I am feeling very good. These key points are places in the course where I can pick up my time on other racers. I like the flats and long sweeping turns where I can gain momentum through the turns and use my strength to explode out of the turn and gain speed. I am approaching my run. I must think now what I have to do to beat these other racers. I've trained all year and I am confident I will succeed. Now, it is up to my mind to prepare myself for the up and coming run. I know what I

have to do both physically and mentally. I am confident I know how to go about succeeding. I have seen the first skiers go down and they look good. But I know I can be just as good. I will succeed. My start is coming up now. I think back to the key places on the course where I have to precisely balance over my skis to go through clean. I know I have to keep my eyes on the course and not the people on the side. I must be clean and smooth through the course to succeed.

I am now in the starting gate. My energy is building and I am getting psyched. The starter gives me the count, 5, 4, 3 . . . I push out of the starting gate, and I ski to the first gate and I am on my way. Think, think. I start to get my rhythm on the first couple gates. Think smooth from turn to turn. On the top part of the course I feel good. I come to the hard turns on the course. I think balance, balance, drive those hands. I feel fast. I will succeed. The following gates are open. I feel clean. I feel good. I feel fast. I know I am doing well. I come to the flats. I must keep my line straight as possible, without sacrificing speed. Let those skis run. I know I'm doing well. I know I'm doing well. Coming closer to the finish now. Going over the last row. Keep on concentrating. I know I am doing well, and I go through the finish. As my time comes out I see that I have done well for my run. Count up nine times better than me. I know I can do better now. I will succeed.

All I have to do is to do the same routine just a little smoother and a little cleaner. I know I can do it. I have prepared for this all year, both physically and mentally. I grab my clothes at the bottom and get ready for the second race. During lunch, I will just relax and have a good time. I just think to myself that I will succeed.

As I go for my second run inspection, I talk with my friends to get extra input on the course so I can correct my mistakes on my first run. The second course seems to be almost the same as the first, maybe a little faster. I feel good about this and I know I will succeed today.

Think fast, fast, where can I pick up speed? I know I can't on the steeps. I must be rounder than on my first run because I know this is where I lost speed on my first run. Round, round, think round. I will succeed. On my free ski run I run on a trail next to the course, making long and fast sweeping turns as if I were running a race course. I feel good and I feel confident that I will succeed. As I wait up for my run, I sit by myself watching the first five racers go down. I go over the course in my mind. I place myself inside their bodies. I try to see how fast, how smooth I can be. I ought to be as clean as possible. I psych myself up as I did in my first run, hopping around, getting ready for the physical aspects of the course. The starter motions me into the starting gate and starts to give me the countdown. Get into the beat . . . 2, 1—I'm off! Rhythm, rhythm, smooth, clean, look for speed. I can feel the snow under

my skis. I feel fast. I feel good. I am confident. I am confident when I come to the steeps. I take the gates round and clean, better than before. I will succeed. Look ahead. My legs are getting tired, but it doesn't bother me. I must drive, drive. I will succeed. The transition onto the flats must be taken well to carry my speed. Yes, I feel the speed gradually gaining as I go skimming across the run. Think fast, fast. Let these skis run, wisping my body against the gates. I am coming over the last hump to the finish. I am extending my body to its limits, driving my body through the gates, looking for the most speed possible. I know I will succeed. I will succeed. I'm almost to the finish now. I get into my tuck and through the finish. Inside I know I have succeeded. I just wait for my time. My time comes up. I can only count six better times on the board. I have succeeded in what I have come here for. I am proud of myself.

Credit: University of South Carolina Sports Information.

Team Motivation

4

Once coaches have met the individual needs of athletes they must dedicate their efforts to development of a cohesive and highly motivated team. This process, though difficult to master, is essential to team success. Coaches must motivate athletes to work together and to sacrifice for the team.

The Keys to Team Motivation

Team success is not determined entirely by motivation. Other factors such as the ability of athletes, scheduled opposition, conditioning level, and even luck are also important. But motivation has a very significant influence on success, and it is a factor that a coach can control. The solutions to athlete motivation will not *always* be found in science. But usually, effective motivation depends upon coaches' abilities to artistically apply principles that are scientifically sound. This chapter provides coaches or aspiring coaches with a scientific basis for motivating their athletes to achieve maximal development and performance.

There are several basic points that are crucial to an understanding of team motivation. Coaches should be well aware of their importance.

Be a Perceptive Observer

Coaches who wish to be effective motivators must become masters of observing the actions and moods of team members. Coaches who carefully observe their athletes will quickly recognize that athletes act and feel in very idiosyncratic ways; therefore, all athletes will not be motivated equally by the same strategies. A major task for coaches is to motivate a group of athletes to function as a team while allowing for individual differences in motivation.

All team members do not perceive a particular motivational strategy in the same manner. But once coaches realize that there are perceptual differences among athletes they can begin to analyze individual athletes and situations in a style that will allow them to become successful. They can begin to ask themselves: "Why is a certain athlete discouraged and walking with a hanging head?" "Is the athlete looking for attention?" "Does the athlete need attention or help from me?" "Should I be tender or should I tell the athlete to stop feeling sorry for himself (pick your head up and act like a winner)?" "Why is the athlete feeling depressed?" "Has the athlete been performing poorly?" "Did I just yell at the athlete?" "Did he just make a crucial error in a big game?" "Did the athlete just fail a test or get rejected by a preferred college?" Obviously, to answer these questions accurately coaches must be perceptive and understanding.

The perceptual approach to motivation (Combs and Snygg 1959), which argues that coaches should try to understand the perceptions of athletes, can be effective. However, this approach demands a commitment by coaches to spend time thinking about the *actions, feelings,* and *thoughts* of their athletes.

Opting for Optimism

Effective motivation demands that coaches opt for optimism. But optimism cannot be expressed through words alone. Every action and behavior must suggest that a coach is optimistic. Clearly, athletes model their coaches if they *believe* them. But they must believe. If coaches' actions belie their words there is little chance that optimistic words will be accepted Often this means that coaches must be *optimistic but realistic.* Unrealistic optimism may lead to frustration or a loss of faith in coaches' leadership. Opting for optimism is extremely important in particularly difficult coaching situations.

For example, coaches who believe that it will take three to five years to build a successful program are better off to say so honestly. But coaches must also explain to their players why it might take so long and should detail how the leadership intends to remediate past problems. At the same time, it should be mentioned that

dedicated effort may lead to success earlier than planned. This approach is effective because it will provide team members with: (1) a rational excuse for past failure, (2) a realistic plan for overcoming past weaknesses, (3) a determined goal orientation, and (4) flexibility in case success does not come rapidly. Yet, the strategy still leaves open the possibility of success coming sooner than anticipated. It is, admittedly, important for coaches to sell their leadership to their athletes. Athletes must believe that their coaches are capable of bringing them success.

Coaches who have a winning reputation have a much easier job. But regardless of past history, *persistent energy must be directed at convincing athletes that improvement and success will eventually come.* When coaches lose this attitude their teams are almost certain to fail.

There is no doubt that it is sometimes difficult for coaches to be optimistic. Indeed, it is far easier to think pessimistically than it is to think optimistically when performance has been poor. Coaches cannot, however, expect their athletes to remain optimistic if they are not optimistic themselves. Coaches are needed most when times are tough. *The coaches' job is to help athletes achieve things they could not achieve by themselves.*

Optimism can of course have its pitfalls. When optimism becomes *blind confidence* it can lead to an ineffective plan for attaining success. Therefore, great coaches take time to honestly critique their programs. They want to find weaknesses and determine strategies for overcoming them. But they do their arguing and planning behind closed doors rather than in front of their athletes. A team plan for the season is presented to the team with all coaches totally committed to it. Discussion of the plan takes place ahead of time. The same strategy should be used at half-time of contests to encourage optimism in athletes. While the athletes are getting their drink and settling down, coaches should meet and evaluate first-half strategy and reach agreement upon changes. By the time the strategy is presented to the team all coaches should have reached a consensus. This leads to an optimistic acceptance of the strategy by the entire team and prevents disagreements on the sidelines.

Sometimes, even a pessimistic attitude by coaches can lead to extra effort by players, particularly confident players who desire to disprove their coaches. When athletes do disprove their coaches, coaches should accept the error and congratulate their athletes rather than respond emotionally in a defensive manner. Occasionally, even the best of coaches have made this error early in their careers. Witness the field goal that decided the acclaimed "best game ever," the 1958 Eastern Conference play-off game between the National Football League's Cleveland Browns and New York Giants.

> No one knows how far the field goal traveled. The driving snow had obliterated the markers at Yankee Stadium when Pat Summerall, standing somewhere around midfield in the closing minutes, drilled the most dramatic three-pointer in Giant history.
> .... The Browns didn't come as close as Vince Lombardi to blocking Summerall's greatest kick. Lombardi, then offensive coordinator of the Giants and prone to regard all placekickers as lazy and untrustworthy, urged coach Jim Lee Howell to try for a first down on the ground. After some sharp exchanges, Howell rejected his advice. Summerall witnessed the argument and, upon returning to the sideline admidst the post-kick bedlam couldn't resist seeking out Lombardi.
> "How about it, coach?" he inquired. Lombardi, who at that moment looked like a twice-crossed consigliere, gave Summerall his most menacing scowl. "You son of a bitch," he growled. "You *know* you can't kick it that far." [Waters 1981, p. 114]

Think carefully about this situation. Even Vince Lombardi, the eternal optimist, defended his ego rather than reward an athlete for believing in himself in a very difficult situation. But the young Lombardi learned and became a highly successful head coach.

First Experiences are Crucial

Great team motivators attempt to anticipate problems that might occur in various situations throughout the season. Potential reactions to these situations are discussed during the coaches first interactions with their teams. There are many explanations for the effectiveness of this strategy: (1) first impressions are very important, and it shows the team that their coaches are aware of the potential hazards in their coaching decisions; (2) it provides athletes with potential problem situations that they might get themselves into and, as such, can help prevent team members from making the described errors, and presents a clear and precise presentation of athlete behaviors and expected coaching responses; and (3) it prevents coaches from leading by episode, in which case, many athletes or their parents will respond in a defensive manner because they perceive that they are being separated out and treated differently.

Great team motivators do everything within their power to make their first experiences with a team extremely positive. They begin to create a positive, enthusiastic, and trusting attitude from the first day. Their first impression delivers a message that says: (1) we will be successful together, (2) we will improve and grow by remaining open to each other's ideas, (3) when problems occur we will talk about them honestly and attempt to solve them rather than keep them inside ourselves and use them as complaints or excuses for failure, (4) we will get excited about what we are doing, but be controlled while doing it, (5) we will be accomplishing our task while attempting to meet the needs of athletes and coaches, and (6) we will experience great joy together and probably suffer disappointment together. Sometimes, we will evaluate and grow from failure and errors, and other times we will learn to laugh at ourselves when our inadequacies prove that we are human. In either case, we must believe in each other at all times and keep striving.

As a result of positive first impressions athletes realize that their coaches care about coaching every athlete. This belief will persist as long as coaches are receptive and interested when athletes come to talk. Coaches can facilitate communication during their first contacts with their athletes by letting all athletes know that their office doors are always open. Many successful coaches believe that any errors that they make in motivating athletes should result from trying too hard or caring too much. One of the all-time great collegiate basketball coaches, Lou Carnesecca of St. John's University, has been described as follows:

His failings, as he himself admitted, were glaring. He was hopelessly disorganized. After more than 30 years, he still didn't understand that basketball was a game. But noboby seemed to bear a grudge. Each of his recruits became an adopted son. He worried about their grades, their love affairs, their families. Even when they'd graduated, he was always there for them, in need. ''Part Mother Hen and partly Father Confession,'' he said. If he sinned, it was only because he cared so much. [Cohn 1981, p. 70]

It is often useful to set up an individual preseason meeting with each member of the team. This meeting can be utilized to establish a positive first impression and to find out as much as possible about each athlete: past sports experience, preferred position, future goals, family background, academic progress, commitment to sports, role on team, and likes and dislikes. This meeting should also be a time for coaches to open up and speak to each athlete about personal tendencies, preferences, and plans for the team. This meeting can lay the groundwork for open communication. However, communication must be continued during every practice session and in various social encounters. *Positive first impressions will endure only if they are regularly reinforced.*

Your Body Moves Count

Often, coaches' body language sends important messages to athletes (see Table 4.1). Coaches must understand the effects of these messsages. Experts in nonverbal communication consider the impact of a message to be 55% dependent on body language. It is believed by such experts that, unless trained, the body does not know how to lie; thus, it is not what coaches say, but how they say it that is most important.

When the head coach walks into the practice area the initial greeting may be, ''Okay, let's bring it in. I want a really good, intense practice today.'' But the way *the coach walks* into the area (a confident, energetic stride or a tired, bent-over walk), the *tone of voice* (an enthusiastic and excited commanding voice or a pleading, whining voice), the *look in the eyes* (excited and wide open or disinterested and half asleep), and even the calm, comfortable, or enthusiastic *movements* of the coaches' arms and hands deliver messages.

Particular body postures, though usually interpreted similarly by different athletes, do not always send the same messages. Different athletes may interpret body language quite differently, depending upon how they are feeling (e.g., nervous or confident) or *thinking* (coach likes me or dislikes me).

Coaches aren't the only ones who send body signals. Athletes also deliver unspoken messages with their bodies. Coaches must learn to accurately read and respond to the body messages sent by athletes. If coaches see that a particular athlete's head is frequently hanging, this may be a sign that the athlete needs some attention. Coaches must know their athletes well enough to understand the meaning of their body signals. Responding to these body signals

Table 4.1: Athletes' Interpretations of Body Signals Sent by Coaches

Coach Speaks in Monotone	Coach Raises an Eyebrow in Response to an Athlete's Question	Coach Walks with Head Down	Coach Clenches Fists During Game
Athlete's Interpretation:	Athlete's Interpretation:	Athlete's Interpretation:	Athlete's Interpretation:
depressed	coach disagrees	concentrating on new	intense
uninterested	doesn't understand	strategy	wants to win
little interest in team spirit	confusion	disappointment	nervous
don't care enough to get	it's up to you—there is	lack of confidence	eager
psyched	nothing more I can do	very serious—no nonsense	concentrating
coach is mad	thinking and/or analyzing	team is losing and there is	sign of encouragement
coach is distracted by	your comments	little hope of winning	if fist is raised
something that has	just made a point that was	psyching self up for the	trying real hard
happened outside of the	of interest	game	struggling to keep
game	surprise	gathering thoughts	emotions under
coach is bored	"So you think you know	wondering what went	control
coach does not enjoy job	more than I do."	wrong	pressure situation
coach has a superior		a real bad day	really into the game
attitude— "I am better		coach has given up on the	ready to hit someone or
and smarter than you."		individual or the team	throw something if
			fist is lowered

can help coaches to motivate all of their athletes in a more effective manner.

Threats and Reprimands for Motivation

Many coaches have for years made use of threats to motivate at least some of their athletes. Threats have varied from "You won't start" and "You're going to lose," to "The whole team will run extra laps if you don't hustle." There are occasional situations in which threats *may* be useful. In such instances, coaches should take time later to explain to athletes why the strategy was necessary. Even then coaches must know which athletes will be helped or destroyed by threats.

Dan Gable, the ex-Olympian champ and present coach of the highly successful Iowa University wrestling team, had the following to say to one of his wrestlers, Ed Banach, before his 1981 NCAA wrestling championship match: "If you don't win tonight, your dream is shattered." Thus psyched, Ed, who had for years dreamed of winning four straight NCAA championships, raced onto the mat and took control with a take-down, a reversal and—bingo!—there was his opponent studying the ceiling lighting arrangement. The fall was recorded at 4:15." [Looney 1981, p. 50]

But the true coaching genuis of Dan Gamble is more clearly reflected in the very different way that he motivated Ed's less confident twin brother, Lou, who was also about to wrestle in an NCAA final in a different weight class. Prior to his final match Gable told him, "You're not going to have any problem!" Both brothers won their matches, partially because Coach Gable knew who would and would not benefit from a threat.

Unfortunately, some coaches rely predominantly upon the use of threats. Eventually, the effectiveness of threats is diminished. Threats may become totally ineffective if they are not followed up. For many athletes threats may work *immediately* in enhancing motivation. Yet, they will be of little value in providing *long-term* motivation. When the threat is removed the motivation of many athletes deteriorates.

Some coaches have found success in motivating athletes by playing upon their intense desire and pride. Although this is not a preferred motivational strategy, it may be useful when used as a last resort. Sometimes, however, coaches go too far with this strategy and the effect is extremely negative.

Kareem Abdul-Jabbar presents an example in discussing his playing days under high school coach Jack Donahue.

"Donahue cajoled and embarrassed his players. His whole thing was trying to motivate you through your pride and your extreme desire not to look bad. Didn't want to look bad in front of Mr. Donahue. He would ask questions like, 'What are you, a stiff? Are you alive? Let me feel your pulse.' Mr. Donahue was great . . . in that respect."
A reservation creeps into his voice.
Donahue once called him out during a game, saying, "You're acting just like a nigger." And although Donahue later said it was to "motivate" him, Abdul has clearly not put that aside. [Knobler 1981, p. 25]

Coaches who use strategies such as threats or embarrassment must recognize the inherent weaknesses in this approach. Above all, coaches must make certain that this strategy does not become their most common motivational technique.

Like it or not, coaches work in an emotionally charged environment. Coaches usually have a strong belief that they know what it takes to be successful. They also realize that their own success will be measured by the performance of their athletes. Consequently, it is to be expected that poor performances and disagreements may lead to an open flow of emotions. Coaches must attempt to respond in-

tellectually to those emotionally charged situations. Sometimes, the best response is to let emotions flow and to verbally reprimand athletes. Other times it is best to remain calm. The key is to maintain control and to understand the advantages and disadvantages of both types of response.

A brief analysis of some of the problems resulting from emotionally charged reprimands will provide a greater insight. The following assumptions can be made concerning reprimands.

1. When overused, reprimands tend to lose their effect as athletes become desensitized.
2. Reprimands may elicit short-term effects, but positive long-term effects are usually minimal.
3. Even the short-term effects of reprimands may be negative, if:
   a. Athletes dislike the coach.
   b. Athletes become scared of the coach.
   c. Athletes lose respect for the coach.
   d. Athletes become anxious and inattentive.
4. Reprimands are particularly counterproductive in nonconfident athletes.

Many coaches and sports psychologists recognize that there may be some benefits to reprimands. They do cause some athletes to "put out." Many athletes interpret a verbal reprimand as an indication that the coach cares or believes that the necessary talent to become successful is present. Such an interpretation occurs most likely when athletes trust and respect their coaches. If, on the other hand, reprimands are interpreted as meaning that talent is missing and there is no way to improve, very negative results can be expected.

It appears that the key is to make certain that energy is directed at improvement rather than anger toward athletes for failing to behave in the desired manner. It is one thing to be critical of performance, it is an entirely different matter to convey to athletes that they are "no good" through anger.

Verbal reprimands can be useful in getting athletes to *pay attention*. Obviously, it is difficult to teach effectively without first getting the attention of athletes. Unfortunately, yelling may get some athletes to pay attention while distracting others. Usually, a simple change in the tone of voice will get the job done with far fewer negative results. A voice change combined with a change in facial body expressions will usually let athletes know when coaches are being serious rather than kidding or providing sarcastic humor.

Also, verbal reprimand can be productive when the reprimand is immediately followed by instruction (Tharpe and Gallimore 1976). Athletes must know what is important. This combination of reprimand and feedback can remind athletes what is important and teach them how to execute correctly.

Usually, a raised voice or repeated emphasis will do a better job than emotionally charged reprimands. But there is no doubt that emphasizing key points is crucial to coaching success and somehow these must be communicated. Dr. James Counsilman, the highly respected and successful swim coach at the University of Indiana, has said the following on this point:

> Let me tell you what I think the X factor is in successful coaching. The X factor is, to quote an old saying, "the ability to separate the wheat from the chaff." Another way of expressing it is to say, "You must be able to recognize the important things and work on them, to minimize the unimportant." Let me give you an example: We have seen mothers and fathers, and a few coaches walking up and down the pool deck as the swimmer is swimming with dropped elbows, overkicking like mad, and he is being yelled at to "kick, kick, kick." In other words, they ignore the important item—the dropped elbows—and emphasize the unimportant by yelling, "kick, kick." [Counsilman 1979, p. 12]

In a similar manner, coaches can have a very positive impact on athletic motivation by raising their voice or changing voice tone to encourage athletes to increase their intensity. When doing so, it is crucial to *remain positively enthusiastic*. Some coaches ineffectively attempt to energize athletes by acting discouraged and disappointed and pleading for increased effort in a whining voice. This approach usually has just the opposite of the desired effect.

Coaches must learn when reprimands are really necessary and useful. Likewise, they must understand how to utilize reprimands and why a simple adjustment in the voice may do the job more effectively. Occasionally, when coaches decide it is important and appropriate they can give athletes a verbal "kick in the pants" and get the desired results.

Cohesiveness: A Key to Maximizing Team Motivation

One of the important influences on team motivation is team cohesiveness. Cohesiveness has the potential to provide the extra ingredient necessary for bringing out the best in team members. Therefore, coaches must understand cohesiveness and how to develop it.

Positive Influences on Cohesion

For years coaches and researchers debated whether cohesiveness causes success or success leads to cohesiveness. A clear-cut answer is yet to be determined. There have been countless examples of cohesive teams becoming highly successful and of successful teams becoming increasingly cohesive. Yet, there are also examples of highly successful teams lacking in cohesiveness and of highly cohesive teams failing.

Cohesiveness can be defined as the extent to which members of a group are attracted to each other or to the group itself. There are several factors that positively influence cohesiveness. Cohesiveness is increased if membership on a team is limited and occurs after passing difficult entrance requirements. Likewise, cohesiveness is promoted if membership is based upon similar values, interests, and beliefs of individual members. Also, small team size, achievement of team goals, and external threats to the achievement of team goals can promote cohesiveness (Middlebrook 1974).

Sometimes, there are exceptions. Paradoxically, losing can on occasion lead to team unity. Likewise, a coach who is disliked by the team or some of the team may cause athletes to unite against the coach.

Interacting Versus Co-acting Teams. In general, cohesiveness is most important to team success in sports that are heavily dependent upon interaction of team members during performance (field hockey, basketball, lacrosse, soccer). In co-acting sports that involve parallel competition (golf, bowling, tennis, swimming) cohesiveness appears to be less crucial to sports team success (Hall 1981). However, even in co-acting sports, when the competition is close, team unity may make the difference between success and failure. Usually, it is safe to assume that increased cohesiveness facilitates team performance.

Limiting Membership. The more selective team membership, the more likely it is that cohesiveness will be increased. This is particularly true if team membership has high status associated with it and gaining membership requires difficulty. When team try-outs are challenging and demand a high level of skill, effort, and competition, cohesiveness will be enhanced. In such circumstances, making and remaining a part of the team becomes highly valued.

Coaches must realize that a difficult entrance requirement also has its negative side. Some players must be cut or placed on lower level teams. Coaches can destroy many of their attempts at developing cohesiveness if they cut members in a heartless and disorganzied fashion. All athletes who are cut should be carefully tested and evaluated, and should find out their status directly from their coaches rather than from a note posted on a door. They should be given advice as to how they might improve themselves. When realistic, they should be in-

vited to try out again in the future (Murray 1981).

Team Aspirations. Coaches must strive to meet both team and individual goals. Appropriate goals can be identified through team discussions, individual coach-athlete discussions, or through questionnaires. Either way, the eventual result must be the establishment of team goals that are acceptable to all athletes.

It is crucially important that coaches and athletes agree upon team goals. Cohesiveness can be hindered if, for example, a coach has a task-oriented goal of winning and team members are mainly participating for social reasons. When faced with this situation coaches must: (1) change the members' attitudes, (2) change their own attitudes, or (3) have both groups change slightly and try to meet both goals (Sherif 1976).

Delineating Roles. Athletes must accept their roles within the team and recognize their importance to team success. Team members need to know exactly what their roles are during practice and competittion. Athletes who are never told their role may feel out of place and unimportant. This is particularly true for substitutes on a team. The more frequently coaches remind their athletes of their roles, the better. Likewise, public statements as to the importance of each role to team success can be beneficial to cohesiveness.

Team Homogeneity. Cohesiveness is enhanced when teams have similar interests, values, and beliefs. Factors such as socioeconomic background, home neighborhood, and religious belief can influence cohesiveness. The impact is positive when there is similarity across team members (Eitzen 1973).

Team Size. It is far easier to influence cohesiveness with smaller groups. Team sports that have a large number of participants (25 or more) may facilitate cohesiveness by separating the team into small groups. In doing so, it is important to bring all members together on a regular basis to prevent splintering of the team.

Mimi Murray, a coach of several national gymnastic championship teams at Springfield

College and a highly recognized sports psychologist, suggests that coaches can foster cohesiveness by:

1. Promoting constant, continuous, and open communication
2. Establishing clear criteria for team selection
3. Emphasizing the team members' shared experiences on the team
4. Establishing team goals
5. Accepting individual personality differences and utilizing each person's strengths while understanding and appreciating their weaknesses
6. Structuring smaller responsibility groups within larger groups through the leadership of other coaches and/or responsible team members
7. Providing opportunities for success through:
   a. positive and negative reinforcement
   b. praising the demonstration of cooperation when losing as well as winning
   c. rewarding team effort, not just individual effort
8. Establishing realistic team and individual goals
9. Delineating each team member's responsibilities to the team
10. Not expecting any more from the team than the coach is willing to give or demonstrate
11. Maintaining awareness of group interaction
12. Listening, hearing, and being receptive to individual and team needs and suggestions
13. Emphasizing the process of goal attainment or achievement, not just the final outcome

The Role of Leaders. Coaches, assistant coaches, and captains all play an important role in developing cohesiveness. Coaches must help team members elect captains that are true team leaders, not merely social leaders. It is ideal if the captains are task oriented with a receptive ear to interpersonal problems and needs.

Teams can only be as cohesive as their coaching staffs. Head coaches are well advised to develop small cohesive staffs rather than larger, conflicting staffs. Athletes will learn of the conflicts if they exist, and such conflicts may undermine all efforts to build a cohesive team. Leaders within a team influence cohesiveness by their very actions. Coaches can emphasize either selfishness or selflessness. It is certain that athletes will respond to behaviors that are emphasized.

Nothing brings a team to the point of accepting that there is no "I in we" like publicly observed competition against a worthy opponent. It has been well documented that competition between teams fosters cooperation within a team. The "we" attitude is fostered by treating each athlete as a valued team member. All athletes must have the same practice and game equipment and follow the same rules. Enforcement of rules must be fair and consistent, and it is preferable that rules be developed by the team members and the coach.

Personal and Team Identity. Many developing athletes constantly struggle for an individual identity and may resist ideas designed to foster similarity. On one hand, coaches must help athletes subjugate themselves for the team's benefit. On the other hand, there is a need to allow individual expression. Each need must be met without destroying the other.

Opportunities for display of individual expression can be occasionally provided in practice and even in contests. If a team has a policy that requires a specific team dress for home or away games, leeway may be given for parts of the dress. For example, teams may have a contest to see who has the most outlandish hat, tie, shoes, or socks. There are endless possibilities.

Speaking in Public. When coaches speak in public they should talk in terms of "we" rather than "I." The one exception may be accepting personal blame for failure and giving the team credit for success. This approach may be needed for insecure teams that lack confidence. Clearly, coaches must be very secure to accept personal blame for team failures. Insecure coaches, fearing that others may feel their team is losing because of the coach, tend to ascribe failure to poor athletic talent on the team. Unfortunately, this approach can destroy the athletes' confidence in their coach.

At award banquets coaches can facilitate cohesion by frequently giving credit for team success to athletes, parents, school staff, and other team support groups. Coaches can be certain that if all of these groups are made to feel important team success will thrive. Banquet speeches should reward the importance of self-sacrificing behavior while praising the individual accomplishments of seniors and assistant coaches in particular.

The late Paul "Bear" Bryant, legendary University of Alabama football coach, emphasized this point when he described his philosophy for creating loyalties and allegiances.

> "There's just three things I ever say. If anything goes bad, then I did it. If anything goes semigood, then we did it. If anything goes real good, then you did it. That's all it takes to get people to win football games for you." [Lyons 1981, p. C5]

Building Positive Feelings

Coaches have developed many strategies for helping athletes feel like valued and important team members. Two swimming coaches, Karl Mohr of the University of California, Berkeley, and Tom Fay of Vanderbilt University, have developed the following "ten commandments" for fostering these positive feelings.

The Ten Commandments*

1. I am committed to your well-being and fulfillment.
2. I will not hurt you.
3. I will not judge you.
4. I will support you.
5. I will accept you.
6. I will listen.
7. I will not make you wrong or make you lose, dominate or invalidate you.
8. I will expand my reality to include and respect you.
9. I will not take it personally.
10. I will be honest, straightforward, and open.

*And in every case I am worthy of the same from you!

Warm-ups. Warm-ups on the court or field should be highly organized and systematic. Warm-ups that are organized can give a team a feeling of unity. It may, however, be desirable to have a more individualized, free-flowing warm-up, either prior to or after the organized warm-up.

Postgame. It is beneficial to have a team come together as a unit at the conclusion of a contest. The team should share both victories and defeats.

During Competition. Cohesiveness can be promoted by instituting general policies for team behavior during competition. For example, during time-out there can be a special strategy for all team members to follow. Many successful teams have all players run off the field or court and go to a specific place for an attentive team gathering. Substitutes as well as active players should have specifically assigned responsibilities.

Star players must learn the importance of giving of themselves for the team. They must be willing to forget about their personal statistics so that a substitute may get an opportunity to perform.

Star players can further benefit team cohesion if, when they are not playing, they become enthusiastic team supporters. Such behaviors enable substitutes to believe that their performance is important rather than meaningless. In turn, the substitutes will be more enthusiastic and supportive when they are not performing.

Substitutes must be constantly treated as valued team members. They must be given roles that are respected and appreciated as being important to team success. It is easy for substitutes to feel that they play "minor roles." Whenever feasible, substitutes should be given playing opportunities. The earlier in the season they get to play, the better.

The points just mentioned suggest that coaches and teammates should be emphathetic and supportive of substitutes. Substitutes must also understand that their coach will listen when they are discouraged, but sulking in public or around team members will not be acceptable. Sulking tends to undermine rather than facilitate cohesion. Often, athletes who sulk will find a sympathetic teammate with whom they can share their misery. The two athletes may form a band that conflicts with the rest of the team. They must understand that this is counterproductive to team success.

Off the Field. While it may be ideal to have a cohesive team, coaches cannot force a team to become cohesive. Team members must develop a respect for each other. Respect may be developed through both on- and off-the-field activities.

Many coaches make visits to their athletes' homes a crucial part of building cohesiveness. Others foster respect by getting the entire team involved in a community project such as working with retarded or physically handicapped children, doing chores for the elderly, visiting hospitals, or working together to prepare athletic fields for competition. Some teams get involved by serving as coaches in local youth leagues.

Constant Reminders. The development of cohesiveness is never guaranteed. Even the best laid and most scientifically designed plans may fail. Coaches must constantly emphasize to their teams that cohesiveness will be crucial to their team's success. Team members must be constantly reminded that it is far easier to be self-centered and critical than it is to be selfless and supportive. Athletes must constantly strive

to help each other in their attempts to become a cohesive unit.

Negative Influences on Cohesion

There is nothing that interferes with the development of team cohesiveness more than coach-athlete conflict or athlete-athlete conflict. Coaches must attempt to understand how their particular patterns of perception may lead to conflict. They must also help team members to understand how their individualistic patterns of perception may cause conflicts.

Interpersonal Conflict: Coach-Athlete. Walter Rejeski, a leading authority on the issue of interpersonal conflict in sports, argues that perceptual divergence is the basis of much interpersonal conflict (Rejeski 1981; Rejeski and Hutslar 1980). Coaches often make inferences about the behavior of their athletes that may not be valid.

Emotionally charged interpersonal interactions have a great likelihood of leading to invalid perceptions and conflict. When an athlete performs poorly at an important moment in a contest, many coaches tend to respond emotionally and to reflect back upon some previous negative behavior that explains the poor performance.

Some coaches harshly and publicly blame the "guilty" athlete when failure occurs. This response often occurs when the unfortunate performance error is made by an athlete who has been accused in the past of having a "bad attitude." In this situation, the coach may perceive that the athlete intentionally lost the contest. This perceptual tendency, called *personalism,* can readily occur in situations in which teams are struggling and the coach begins to feel paranoid about team acceptance and job security.

Such biased forms of feedback may bias coaches' future perceptions of certain athletes and serve to sustain athletes' undesired behaviors and promote more serious problems. If coach-athlete conflict continues, it may lead to teammates concluding that if they make a crucial error they will be similarly blamed by the coach. For a few exceptional athletes this may facilitate performance. For most it will cause increased anxiety and a resultant decrease in performance.

Failure-induced Conflict. It is not uncommon for team failure to lead to conflict between coaches and athletes. There is a marked tendency for coaches and athletes to accept personal responsibility for success and blame failure on others (Bird 1977; Roberts 1977). Coaches may feel that they are doing a great job of coaching, but that they have been given inferior athletes. At the same time, athletes may perceive they would be winning if only they had a more skilled coach. Athletes may argue that the conditioning program or team strategies are inferior to those of the opposition. Many athletes may believe that the wrong athletes are performing in competition. Team failure provides them with the desired justification for their view: "I am better than those playing and if I played we would win."

As conflict grows, so does frustration. Coaches may blurt out: "You do your job and I'll do mine. Your job is to play and mine is to coach. Let me worry about what works and what doesn't!" Unfortunately, when the team has deteriorated to this level of conflict, an emotionally charged statement will not be effective. Athletes are usually thinking: "If you (coach) would do your job we wouldn't have to worry about what works and what doesn't and we *could* stop worrying and just play!"

Without an understanding and appreciation of personal perceptions, coaches will have difficulty preventing and/or resolving coach-athlete conflict. More than likely, emotionally charged responses will be counterproductive to cohesiveness.

Athlete-Athlete Conflict. Athlete-athlete conflicts occur for many and varied reasons. Within sports teams, particularly those lacking in homogeneity, there is a wide variety of attitudes, values, beliefs, and abilities. Some athletes believe that dedication and hard work are the only means for success. These athletes may believe that others who do not adhere to this belief should not be on the team, let alone be starting in their place.

Athletes value different things. Some value social interactions and friendship; others value using sports to get a scholarship to college or a "shot" in the pros. When team members disagree on these values conflicts are likely.

Athletes from divergent socioeconomic or political backgrounds have beliefs that may breed conflict. Coaches must make certain that they are aware of these potential producers of conflict. Then they can work toward the development of athletes who are willing to accept the views of teammates and work *for* rather than *against* the best interests of the team.

Summary

All teams must be motivated to function as part of a highly motivated and cohesive group. A scientifically based approach can help coaches accomplish the task of promoting team cohesion.

Several keys to motivation have been identified. Specifically, cohesion may be developed through use of a perceptual approach to motivation and by constant emphasis on optimistic thoughts and behaviors. In general, threats and reprimands are counterproductive, although their judicious use can be productive.

Team cohesiveness plays an important role in team motivation. Cohesiveness can be increased by limiting team membership to those who past stringent entrance requirements. Likewise, cohesiveness is greater in smaller, more homogeneous groups and in groups that have definite goals, particularly if attainment of these goals is threatened by an opponent.

A key aspect of the coach's job is the development of team cohesion. Through an awareness of the factors that positively and negatively affect cohesiveness coaches can build their teams into units that are highly motivated.

References

Bird, A.M. Applications from attribution theory: Facilitating sport group performance. Paper presented at the joint NACPEW/NCPEAM Conference. Orlando, Florida, January, 1977.

Cohn, N. Willie Mays, Pete Rose, and Lou Carnesecca: Their brilliant careers. *Inside Sports,* 3(Feb.): 64–71, 1981.

Combs, A.W., and Snygg, D. *Individual Behavior, A Perceptual Approach to Behavior.* Rev. Ed. New York: Harper and Brothers, 1959.

Counsilman, J. The X-factor. *Swimmers Coach,* (Nov.–Dec.): 10–12, 1979.

Eitzen, D.S. The effect of group structure on the success of athletic teams. *International Review of Sport Sociology,* 8:7–17, 1973.

Hall, E.G. Team cohesiveness, competition, and success. In *Psychological Considerations in Maximizing Sport Performance.* Edited by L. Bunker and R. Rotella. Charlottesville: University of Virginia, Department of Health and Physical Education, 1981.

Knobler, P. Not just another pretty face. *Inside Sport,* (Feb. 28): 20–27, 1981.

Looney, D.S. Lookalikes do alike. *Sports Illustrated,* (March 23): 48–50, 1981.

Lyons, W. Bryant aims at mark he doesn't care about. *The Charlotte Observer,* (Fri., Nov. 13): C 1–5, 1981.

Middlebrook, P. *Social Psychology and Modern Life.* New York: Alfred E. Knopf, Inc., 1974.

Murray, M. Cooperating and cohesiveness: Setting a winning personal environment. In *Psychological Considerations in Maximizing Sport Performance.* Edited by L. Bunker and P. Rotella. Charlottesville: University of Virginia, Department of Health and Physical Education, 1981.

Rejeski, W.J. A model of attributional conflict in sport. In *Psychological Considerations in Maximizing Sport Performance,* Edited by L. Bunker and R. Rotella. Charlottesville: University of Virginia, Department of Health and Physical Education, 1981.

Rejeski, W.J., and Hutslar, S. The mediatorial role of expectancies in the acquisition and performance of sport skills. *Journal of Sport Behavior,* 4:18–23, 1980.

Roberts, G.C. Children in competition: Assignment of responsibility for winning and losing. In *Proceedings of the NCPEAM/NAPECW National Conference,* 1977. Edited by L.I. Giduilas and M.E. Kneer. Chicago: University of Illinois at Chicago Circle, Office of Publications Services, 1977.

Sherif, C.W. The Social Context of Competition. In *Social Problems in Athletics.* Edited by D.M. Landers. Urbana, Illinois: University of Illinois Press, 1976.

Tharpe, R., and Gallimore, R. What a coach can teach a teacher. *Psychology Today,* (Jan.): 75–78, 1976.

Waters, H.F. The boys in the booth. *Inside Sports,* (Feb. 28): 108–116, 1981.

Recommended Readings

Atkinson, J.W. *An Introduction to Motivation.* Princeton, New Jersey: Van Nostrand, 1964.

Atkinson, J.W., and Raynor, J.O. *Motivation and Achievement.* Washington, D.C.: V.W. Winston and Sons, 1974.

Bandura, A. *Social Learning Theory.* Morristown, New Jersey: General Learning Press, 1971.

Beier, E.G. *People Reading: How We Control Others, How They Control Us.* New York: Stein and Day, 1975.

Cofer, C.N. *Motivation and Emotion.* Glenview, Illinois: Scott, Foresman, 1972.

Cratty, B.J. *Social Psychology in Athletics.* Englewood Cliffs, New Jersey: Prentice-Hall, Inc., 1981.

Heider, F. *The Psychology of Interpersonal Relations.* New York: Wiley, 1958.

Horner, M.S. Toward an understanding of achievement related conflicts in women. *Journal of Social Issues,* 28:157–175, 1972.

Maslow, A. *Motivation and Personality.* New York: Harper & Row, 1954.

Maltz, M. *Psycho-cybernetics.* New York: An Essandess Special Edition, 1960.

McClelland, D.C. *The Achieving Society.* Princeton, New Jersey: Van Nostrand, 1961.

Rushall, B.S., and Siedentop, D. *The Development and Control of Behavior in Sport and Physical Education.* Philadelphia: Lea & Febiger, 1972.

Singer, R.N. *Motor Learning and Human Performance.* New York: MacMillan Publishing, 1975.

Willis, Joe D., and Bethe D. Achievement motivation: Implications for physical activity. *Quest,* 13:18–22, 1970.

Credit: From R. J. Sabock: *The Coach*, 2nd ed. Philadelphia, Saunders College Publishing, 1979.

Understanding Competitive Stress

5

Stress, pressure, tension. Some athletes thrive on pressure. Others wither in its mere presence. Stress gives participants the "kick" that makes competition so enjoyable and challenging. It can also cause athletes to fall flat on their faces. Pressure-filled performance situations can make coaches and athletes heroes or goats.

Athletic teams must perform in stressful conditions during the competitive season. Sometimes, stress will appear when least expected.

Likewise, teams must be ready to perform efficiently when they are bored by an over-matched opponent. If a team is unprepared, an "upset" or the development of sloppy habits may occur.

There are many aspects of stressful performance that coaches must thoroughly understand if they are to best prepare their athletes for competition. The following are some of the more important issues:

1. How does stress influence performance?
2. What are the greatest sources of stress on athletes and coaches?
3. Do off-the-field sources of stress influence performance?
4. How do coaches' behaviors affect a team's stress level?
5. How does team performance affect a coach's level of stress?
6. How does stress lead to anxiety and poor concentration?
7. How should coaches best respond to pregame, during-game, and postgame stress?
8. Fear: Why does it sometimes lead to courageous performance and sometimes to "choking"?
9. Why does stress lead to increased assertiveness on one occasion and intimidation on another?
10. How does team cohesiveness help athletes perform under stress?
11. How do courageous athletes influence other team members?
12. How and why does boredom lead to disinterest, poor attention, and upsets?

Certainly, there are no clear-cut answers to these questions. But there is an abundance of scientific literature that can help coaches make better decisions relative to preparing their athletes for stressful performances. This chapter provides scientifically based guidelines for helping athletes cope with competitive stress.

Stress, Anxiety, and Arousal

Three of the most complex and confusing terms in the field of sports psychology are stress, anxiety, and arousal. Far too often, they are used as if they all mean the same thing. They do not. As a matter of fact, they do not even necessarily occur together. In some competitive situations neither anxiety nor arousal will be elicited. Some competitions lead to increased *arousal* (physiological changes) without *anxiety* (psychological concerns, such as worry or fear). However, whenever anxiety is increased arousal will also be elevated. (See Table 5.1.)

For our purposes, *stress* will be defined as any situation that has the potential for eliciting increased anxiety and arousal. If these changes do not occur in response to the real or imagined situation, then the situation is not stressful. It must be recognized that a situation that induces a stress response in one athlete does not necessarily elicit a stress response in other team members. This means that each athlete will respond differently to stress and, therefore, must be coached in an individualized manner.

Anxiety

Anxiety has typically been viewed as a personality variable that can have a tremendous influence on learning and performance of sports skills. Anxiety has been described in various ways, including "an emotional state, with the subjectively experienced quality of fear or a closely related emotion (terror, alarm, fright, panic, trepidation)" (Lewis 1970, p. 77). Sometimes, a distinction has been made between fear and anxiety, "then fear refers to feelings of apprehension about tangible and predominantly realistic dangers, and anxiety to feelings of apprehension that are difficult to relate to tangible sources of stimulation" (Rachman 1978, p. 6). Here, fear and anxiety will be considered as similar terms.

Anxiety involves negative thoughts about performance and is often, but not always, accompanied by performance decrements. The description of state anxiety presented by Martens (1977) emphasizes this point: "*State anxiety is an existing or current emotional state characterized by feelings of apprehension and tension and associated with activation of the organism.*" However, athletes sometimes have subpar performances and teams lose contests because prior to the game they were not at all anxious. As a matter of fact, their "minds were elsewhere." Knowledgeable coaches and athletes who anticipate this situation can prevent a problem by inducing state anxiety. Such warnings as "You had better start thinking about tonight's game or you will embarrass yourself," and "You had better not take this team too lightly, they could really surprise you" are attempts to increase pregame levels of state anxiety. The intent is to regulate the thought pro-

Table 5.1: Common Physical and Psychological Responses to Anxiety

Psychological	Physical
Mental Confusion	Nausea
Feeling of Panic	Frequent Urination
Attentional Narrowing	Loose Stools
Depression	Nervous Body Movements
Loss of Control	Insomnia
Loss of Attentional Flexibility	Rapid Breathing
Dizziness	Accelerated Heart Rate
Feeling Tired	Increased Blood Pressure
	Increased Sweating
	Increased Adrenalin Secretion
	Increased Muscle Tension
	Pupil Dilation

cesses in overconfident athletes whose attention is not directed on the contest. In other words, athletes who lack pregame anxiety may have as many problems directing attention as will overanxious athletes.

Some coaches may fail to effectively prepare athletes for a contest when they treat all athletes the same (i.e., *generalization*). They mistakenly treat overly anxious and overly relaxed, unprepared athletes in a similar fashion. Likewise, errors are made when coaches prepare their teams based on their perceptions (anxious or confident) rather than on the basis of their athletes' true feelings.

The Interaction Model of Anxiety

Every athlete has a particular level of internal anxiety *(trait anxiety)* that is specific to his own personality and reflects a chronic predisposition or trait (A-trait). This is contrasted with the aforementioned state anxiety, a component of transitory emotional functioning (A-state). The temporary state of anxiety is generally categorized by consciously perceived levels of tension and apprehension, which may be linked to various autonomic nervous system reactions (i.e., increased heart rate, elevated blood pressure, rapid respiration rate). This two-process concept of anxiety is sometimes referred to as *Spielberger's State-Trait Theory* (Spielberger, Gorusch, and Lushene 1970), and emphasizes the interaction of personal characteristics (trait anxiety) with certain situational characteristics (state anxiety). For example, athletes who are high in A-trait anxiety perceive ego-involving situations as threatening and, therefore, respond with a higher A-state arousal than would persons with lower A-trait anxiety levels. Highly anxious individuals tend to be self-centered and to focus frequently on self-worry and self-evaluation.

The interaction model of anxiety is based on the complex interaction of A-trait and A-state factors (Endler 1975). Five different facets of A-trait have now been identified: *interpersonal ego-threat, physical danger, ambiguous* and *innocuous daily routines,* and *social evaluation threat* (Endler and Okada 1975). This theory has been used to predict that when situational variables match or are congruent with facets of the personality there will be an interaction that causes changes in state anxiety. For example, one could predict interpersonal ego-threat A-trait will interact with a congruent ego-threatening situation to cause a change in anxiety (A-state), but would not interact with a noncongruent physically dangerous situation.

This interaction (person by situation) model has great implications for sports. For example, in swimming, the ego-threatening or social evaluation aspects of a competitive swim meet might be expected to produce increased anxiety in athletes who are highly anxious regarding social evaluation. Both of the factors would also interact with the athletes self-perception at that point in time (self-efficacy), their *perception of the opponent* and their *potential for success* if they play well (controllability and predictability), and *their expectancy* based upon past experiences. Simultaneously, a coach could predict that the A-state increases would be greater for higher A-trait athletes than for low A-trait participants. So the likelihood would be greater that the higher A-trait athlete would experience a performance decrement.

The Perception of Stress

Stress typically involves the "perception of a substantial imbalance between environmental demand and response capability, under conditions in which failure to meet demand is perceived as having important consequences and is responded to with increased levels of state anxiety" (Martens 1977, p. 9). But stress is not necessarily bad for sports participants. It can function as a crucial motivating and driving force.

In order to understand this point, coaches must realize the important role played by *cognitive processes.* It is athletes' *interpretations* of situations that influence how they react to them, both psychologically and physiologically. So athletes' perceptions of situation are important determinants of behavior. Because many perceptions do cause an emotional reaction athletes must develop an appropriate way of appraising situations.

In general, both emotional experience and bodily changes often follow the perception and interpretation of a situation as stressful. These emotional "feelings" have motivational properties that can cause athletes to either effectively or ineffectively manage the situation.

But how do athletes read these emotional reactions? Most likely, the physiological responses provide information about the intensity of their emotional responses, but don't help much in identifying the quality of the emotion (i.e., which emotions are being experienced). A process known as *cognitive labeling* does this job. The particular cognitive label given is based on the situation in which the emotion occurs. It is this cognitive process that determines if the physiological arousal will be called fear, courage, anger, joy, or whatever (Schacter, 1971).

The challenge of sports competition often produces strong emotional responses that are cognitively appraised. This appraisal is based on knowledge about past experiences as well as future expectations. When faced with a competitive situation, athletes often ask themselves the following questions: "How important is the contest to me?" "Have I competed with this person or team before?" If yes: "How did I do?" If no: "Who are they similar to that I have competed against?" "Where can I find out more information about them?" "Can I effectively manage the situation?" "Am I confident or am I anxious?" "Should I approach the situation or should I avoid it?"

The resulting perception helps athletes describe the situation that, in turn, can arouse or fail to arouse the individual and influence performance. Athletes may respond by being underaroused, "psyched-up," or "psyched-out."

A classic example was presented recently in an interview with Arnold Palmer, the golfing legend. In recalling his thoughts during a championship year in the British Open, he described how the weather was windy, wet, and very cold. These conditions upset and bothered the performance of many of the professional golfers. But Palmer loved the conditions. He interpreted them as being to his advantage because many others couldn't or wouldn't effectively deal with them. His perception aroused him to a level that he interpreted in a way that gave him confidence and helped him to concentrate. The same conditions destroyed many others.

Adaptation to Stress

Fortunately, the body and mind have a tremendous ability to adapt to stress. One of the leading researchers on stress, Hans Selye (1974), has developed an all-encompassing term for the stress adaptation process called the "General Adaptation Syndrome"—(G.A.S.: *general*, because it is produced only by agents that have a general effect upon large portions of the body; *adaptive*, because it stimulates defense and thereby helps prepare the body for hardships; *syndrome*, because its signs are coordinated and partly dependent upon each other). This entire syndrome evolves through three stages: (1) the alarm reaction, (2) the stage of resistance, and (3) the stage of exhaustion. Anytime that a stressful stimuli is experienced or is perceived as being experienced, an alarm reaction is set off with physiological and psychological responses that typically cause a loss of appetite, strength, and ambition.

Continuous exposure to any noxious agent capable of setting off this alarm reaction is followed by a stage of adaptation or resistance. When in the resistance stage the body returns to a homeostatic balance and copes successfully with the stressor that initiated the alarm reaction. However, it appears that after prolonged exposure to any noxious agent the body loses its learned capacity to resist, and enters the stage of exhaustion. Exactly how long the body can maintain itself in the third stage is unknown. But Selye (1974) proposes that an organism has a finite level of energy that it can use to resist stressors. How long an organism can last in the third stage depends upon the amount of *adaptation energy* the organism has, and also on the severity of the stressor. Eventually, if an athlete (or coach) faces continuous exposure to the stressor complete exhaustion results.

Psyching Up but Not Out

Clearly, stress plays a major role in sports performance. Thus, it is essential that coaches be prepared to help athletes manage the stress that is associated with competition. The major goal in stress management for competition is to ensure that each athlete is mentally and physically prepared in a manner that is ideal for the individual, situation, and sport. This is a most difficult task for coaches, since it is not easy to differentiate between athletes who are bored and unprepared and those who are "psyched-out."

Obvious behaviors such as excessive quietness or silliness, yawning, or inattention are typically witnessed in bored, and "psyched-out" as well as "psyched-up," performers. It is easy for coaches to misread these behaviors and to respond with the wrong coaching strategy.

Effective coaches attempt to interpret these behaviors accurately, based upon their knowledge of stress and their familiarity with each athlete they coach. If these coaches feel certain athletes are ready to compete, they may leave them alone. If they feel others are not ready, a pep talk may be provided. If they perceive that some athletes are anxious and scared, words of calming confidence may be delivered.

However, many coaches make only poor guesses. They do not know what to look for in making their decisions. So they take their chances and live with their mistakes. Other coaches do not even try to respond to their

team's needs. They always get their team ready the same way. Often, they do what they are most comfortable doing. Coaches who are energetic and enthusiastic often prefer to give a "fired-up" pregame or half-time pep talk to get the team "up" because they enjoy giving it. Little thought may have been given to whether or not the team or individual athletes need to be "psyched" higher. Coaches should be aware that the pep talk has been given so routinely that it no longer affects team members.

Similar criticisms could be made of quiet, introverted coaches who tend to display a calm demeanor in the locker room. This strategy is particularly limiting when a team needs a pep talk and the coach feels unable to provide it. Coaches who cannot fulfill this need are just as lacking as coaches who cannot calm down when such a response is needed.

Misinterpreting Winners

Sometimes coaches pick up ineffective habits when they misinterpret the actions of highly visible coaches. For years coaches have imitated Knute Rockne's fabled "get one for the Gipper" speech, but many coaches have failed to recognize several important characteristics of Rockne's team: (1) his Notre Dame football team often won by 50 points or more, (2) their constant success led to frequent boredom and disinterest in upcoming opponents (their main problem was overconfidence rather than fear or anxiety), (3) his team was typically composed of many of the most talented players in the country, (4) his players were mature, advanced athletes, (5) football, in general, may require a higher level of arousal than many other sports, (6) players on his team who held "finesse positions" (quarterback, receivers, halfbacks) often blocked out his pep talks so that they did not get "too high."

Certainly, most coaches do not have a situation that even approximates Rockne's. Attempts to increase arousal such as throwing chairs, pounding on lockers, eating frogs, or playing

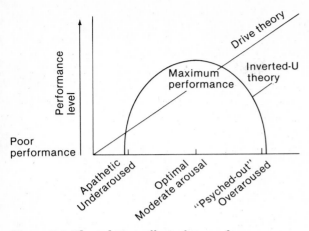

Figure 5.1 The relative effect of arousal on performance based on the drive theory versus the inverted-U theory.

school fight songs may be counterproductive. This is not to say that they are ineffective if used at the *right time,* in the *right place,* with the *right individuals.* But coaches must be cognizant that the impact of such actions may not always be positive.

For many years coaches were taught that there was a direct relationship between increased arousal and performance. It was believed that as arousal increased performance would improve. This belief was based on a now outdated concept known as *drive theory.* Current scientific thinking is based on a new, improved concept known as the *inverted-U the-ory,* which suggests that there is an ideal level of arousal that is required for maximal performance (see Figure 5.1). A level of arousal that is above or below this ideal level will lead to less than optimal performance. A goal for coaches, then, is to help athletes identify and maintain this ideal level. To do so many related factors must be understood.

Arousal and Confidence

An understanding of stress and sports performance would not be complete without rec-

ognition of the important role of confidence. Confidence is the factor that causes athletes to label their arousal as excitement or fear.

Arousal is an emotional experience that is interpreted cognitively. Confident athletes may interpret the uneasiness, the butterflies, and the tingling sensation just prior to a contest as the excitement that means they will perform well. Confident athletes interpret their emotions in a positive, self-enhancing fashion.

When confidence is lacking, however, the very same initial arousal level is interpreted as scary and fearful. The arousal leads to anxious thoughts, which, in turn, may lead to increased arousal and, at some point, to an overaroused and "psyched-out"athlete.

Unfortunately, despite the common belief that self-confidence is a never-changing quality, in fact, it varies from moment-to-moment (one game to the next or even within a particular contest) and across various tasks (from basketball to lacrosse). These transitory self-confident expectations are typically labeled *self-efficacy* and describe expectations of personal effectiveness. Both "confident" and "non-confident" athletes can quickly change their self-efficacy expectations, depending upon against whom they are competing on a certain day and how they are performing at various moments in a contest. Such fluctuations in self-efficacy are observed in professional athletes, and it can be expected that these variations will be even greater for younger and less skilled athletes.

A related factor in self-efficacy expectations is the *perceived difficulty* of the athletic challenge. A wide variety of mental blocks (four-minute mile, 7-foot high jump, 18-foot pole vault, and many other personal mental barriers) reported by athletes increase their perceptions of stress and most likely decrease their chances of attaining their performance potential.

There is little doubt that self-efficacy plays a crucial role in sports performance under stress. But coaches must remember that much more than self-efficacy is needed to be successful in the world of competitive athletics. Self-efficacy can help and is probably necessary for sports success, yet "success" as determined by the won-loss record will also be determined by physical skill, effort, talent, and maybe even a little luck. This point is made perfectly clear in the example of an 18-year old American boxer in the 1979 Pan American Games named Rufus (Bubba) Hadley, who just prior to his semifinal bout with Teofilo Stevenson (possibly the greatest amateur boxer) said, "He's just another man, and I don't know any reason why I should fear another man." In the words of a *Sports Illustrated* magazine reporter, John Papanek, "Reason One: Few have ever gone the full three rounds against Stevenson. Reason two: the second time Stevenson threw that right hand at Bubba, Bubba bounced off the canvas. Only 1:39 of the first round had elapsed." (Papanek 1979). Of course, it's possible that Stevenson was lucky or that Hadley's statements defied his true feelings. It is one thing for an athlete to say he is confident and quite another to believe it.

Athletes appear to possess quite diverse levels of self-confidence. They range from *overconfidence*—thinking they are better than they really are, to *underconfidence*—thinking they are less able than they really are. Somewhere in the middle are the athletes who have realistic confidence. Both overconfidence and underconfidence present problems to performance under stress. Underconfidence can prevent athletes from performing to their potential. Usually, it increases stress because of a perceived discrepancy between task demands and personal abilities. Such situations cause athletes to feel threatened.

Overconfidence, on the other hand, reduces the amount of threat perceived in a competitive situation. As a result, overconfident athletes enhance their ability to perform on the day of competition regardless of the high quality of opposition. Overconfident athletes work against themselves, however, when their excessive confidence causes them to: (1) fail to prepare themselves for competition, (2) "go to sleep" after getting an early lead in competition, or (3) attempt to play beyond their abilities.

Overconfident athletes are capable of upsets against supposedly superior opponents, but are also susceptible to being upset themselves. Overconfidence may lead to this weakness because it can produce a lack of attention directed at the upcoming competition. It is typically characterized by a complete absence of positive as well as anxious thoughts related to the possibility of poor performance. Such thoughts can help direct attention during competition. Perhaps the ideal is to develop athletes who are realistic in their confidence levels during practice with a movement toward overconfidence during competition.

Fear and Courage

Confidence is a most important factor in determining whether fear leads to uncontrolled anxiety or courageous performance. Certainly, a performance could not be considered courageous if fear was not present initially. Fear, when combined with confidence, often leads to *assertive* performance.

On the other hand, when fear is combined with uncontrolled anxiety it often leads to *intimidation*. In many sports this is inconsistent with effective performance. Coaches must constantly be aware of the important role of confidence. By producing assertive behavior confidence may lead to intimidation of the opposition, which causes increased assertiveness and confidence and, ultimately, the desired success.

Experience and Inexperience

Experience means more than the number of years an athlete has been competing. Years of constant failure may do more harm than good. Experience without learning from one's errors may be lacking in usefulness. On the other hand, experience that is filled with success and a few failures may be ideal. Knowledgeable coaches have recognized for years the advantages of early success experiences in the development of self-confidence. Notice how top-rated teams at the collegiate level "pad" their early season schedules whenever possible.

Likewise, coaches of athletes associated with an individual sport such as Sugar Ray Leonard in boxing and Tracy Austin in tennis realized the importance of "bringing their athletes along slowly." This simply means that an abundance of early success was ensured by proper selection of opponents. Such planning enhances confidence and ensures that, when and if failure does occur, it will usually be a close loss that will do little to destroy confidence.

In some well-established programs young athletes can be brought along slowly. In such situations, athletes can be inserted in carefully selected situations designed for success and can be gradually inserted in more and more stressful situations. But often, inexperienced athletes must play in a contest with experienced players. Coaches must realize that although the skill levels of younger and older athletes may appear to be similar in practice, a considerable discrepancy may exist when performance is required in a stressful situation.

It is indeed likely that inexperienced athletes will be nervous, intimidated, and even "psyched-out" the first time they play at home, play away from home, play an important opponent, or play in a regular season or postseason tournament. In general, then, these players experience increased levels of stress and need to be prepared for competition differently than if they were seasoned veterans.

In general, fears diminish as a result of repeated exposure to a stressful situation. A particularly helpful approach is to employ mild or toned-down versions of the frightening experience—a process known as *habituation*. Habituation is facilitated by regular and short presentations of the stressful stimulus that apparently causes an emotional adaptation to the situation.

Thus, it would be beneficial to put less experienced players into contests for short time periods early in the season and only gradually play them in crucial or difficult situations. Similarly, it would be ideal to have players travel with the team for a year and get used to stress-provoking situations, such as bus trips, playing unknown teams, playing in front of strange crowds, or on an unfamiliar playing surface. In doing so, these stressors would be less likely to interfere with performance. When it is impossible to delay playing inexperienced players, habituation can be facilitated by providing information about the forthcoming stressor well in advance of the situation. This advanced knowledge positively affects expectations and responses.

Sensitization

Sometimes, experience or repeated exposure to a stressor leads to increased rather than decreased stress. This phenomenon is labeled *sensitization*.

Anxiety can be viewed as varying along a continuum; at one end fear is habituated, while at the other end it is sensitized. Prolonged fatigue, a decline in physical conditioning, a traumatic experience (e.g., injury, "choking" in a crucial situation), or a "near miss" experience (e.g., almost "pancaking" on a 3-meter dive) all have the potential for increasing an athlete's sensitivity to a competitive situation that had previously been habituated.

A most pervasive senstization effect is likely to result from a negative experience such as failure. Coaches must keep in mind that an athlete need not fail in terms of winning or losing to consider an experience a failure. Indeed, an athlete's personal interpretation of a situation (which may be quite different from the coaches') may be of equal or greater importance than the actual outcome.

Athletes may become increasingly sensitized to stress as a result of failing to improve performance despite continued practice and experience (i.e., a performance plateau). As mentioned previously, this is an important and often misunderstood cause of stress for overachieving athletes. Such individuals typically have an abundance of anxious thoughts prior to competition, which can lead to interfering anxious thoughts during competition, which, in turn, can result in anxious thoughts and sleepless nights following competition, leading to fatigue and poor practice and more precompetition anxious thoughts.

The Stress of Emotions

Emotions play a significant role in sports performance. Emotions are feelings that appear in response to the surrounding world. In essence, then, they are reactions to experiences.

Early in life athletes learn when something feels good or bad. These feelings function as internal feedback devices that help people to make such decisions as whether to approach or to avoid hard work. People experience many emotions: love, anger, sadness, joy, fear (worry), shame (guilt), pride, and surprise. All other emotions can be traced back to these basic emotions.

Certainly, all athletes do not experience emotions in a similar manner. A situation may cause one athlete to respond with joy and another with shame. Emotions have *qualities* that can help coaches understand athletes' emotions. *Emotional personality* describes how athletes usually feel or their typical mood. Some athletes are usually happy, and filled with joy and energy. Others may normally be unhappy or depressed.

Another quality pertains to the ability to control emotions. Emotional control may vary from maintaining calm to allowing emotions to flow openly. While all athletes can develop emotional control, some are more naturally skilled at it. The final emotional quality is emotional flexibility. This refers to how easily different emotions can be experienced.

These emotional qualities play a most important role in stressful performance. Coaches can be certain that under pressure emotions will occur. A great win may lead to elated and proud performers. A tough loss or a slump may lead to depression and shame. Failing a test in school on the day of a big game can lead to emotions capable of hindering optimal performance. Likewise, an athlete who finally gets his first chance to start may demonstrate positive emotions that can lead to a superior performance.

Attention and Concentration

To be successful in sports athletes must have highly developed concentration skills. No skill is more important. By its very nature, anxiety is contradictory to concentration during competition. Precompetition anxiety, however, can serve to aid concentration rather than hinder it. So a key is to help athletes use anxiety as a means of facilitating concentration.

When confronted with an evaluative situation, anxious athletes are distracted by their own preoccupation with self-centered, interfering thoughts. Because of the nature of anxiety it does not matter if anxious athletes are really being evaluated or just perceive that they are being evaluated. In either case, concentration will suffer.

It is generally accepted that highly anxious individuals respond to stress with habituated, personalized responses of a self-deprecatory kind. These responses, in turn, interfere with efficiency and attention. Individuals with low-anxiety levels are more likely to respond to stress with increased attention and with effort directed at the task.

Attentional Factors

Different sports and different situations within a given sport demand various attentional foci. Some situations may require athletes to attend to several cues in rapid succession. Robert Nideffer, an innovative sports psychologist, argues that such attentional demands are complicated not only by anxiety and arousal but also by each athlete's own unique attentional style (Nideffer 1976).

For maximal performance athletes must produce the proper attentional style for the given situation. It would be ideal for athletes to have *control* over their attention and to tailor it effectively to each situation. This control, called *attentional flexibility*, is essential for concentration. If flexibility breaks down so will concentration.

Nideffer has conceptualized attention as being primarily a combination of two factors— *width of focus* and *direction of focus*. Width of attention can be either *broad* or *narrow*. Direction can be either *internal* (athlete's own thoughts and feelings) or *external* (attending to objects and events that are outside the athlete's mind and body). Appropriate attentional techniques vary from sport-to-sport, from situation-to-situation, and from moment-to-moment. For example, when basketball players lead a three-on-two fast-break they must focus on several different cues sent out by several different players on both teams in order to make an effective play (i.e., broad-external focus). On the other hand, when they shoot a jump shot at the end of the break they must focus on the target (rim or backboard) at the moment of release (narrow-external focus). During a time-out a floor leader must bring together a storehouse of information for teammates (game score, time left in game, defense to play, offense to run, and so forth) and this task demands a broad-internal attentional focus (see Figure 5.2).

In his thought-provoking book, *The Inner Athlete*, Nideffer makes the general suggestion that "the more complex and rapidly changing the situation, the more attention must be externally focused and conversely, as the need for analysis or planning increases, the more internal and reflexive focus must become" (1976, p. 48). He further argues that the categories may be broken into four basic attentional styles— *broad-internal*, *broad-external*, *narrow-internal*, and *narrow-external*—which are formed by combinations of the two factors, width and direction. Everyone's attentional style is some combination of these four styles, with the tendency for a particular style to dominate, particularly under stress.

Understanding Different Styles

Athletes who tend to have a broad-internal style tend to think about and analyze information very well. This tendency is helpful for athletes who must self-correct and self-coach themselves. Likewise, it is quite beneficial to a

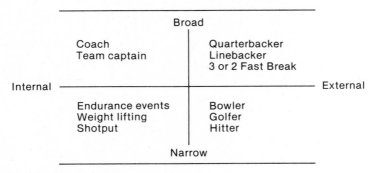

Figure 5.2 Attention focus (from Nideffer 1976, p. 49).

coach who must bring information together and make decisions effectively. But if this approach continues when other attentional styles are needed during competition problems are assured. Individuals with a broad-internal inclination sometimes "think too much."

Those who have a broad-external attentional style tend to be skilled at picking up a variety of cues from the environment. A broad-external focus can be very beneficial if an athlete is leading the fast-break in basketball, lacrosse, or field hockey, looking for an open receiver in football, or analyzing an opponent's wrestling skills. But this attentional inclination can also become a problem if too much irrelevent information is absorbed, if attention must suddenly be narrowed or internalized, or if the athlete gets too far ahead in this thinking (thinks of the next move required prior to initiating the one preceding it). Additionally, such athletes often fail to analyze and learn from past experiences.

Athletes who are inclined toward a narrow-external attentional style are able to block out distractions and concentrate on one or very few environmental stimuli. This style is very helpful in situations in which optimal performance requires concentration on an external object (shooting in basketball, field-goal kicking, hitting a baseball, penalty kicking in soccer, hitting ground strokes in tennis, and so forth). Such an attentional tendency can be quite helpful in blocking out crowd noise and other environmental distractions. If athletes with this attentional tendency focus on the appropriate cue they are effective, but they may be prone to errors of *under-inclusion*. The quarterback who sees only one receiver and the defensive player who sees only the one player he is assigned to guard are hindered by their narrow-external attentional style.

Finally, the narrow-internal attentional tendency helps athletes direct attention inward and focus on a single thought or feeling. This may be quite helpful to athletes in endurance events (distance swimming, running, bicycling, cross-country skiing). Such a style may also

help athletes block out the pain experienced during a hard, tiring practice session and to cope with an injury or treatment of an injury (e.g., immersion of a foot in ice). But if athletes are lacking in self-efficacy and are constantly dwelling on self-defeating thoughts, the narrow-internal focus can be extremely detrimental to their performance.

Because of the nature of competitive sports athletes are constantly required to call upon different attentional styles. It would be impossible to identify a sport that would require the use of only one style during the learning and performance of the activity. Thus, athletes wishing to maximize their performance potential can benefit from increased awareness of their attentional tendencies and from development of flexibility in their attentional style.

Anxiety and Attentional Flexibility

Anxiety typically causes athletes to *decrease* their attentional flexibility. High anxiety makes it more difficult to willfully control and direct attention. Apparently, it narrows the athlete's ability to use the available cues. In addition, when highly anxious, athletes tend to use their preferred attentional style even more frequently. If the preferred style happens to be appropriate, this tendency is beneficial; if it is not, concentration and performance suffer.

Highly anxious athletes may focus on one cue and ignore other more relevant cues. However, on a more positive note, they may concentrate on just the relevant cue(s) and ignore irrelevant distractions. Conversely, those low in anxiety may find it easier to attend to all relevant cues, but they may also be distracted by irrelevant stimuli.

Seemingly, then, high anxiety may occasionally be advantageous for concentration, but this advantage is greatly outweighed by the disadvantages. A person low in anxiety may be distracted by irrelevant cues, but probably not as often as the person high in anxiety is distracted by his own anxious thoughts. Because the attention of a highly anxious athlete is diverted inward toward the perception of anxiety, less attention is available for task-relevant cues and, therefore, performance suffers.

Conceptually, every task has both relevant and irrelevant cues. Recall that anxiety tends to reduce the number of cues to which an athlete can attend. Because task-relevant cues are the first to drop from attention, performance improves with increases in arousal. However, when all irrelevant cues have been excluded, further increases in arousal can only affect task-relevant cues and, thus, proficiency will be retarded.

As stated previously, highly anxious athletes may perform poorly under stressful conditions because attention is directed inward toward thoughts, but under low-stress conditions these athletes may perform better because attention is directed to task-relevant stimuli. In contrast, athletes of low anxiety may perform poorly under low-stress conditions but perform well under high-stress conditions because attention is directed to task-relevant stimuli.

Boredom and Attention

Coaches often experience their greatest stress when they feel that their team is not ready for a competition it is favored to win. An upset is imminent. It is ironic that with all the "spine tinglers," crucial plays, and big games "laughers" could cause stress in coaches.

Clearly, such competitions need not be stressful. But experienced coaches know full well that boredom can be just as counterproductive as excessive anxiety. At least with anxiety, athletes are interested and motivated. Athletes who are disinterested in an upcoming contest typically do not even try to concentrate.

Attentional problems resulting from boredom usually begin well in advance of the scheduled contest. In the days prior to competition little if any thought is directed at the upcoming competition. As a result, athletes may enter competition physically and mentally un-

prepared. If the opposition is good enough an upset may occur.

In many sports it may not be possible or desirable to concentrate and be "up" for every game. So coaches and athletes must learn how much concentration and preparation is needed for each contest. Getting too "up" for too many games may cause a team to peak too early and play "flat" when they cannot afford it. But failure to get "up" frequently enough can result in upsets.

Boredom usually causes attention to drift to matters unrelated to competition. Other issues may become more challenging and interesting. The longer attention strays, the more difficult it will become to get athletes "into" the contest. Peak concentration is not something that can be easily turned on when needed. It must be slowly and consistently developed.

Boredom during competition should not be overlooked as an important aspect of competitive stress. When lack of concentration becomes obvious and an upset is imminent, stress will certainly occur. The stress response may be enough to get a team to survive and "pull a contest out," but often it is too late.

Stress Has Many Faces

Stress attacks athletic teams from many different directions. Athletic contests, by their very nature, are stressful. Most contests end with an easily identifiable winner and loser. In team sports athletes may be labeled as starters or substitutes. Usually, substitutes desire to be starters. Coaching staffs often have head coaches and assistant coaches who are striving for head coaching opportunities. Sometimes, competitive stress may cause head coaches to wish, at least for the moment, that they could return to their assistant coaching positions.

Sports presents athletes with widely varying degrees of stress. It is far more stressful to come to bat with the winning run on base in the ninth inning than it is to come to bat with the team comfortably ahead. Similarly, it is more stressful to have to make a crucial coaching decision in the last moments of a closely contested competition than it is to make one when the outcome is already decided.

Many Unanswered Questions

Any competitive situation that causes athletes to ask, "Can I handle this situation?", "Am I good enough?"; or coaches to wonder, "Is my decision the right one?", "Have I prepared the team for this situation?" can lead to increased stress. In sports such questions will be quickly, objectively, and publicly answered. There is no escaping the answer. Indeed, this is what competitive stress is all about. This also explains why the fear of failure, the hope of success, and the fear of success (explained in Chapter 3) play such a vital role in understanding athlete motivation.

Fear of the Unexpected

Any discussion of competitive stress would be incomplete without mention of the stress experienced on account of fear of the unexpected and unknown. Many athletes and coaches take great pride in preparing in such detail that they are in total control of competitive situations. However, one cannot prepare for every eventuality and, thus, unexpected factors can ruin the best laid plans.

In a similar manner, sports participants often experience unusually high levels of stress when they encounter opponents against whom they have not previously competed or on whom there is no available scouting report.

The Demand for Improvement

Competitive stress can take many forms. The constant growth and improvement demanded for athletic success is a prevalent source of pressure. An extended rest or vacation may mean the possibility of falling behind others. If a coach overlooks a few important points a team may be outcoached and defeated. If success in sports were easy or attainable without constant effort and growth it probably would not be stressful; but it would not be desired or admired either.

The daily physical and mental demands for practice may be quite strenuous. Athletes must challenge their bodies to push a little harder and their minds to concentrate a little longer in the face of greater and greater challenges. In meeting these challenges there is the everpresent possibility that, if athletes push too hard, they might injure their bodies; but if they fail to push hard enough they will fall short of meeting an unknown potential and be surpassed by competitors. If athletes fail to challenge their minds to more and more difficult pressures and distractions they may not be ready for competition.

Every successful athlete or coach has highly developed ego-strength. Ego-strength facilitates belief in oneself in the face of stiff competition. But every time competition occurs, the ego is challenged. The ego, although it must be strong, must be able to cope with the inevitability of failure, which will be witnessed by friends and foe alike.

Society Loves Winners

Stress also comes from the *social environment*. Most of the problems mentioned occur as a result of social evaluation. In American society, the rewards clearly go to the winners. Coaches and athletes know the joys of going to class after a satisfactory performance; they also know the grilling that is likely to follow a less than satisfactory performance. School recognition, awards, peer approval, extensive newspaper coverage, and even the opportunity for higher level participation are granted to those who are successful. The mere fact that these valued prizes are available contributes to competitive stress.

Parents can become an important source of stress. Parents who push their children and love them only when they are successful compound the stress experienced by young athletes.

Likewise, parents who denigrate their child's coach add to the athlete's problems. But parents who learn to listen attentively to their young athletes and respond with encouragement and support can significantly assuage the amount of stress their young athletes must manage.

Academic Pressures

Academic grades often become an important source of social stress in school-age athletes. Athletes who are distracted in practice by anxious thoughts of the test they just failed may suffer a decline in their sports performance. This is, however, a two-way street. Athletic stress may cause academic problems, which if they become serious enough may add to competitive stress.

The pressures for academic grades may come from coaches, teachers, and parents. Athletes who are concerned about their futures may put pressure on themselves. The greatest stress appears to occur when both teachers and coaches demand that their charges commit themselves 100% to their respective activities. This is a demand that is often made, but that is impossible to meet.

The stress of this situation causes many athletes to attempt to resolve their dilemma by choosing one or the other. Other athletes may give up their social life in an effort to do the best they can at both; the loneliness involved in this decision may serve only to give athletes greater stress to manage. On the other hand, many who choose this route are quite comfortable with their choice as long as they receive their cherished success; but if they do not succeed, tension and unhappiness with their chosen lifestyle may result.

Coach Pressures

For many athletes a major source of stress may be coaches. Coaches have virtual control over athletes' success or failure. Coaches decide on who will start, who will substitute, and who will make the team. Coaches are the major

source of praise and punishment; they can encourage and fill athletes with confidence or they can discourage and destroy confidence. Sports psychologists report that one of the most difficult sources of stress for athletes to manage occurs when they play for coaches who do not believe in them. This situation is particularly difficult when there appears to be every reason for belief in the athlete's abilities.

Self-induced Pressure

Athletes themselves are oftentimes their own greatest source of stress. In their attempts to reach their potential, athletes often place unrealistic and self-defeating pressures upon themselves. When fans and others treat athletes as if they were godlike, athletes sometimes begin to think they are just that. In the process, they may forget they are human and, thus, subject to error.

Athletes' efforts to improve often cause them to feel unsatisfied with their performances. The great feelings athletes get from success and the terrible feelings they get from failure may cause athletes to irrationally associate winning with being a good person and losing with being a bad person. Soon, their self-worth becomes intimately tied into their sports performance. This can be highly stressful if success does not come in large and frequent doses. Even in very successful athletes this viewpoint may cause serious problems when their athletic career ends.

Another significant source of stress is poor athletic performance by an individual or team. Poor performance is particularly stressful if it causes coaches to become stressed and they, in turn, add to the pressures athletes are already experiencing.

Stress Changes with Experience

All athletes experience the anxious thoughts that so frequently occur in response to stress. Throughout the course of one's athletic career, however, the sources of stress and the kinds of anxious thoughts experienced change.

It is generally assumed by learning theorists that children are born without fears or anxieties. They tend to view children as being a *tabla rosa* (Lat. "a blank slate") at birth, with all fears and anxieties being learned. In which case, young athletes learn their anxieties from messages delivered from parents, siblings, peers, coaches, or personal experience. These anxieties need not be intentionally transmitted. They are often indirectly and unintentionally taught as a result of *modeling* (imitation).

Coaches who have taught sports activities such as diving, football, or gymnastics to children recognize the absence of fear in the very young. If fear is present, it is usually quite easy to convince youngsters that there is little or no reason for fear.

Move to a New Level

At each level of advancement in sports the stress present may lead to recurring anxieties. As athletes are initiated to the new level (first year in little league, high school, college, pros, and so on) they tend to have fears and doubts about their ability to successfully compete at the new level. Often, "rookie" athletes place veteran players on a pedestal, and the veterans do everything within their power to maintain this inflated image. At this point in their careers many athletes are stressed by the possibility of *rejection* or *disapproval* by coaches and/or teammates.

Problems of Advancement

Once the pressure of making the team subsides the stressors again change: "How good will I be?" "Will I play regularly?" "Can I play my style or will I have to change?" Likewise, established athletes must deal with incoming players: "How good are they?" "Will one take my spot on the team?" Even more stressful for some athletes is the hiring of a new coach: "Will the new coach have confidence in me?" "Will I fit into the coach's plans?"

Certain stressors may be encountered by athletes as they approach the end of their careers. In spring sports, athletes in their last year in school may struggle with the common ailment called "senioritis." This problem is characterized by athletes worrying that they may not be admitted by the college that they desire, may not graduate, or may fail to get a job after graduation. This stressor is usually most pronounced for students who have not concerned themselves with academic work and future plans earlier in their careers. When such athletes realize they are in trouble in the spring of their senior year the resulting anxieties often interfere with motivation and concentration; hence, the term "senioritis."

Life at the Top

Many people erroneously think that once you make it to the top of a career the pressure eases. For most it does not. Certainly, for some professional athletes financial pressures are eased. For others success causes new and different problems. Difficulties with financial management may be very stressful for new professional athletes.

For most professional and high-level amateur athletes a career is short and intense. Many weeks away from home with constant travel and abnormal hours are a newfound difficulty. Loneliness is everpresent. High-level athletes often delay marriage until after their athletic careers. Some avoid any type of meaningful relationship in order to avoid the pain of separation.

In general, professional athletes experience all of the stress-related problems discussed with the exception of the academic pressures. The life of the high-level athlete is not easy and glorified as often imagined.

Identity Crises

In the contemporary world of sports there is an increased frequency of athletes suffering from an "identity crisis" at the end of their playing careers. Many athletes find that it is extremely stressful to be suddenly stripped of their identity as an athlete. The result may be a short period of loneliness and confusion, followed by adaptation, formation of new friendships, and adoption of a new lifestyle. However, in extreme cases, failure to adapt can precipitate severe depression or even suicide.

Even Stars Experience Stress

Far too often, it is assumed that only struggling athletes experience the negative effects of stress. In reality, highly gifted athletes have just as many, if not more, sources of stress than other athletes. Instead of struggling to get coaches to believe in them, these athletes must constantly strive to live up to the often exaggerated expectations of coaches, teammates, and others. Sometimes, this pressure becomes so great that athletes develop a "fear of success," in which they undermine performance so that they will not be asked or expected to repeat high-level performances.

The success of a team is often dependent upon the performance of star players. This can become a source of stress, especially when team performance is far below standard. Also, these athletes are expected to be positive models for younger athletes and the ideals of athletics. In this role, they are readily recognizable. They cannot go out on a date, walk the streets, or even go to class without being recognized as an athlete. As such, they are frequently and openly praised or criticized.

Being Average

To athletes who possess average athletic abilities, the problems of the gifted seem insignificant. They may practice twice as much with far greater intensity, and yet still perform far below the level of gifted teammates or opponents. They spend time learning strategy. They

become intelligent athletes and constantly provide inspiration for the team. Yet, the fans do not seem to appreciate these skills. When things are going poorly even the coach turns to the star on the team.

Average athletes, despite tremendous dedication, often have quite little margin for error. One or two errors in a game and they are benched. The star, however, may repeatedly make poor plays and still stay in the game. Average players often want success a great deal, and they may become quite frustrated as they realize that success will elude them no matter how hard they try. With frustration, jealousy of more talented athletes may develop.

Performance Before Spectators

It is common for athletes to experience stress when they perform in front of spectators. This is particularly true for athletes who lack confidence. However, when performance is going well the presence of an audience can be beneficial.

To understand the impact of an audience upon performance coaches must be aware of individual perception. Athletes who participate in less popular sports often have to play without an audience. Such athletes often express stress and frustration at the lack of audience interest in their performance. However, these same athletes may express relief at the lack of an audience following a poor performance.

Prior to the start of every season teams and their fans have expectations for the upcoming season. When these expectations are not met early in the season stress may easily become distress. Athletes may put unnecessary pressures on themselves that may further hinder performance.

Coaches often respond to fan demands when their team is performing poorly by changing line-ups, hoping to "shake-up" the team and turn the season around. This is a strategy that can be useful if poor performance is due to lack of readiness for competition. If this is not the reason a disastrous season may result from this coaching ploy.

Audience Make-up. All audiences are not the same. Many coaches inaccurately assume that the larger the crowd the more stressful. This is not necessarily true. A very small audience of "significant others" such as parents, family, friends, classmates, and college or professional scouts can produce far more stress than a large but unknown crowd. But these same individuals also can be an extremely positive source of motivation.

Partially for this reason, most athletes are more comfortable and confident when they compete in front of a friendly, home crowd. The pressure of playing away contests before hostile and sometimes abusive crowds can be immense. If athletes are not skilled at handling such pressure, concentration may focus on the crowd rather than on the sports task. Audience-related distractions can lead to: (1) concern over *audience evaluations* of performance, and (2) abnormally aggressive play that may cause excessive penalties and inefficient performance.

Crowd Proximity. In some sports athletes must compete with fans "right on top of them." When fans are close, athletes both feel and hear them. They may hear every spoken word and even know who said it. Such situations may lead to increased chances for negative emotions and distractions.

Many schools that have built large indoor athletic facilities have found that their previously enjoyed home-court advantage has been eliminated. Visiting teams are not so easily intimidated when fans are well-removed from the court. Many schools have added portable seats closer to the floor for vociferous fans, the main goal of which is to increase the pressure and produce stress in visiting opponents.

Fanatics. Athletes must be prepared to deal with fanatics who are "best friends" when performance is going well and "worst enemies" when it isn't. Because of the difficulty in trusting fans, many athletes isolate themselves from them. Others learn to positively utilize fans' ac-

colades when they are successful and avoid them when they perform poorly. Ultimately, athletes must learn to identify their real friends because sooner or later they will be needed.

Errors Before a Crowd. No one enjoys making errors in front of a crowd. Fans may taunt error-prone athletes with verbal abuse. In some sports it is far more troublesome to make an error than in others. In team sports, because of the many players on the field, it is easy to have an error go undetected. In those sports in which athletes are all alone there is no escaping the error. Everyone notices.

The stress experienced in these situations is greatly influenced by the reaction of the coach. An abusive reprimand by the coach in combination with the taunts of a crowd can raise competitive stress to a debilitating level.

Summary

Stress is a major influence upon sports performance. Thus, coaches must understand the difference and interactions among stress, anxiety, and arousal. Special consideration should be given to the interactional model of anxiety and the crucial role played by perception in labeling and responding to events in the athlete's environment. The General Adaptation Syndrome of Selye describes the typical response to stress.

It is important that teams be "psyched-up" not "psyched-out" prior to competition. Special attention should be directed to the role of self-confidence in interpreting arousal in either a positive or negative manner. The inverted-U theory of arousal and performance suggests that there is an optimal level of precompetition arousal. Experience and emotions should be considered in designing pregame preparation strategies.

Arousal and anxiety can profoundly affect the athlete's attention. Self-awareness of personal attentional styles and attentional flexibility are traits that should be fostered.

There are many sources of stress facing athletes. These include self, competition, coach, and other induced variables. Stress is a phenomenon that changes as athletes move from a lower to a higher level of performance. "Life at the top" can be as stressful as the struggles encountered by average athletes.

Finally, the pressure caused by expectations, the desire of setting records, and the necessity of competing in front of fans contribute importantly to competitive stress. The sources of stress are many and varied. Coaches must be aware of and sensitive to athletes' needs as they attempt to deal with these sources of stress.

References

Endler, N.S. A person-situation interaction model for anxiety. In *Stress and Anxiety*. Vol. V. Edited by C.D. Spielberger and J.G. Sarason. Washington, D.C.: Hemisphere Publishing Co. (Wiley), 1975.

Endler, N.W., and Okada, M. A multi dimensional measure of trait anxiety. The S-R inventory of general trait anxiousness. *Journal of Counseling and Clinical Psychology*, 43:319–329, 1975.

Lewis, A. The ambiguous word "anxiety." *International Journal of Psychiatry*, 9:62–79, 1970.

Martens, R. *Sport Competition Anxiety Test*. Champaign, Illinois: Human Kinetics Publishers, 1977.

Nideffer, R.M. Test of attentional and interpersonal style. *Journal of Personality and Social Psychology*, 34:394, 1976.

Nideffer, R.M. *The Inner Athlete: Mind Plus Muscle*. New York: Thomas Crowell, 1976.

Papanek, J. A new bunch punches in. *Sports Illustrated*, (Jul.): 30, 1979.

Rachman, S.J. *Fear and Courage*. San Francisco: W.H. Freeman and Co., 1978.

Schacter, F. *Emotion, Obesity, and Crime*. New York: Academic Press, 1971.

Selye, H. *Stress Without Distress*. Philadelphia: J.B. Lippincott Co., 1974.

Spielberger, C.D., Gorusch, R.L., and Lushene, R.E. *Manual for the State-Trait Anxiety Inventory*. Palo Alto, California: Consulting Psychologist Press, 1970.

Recommended Readings

Bandura, A. Self-efficacy: Toward a unifying theory of behavioral change. *Psychological Review*, 84:191–215, 1977.

Bunker, L.K. The effects of anxiety on performance—Psyching them up, not out. In *Sport Psychology: From Theory to Practice*. Edited by L. Bunker and R. Rotella. Charlottesville: University of Virginia, pp. 3–22, 1978.

Endler, N.S. A person-situation interaction model for anxiety. In *Stress and Anxiety*. Vol. V. Edited by C.D. Spielberger and J.G. Sarason. Washington, D.C.: Hemisphere Publishing Corp. (Wiley), 1975.

Landers, D.M. Motivation and performance: The role of arousal and attentional factors. In *Proceedings of the NCPEAM/NAPECW National Conference*. Chicago: University of Illinois at Chicago Circle, Office of Publications Services, pp. 216–228, 1977.

Lazarus, R.S., Bkaer, R.W., Broverman, D.M., and Mayer, J. Personality and psychological stress. *Journal of Personality*, 25:559–577, 1957.

Mandler, G., and Sarason, S. A study of anxiety and learning. *Journal of Abnormal and Social Psychology*, 47:166–173, 1952.

Martens, R. Anxiety and motor performance: A review. *Journal of Motor Behavior*, 3:161–179, 1971.

McGrath, J.E. A conceptual formulation for research on stress. In *Social and Psychological Factors in Stress*. Edited by J.E. McGrath. New York: Holt, Rinehart and Winston, 1970.

Nideffer, R.M. Test of attentional and interpersonal style. *Journal of Personality and Social Psychology*, 34:394, 1976.

Rachman, S.J. *Fear and Courage*. San Francisco: W.H. Freeman and Co., 1978.

Seligman, M.E.P. *Helplessness: On Depression, Development and Death*. San Francisco: W.H. Freeman and Co., 1975.

Selye, H. *The Story of the Adaptation Syndrome*. Montreal: Acta, Inc. Medical Publishers, 1952.

Wine, J. Test anxiety and director of attention. *Psychological Bulletin*, 76:92–104, 1971.

Credit: Courtesy of Kit Brooking.

Preparation for Competition: Make It Complete

6

A key to effective management of a team's competitive stress is preparation. Preparation is effective because it enhances confidence and allows athletes to feel that they "have been there" prior to experiencing an actual competitive situation. Coaches can *innoculate* athletes and thereby enhance their abilities to deal with competitive stress through careful preparation (Meichenbaum 1979).

To be successful in this endeavor coaches must be masters at anticipating difficult and problematic situations. Teams whose coaches fail to successfully anticipate future competitive situations typically respond with *confusion* and *uncertainty*, which results in a *lack of confidence* in themselves and their coaches. Teams that are fully prepared are more likely to respond to game situations with confidence.

While effective preparation is a key ingredient in success, it must be realized that it is possible to become so detailed in team preparation that practices become boring and inefficient. Coaches can *overprepare* and take all the fun out of practice. This in itself can become stressful for team members. Coaches must strike a balance between overpreparation and underpreparation; perhaps leaning in the direction of overpreparation as long as practice remains fun. In attempting to attain this balance, coaches should keep in mind that if they have teams of modest talent or are "building a program" a tendency toward overpreparation may be more effective. But at some advanced levels of skill and team development, overpreparation may prevent a team from performing up to its potential. Overpreparation, by prescribing a response to all situations, can prevent gifted athletes from responding in creative and more effective manners.

The Basics of Preparation

Team preparation begins in the preseason with a careful evaluation of the physical and mental skills of potential team members. Team strategies and practice plans are designed in response to this evaluation. Such an approach helps assure that practice and competitive strategies are effective, and that the team will be ready for any situations that they are likely to face.

Typically, there is limited preseason practice time. Every situation likely to be faced cannot be prepared for or even anticipated. Coaches must then make certain that: (1) their teams are prepared for early season opponents (this greatly influences team confidence in the coaches), and (2) team strategies will be effective against a wide range of opposition strategies. Once these concerns are met, coaches can go about the business of coaching their teams to *execute* strategies and fundamentals.

The Will to Prepare

An initial task of all coaches is to help their teams develop the will to prepare. Preparation necessitates an eye for detail and a willingness to practice with *concentration* and *intensity*. It also requires patience and an understanding of why preparation is necessary. Coaches must be willing to teach their athletes *why* preparation is important.

It is certainly easier to develop the will to prepare when there has been repeated success associated with it. In the absence of such success, coaches must invest extra effort to maintain a positive approach to the necessity of preparation. Coaching a mediocre or losing team demands more effort, more thought, and more thorough preparation; sometimes without immediate success. Coaches must help their athletes develop the willingness to pay this price. They must begin by setting an appropriate role model (Bandura 1969, 1974).

Athletes Must Believe

Even within the same sport and at the same level coaches can achieve success with a wide assortment of coaching strategies. The exact technique employed may not be as important as getting the team to prepare and execute whatever the coach believes will lead to success.

Coaches must get their athletes to fully accept their beliefs. To accomplish this, coaches must be well aware of all the strengths and weaknesses of their chosen strategies so that they can anticipate the reasons for skepticism in athletes. Presenting this information to team members is the first crucial step toward acceptance and belief. It shows athletes that their coach is conscientious and knowledgeable, and is capable of leading them to success.

Unless a particular coach has a long record of success it is quite natural for athletes to question strategies that are new to them. Acceptance usually involves progression through an *awareness stage* to an *interest stage* during which athletes will begin to look for more information about the strategies. A third stage eventually follows, called the *evaluation stage,* during which athletes compare the new approaches to other familiar approaches. The evaluation stage overlaps with a *trial stage* during which athletes try out the strategies and form favorable or unfavorable impressions. Eventually, athletes accept or reject the coach's ideas. Acceptance usually leads to complete belief, if the coach's behavior and team performance continue to support the belief (Rogers and Shoemaker 1971).

It should be noted that coaches go through a similar process in choosing and believing in their team strategies. This process is not neat and exact. Evaluation always continues and leads to greater belief or questioning. Refinement probably never ends.

Some athletes may immediately accept anything their coaches tell them. These athletes do not go through the process described previously, and are unlikely to cause problems related to believing in their coaches unless the strategies are consistently ineffective.

Coaches Build Acceptance and Belief

Sometimes, it is difficult to get a team to believe in their coaches and to diligently practice a particular strategy. This may be particularly true with teams that have only average talent. However, this task can be accomplished.

For example, the basketball coaching staff at the College of William and Mary, comprising the brothers Bruce and Barry Parkhill, work with such a team and have been quite successful even against teams with far superior physical talent like the University of North Carolina and Virginia Polytechnic and State University. These coaches have achieved success by getting their teams to accept and believe in a slowed down, disciplined offense and a solid defense. They have spent the time and energy necessary to convince their teams that their way is *the way* that it can be successful. Their teams accept their abilities realistically, and believe they will win with strategy and execution that will frustrate less disciplined teams.

A typical reaction followed a 48–46 William and Mary upset victory over Virginia Tech. Charlie Moir, the Tech coach, responded to defeat by stating, "It's not fun playing this type of game. . . . It's really tough to play William and Mary; they'll keep you on defense 28 . . . 30 . . . 32 minutes a game. Not to take away from Bruce Parkhill—he had his team well prepared, they played well and with more confidence that we—but I would just prefer not to play at that pace" (Steele 1981, D-1). A star player for William and Mary responded to these criticisms in a manner that expressed his team's belief in their preparation strategies: "They could either beat us at our own game or force us to play their game; they couldn't do either." Coaches who get their athletes to believe in such a system are likely to develop teams that play to their potential.

Often, coaches must encourage athletes to believe in a system or approach that differs from those they have previously encountered. Gifted athletes may be particularly resistant to acceptance of a new system.

Coach Joe Morrone, soccer coach at the University of Connecticut, has had much success largely due to his ability to manage such situations. The following is an example of his success in getting a talented player to believe in and adjust to his system.

Soccer player Pedro DeBrito acquired his extraordinary skill in the streets. "I had to go through a new learning process when he arrived at UCONN two years ago," DeBrito recalls. "It was hard at first . . . Coach Morrone asks you to do so many things—I just wasn't used to it at first. Now there's nothing to it."

"The first year was difficult for him," concurred Morrone. "I'm asking some of these kids who have never returned on defense to do so. But now, for example, Pedro's one of our best defensive players. Last week against North Carolina State they had two Nigerians who were as fast as greased lightening. Pedro came to me and said, 'Coach, let me play one of them.' So I did, and he did a great job."

In 1981 Pedro DeBrito led the University of Connecticut to the NCAA soccer championship and was the first player drafted by the Tampa team of the North American Soccer League. [Stout 1980, p. 4]

Anticipation: A Key to Preparation

There is no way to fully prepare a team for competition unless a coach directs attention to the future and anticipates problems that might occur. This is the first step in preparing to meet them. In a way, anticipation is a form of "positive worry" or "useful anxiety." Coaches who never worry about the future probably do not adequately prepare their teams.

Coaches must use "positive worry" to help them get ready for competition. Imagination is one of the most effective psychological strategies available for anticipating and preparing for the future. By imagining upcoming situations and possible positive and negative occurrences coaches can increase their readiness skills. It is easier and more natural to develop these skills through normal experience. However, through imagination coaches can avoid some of the failures associated with trial and error. Coaches must learn from the mistakes of others and endeavor to avoid the same mistakes.

Preparing for the Worst

Athletes need to be prepared for the worst things that could happen during competition. In football, when the quarterback misses the handoff to a back on an important play he had better have been taught to keep the ball and follow the back into the hole. In basketball, when a player has a wide open lay-up, trailers had better have been taught to follow in case the shot misses. In baseball and softball, hitters should have been taught to run out infield grounders in case they are misplayed.

Coaches must prepare every athlete on their teams, not just the starters and first line of substitutes. At some point in the season the last player on the team may play a crucial role in team success or failure.

Many athletes need to be prepared to keep their composure in the event that the team experiences repeated failure. Athletes need to be made aware in advance that there is a tendency to blame others for failure and for team cohesiveness to breakdown. Sports is difficult when teams fail. When losing, every break may seem to go the other way. Athletes must be ready for these situations.

Preparing teams for the worst is not negative thinking; it is realistic thinking. Athletes must be taught how to respond in an effective manner when situations that could destroy effective functioning do occur. Talking to athletes only about the negative consequences is negative thinking. But preparing athletes for difficult situations through useful drills is preparation for success under competitive stress.

Out-of-Season Preparation

Preparation cannot be complete if it is not initiated until the first day of practice. Much preparation must occur during the off-season. Preseason preparation may appear in the form of an off-season conditioning program or it might involve individual goal-setting programs designed to further develop athletes' strengths and remediate weaknesses.

Coaches must also use the off-season to prepare for the upcoming season. There are coaching clinics to attend, game films to view and evaluate, personnel to study, and books to read. Coaches who "go to sleep" in the off-season are likely to be outcoached by others. However, out-of-season preparation should start and finish well in advance of the season. The last week or two prior to the commencement of team practices should be reserved for rest and relaxation so that energy and enthusiasm for the long season ahead can be assured.

Preparing a Disciplined Team

Many psychologists frown upon coach-imposed discipline. There seems little doubt, however, that success in sports requires that athletes follow coaching instructions that are given during competitive pressure. Athletes must be taught why this discipline is needed. They must understand that the privacy of the coach's office is the place for discussion of strategic decisions. Crucial game situations require that coaches make decisions and athletes follow them.

This approach does not preclude practice games in which players coach themselves and learn to make their own decisions. If athletes were truly prepared for any situation in practice they would be capable of self-coaching and self-disciplining themselves. The attainment of such objectives would be admirable and useful for every team.

Special Considerations in Team Preparation

There are a number of special factors that coaches should consider in preparing their teams for competition. Attention to these factors can make the difference between losing and winning an athletic contest.

Underestimating and Overestimating

Care must be taken to avoid either underestimating or overestimating the abilities of a specific opponent.

Underestimation can lead to ineffective team performance due to a lack of readiness. Overestimation causes performance to suffer because coaches lose confidence and decide to change strategies that their teams have been executing well. New strategies may be intelligently designed but ineffective because execution suffers. Many coaches *beat themselves* when they make such specific and last-minute changes for a particular opponent. There are two exceptions. One occurs when teams are involved in postseason competition and there is an extended time period for preparation. In this case, specific short-term preparation can be very productive.

The other exception occurs when coaches feel that their only hope for success is to change. Often, however, this type of change backfires and causes dissension and a loss of faith in leaders. Most athletes can learn to accept failure if they have played well. Losing with a strategy that was only practiced for an hour or two is quite unacceptable. Coaches must think very carefully about the consequences of last-minute changes.

Setting the Tone

Many successful coaches begin early season practice by developing a "mind-set" for themselves and their athletes that places an emphasis on the joy of and need for preparation. Chuck Knoll, coach of the Pittsburg Steelers, has stated, "The one nightmare I always was going into a game unprepared" (Zimmerman 1980, p. 29). Paul "Bear" Bryant, former

football coach of the University of Alabama states, "I get a kick out of going to practice every day. That's where the fun is—when you're preparing, and playing" (Siner 1980, B-7). Ron Bata, the highly successful baseball coach at the University of Southern California, emphasizes preparation by sitting his entire team down at third base on the first day of practice and discussing with them everything that could possibly happen at third base. On the next day of practice he repeats the same procedures at second base. Coaches cannot expect their athletes to emphasize preparation unless they do so with both *their words and their actions*.

Consistency and Routines

Consistently is an important factor in athletic performance. Unfortunately, consistency does not come naturally to many athletes. Consistency must be taught. Coaches must recognize that anxiety may cause athletes to forget their fundamentals and perform poorly.

One of the more productive psychological strategies for improving consistency requires the mastery of preset *performance routines*. The repeated practice of performance routines has at least two important desensitization effects. First, routines have a calming effect on athletes by causing them to feel that they have been in the situation many times in the past. Athletes, like others, are more relaxed and less distracted in situations in which they are familiar. The second effect is caused by the fact that routines provide athletes with a *specific attentional focus* that prevents their minds from focusing on the stressful situation in which they must perform.

Routines may be utilized in many situations. There may be specific practice routines for starting practice, ending practice, and breaking into drills. There may be individualized or team pregame routines, locker room routines, warm-up routines, time-out routines, half-time routines, and/or specific performance situation routines. Many teams make effective use of routines for practice on the day before competition. In doing so, coaches get the team in the habit of preparing for every contest in a consistent manner. Routines can promote consistency by ensuring that teams avoid underpreparing for an inferior opponent and avoid overpreparing for a superior opponent.

In particular performance situations, such as penalty kicking in soccer, field goal kicking in football, warming-up goalies, free-throw shooting in basketball, pitching in softball or baseball, serving in tennis, or high jumping in track and field, athletes should be helped to develop very exact performance routines. They should be taught to practice the entire routine every time they practice the skill until it becomes natural and automatic.

It is not necessary (although it may be helpful) for all athletes to have the exact same routine. What is important is that all athletes have a routine that will help them during stressful competitive performances.

Simulations: You Don't Play the Way You Practice, You Practice the Way You Play

The psychological training technique known as *simulation* or *model training* (Vanek and Cratty 1970) is intended to prepare athletes to effectively manage stress by anticipating potential stressors and then replicating them repeatedly in the practice environment. This technique can be highly effective and has been used with success in space flight missions, civil defense, community disasters, and various stressful performance situations other than sports.

Many coaches use preseason scrimmage games that are open to spectators to help habituate their athletes to upcoming competitive situations. Others use their second team to play the opposition's role. Some coaches make a point of arriving at an away game early so as to acclimatize athletes to the strange and potentially anxiety-inducing and distracting situa-

tion. Lefty Driesell, basketball coach at the University of Maryland, utilizes a tape recording of screaming fans during practice to get ready for upcoming crowds. It should be noted that at least one notable university football coach overused this idea the week of an important contest with the result that the starting quarterback lost his voice on game day from constantly screaming signals over the simulated crowd noise during practice all week.

Audience and Co-action Effects.

Simulations are most effective when they make use of *audience effects* (fans, parents, peers) and *co-action effects* (teammates, coaches). Audience simulations can include friendly, hostile, and neutral crowds in a large wide-open playing area as well as in small, confined areas. Practice scrimmages can easily be arranged in which supporters are asked to attend an open scrimmage and role play the fan behaviors of another school. Fans can be challenged to attempt to distract performers during scrimmage as long as they stay within the bounds of sportsmanlike conduct and do nothing dangerous. Athletes must understand that the situation is designed to challenge their concentration and emotional control and to get them ready for future situations.

During these same simulations team members should practice responding to teammates in a manner consistent with ideal game day behavior. This means that all athletes and coaches realize that their responses (verbal and nonverbal) influence the concentration and confidence of other team members. Athletes should practice being encouraging and enthusiastic in supporting one another during the scrimmage. When appropriate behavior does not occur coaches should utilize the opportunity to educate and increase the awareness of their players. It is best to use the "teachable moment" rather than wait until the contest is over. After the contest athletes may have forgotten how they behaved.

Vary the Conditions. Simulations can include various conditions that can distract athletes' attention and, thus, interfere with performance. These conditions may include practicing: (1) in extremely windy, hot, cold, or wet situations, (2) with strange equipment, (3) with unusual or abnormal field or court conditions, and (4) with a modified or abbreviated warm-up period. Practicing game situations, such as being tied, ahead, behind, or late in a contest, are also useful for desensitizing athletes to the stress inherent in sports competition (Cratty 1981; Wolpe 1958).

Simulations, however, should not be only physical in nature. Viewing game films or pictures of an upcoming opponent, the anticipated playing environment, and the expected crowd can also be effective. Application of simulations is limited only by the imaginations of coaches.

Ideally, simulations should be implemented only after basic strategies and fundamentals have become automatized. Earlier use of simulations is likely to add confusion and anxiety (Kauss 1980). When these strategies are used during the week of a game coaches should emphasize appropriate responses, not expected distractions.

Likewise, coaches should avoid building up the opposition to the point that athletes begin to feel that their task is impossible. When this is done the effectiveness of simulations is seriously undermined.

Preseason Scrimmages

Preseason scrimmages, no matter if they are conducted within the team or against outside opposition, are important to team success. They prepare the team by building confidence in team abilities, strategies, and execution.

Oftentimes, preseason scrimmages do not go smoothly. Execution may break down, strategies may backfire, and athletes (and coaches) may begin to second-guess. This response must be anticipated. Prior to the scrimmage athletes should be reminded to concentrate and give

their best, but to realize that it is still early in the preseason. At this point, team preparation is not yet complete, so there should not be too much concern over results.

Postgame analysis should include praise for effort and concentration, including frequent reminders that the talent necessary for success is present. In addition, points of strength should be emphasized. Weaknesses can be presented in a manner that allows athletes to know the coach is aware of the problems, but is not overly concerned by them. For example, when teaching a pressing team defense that falters, coaches might say, "At times the defense looked real good. At other times it really broke down. We are just going to have to work extra hard on getting the help side people in position. When we did we forced the turnover. Does everyone understand their responsibilities?"

Preseason scrimmages must be looked at as opportunities for learning and testing out strategies and competitive performance. Coaches must help make certain that scrimmages facilitate team improvement rather than hinder it.

Typical Athlete Problems

Coaches can help themselves prepare their athletes for competition by realizing that certain signals sent by athletes are filled with important information. Coaches must anticipate these signs and utilize them.

Looking for Telltale Signs. When most of the athletes on a team show up for practice appearing and acting lethargic they may have been pushed hard enough and may need a day off or an easy practice. Athletes who act depressed and walk around with their heads hanging are often asking for attention and help from their coaches. An entire team that fails to attend with interest when the coach is speaking may be trying to tell the coach that the talk has lasted too long and that they are ready to move.

There are no clear-cut interpretations of the signals that athletes send. Nonetheless, coaches should be alert to these signals and must be prepared to respond to them.

Constant Failure. Athletes who have been performing poorly may be frustrated and depressed. Oftentimes, it is quite natural for coaches to respond with criticism and discouragement. Usually, such coaches intend to "snap the athlete out of it" and find out if they are "tough enough" to overcome adversity. This approach may be effective, since athletes need mental toughness during practice and competition. However, constant "putdowns" will destroy many athletes.

Coaches must know their athletes well enough to be able to develop mental toughness without destroying and frustrating them. This does not mean coaches should always avoid driving athletes to the point of frustration. Often, coaches must take them this far to find their limits. The most important point is that when athletes reach the point of frustration coaches must read their behaviors and back off. Athletes must then be given support and encouragement if they are to continue to grow and improve.

Constant Success. Despite the fact that self-confidence is very important to success in sports there are times, particularly in practice, when too much confidence can become a problem. Coaches must recognize that athletes can have problems in dealing with too much success. A problem has arisen if athletes begin to appear lazy, "holier than thou," or are no longer coachable.

When this situation occurs coaches should discuss the problem with athletes and should establish new and more challenging goals. If these basic strategies do not work coaches may need to carefully monitor adherence to team rules and policies. Every attempt must be made to maintain self-confidence while making certain the athletes continue to function within the team framework.

The Midseason Blues. On most teams at least some athletes experience a letdown sometime around the middle of the season. The excitement of the preseason has long since dissipated and the end of the season is far in the future.

Athletes may begin to feel stale and weary from the dedication and discipline necessary for sports success. These problems may be exaggerated if the early season has brought failure and disappointment.

Coaches must anticipate this potential problem and be prepared to deal with it. A break in normal routines may be needed. A day or two spent talking about and reviewing team goals may be quite useful at this point in the season. Revision of intermediate and long-term goals for practice and competition can help revive enthusiasm. Tom Fay, Editor-in-Chief of *Freestyle Magazine* and swim coach at Vanderbilt University, suggests the following for what he calls the "blahs."

> "Next you must re-tune your body. Examine your eating, sleeping and workout habits to make sure you are sticking to good discipline and good habits. Quit eating those little "extra" snacks that seem so tempting when boredom sets in. Be more conscious of the little things you are doing wrong in workout, for example, one hand turns on butterfly and breaststroke, improper finishes on repeats, slacking off in the middle of a set to "save up" for the last one. Bad habits, even practiced for a short time, will hamper you later and are never as easily broken as begun!
>
> "Check your sleeping habits to make sure you are getting enough rest. During the season, without proper rest, it is all too easy to get sick or catch a nagging cold. Allowing yourself to become physically unable to perform at your peak is doing yourself and your team a disservice. Be wise and sensible, then, in rest as in play." [Fay 1979, p. 28]

When team members are experiencing the "blues" or the "blahs" it is often useful to have a team meeting designed to put the importance of sports into perspective. Often, at this point in the season athletes have concentrated so much on their sport that other things in life get overlooked or appear unimportant. Young athletes may need help in rediscovering balance in their lives.

Nonsport Problems. Frequently, in today's ever-changing world many of the most difficult problems that influence athletes' performances are not directly related to sports. They may include problems with school, parents, or peers. Coaches may not be in a position to solve such problems for athletes. However, coaches must be close enough and responsive enough to their athletes to recognize the problems and at least provide a receptive ear. This alone will greatly reduce the stress faced by athletes. When problems are beyond the coach's abilities they should find an expert who can help.

Captains and Assistant Coaches

Captains and assistant coaches can be invaluable in helping head coaches meet the needs of athletes. These assistants can inform coaches of whether the team is "up" or "down" and can provide valuable information about interpersonal problems that may arise on the team. These persons should function to facilitate communications between athletes and the head coach.

During the preseason captains and assistants should be prepared to deal with athletes who will come to them with problems during the coming season. At this time, assistants should be alerted to the possibility that athletes may approach them with complaints about the head coach. This is a particularly sensitive situation for which assistants must be properly prepared. When approached with a complaint about the head coach assistants could respond so as to gratify their own egos by agreeing with the athlete's complaints and perhaps even suggesting that if they were the head coach things would be different or better. Needless to say, this type of response can be extremely detrimental. It would be much preferred that the assistant re-

spond to this situation by listening to the athlete, by informing the head coach of the problem, and by suggesting possible solutions. However, if an athlete speaks in confidence, it usually is best that confidentiality be honored. Nonetheless, assistant coaches should always take care to avoid eroding the position of head coaches. They must be supportive helpers. Captains and assistant coaches often have crucial but thankless responsibilities. To be effective they must be selfless and team-oriented.

Summary

Preparation is one of the more effective strategies for innoculating athletes to stress. Anticipation of problematic events is crucial to preparation skill. Anticipation of and preparation for stress can prevent confusion, uncertainty, and the resulting lack in confidence.

Team preparation requires the will to prepare. In addition, athletes must believe in what their coaches ask them to execute. Athletes typically advance through an awareness stage, an interest stage, an evaluation stage, and a trial stage in coming to accept their coaches' strategies. Teams must be prepared for the worst and the unexpected. Likewise, teams must be disciplined in order to accomplish the necessary preparation. Overestimation and underestimation of opponents must be avoided whenever possible.

Coaches can emphasize preparation by both their words and their actions. Two of the most useful preparation strategies are simulation and routines. Together these strategies can prepare a team to perform in front of various audiences and under differing playing conditions.

There are a host of special practice considerations that can be prepared for and managed effectively. These include preseason scrimmage failures and frustrations, telltale signs of problems, constant failure, constant success, midseason blues, nonsport problems, and problems with captains and assistant coaches. Potential problems that are anticipated and dealt with properly can actually enhance feelings of confidence and control. Proper preparation can prevent these situations from producing uncontrollable stress and performance decrements.

References

Bandura, A. Behavior theory and models of man. *American Psychologist*, 29:859–869, 1974.

Bandura, A. Social learning, modeling. *Principles of Behavior Modification*. New York: Holt, Rinehart and Winston, 1969, p. 9.

Cratty, B.J. *Social Psychology in Athletics*. Englewood Cliffs, New Jersey: Prentice-Hall, Inc., 1981.

Fay, T. It's tune up time. *Swimmer's Magazine*. (Feb./Mar.): 28–29, 1979.

Kauss, D.R. Peak Performance: Mental Game Plans for Maximizing Your Athletic Potential. Englewood Cliffs, New Jersey: Prentice-Hall, Inc., 1980.

Meichenbaum, D. *Cognitive Behavior Modification: An Integrative Approach*. New York: Plenum Press, 1979.

Rogers, E.M., and Shoemaker, F.F. *Communication of Innovations*, 2nd ed. New York: Free Press, 1971.

Seele, S. ZZZZZ–Tribe lulls Virginia Tech into nightmarish sleep. *The Daily Progress*, Charlottesville, Virginia, Thurs., Jan. 22, 1981, D-1.

Siner, H. Being a legend tough on Bear. *The Daily Progress*, Charlottesville, Virginia, Fri., Dec. 5, 1980, B-7.

Stout, J. Morrone eyes final four. *The Connecticut Alumnus*, (Nov.): 54 (no. 3), 1980.

Vanek, M., and Cratty, B.J. *Psychology and the Superior Athlete*. New York: Macmillan, 1970.

Wolpe, J. *Psychotherapy by Reciprocal Inhibition*. Standord, Conn.: Stanford University Press, 1958.

Zimmerman, P. The teacher. *Sports Illustrated*, (July): 28–35, 1980.

Recommended Readings

Cratty, B.J. *Social Psychology in Athletics*. Englewood Cliffs, New Jersey: Prentice-Hall, Inc., 1981.

Kauss, D.R. *Peak Performance: Mental Game Plans for Maximizing Your Athletic Potential*. Englewood Cliffs, New Jersey: Prentice-Hall, Inc., 1980.

Meichenbaum, D. *Cognitive Behavior Modification: An Integrative Approach*. New York: Plenum Press, 1979.

Credit: University of South Carolina Sports Information.

Mastery of Sports Skills: Designing Effective Practice Sessions

7

There is little doubt that great coaches are great teachers. There is no one, perfect teaching technique. However, research has identified a set of guidelines that can greatly facilitate learning by athletes. Over the last 20 years we have witnessed a rapid expansion of knowledge pertinent to the psychological aspects of motor learning (i.e., mastery of movement skills). This chapter focuses on information that is most relevant to designing and implementing practice sessions. The techniques discussed in this chapter, if applied in a manner that is consistent with the principles discussed in the foregoing chapters, can lead to efficient skill advancement by athletes.

A Basic Framework

Although many theories of skill acquisition have evolved, emphasis here will be given to applications of the work of Schmidt (1975) and Gentile (1972). Their ideas are both useful and widely accepted. Interested readers may wish to review the writings of Adams (1971), Bernstein (1967), Marteniuk (1976), and Stallings (1982) who have been leaders in the growth of knowledge in motor learning.

Schema Theory

Schmidt (1975) has proposed a model that describes the manner in which an athlete goes about learning a movement skill. This model, termed the "schema theory," is based on three premises. A first premise holds that athletes cannot store the multitude of *specific* motor responses that they are capable of executing. Instead, the "motor memory" contains a smaller number of generalized "schemas" that can be applied in many situations. A second guiding principle indicates that when athletes are confronted with a motor task, a general classification of movement (schema) is first called upon. Subsequently, a specific response is molded to the demands of the task. A third premise states that skill learning takes place as performers reduce differences between actual performance at a given time and the "model of movement" that is ideal to the performance situation.

Gentile's Working Model

Gentile's (1972) efforts have been particularly useful for practitioners. Her working model agrees in principle with the "schema theory" and attempts to deal with solutions to problems that occur in practice. Gentile argues that when athletes attempt to execute a skill there are four possible response interpretations that they might make:

1. If the skill was executed with desired results, and the execution "felt correct," the conclusion is that "all is well."
2. If execution "felt correct," yet the results were disappointing, the result is that "something is wrong."
3. If the execution "feels wrong," but satisfactory results are obtained, the response is surprise or questioning one's feelings.
4. If it is believed that the skill was executed incorrectly, and the results were disappointing, the athletes are likely to view that "everything is wrong." Improvement is needed.

Coaches must constantly deal with these responses while keeping in mind that there may be dramatic differences between coaches' and athletes' perceptions of form and of results that may interfere with improvement. Coaches should initiate the learning process by determining how much experience athletes have had with specific skills important to the sport being played. Likewise, experience with other similar sports that might facilitate or interfere with learning should be explored.

Athletes typically advance through three stages of skill development: *beginner, intermediate,* and *advanced.* Although it is difficult to identify these stages with absolute precision, coaches should provide feedback that is appropriate to the athlete's developmental level.

Robert Christina, an expert in motor development at the Pennsylvania State University, has suggested a framework for understanding the differences among these developmental stages (Christina 1981).

Beginner Stage

During the beginning stage of learning athletes strive to understand the techniques that their coaches have just introduced, demonstrated, and explained. Energy is devoted to developing an image and a feel of the movements required so that coordinated execution can be developed. Basically, athletes at this beginning stage understand and practice *one part* of a complex skill or sport until it is well learned and automatized. This is followed by the learning of a new skill part. Eventually, the parts are put together into coordinated movement.

At the beginner stage errors may be frequent. Performance is far from flawless. Attempts at execution demand the total attention of athletes. Coaches must be careful not to provide too much feedback to beginners. *Specific, simple,* and *understandable* feedback is crucial to effective learning at this early stage of learning. When feedback is provided athletes should stop practicing and should attend carefully to the coach's new instructions.

Intermediate Stage

The intermediate stage is dominated by planning and implementing effective practice strategies. Only "perfect practice will make perfect." Coaches play a most important role in insuring that athletes: (1) are motivated to learn, (2) attend to the relevant cues and/or strategies, (3) receive feedback about what they are doing correctly and incorrectly as well as how their errors can be improved, and (4) receive reinforcement. These factors are not, however, influenced only by coaches. Feedback and compliments from teammates and intrinsic feedback from successful performance are also important sources of influence. A team attitude that fosters helping and supportive behaviors can be helpful to this process.

At the intermediate stage performance is not yet proficient and athletes must continue to improve their understanding of the technique. As athletes progress through this stage they will manifest: (1) a decreasing need for direct attention to the execution of technique, (2) the gradual elimination of extraneous movements and errors, and (3) improvements in speed and coordination. Repetitive drills are particularly useful during this stage.

Advanced Stage

Athletes at the advanced stage must be coached in a way that allows: (1) development of their skills so that they can be consistently repeated under various practice and competitive situations, and (2) continued development of skills to a more advanced level.

Advanced athletes understand their skills well enough to execute self-correction to a great extent; but at times, they still require technical coaching to make certain corrections. Coaches must provide practice conditions that require *full attention* and *self-discipline* so as to prevent the development of bad habits. Advanced athletes perform skills more automatically and, consequently, more attention can be given to game strategy and other issues.

Performance at the advanced level is faster and smoother. Improvement will level off and develop much slower. Much of the improvement that does come involves becoming a "smarter athlete" who is able to respond more readily to new and challenging situations. At this stage coaches must structure practices that require performance of skills at full speed under stressful competitive situations.

Team Advancement

Teams, like athletes, advance from lower to higher levels of skill performance. Teams with advanced skill levels are able to devote much more of their practice time to strategy, complicated offensive and defensive maneuvers, and training and conditioning. Less advanced teams must spend much more of their practice time on skill development.

Less advanced teams may have to forego early season success for the sake of skill development. In such cases, coaches and teammates must patiently await results that may not come until later in the season. Teams that survive negative early season performances are likely to improve throughout the season. When this occurs teams can achieve peak performances at the time of postseason or championship competition.

Setting the Environment for Learning

Improvement occurs most effectively when coaches create an environment conducive to learning. Setting this environment is the first step in designing effective practice sessions.

Points of Emphasis and Execution

Prior to the first day of practice coaches must decide what they will teach. Usually, there are two to four weeks between the first day of practice and the start of the regular season. The typical two hours per day of practice time provides insufficient time to teach everything desired. *Therefore, coaches must identify certain important points to emphasize.* Attention should be directed toward proper execution of these skills on a daily basis. These skills will eventually become *characteristic of the team.*

There is no magic strategy for deciding which skills to emphasize. Certainly, even within the same sport coaches who are successful emphasize different points. One baseball coach may win with pitching, bunting, and baserunning, while another may win with fielding and the power hitting. One basketball coach may win with defense and another may win with offense. Somehow, coaches must study their sport carefully, understand their personal areas of expertise, identify the abilities of their atheletes, and then design practice strategies that result in mastery of fundamental skills. Fundamentals must be accepted by the entire team, including all players and coaches, in order for them to be executed consistently. Once these key skills have been accepted, all that remains is effective teaching of the fundamentals and repetition via concentrated drilling.

Perfect Practice Makes Perfect

Beginning on the first day of practice, team members *must* understand that practice time is limited and should not be wasted. It must be clear that success is achieved through perfect execution of what is practiced. The team must realize that they can achieve success only through proper execution of fundamentals.

It must be clear that half-hearted efforts in practice will not be tolerated. This approach sets the mood for the self-discipline and concentration necessary for competition. While this approach may need adjustment for younger, less mature athletes, it is a necessity for quality practice. If sloppy practice does occur it should be stopped and discussed. Athletes must understand that sloppy practice will cause problems later in the season.

The Center for Error Detection and Correction

On the first day of practice athletes begin to form impressions of their coaches and the practice environment. Coaches must make it clear that practice is a serious time and, yet, is also a time for growing, learning, closeness, and fun.

Athletes should be told that practice is considered *the center for error detection and correction.* Everyone makes mistakes in practice. These errors are fine, since they can allow each athlete to improve. Coaches should only ask that when mistakes are pointed out and correc-

tions are given each athlete attempt to improve until the frequency of mistakes is drastically reduced. Coaches should provide personal examples of the fact that athletes, like coaches, are human and will always make errors. The team's goal should be to grow from errors rather than be destroyed or held back by them.

Encouraging Questions

Athletes should be encouraged to ask questions about any instructions that are unclear to them or inconsistent with what they have been taught by other coaches. Athletes should know that there may not always be time during practice to answer every question, but that their questions are welcomed during breaks or prior to or after practice. It must be clear to athletes that practice is the time for questions. There is no room for uncertainty during competition.

Even though the coach is in charge, learning and improvement must always be a two-way street. Listening to and responding to initial questions is crucial to establishing the desired environment. Likewise, coaches should make themselves available to athletes prior to or after formal practice, whenever facilities and time allow. These times are ideal for giving athletes individualized attention to weaknesses or for working on a new skill.

Practice Is a Privilege

Practice must be serious. Effective coaches demand concentration and "hustle" while still finding moments for humor and personal interactions. Athletes should view practice and team membership as a privilege, not a right. Each day athletes must earn the privilege of returning for the next day. It can only be earned through "hustle" and effort.

Let each athlete, no matter if he/she is the first or last player on the team, know that laziness will not be tolerated. When athletes fail to "hustle" they should expect that their coach will be upset with them. But they should realize that their coach is upset at them for wasting their ability and the team's time rather than on account of a lack of concern for such athletes.

The Coaches' Attitude Is Contagious

Coaches must go into each practice session with an enthusiastic attitude. Practices tend to go as well as the coach makes them go. Bad days are wasted days, not just for coaches but for the entire squad. The coaches' attitude is contagious and can be a great source of power.

Successful coaches consciously select the atmosphere they wish to create for a particular practice session and plan strategies accordingly. Enthusiastic and well-prepared coaches, through their words and actions, seem to say, "I can't wait to start practice. I have so much to teach you today. I have a definite plan for today's practice." Athletes respond to this energy because they know their drills will ensure learning and fun.

Practice Considerations

Several key factors influence the learning of skills by athletes. Proper attention to these factors can optimize the efficiency of a team's practice sessions.

Length of Practice

There is no hard and fast answer concerning the ideal length of time for practice. Certainly, a tennis team can effectively practice twice a day for two hours per session. At other times, perhaps in the middle of the season, a single one-hour session is a bit too much.

John Lawther, a leading expert in motor learning, suggests that coaches consider the following factors in designing practice sessions: (1) the age of the athlete, (2) the complexity and strenuousness of the sports skills being practiced, (3) the specific purposes of the particular practice, (4) the level of learning already attained, (5) the experiential background of the learner, and (6) the total environmental conditions, including other demands and distractions, and activities between practices. For school-age athletes environmental conditions might include proximity to exams, closeness to a long bus trip, or time in the season (first week of practice, middle of season, week before postseason tournament) (Lawther 1977).

Clearly, *fatigue* and *interest* are crucial factors to consider in making decisions concerning the ideal length of practice. Coaches must be acutely aware of the necessity of reading their athletes' behavior. When athletes act *lethargic* and *inattentive* practice is no longer productive. A decision must then be made to either end practice and start again the next day, end practice and take a day or two off, or take a few minutes' break to get a drink.

It is almost impossible to force athletes into practicing. Attempts to do so work against effectiveness and ruin the enjoyment of practice. Practice sessions should force athletes to improve their concentration skills, but should not lead to excessive fatigue. Insufficient challenge leads to underdeveloped athletes. Practices that are too long or stressful become sloppy and inefficient.

In general, for older and more advanced athletes, the available research suggests that lengthy and continuous practice of one activity (*massed practice*) can be quite effective. With younger, less developed athletes, practice sessions and drills should be more frequently separated with rest periods or with practice of other activities (*distributed practice*).

Overlearning

Another factor that must be considered relative to the length of practice is overlearning. Overlearning involves practicing a skill so that it can be performed "automatically." A goal of practices should be to achieve overlearning without encountering boredom.

In working toward this goal, coaches should first observe whether or not all athletes can execute the desired skills repeatedly on the same day and on different days without a decrease in performance level. This indicates whether or not the skills have been learned. Once it is believed that the skills are learned, coaches must decide how much overlearning is required to make certain that skills are remembered. Usually, overlearning should continue until coaches are assured that the skill can be performed under conditions of competitive stress.

Once coaches are comfortable that athletes have attained this level of overlearning, concern must turn to avoiding boredom. Occasional practice of overlearned skills is needed, but too much review leads to boredom. At this point, new skills should be added to stimulate players and promote team development.

Part Versus Whole Teaching Methods

Sports skills can be taught in their entirety (whole method) or can be broken down into smaller parts for instructional purposes (part method). In general, if an activity is complex and difficult to learn it is best to analyze the skill and practice each part separately. As a part is learned another part is added until the whole skill can be practiced at once. Sports skills, such as the tennis serve, golf swing, swimming strokes, and the jump-shot in basketball, may be taught by either the whole or part method. In general, older, stronger and more coordinated athletes learn effectively with the whole method. If coaches are uncertain regarding which method is best they should experiment by letting athletes try the whole skill first and then determine whether or not the skill must be broken down.

Regardless of which method is selected, learning is facilitated by first presenting the entire skill to athletes so they can develop a clear picture of the complete movement. This helps athletes formulate a plan and know what they are working toward. This is important to both learning and motivation.

Effective Demonstrations

Demonstrations always play an important part in skill development during practice. Successful demonstrations have several basic characteristics. First, athletes must attend to important aspects of the skill being demonstrated. Second, the duration of the demonstration should not exceed the athletes' attention spans. And third, steps must be taken to ensure that athletes remember the demonstration.

Some coaches are skilled in a sport and can effectively provide the demonstration themselves. Others can bring in someone else or utilize a film. No matter who provides the demonstration, it must be obvious to athletes that the skill is worth developing. Once this impression is formed through a full-speed demonstration, it may be repeated several times in slow-motion with *attention intentionally directed* at a few key points. The younger the athletes, the shorter the attention span and the fewer points to which attention can be directed at one time.

Memory can be helped by emphasizing that: (1) the skill demonstrated will be crucial to future success in competition, (2) many athletes at advanced levels utilize the skill, and (3) there will be rewards for individuals who develop the skill demonstrated.

Avoid Overanalysis

It is easy for competent and enthusiastic coaches to provide athletes with far too many cues for learning. Coaches must remember that their level of skill proficiency and understanding is far beyond that of many developing athletes. This may be a particularly pertinent problem for gifted athlete-coaches who acquired their skills quite easily. All athletes may not comprehend dissected skills as easily as such coaches did.

Provision of too many learning cues can result in "paralysis by analysis." However, as soon as athletes can consistently demonstrate the desired general movement pattern more learning cues can be provided. A key is to find an effective middle ground that avoids both bombarding athletes with too many cues and waiting too long to provide additional information.

Reading Cues

To be successful athletes must learn to develop the ability to "read" the important cues in their competitive environment. Often, there are far too many cues available to focus on all of them during performance. As athletes become more experienced and their performance improves they should learn how to attend to the most important cues.

The development of the ability to "read" cues is based upon *alertness and duration of attention, limited storage capacity,* and *selective attention.* To be alert athletes must keep their eyes and ears open and receptive. Only a limited amount of information can be dealt with at any one time because even athletes have limited storage capacities. Athletes must, therefore, be selective about the information to which they attend.

Coaches need to help their athletes attend to the *salient cues* in their environment. Instead of simply teaching the physical skills, coaches should also teach athletes which cues to read and how to read them. By combining the specific teaching of these cues with the learning that comes from playing experience athletes learn how to "read" situations and anticipate what will happen next.

Athletes who develop such abilities are often considered to have "great reactions." Athletes in sports such as soccer, lacrosse, field hockey, or football quickly learn the importance of watching the opponent's hips rather than the head; in receiving serves in tennis athletes improve their reactions by attending to the ball in the hand rather than other body parts.

By attending to salient cues advanced performers anticipate movements earlier and respond sooner, and in this way may be perceived to be quicker. The quarterback in football and the floor/field leader in other sports must "read" the defense and know early what will occur. The early detection of these cues reduces the information processing demands, and leaves more time for deciding what action to initiate.

A Picture and a Feel

To master a sport skill athletes must have a picture of what the skill looks like and what it feels like when executed correctly. Coaches must help athletes attend to both of these sensations.

Earlier, strategies were detailed for developing visual pictures. Feeling can be developed by questions such as: "Could you *feel* the full extension at release?", "Could you *feel* the stretch in your left side at the top of the backswing?" Because athletes tend to use their eyes to the exclusion of feel, strategies such as *blindfolded* or *slow-motion* performance can also facilitate the development of feel.

It is often useful to ask athletes to avoid observing the results of their performance. By doing so it is easier for athletes to focus on feeling rather than their results. Athletes may then be asked to predict the accuracy of their performance based upon their feelings.

Speed Versus Accuracy

In many sport skills successful performance requires both speed and accuracy. In teaching skills of this sort (e.g., throwing, kicking) coaches must decide whether they should: (1) initially teach the skill in slow motion with emphasis on accuracy, (2) emphasize speed, allowing accuracy to come later, or (3) emphasize speed and accuracy equally.

Evidence supports the notion that speed with a gross accuracy should be emphasized early in learning. The emphasis on speed ensures that the skill movements are learned correctly. Once speed is produced consistently, it will be easy to produce accuracy. By practicing with a large target the frustrations possibly encountered as a result of inaccuracy are greatly reduced.

When accuracy rather than speed is emphasized early in the learning process problems may arise. Athletes may become so concerned with accuracy that they may try to achieve it using a poor movement pattern. It is much more difficult to change the pattern at a later date. Anyone who has tried to teach an older athlete who has a push throwing motion or "throws like a girl" is aware of the difficulty of changing that motion. A correct throwing motion has nothing to do with being male or female, but rather is a result of a failure to emphasize speed early in the learning process. However, coaches should remember to be sensitive to the frustrations that may occur with the initial emphasis on speed and the resulting inaccuracy. Extra help and even individualized practice unencumbered by observing teammates may prove helpful by reducing socially induced stress and allowing the athlete to practice in an efficient manner.

Feedback for Improvement

Improved performance of sports skills occurs as a result of two important sources of feedback. Feedback may come internally from the athletes themselves as well as from *external sources* such as coaches or teammates.

There is a tendency for most athletes to rely solely upon the results of their skill execution. This can be an accurate and useful source of information. However, there are many times when athletes are so result-oriented that it is difficult for them to focus on the skill pattern. Coaches must help athletes by providing cues that link cause with effect. The ultimate goal is to develop self-correcting athletes who can, for the most part, function independently.

When actively working with athletes on skill improvement coaching comments such as "nice shot," "super hit," or "that's lousy" are quite useless to athletes. What is needed is specific information that helps athletes develop a framework for repeating a "nice shot" or correcting a "lousy shot." They already knew it was either nice or lousy. There are, however, times during actual competitive performance when coaching comments regarding obvious performance results are extremely useful to motivation and confidence.

The Use of Praise

Praise, like other types of feedback, provides athletes with information. It helps athletes to realize which types of behavior and performance are worthy of satisfaction. For most athletes praise is a more powerful tool. But if it is overused or easily dispensed for a half-hearted or sloppy performance, praise may become ineffective and lose its potency.

When even advanced athletes are learning a new skill, frequent praise may be given for closer and closer approximations of the desired skill. Such feedback lets athletes know they are on the right track. When athletes begin to "get it," enthusiastic comments such as "super," "that is it," or "that's the idea" can be effective.

As the skill progresses gradually to the intermediate or advanced stage, praise should be given less frequently (schedule of reinforcement). The reduced praise indicates to athletes that the correct skill execution is now expected. Self-correction and self-direction are encouraged and only exemplary performance should be praised.

In general, coaches attempt to get their athletes to generate outstanding efforts in order to *earn* praise. In this way athletes are urged not to become complacent with their present level of execution. Error elimination is the desired goal and movement in this direction should indeed be praised.

Providing Useful Feedback

Practice involves constant performance by athletes and observation by coaches. Evaluation of practice attempts and provision of useful feedback are two of the most important functions of coaches.

Too Much or Too Little. Coaches who fail to give feedback are of little use, while coaches who provide too much feedback also experience difficulties. Feedback must be presented in an understandable manner. Coaches should only give corrective feedback when they are quite sure of the cause and solution of the error. Frequent, inaccurate feedback will cause most athletes to "tune the coach out." Future attempts at helping will fall on deaf ears.

When coaches observe athletes making many errors at the same time a decision on where to start correction will have to be made. It was previously mentioned that too many thoughts would lead to "paralysis by analysis." *It is usually best to begin where the problem originates.* Typically, this will be a step or two ahead of where the problem becomes obvious. For example, a tennis player may be observed hitting the forehand off the back foot, which is less efficient than stepping into the ball with the front foot. The problem, however, originates earlier than ball-racket impact. It may originate in late racket preparation.

A key is to decide whether or not one error is leading to another. If this is the case, one should begin by correcting the initial error. If this is not the case, coaches must rely upon their experience to decide which error should be corrected first. Usually, the error that will cause the greatest improvement and, thus, increase motivation should be corrected first.

Feedback Must Be Heard and Repeated. Feedback should first and foremost be given in a voice that can be heard. It should carry information relevant to skill progress or motivation. Skill practice must be *intense* and *repetitive.* Coaches' feedback should help maintain intensity and make certain that skills are repeated correctly.

Begin with a Compliment. In general, it is best to initiate feedback by complimenting athletes on their effort and on any aspects of the skill that were performed correctly. This assumes that such feedback is honest and accurate. Depending on the sensitivity and motivation of athletes, there are times when it may be necessary to look the athletes in the eyes and say, "You didn't even try and your execution is totally wrong. Let's get into this. We have got to start over from the very beginning." Athletes usually know when they tried (especially more mature athletes) and know when praise is undeserved.

Athletes can be encouraged to practice by ensuring them that improvement eventually will result. Also, athletes must be given some time frame for accomplishing the desired performance level.

Feedback Should Be Immediate. Ideally, feedback should be given as soon after performance as possible. This will make the feedback more pertinent and, thus, meet a more receptive athlete. When athletes have been working with the same coach for an extended time period it is often possible for the coach to communicate skill instruction entirely through nonverbal behavior. A coach may communicate a need for follow-through to a field goal kicker by raising his leg high or indicate the need for footwork by a series of quick short steps. This is a special type of communication that develops when coach and athlete respect, trust, and understand each other fully.

Sarcasm. In some sports environments, such as at the college level, sarcasm is a fully accepted form of feedback. It can be an enjoyable mental game for mature and confident students. However, sarcasm must be used judiciously when coaching young athletes who lack confidence. The coach must be certain that sarcasm facilitates establishment of a positive learning relationship rather than destroying such a relationship.

Special Practice Considerations

Besides the factors already discussed, there are several special phenomena that frequently arise as athletes develop. Coaches must manage these situations in a satisfactory manner if they wish to optimize the skill acquisition of their athletes.

Plateaus

When athletes are at the beginning stage of development progress comes in leaps and bounds. This is an easy time to enjoy being an athlete. However, with development to the advanced levels progress slows down and becomes more difficult. At times, progress may appear to be at a standstill—*a plateau.* Athletes may respond by becoming discouraged. They may start wondering if they have reached their potential or if future practice is worth it. A coach's aid is needed.

Athletes must be helped to realize that plateaus are a natural part of sports. Everyone who has achieved the advanced stage has gone through them. Plateaus are frustrating, but must be worked through. It is self-defeating to think that potential has been attained. Usually, a stumbling block on the way to a new level of proficiency is only temporary.

Oftentimes, plateaus can be solved in a relatively short time if the cause can be identified. For some the answer will be working harder. For others a few days rest is required. It is not uncommon for plateus to result from a flaw in skill mechanics or perhaps a mental barrier that needs correcting; a plateau may be due to poor conditioning. Frequently, athletes get into plateaus because they emphasize practice quantity while overlooking practice quality. Such athletes may need to develop a more serious attitude toward their practice.

Occasionally, plateaus can make very high-level athletes feel that their potential has been attained. Coaches can assist athletes by helping them evaluate their progress fairly. As athletes reach higher performance levels a slower rate of progress is expected. So even very small gains may be quite significant. Athletes must be helped to accurately recall their progress.

Sometimes, athletes overlook the great strides they have made.

When an entire team seems to have plateaued or even slipped backward coaches should realize that they may be bored or "stale." Something different must be done to make practices novel and exciting. Concerns regarding boredom and staleness have increased steadily as year-long training and specialization have become common in more and more sports.

Making Changes in Technique

Perhaps one of the most difficult challenges that coaches face involves trying to change the technique of an athlete who has previously learned an inefficient technique. This problem is particularly difficult if the athlete in question has had considerable success with the old technique and the particular coach has not had a lot of experience in developing high-level athletes.

Prior to making a decision coaches must be certain, at least to their own satisfaction, that the *change in techniques will benefit the athlete* even if it requires time and frustration. Such decisions can seldom be made with absolute certainty. So it is often helpful to ask more experienced coaches or experts to observe the athlete's performance and offer opinions concerning the feasibility of change. Decisions regarding technique changes should be made only after considering the athlete's potential for advancement in the sport, the advantages and disadvantages of changing the technique, and strategies for making the change.

Coaches must determine whether or not the athlete is capable of making the change in question in the amount of time allowed. Certainly, the best time for initiating a change is shortly after the completion of a season so that there is plenty of time to make the change without undue pressure and frustration.

It is not uncommon for athletes who are asked to make a complex change just prior to the start of a season to feel extremely tense.

When initial competitive results are not entirely successful, as is usually the case, athletes may very much desire to go back to their previous technique. The old technique may feel far more comfortable than the new one. Coaches must anticipate this feeling and help athletes resist the self-defeating urge to return to their previous technique.

Athletes need to realize that they may have to "play through" certain competitions. This means that they may have to be willing to allow performance results to suffer temporarily in order to reap future payoffs. It is important that athletes appreciate this point so that they avoid an undesirable loss of confidence. Athletes must constantly be reminded that performance that surpasses their previous best performance is likely to follow in the near future.

Practice and Game Films

Practice and game films can be highly effective teaching tools when they are used correctly. Practice films or videotapes can be direct and immediate sources of feedback. Coaches, however, must take the time to help athletes identify their mistakes as well as the correct aspects of their techniques. If the attention of athletes is not appropriately directed much time may be wasted by focusing on the wrong or less important aspects of performance. This issue may be particularly troublesome in sports that involve a ball and a goal because athletes may focus on the ball rather than execution of technique.

Reviewing game films has become increasingly popular, and with the development of fast-rewind and slow-motion projection capabilities it has become increasingly useful. It is possible that frequent observation of game films may be far more beneficial to highly successful teams. Viewing films is enjoyable and confidence-enhancing for athletes who observe themselves performing successfully. The search for flaws in execution is likely to be met with enthusiasm for further improvement. But this is not necessarily the case for losing teams.

It is neither fun nor confidence enhancing to repeatedly view one's inept performances. Athletes in such situations quickly "tune out" and learn little.

Films can and should be used even in a losing situation, but care must be taken to isolate a few important errors that need to be corrected. Most athletes can handle this approach and will respond positively. Films can be made available for athletes to view on an individual basis. Many athletes are more relaxed and willing to study their errors when they are alone.

Also, films can be edited so as to isolate particular aspects of team performance, such as offensive plays, defensive plays, fast-break offense, slow-down offense, or pressing defense. Many athletes benefit from films that are individualized specifically for them. For example, athletes might view a film of only their own play in past games or they may view a film of only their best plays from the past year. Such a film can be great for confidence as a contest nears. Finally, viewing a game film against an upcoming opponent can be beneficial, particularly if that team is victorious in the game viewed. These films will be especially useful if the audio-visual specialists make a point of filming the locker rooms, the playing fields, and the audience during competition. More information on use of filming procedures is provided in Chapter 14.

Providing Transfer of Training

Most athletes have had a variety of experiences playing an assortment of sports. Coaches can utilize these experiences when they teach new skills. Athletes can be reminded of similarities between a skill being learned for the first time and another already mastered skill. Similarities between throwing a baseball and serving a tennis ball can be pointed out with specific attention directed at feeling the movement.

Transfer also occurs when athletes move from one level of competition to the next. It is important that skills be taught and practiced in a manner that will effectively transfer to the next level. Soccer, field hockey, lacrosse, or basketball players must practice shooting at full speed as it must be executed during competition. Athletes who are continually allowed to stand still and shoot in practice are building a skill that will not transfer. Athletes should be urged to supplement such practice with real-game practice.

Negative transfer can occur in the learning phase of skill acquisition when two skills are somewhat similar but confusing, such as the forehand shots in tennis and badminton. Both skills require tracking skills and the manipulation of an implement; but badminton requires a loose, flexible wrist, while tennis demands a firm wrist. This situation can be confusing and, thus, inhibit learning. Coaches must help athletes understand and feel the differences between two similar skills.

The Role of Conditioning

Success in sports often demands skillful execution under situations that demand *physical fitness*. Both skill development and fitness enhancement should be considered in designing practice sessions. If one goal must be given a lower priority in early season practices, it will be skill execution. Drills may be of such high intensity that skill performance may deteriorate. Nonetheless, at this point in the season athletes need to be encouraged to push themselves even if performance does suffer.

As the competitive demands of sports advances, it becomes increasingly obvious that out-of-season conditioning is a necessity. Strength, endurance, and flexibility are prerequisites to successful performance of many sports skills. The absence of these prerequisites may cause athletes to adopt movement patterns that are less than optimal in order to perform at high speed for the required time period. Sloppy or inefficient patterns may soon become ingrained.

Athletes who are fit prior to the first day of practice can reduce the risk of such errors occurring. Concentration and rate of improvement may also be enhanced by adequate fitness levels. Detailed guidelines for development of fitness in athletes are provided in Chapters 21 and 22.

Out-of-Season Practice

There are probably few situations that provide more frustration than the first day back to practice after an extended lay-off. The athlete may be incapable of performing skills that were previously mastered. This may lead to a loss of confidence.

To avoid such difficulties, at the end of a season athletes should be encouraged to: (1) take a short break, (2) practice regularly during the off-season, but with a reduced practice length, and (3) find an activity to help them maintain or enhance their fitness level.

Athletes may become overly dependent on encouragement by their coaches to practice in a productive manner. Some may grow so reliant upon their coaches that without the coach they become sloppy and pick up bad habits. Again, the value of teaching athletes to self-direct and self-coach themselves becomes apparent. Out-of-season practice without concentration may cause more problems than it cures. Athletes must be reminded repeatedly of the need for perfect practice during the off-season.

Summary

The speed with which athletes acquire movement skills is greatly dependent upon the effective design and implementation of practice sessions. While effective coaches do not all practice in a similar manner, their teams do follow basic guidelines. Of particular utility for coaches are the theories of motor learning advanced by Schmidt (1975) and Gentile (1972).

Athletes and teams tend to progress through sequential stages of skill development. Practice planning and teaching strategies must be modified as athletes advance through these stages.

Effective coaches recognize the importance of establishing an environment conducive to learning. They emphasize important points and direct practice time and energy toward the consistent execution of these points. Eventually, these attributes become characteristic of the team. Effective coaches recognize the importance of perfect practice, but they also foster an attitude that practice is a place for error detection and correction. This attitude is encouraged by enthusiastically soliciting questions and behaving in a manner that causes athletes to feel that practice requires concentration and intensity.

In designing practices coaches should consider the options and apply knowledge regarding overlearning, part versus whole-learning methods, demonstrations, and avoidance of over-analysis. Athletes must learn to read cues, must develop both a picture and feel for a skill, and must properly balance speed and accuracy in learning certain skills.

Feedback is an integral aspect of skill improvement. While the possibilities for feedback are endless, special attention should be directed toward the proper use of praise. To be productive feedback must be heard and repeated, should be given immediately, and should begin with a compliment.

Coaches may encounter certain special problems in helping athletes master skills. Athletes may encounter performance plateaus and may need to make significant changes in technique. Acquisition of skills may be affected by transfer and by physical fitness level. All of these factors influence the quality of practice sessions. While there are no magic answers, attention to certain basic guidelines can facilitate skill mastery by athletes.

References

Adams, J. A closed-loop theory of motor learning. *Journal of Motor Behavior,* 3:111–150, 1971.

Berstein, N. *The Coordination and Regulation of Movements.* London: Pergamon, 1967.

Christina, R., R. Martens, J. Harvey, and B. Sharkey. *Coaching Young Athletes.* Champaign, Illinois: Human Kinetics Publishers, 1981.

Gentile, A. A working model of skill acquisition with applications to teaching. *Quest,* 17:3–23, 1972.

Lawther, J. *The Learning and Performance of Physical Skills,* 2nd ed. Englewood Cliffs, New Jersey: Prentice-Hall, Inc., 1977.

Marteniuk, R.G. *Information Processing in Motor Skills.* New York: Holt, Rinehart and Winston, 1976.

Schmidt, A. A schema theory of discrete motor skill learning. *Psychological Review,* (July) 4:82, 1975.

Stalling, L.M. *Motor Learning from Theory to Practice.* St. Louis: C.V. Mosby Co., 1982.

Recommended Readings

Bunker, L. Teaching for transfer and decision making. *Proceedings of Sport Psychology Conference.* Edited by L. Bunker and R. Rotella. 1978. Charlottesville: University of Virginia Department of Health and Physical Education, 1978.

Gentile, A. A working model of skill acquisition with applications to teaching. *Quest,* 17:3–23, 1972.

Gould, D., and Weiss, H. *Teaching Sport Skills to Young Athletes.* East Lansing, Michigan: Youth Sport Institute, 1980.

Martens, R., Christina, R., Sharkey, B., and Harvey, J. *Coaching Young Athletes.* Champaign, Illinois: Human Kinetics, 1981.

Schmidt, A. A schema theory of discrete motor skill learning. *Psychological Review,* (July) 4:82, 1975.

Singer, R. Different strokes for different folks: Teaching skills to kids. In *Youth Sports Guide for Coaches and Parents.* Edited by Serry Thomas. AAHPERD Publications, 1977.

Smith, R., Smoll, F., and Curtis, B. Coach effectiveness training: A cognitive-behavioral approach to enhancing relationship skills in youth sport coaches. *Journal of Sport Psychology,* 1:59–75, 1979.

Credit: Courtesy of Randy Lanier.

Social-Psychological Influences on Sports Performance

8

Sports teams do not exist in isolation. They are intimately influenced by the communities in which they exist, and in turn, sports teams impact upon the communities of which they are a part. The community includes various groups of people, some of whom are associated with the team and others who are not. Various groups, such as the families of athletes, peers, the school faculty, fans, and potential fans, can play a most important role in team success.

Athletes' Families

Teams often include athletes from a wide range of family backgrounds. It is important that coaches understand how these vastly different family backgrounds can influence athletes' attitudes, desires, and motivations.

Coaches can facilitate development of this insight by arranging a parent-coaching staff meeting prior to the start of a season. This is an ideal opportunity for coaches to explain their coaching philosophies and expectations. Such meetings allow coaches and parents to become acquainted with one another.

Parental Attitudes

Many families feel that sports is a very important part of life. Some parents may simply wish to have their children take part in sports to keep them out of the many dangers present in contemporary society. Other parents aspire for their children to excel in sports. Many such parents feel that their children's success or failure in sports is a direct reflection on their own success as parents and their children's success as people. Parents who hold this attitude often impose a great deal of pressure upon their children.

Often, parents who put pressure on their children to excel in sports may have spent an abundance of time playing and practicing with them during the children's formative years.

Money may have been freely invested in summer camps and in providing lessons and equipment.

Coaches should expect children to adopt their parent's attitudes toward sports. Coaches can carefully observe how their athletes react to parental pressures. Some athletes respond to the pressure as an exciting challenge that they love. Others become overly concerned with failure and the fear of disappointing their parents. Coaches need to be sensitive to these reactions and respond in a way that will be most helpful to their athletes.

A Sense of Self-Worth

Oftentimes, parents teach young athletes that sports is the only way in which to establish positive self-esteem. Children of such parents must be helped to put sports into its proper perspective. This assistance will be particularly needed if success is not forthcoming for the athletes.

Sibling Effects

Athletes who have had older siblings excel at sports may experience special pressures that coaches must appreciate. This situation may also provide these athletes with the ideal environment for sports success.

It is commonly found that firstborn children are less interested in participation in contact sports. This is apparently a result of parental anxieties over the safety of their first child. When firstborn children experience difficulty in contact sports they must be helped to overcome their fears of injury learned from their families.

Frequently, when siblings, particularly twins, are members of the same team the success or failure of one may greatly affect the other. It is not uncommon for one sibling to value the other sibling's success more highly than team success. However, some siblings become very competitive with each other, which may undermine team effectiveness.

Parenting Style

It is useful to know whether an athlete's parents utilize a humanistic or authoritarian parenting style. This may have important implications for the coaching style most suitable for particular athletes.

The parenting style may be significantly affected by the family's socioeconomic level. Many higher socioeconomic level families are taught through a democratic process that places great emphasis on children understanding why certain behaviors are necessary. Lower socioeconomic class athletes may have been taught by more authoritarian strategies dominated by power, threat, and punishment.

In today's fast-paced society, many athletes across all socioeconomic lines may have received little or no feedback from their parents as to how to behave or why they should behave in a certain manner. An understanding of these parental influences will help coaches to appreciate the problems that their athletes may experience in accepting team rules and regulations. Coaches should observe the way in which parents and their children interact. Such interactions can provide important cues that can facilitate coaching effectiveness.

Community Influences

The sports community consists of all those individuals within the athletes' immediate environment. Various community members within the school, including school administrators, teachers, student body, janitors, team managers, scorers, cheerleaders, pep band members, sports journalists, and sports broadcasters, can have a significant impact upon team performance. Effective coaches find ways to obtain the support of these community members.

Increased Status

Members of teams that receive support from community members experience an increase in status. As a result, athletes have more incentive to improve and attain success. Enhanced status and incentive typically lead to increased interest in attaining team membership. This situation often results in increased competition within the team. Parents may become more interested in preparing their children to compete successfully for the few available team positions. When this situation becomes extreme many coaches initiate additional subvarsity programs to allow more of the desiring athletes to participate. Growing interest among athletes often leads to members of the community volunteering to serve the team in various capacities (e.g., volunteer assistant coach, booster club officer, team physician).

Creating School Spirit

As enthusiasm grows teachers often become interested in and actively supportive of the athletic program. In some particularly successful programs coaches plan special preseason trips that are available only to those team members with at least a B average (for high school). Such demonstrations of support for academic achievement can enhance the enthusiasm of teachers, parents, and school administrators for athletics. Pep rallies may be organized and become increasingly popular. Increased excitement is created in those who participate, such as cheerleaders, pep band members, manager, and so forth. The enhanced status awarded these positions increases enthusiasm and identification with the team. With time, sports journalists and broadcasters become more and more interested in the team.

Such school spirit–building programs frequently cause athletes to experience elevated self-esteem. They like the way they feel, which gives them increased incentive to practice for the upcoming season; in turn, this leads to more skilled teams. As this extremely positive social-psychological cycle evolves, positive *school spirit* develops. It results from a psychological process labeled *contagion*. Building school spirit may not be easy. It will take *commitment*, *time*, and *energy*. But strong school spirit has a most pleasing effect on team performance.

Argue behind Closed Doors

Typically, teams are able to build school spirit because others are impressed by the commitment made by the entire team, including coaches and players. Head coaches must make sure that all staff members feel comfortable about critically discussing coaching strategies during coaching meetings.

If assistant coaches are not able to speak their mind during meetings their thoughts of disagreement will come out at some other time. Assistant coaches who complain in private to athletes undermine team spirit. Complaining during competition undermines both team and school spirit. Spectators quickly recognize dissension and lose respect for self-centered assistant coaches who value themselves more than team success. Likewise, head coaches who are too narrow-minded to listen to their assistant coaches are unlikely to gain the solid support of the community.

Other Interests in Life

Another factor that can detract from school spirit occurs when coaches believe that their teams are the only activities of any importance in athletes' lives. Coaches must realize that there are other important activities.

Whenever possible, team members should be encouraged to show that athletes care about other school activities. Athletes are often popular peer leaders in schools. Their involvement in other activities can make the activities attractive to other students, which, in turn, may help make the other students successful and popular.

Emphasize Student-Athletes

There is nothing more highly valued in most schools than student-athletes. But far too often, coaches build programs that place all of the emphasis on athletics. Athletes may totally avoid academic interests when this orientation is combined with increased recognition and popularity.

Coaches who build long-lasting school spirit make certain that their athletes perform in the classroom. This emphasis is most crucial for those athletes whose families do not give them support or encouragement.

Coaches who constantly interact with other teachers will be much more likely to generate support from the faculty. There have been far too many cases of outstanding athletes failing to learn such basic skills as reading or writing. Coaches who allow this type of problem to exist within their teams show a complete disregard for their athletes and the overall purpose of schooling.

Helping Others Less Able

Athletes tend to be healthy and fortunate people. They can be a very positive community influence if they occasionally involve themselves in community projects designed to help others less fortunate than themselves. Such projects may include helping the elderly, setting up a special day for teaching the retarded, getting involved in the special Olympics, or being of service to the poor.

Activities of this nature have a dual function. On one hand, they set a very positive model in the school and community. On the other hand, the athletes themselves benefit. Service activities may be particularly valuable for poorly motivated athletes. It is difficult for athletes to feel sorry for themselves when they are regularly working with less fortunate individuals.

Blacks in Sports

Since the early 1800's blacks have played a crucial role in the world of sports. In recent years, many sports have been dominated by outstanding black athletes.

Discrimination in Sports

Current research evidence documents that there has been discrimination against black athletes in the world of sports. *Discrimination*, the unfavorable treatment of a person or group, is typically a result of *prejudice*, an unfavorable feeling or attitude toward a person or group.

Despite the oft-stated view that sports facilitates *integration*, the evidence is clear that sports, while playing a role, certainly has not been a leader in initiating this type of social change. This finding is not surprising considering the fact that sports has a conservative tendency and is prone to mirror the values of the greater society.

The information in this section is presented for the purpose of helping coaches to increase their self-awareness and, hopefully, to prevent any prejudices that they may have from leading to discrimination on their teams. Ultimately, each coach must decide if his/her coaching decisions are based upon prejudice or upon performance.

Stacking

It has been repeatedly discovered that discrimination across playing positions occurs within athletic teams. The phenomenon referred to as *stacking* (Edwards 1973) is particularly evident in collegiate and professional sports. In team sports, such as football and baseball, there has been a disproportionate concentration of black athletes in specific team positions. As a result black athletes have been permitted access to a limited number of roles within a team. Many central positions on a team have been denied to blacks.

For example, white athletes have been over-represented in the central positions in football (quarterback, center, offensive guard, linebacker) and baseball (infield, catcher, pitcher).

Blacks have been primarily distributed in the peripheral positions (Loy and McElvogue 1970).

Impact of Stacking

The ramifications of stacking may be long lasting. Many peripheral positions rely to a great extent upon speed and quickness, which slow with age. As a result, playing careers of blacks may be shorter than for white athletes. For professional athletes this has the effect of reducing lifelong earnings and decreasing pension funds. The effects are amplified by the reduced opportunities for black athletes to make advertising endorsement money and to gain managerial or coaching positions. The latter situation is apparently related to the fact that many such jobs go to ex-athletes who occupied central playing positions. Between 1971 and 1958 more than 75% of all managers in baseball were former infielders or catchers (Eitzen and Yetman 1977).

Explanations for Stacking

Many sociological, psychological, and biological explanations have been developed for the purpose of explaining the causes of stacking. Each provides insight into the problem.
Sociological Views. The *stereotyping hypothesis* suggests that stacking is a result of the perceptions of managers regarding the physical, psychological, and social abilities of black athletes. It is believed that these views combine with managers' perceptions of the different abilities required for various playing positions. The available evidence suggests that many coaches have beliefs about black athletes that are not valid, but that influence their coaching decisions regarding these athletes.

The *interaction and discrimination hypothesis* supports the notion that coaches and athletes view intimate relations between blacks and whites in a negative manner. As a result minority members have been excluded from central positions that often demand a high degree of interaction with other athletes. This view is sup-

ported by a perception by coaches that blacks possess undesirable characteristics (Leonard 1980).

The *outcome control hypothesis* argues that white coaches and players hold prejudiced beliefs that blacks are not able to execute the responsibilities of control, leadership, and authority. These views coupled with the myth of black intellectual incompetence causes coaches to keep blacks out of central positions (Edwards 1973).

Another view, the *prohibitive cost* hypothesis, suggests that the expense of training young athletes for certain positions combined with the low socioeconomic standing of many blacks is responsible for differences in playing positions. There is limited support for this view, which argues that blacks have gained access to central positions as their socioeconomic status has improved (Medoff 1977).

The *differential attractiveness of positions hypothesis* argues that black athletes themselves may play an important role in the discrimination process. This view suggests that minority members perceive positions differently and make choices on the basis of these perceptions. Black athletes may choose to play positions that provide the best opportunity for success and recognition. This is evidenced by the many black high school and college quarterbacks who have asked to be moved to wide receiver positions to enhance their chances of making it in the college or professional ranks.

The final sociological explanation, the *role modeling hypothesis,* indicates that young black athletes imitate successful black athletes who preceded them. Most black models play peripheral positions and, thus, the situation tends to perpetuate itself.
Psychological Views. There are far fewer psychological explanations for stacking. The first hypothesis argues that blacks excel at *reactive* tasks that require immediate responses at the right time to changes in the stimulus situation. This view argues also that whites excel at *self-paced* activities that allow athletes to respond whenever they choose to do so to a rel-

atively static and unchanging stimulus (Jones and Hochner 1973). These authors argue that the hypothesis in question may account for blacks' overrepresentation at reactive playing positions such as the outfield in baseball and wide receivers and cornerbacks in football, and their underrepresentation in self-paced activities such as golf and bowling. It does not, however, explain blacks' underrepresentation in such reactive individual sports as auto racing, fencing, skiing, or tennis. Certainly, the prohibitive cost hypothesis should be considered in these instances.

A second psychological view is the hypothesis that *blacks and whites have personality differences*. The supporters of this view (Jones and Hochner 1973) argue that personality influences an athlete's sports preferences and preferences influence personality. Relative to whites it is believed that blacks: (1) emphasize an individualistic rather than a team orientation; (2) stress style or expressive performance over success or technical performance; and (3) reflect a personalized power orientation associated with individual winning instead of a power orientation correlated with team winning.

The evidence in support of this hypothesis is lacking. Prejudicial views in support of it are abundant.

Biological Views. A typical explanation for the stacking of black athletes into certain playing positions as well as for the domination of blacks in many sports and positions is that blacks are naturally superior athletes endowed with physical advantages (Norman 1968; Jordon 1969; Malina 1972). The biological-physiological differences cited have been many and varied. The arm and leg length of blacks has been utilized to explain dominance in track and field events, outfield playing in baseball, and wide receiver and defensive back positions in football. On the other hand, their higher specific gravity (leanness) has been cited as the cause of the black athletes' lack of success in swimming events. These views are open to criticism. Most of the differences are average differences and fail to consider within-race variations as well as the similarities across different races.

Black Dominance in Sports

There is an abundance of evidence that demonstrates a dominance of black athletes in many aspects of contemporary sports. Many possible explanations of this phenomenon have been offered. Coaches should understand these theories because of their potential effect on coaching strategies.

Race-Linked Differences. It has been argued that black athletes are successful because of their psychological inclination to be "calm, cool, and collected" under pressure (Kane 1971). At best, the research on this point has been contradictory with some data supporting the argument and some suggesting that blacks are more "uptight" because sports is their only hope of success. Harry Edwards (1973), the noted sports sociologist, believes that the view of the black athlete being cool under pressure may tend to become a self-fulfilling prophecy.

Another explanation argues that black dominance is due to the survival of the fittest. Many successful black athletes, including Yale-educated Calvin Hill, have supported this notion, but there is little scientific support for it.

Matriarchal Explanation. Many have contended that the predominantly matriarchal black family structure is responsible for the black athletes' sports success. This argument rests on the contention that blacks strive to fill the social and emotional void left by absence of the father by developing a close relationship with their coach. This view suggests that the coach, as a surrogate father, may lead black athletes to outperform their white counterparts.

While this situation has important implications for coaches of black male athletes, it is not a very acceptable explanation for black dominance in sports. In reality, there are more whites who come from matriarchal families. In addition, black athletes do not always form a close relationship with their coaches.

Cultural Causes. Many scientists accept the view that the domination of sports by black athletes may be largely a result of various sociological causes. There has been little attempt to rank these sociological causes in their order of importance.

The occupational discrimination that has occurred in American society has caused many blacks to put their energy into socially acceptable activities such as sports. The availability of certain types of playing equipment and fields probably have been influential in determining the sports in which black athletes excel. In addition, many black athletes have seen sports as an opportunity to "make it." For some this has proven to be true. For many others sports interests have interfered with academic interests.

This is not a surprising finding considering the relative popularity of sports in most schools in the United States. Many blacks who may have experienced academic failure or mediocrity early in their schooling while at the same time gaining recognition through sports performance, may have understandably concluded that they are talented in sports; thus, they have focused their energies in that direction. This is analogous to many academically gifted students who early in life dream of athletic success, but when they find that their athletic abilities are limited decide to put their energies into academic work.

The problem lies in the fact that there are far more opportunities for career success for those who achieve academic success than there are for those who attain only athletic success. However, the few who do make it in sports receive very enticing rewards.

This problem again points to the very important role that coaches play in making certain that their athletes receive an education and learn a process for achieving success in sports that has carry-over value to other areas of life. This is the best way to ensure upward mobility for black athletes.

Aggression in Sports

Many sports require behaviors that may be labeled as aggressive. The amount of aggressive behavior that is acceptable and required varies greatly, depending upon the competitive level and the type of sport.

Cratty (1981) has suggested that both the *amount* and the *type* of aggression desired for optimum performance may be placed on a scale (see Figure 8.1). In general, at the higher levels of competition more extreme levels of aggressive behavior are demanded and considered acceptable. In recent years, however, it has become apparent that increasingly aggressive behavior is being actively encouraged with younger and less skilled athletes. The effects of this change are yet to be completely evaluated.

Because aggressive behavior does play an important role in sports success, coaches must understand how to teach their athletes: (1) to develop aggressiveness, (2) to keep increased aggressiveness *specific* to sports performance,

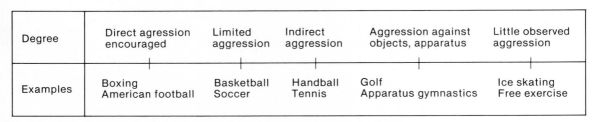

Figure 8.1 A scale depicting varying amounts of aggressive behavior in sports.

and (3) to keep aggressive urges under control so that they do not lead to unnecessary injury to themselves or other athletes.

Defining Aggression

Coaches must understand aggressive behavior. Aggression has been defined as "any form of behavior directed toward the goal of harming or injuring another living being who is motivated to avoid such treatment" (Baron 1977, p. 7). Based on this definition, injury to others may be included as a part of aggressive behavior. Clearly, one may question if this is what is or should be required of athletes.

Zillman (1977) has dichotomized aggressive behavior in a manner that makes it more relevant to sports. Aggression can be viewed as being either "annoyance-motivated" or "incentive-motivated." Annoyance-motivated aggressive behavior is undertaken in response to an aversive stimulus. Incentive-motivated aggressive behavior, on the other hand, is performed in the pursuit of a goal. In incentive-motivated behavior the goal is of primary importance and the injury caused in its attainment is incidental. In annoyance-motivated aggressive behavior the goal is to injure another person. It appears that incentive-motivated aggressive behavior may be the effective and desired kind of aggression in sports performance in which intimidation may play a crucial role in success.

Theoretical Views of Aggression

Initially, aggression was viewed as an instinctive behavior. Freud (1920) believed that aggression was a necessary redirection of man's desire for self-destruction. Later, the ethologist Konrad Lorenz (1966) proposed that aggressive behavior was the result of an accumulated and innate drive to aggress (attack) in combination with an appropriate aggression-releasing stimulus. Lorenz believed that much social violence could be eliminated through gun control because unlike other animals, humans are able through the use of man-made tools to kill from

a distance. Many animals who must fight with their claws and teeth will read "postures of submission" and end an encounter short of death unless they are fighting for food.

Basically, instinct theories suggest that the only way to control aggressive behavior is to vent it. Sports is often viewed by such theorists as an excellent way of doing so and many sports were popularized when instinct theories of aggression were dominant. Recent research findings disagree with the view that there is a *cathartic* discharge of the aggressive urge when it is expressed openly. Today, there is little support for this notion.

Another view of aggression, which remains acceptable today, argues that aggression is a result of an elicited drive. Dollard, Miller, and Sears, et al. (1939) suggest that the drive is elicited by *frustration* (Frustration-Aggression Hypothesis). Berkowitz (1962) attributes aggressive acts to the presence of aggressive *cues* in the environment that elicit a drive to harm or injure.

The aforementioned theories are quite pessimistic. They see people as either having aggression instinctively within themselves or being driven to aggress by outside sources.

Another theory, the *Social Learning Theory* (Bandura 1973) will be discussed in depth because it argues that it is possible to control the amount and kind of aggressive behavior and because it is the most widely accepted view today. The implications for coaching are many.

Bandura's approach to aggression is optimistic. It holds that humans possess the ability to aggress and that activation of aggression is dependent upon appropriate stimulation. Further, however, social learning theory suggests that it is possible to exert personal control over the *type* of aggressive behavior, the *frequency* of expression, and the *targets* of aggression.

Controlling Aggression

The Social Learning Theory implies that athletes can learn to increase or decrease aggressive behavior as it is appropriate and desired.

The learning of aggressive behavior involves a three-step process involving the *acquisition, instigation,* and *maintenance* of behavior. Elimination of any of these steps could lead to inappropriate or improperly expressed aggression.

Aggression can be acquired through either *direct experience* or *observational learning.* Learning through direct experience is dependent upon reinforcement (instrumental conditioning). That is, behaviors that are reinforced will be repeated and those that are not will be eliminated. Reinforcement may come from coaches, teammates, opponents, fans, or feedback on effectiveness of behavior for attaining the desired goal.

Fortunately (or unfortunately) much learning can also occur through observation of others, either directly or indirectly (television, and so forth). Athletes may observe other athletes and imitate aggressive behaviors that are rewarded (winning, intimidation, recognition). Through observation athletes learn which behaviors are appropriate and rewarded.

Instigation, the second factor in this process, is effected by four antecedents of aggression: (1) modeling influences, (2) incentive inducements, (3) instructional control, and (4) the presence of an audience (Bandura 1973; Baron 1977).

Modeling happens primarily as a result of contagion when athletes view other athletes who experience success through, in this case, aggressive behavior. It appears that this is more important than presenting a model that is physically or maturationally similar to the observer (Epstein and Rakosky 1975). Coaches must remember two relevant points. First, a similar model may help get athletes attention; second, if athletes are more socially than task motivated, they may learn to *decrease* aggressive behavior when they observe aggressive acts.

Aggressive behavior can be increased when it leads to the attainment of a goal. In sports, incentive-motivated aggression is of primary importance, and leads to an increase in aggressive behavior if the goal is perceptible and considered important (Buss 1966; Duquette 1981).

The third element, instructional control, occurs when athletes have such respect for their coaches that they do what they are told to do. Coaches are in a position of tremendous power; therefore, they must utilize this power for instructional control wisely. Instructional control can also be influenced by groups of significant others. Teammates can dare and excite others such that they increase their aggressiveness (Borden 1973).

The final instigator of aggression is an audience. Audiences can function to either facilitate or hinder aggressive behavior. To understand the influence of an audience, it must be realized that the make-up and *expectations* of the audience are far more important than its mere presence (Borden 1973).

Thomas Duquette, a successful lacrosse coach, who was also a four-time collegiate All-American, a professional lacrosse player, and a sports psychologist, provides the following example of fan expectations of professional box lacrosse.

> Box lacrosse was promoted as violent, the fans expected violence, and they got violence. The sport was inherently rough, but the fans demanded excessive violence and they got it. [Duquette 1981]

Finally, coaches need to realize how to maintain aggressive behavior once it has been learned. *Reinforcement* appears to be the key. Initially, coaches must provide constant and immediate rewards each time athletes are aggressive. Care should be taken to reward attempts at being aggressive even when the results are not as successful as ultimately desired. Later, rewards from coaches should become more intermittent.

Aggression is best maintained and regulated through *external rewards, vicarious reinforcements, self-reinforcements,* and *neutralization of self-punishment* (Bandura 1973).

Duquette (1981) has suggested that reinforcement can take the form of a pat on the back or a tangible reward for behaving aggressively. Dangers begin to creep in with the neutralization of self-punishment, which has an important role in reducing violent behavior in the social setting. Eliminating this self-control mechanism is potentially dangerous. Athletes must be carefully taught in which situations aggressive behavior is *appropriate, why* it is acceptable, and the *extent* to which it is acceptable. Athletes must also be taught to *maintain emotional control* if and when they behave aggressively. If these recommendations are not followed coaches run the risk of seeing their athletes' aggressive behavior spill over into other activities with the resulting problems for society and athletes.

Specific Problems

Regular application of the ideas presented here increases the likelihood of athletes developing a healthy form of aggressive behavior. Nonetheless, some athletes may still present problems to their coaches. Some of these problems and suggested solutions are addressed in the following discussion.

For many athletes who experience problems in *displaying aggression*, cognitive intervention strategies can be useful. McAuley (1981) has presented several applications of this approach (see Box 8.1).

Cratty (1981) has listed several situations that could lead to heightened aggression and to potentially dangerous problems:

1. An unfit player
2. A player in front of a hostile crowd
3. A player on a losing team, in a closely contested game
4. A team within the upper part of the standings playing one lower in the standings
5. Competition between teams whose backgrounds are divergent in race or ethnic make-up
6. A past background of hostility between the two racially or ethnically different teams and/or the political climates they represent
7. The presence of an aggressive act by another that is either not punished or results in an advantage

Anticipation of these aggressive problems allows the coach to develop strategies for preventing excessively aggressive behavior.

Making Decisions about Aggression

When teaching aggressive behavior coaches must pay close attention to the *norms* for their sport. Sports are governed by rules and regulations. Athletes must be taught to abide by these rules rather than to break them without getting caught. Winning is not worth teaching immoral and potentially dangerous behaviors.

Coaches must also be certain to provide role models appropriate to their reference group. When this is not done, even young athletes can be expected to model the most aggressive professional athletes who are readily visible. Ultimately, coaches must ask themselves if their teachings are *legitimate* and *morally acceptable*. Violent behavior of any sort cannot be tolerated. This would only serve to dehumanize a very humanistic endeavor.

Controlling Fan Violence

There are far too many examples of violent fan behavior at every level of sports. Something must be done and coaches must accept their role in controlling violence. While there is no one, simple answer to this problem, there are several guidelines for controlling fan violence. To begin with, coaches should remember that violent behavior is learned and, therefore, can be controlled by eliminating factors that increase its occurrence.

Violence is often elicited by conditions in the social environment. Frustration resulting from team failure can lead to fan violence. This is particularly true if coaches respond to apparent failure with uncontrolled emotion and verbal attacks on officials or opponents. Coaches can certainly incite a crowd to behave violently; so coaches have a responsibility to behave appropriately.

Box 8.1 Self-instructional Strategies for Facilitating Healthy and Effective Aggressive Behavior

Self-Defeating	Self-Enhancing
1. *Soccer* "I'm scared to dive into the goal mouth to head the ball for fear of being kicked in the head."	"My job is to score goals and I have to go after the ball. If I time it right there is less chance of me getting kicked. However, if I do, that's a risk I have to take."
2. *Basketball* "My rebounding is very weak because I am scared of being elbowed or pushed off balance, which may cause an ankle injury, and then I'll be out for the season."	"If I use my judgment ability and use all of my body to protect myself when rebounding, I stand more chance of getting the ball, improving my rebound, and less chance of getting injured."
3. *Lacrosse* "My opponent really gave me a hard time in the last game. I'm going to tear him up this time!"	"I have to play hard but I must not lose my temper, otherwise I won't be able to concentrate and attend to the game, giving the opposing team an advantage."
4. *Skiing* "The last time I competed on ice I had a bad fall. I don't want to injure myself again."	"If I ski wide and overcautiously I will lose seconds and may even fall. I've skied lots of times on icy courses and I must ski hard and competitively as I have done in the past."
5. *Tennis* "I don't want to attack the net following a good serve in case my opponent lobs me as I have a poor overhead."	"If I practice my overhead I can combine it with my good serve and attack the net, which will strengthen my game considerably."
6. *Racquetball* "I don't want my game to be more aggressive as I may get hurt diving for a ball or hit by the ball when I go to the front."	"'Going to ground' and 'getting to the front' are essential parts of the game. The chances of me winning more big points by doing so are far greater than the chances of my getting hurt."

Likewise, athletes must know that they are subject to very strict and immediate punishments for fighting or other violent acts. Once established, such rules must be enforced. It is well documented in the research that exposure to aggressive models serves as a catalyst for overt aggression. Coaches who teach their athletes nonviolent responses must make certain that officials will immediately enforce penalties for violent acts.

A wide range of environmental influences can lead to violence. For example, loud or irritating noises, uncomfortably warm temperatures, crowded conditions, or seating of opposing fans next to each other can precipitate violence. Personal influences like the effect of drugs, alcohol, or an injury may lead to heightened violence.

Coaches can best control violence by preventing its occurrence in the first place. This can be facilitated by making changes in some league rules, and by increasing the severity of punishments for players, coaches, and fans who are violent. Also, coaches can help by putting constant pressure on sports journalists and broadcasters to avoid overpublicizing acts of violence.

Dean Smith, the highly successful basketball coach at the University of North Carolina, provides an ideal model for controlling fan behavior.

> Smith took to the courtside microphone to urge the crowd to refrain from profanity and the waving of hands behind the Virginia basket when a player went to the line.
>
> "We never have obscene language or the waving of arms here," said Smith. "It was disappointing we did today, but we never will again. Maybe they were new students, but I'm proud of how our fans have behaved and don't want that to change." [Godwin 1982, p. 1]

Summary

There are a wide variety of social-psychological factors that influence sports performance. Coaches need to be aware of these influences if they wish to enhance their chances of having a happy and successful team.

Athletes' families exert an important influence. Parents direct a child's interest, attitudes, and sense of self-worth. Knowledge about siblings and parenting styles can aide coaches in their coaching decisions.

A variety of community members play a role in team success. Creation of increased status for athletes and school spirit can be invaluable aids to coaches. Coaches can best facilitate the development of these positive attributes by arguing only behind closed doors, supporting other school activities, emphasizing the development of scholar-athletes, and planning team activities designed to help the less fortunate.

Another pertinent social-psychological influence is the role of black athletes in sports. Historical evidence has been presented that suggests that black athletes have been discriminated against. One form of discrimination, stacking, has had significant influence on the advancement of black athletes in sports. A number of sociological, psychological, and biological explanations for stacking have been advanced.

In spite of prejudicial treatment black athletes have become dominant in some sports. Possible explanations for this dominance include race-linked biological differences as well as various sociological and psychological factors.

Aggression has become an important issue in sports. The amount of aggressive behavior that is acceptable and required varies greatly, depending upon the competitive level and the type of sport. Aggression has been defined in many ways, but it can be dichotomized as annoyance-motivated and incentive-motivated behavior.

A number of theoretical views on aggression have been developed. These include the Freudian theory, the innate drive–releasing stimulus theory, the Frustration-Aggression hypothesis, and the Social Learning Theory. The Social Learning Theory has particularly important practical implications for teaching and controlling aggressive behavior in athletes. Fan violence is an increasing problem in sports. Coaches play a significant role in controlling this and other forms of aggressive behavior in sports.

References

Bandura, A. *Aggression: A Social Learning Analysis*. Englewood Cliffs, New Jersey: Prentice-Hall, Inc., 1973.

Baron, R.A. *Human Aggression*. New York: Plenum Press, 1977.

Berkowitz, L. (Ed.). The frustration-aggression hypothesis revisited. In *Roots of Aggression*. New York: Atherton Press, 1969.

Borden, R.J., and Taylor, S.P. The social instigation and control of physical aggression. *Journal of Applied Social Psychology*, 4:354–361, 1973.

Buss, A.H. Instrumentality of aggression, feedback, and frustration as determinants of physical aggression. *Journal of Personality and Social Psychology*, 3:153–162, 1966.

Cratty, B.J. *Social Psychology in Athletics*. Englewood Cliffs, New Jersey: Prentice-Hall, Inc., 1981.

Dollard, J., Miller, N., Sears, R., et al. *Frustration and Aggression*. New Haven, Connecticut: Yale University Press, 1939.

Duquette, B.T. Aggression in sport. In *Psychological Considerations in Maximizing Sport Performance*. Charlottesville: University of Virginia, Department of Health and Physical Education, 1981.

Edwards, H. *Sociology of Sport*. Homewood, Illinois: The Dorsey Press, 1973.

Eitzen, S.D., and Yefman, N.R. Immune from racism. *Civil Rights Digest*, 9(Winter):3–13, 1977.

Epstein, S., and Rakosky, J. The effect of witnessing an admirable versus an unadmirable aggressor upon subsequent aggression. *Journal of Personality*, 44:560–576, 1975.

Freud, S. *A General Introduction to Psycho-Analysis*. New York: Liverright, 1920.

Godwin, J. Unsung Braddock rescued No. 1 UNC. *The Daily Progress*, Charlottesville, Virginia, Sun., Jan 10, 1982, D-1.

Jones, J., and Hochner, A. Racial differences in sports activities: A look at self-paced versus reactive hypothesis. *Journal of Personality and Social Psychology*, 27:86–95, 1973.

Jordan, J. Physiological and anthropometrical comparisons of Negroes and Whites. *Journal of Health, Physical Education and Recreation*, 40(Nov/Dec.):93–100, 1969.

Kane, M. An assessment of black is best. *Sports Illustrated*, 34(Jan. 18):72–83, 1971.

Leonard, W.M. *A Sociological Perspective of Sport*. Burgess Publishing Co., Minneapolis, Minnesota, 1980.

Lorenz, K. *On Aggression*. New York: Harcourt, Brace, and World, 1966.

Loy, J.W., and McElvogue, J.R. Racial discrimination in American sport. *International Review of Sport Sociology*, 5:5–23, 1970.

Malina, R.M. Anthropology, growth, and physical education. In *Physical Education: An Interdisciplinary Approach*. Edited by R. Singer et al. New York: MacMillan, 1972, pp. 237–309.

McAuley, E. Strategies for dealing with aggression in sport. In *Psychological Considerations in Maximizing Sport Performance*. Charlottesville: University of Virginia, Department of Health and Physical Education, 1981.

Medoff, M.H. Positional segregation and professional baseball. *International Review of Sport Sociology*, 12:49–54, 1977.

Norman, S.L. "Collation of Anthropometric Research Comparing American Males: Negro and Caucasian." Master's thesis, University of Oregon, 1968.

Zillman, D. *Hostility and Aggression*. Hillsdale, New Jersey: Lawrence Earlbaum Associates, 1977.

Recommended Readings

Bandura, A. *Aggression: A Social Learning Analysis*. Englewood Cliffs, New Jersey: Prentice-Hall, Inc., 1973.

Berkowitz, L. *Aggression: A Social Psychological Analysis*. New York: McGraw-Hill, 1962.

Duquette, B.T. Aggression in sport. In *Psychological Considerations in Maximizing Sport Performance*. Charlottesville: University of Virginia, Department of Health and Physical Education, 1981.

Edwards, H. *Sociology of Sport*. Homewood, Illinois: The Dorsey Press, 1973.

Kane, M. An assessment of black is best. *Sports Illustrated*, 34(Jan. 18):72–83, 1971.

Loy, J.W., and McElvogue, J.R. Racial discrimination in American sport. *International Review of Sport Sociology*, 5:5–23, 1970.

Zillman, D. *Hostility and Aggression*. Hillsdale, New Jersey: Lawrence Earlbaum Associates, 1977.

Credit: University of Virginia Sports Information.

Coping with the Stresses of Coaching

9

The many demands of coaching and the competitive nature of sports can cause coaches to live their lives under constant stress. In general, when stress is kept to a manageable level it acts as an exciting stimulant for coaches. It attracts them to coaching and keeps them enthusiastic about their work. But when the stress of coaching becomes excessive and chronic it may work against the success and happiness of coaches.

Stress may lead to a contemporary phenomenon called "burn-out." When coaches experience burn-out they frequently doubt their ability to lead and coach effectively. In addition, the abilities of assistant coaches and athletes may also be questioned. Coaches may believe the athletic director and the school or organization constitute a situation in which success cannot be achieved. Coaches who experience burn-out come to perceive their coaching situation as impossible.

Understanding Burn-out

Coaches who experience burn-out find that they tire more easily and do not have the energy they once had. They often feel helpless, irritable, and lacking control over their environment. Burned-out coaches or coaches on the verge of burn-out lose patience and have a diminished tolerance for frustration. Typically, these coaches become closed-minded and inflexible. The amount of time spent on coaching duties may be increased, but less is accomplished.

Eventually, coaches who burn-out become rundown, overtired, and depressed. They may have frequent headaches or other physical ailments. Failures that were once attributed to correctable weaknesses are perceived as impossible obstacles. Initially, such coaches blame failures on the quality of their athletes or the opponents on the schedule. But eventually, these coaches internalize failure and blame themselves for all problems. Clearly, something must be done if such coaches are to avoid crises.

Risk Factors for Burn-out

Burn-out occurs most frequently in the most dedicated and concerned coaches. It may be experienced by coaches who win as well as coaches who lose consistently. Burn-out is not something that is reserved for coaches at the collegiate or professional level. Nor is it a phenomena shared only by "major" sports coaches. Coaches in any sport and at any level can suffer from it. Burn-out is related more to individual factors than to job demands.

Coaches who have a great need to feel that they are successful are prone to burn-out. When confronted with a difficult challenge, coaches high in the need for success respond by working harder and longer. Sometimes, such coaches stay up all night; at times, in the coaching office so that others will realize that they have not given up and that failure is not due to a lack of effort.

Often, the enthusiasm and dedication shown by these coaches causes others to approach them constantly for help. Others know that these coaches will make things happen, solve problems, and get the job done. Soon, they are overwhelmed with commitments. In the beginning, these coaches enjoy being needed and find it difficult to say no. Later, this source of joy becomes a stressor.

A coach who is strongly motivated often attains success and begins to believe that the only way to get things done correctly and on time is to do things himself/herself. Others may be perceived as either unwilling or unable to carry out tasks the right way. Thus, such coaches may choose to do all the scouting, scheduling, and directing of developmental programs. Coaches who manifest these behaviors often become highly successful. It is easy to see why athletic directors, parents, and athletes love such coaches.

The problem of burn-out may be even more of a concern for the success-motivated "minor" sports coach. Often, schools are not excited about having a success-motivated person coaching their "minor" sports. Steps may be taken that frustrate efforts to build a great program in a sport that the athletic director feels is unimportant. The highly motivated coach often views this as just another obstacle that must be overcome by working harder.

Often, the spouse and family of success-motivated "minor" sports coaches complain that they are never home. But unlike the spouses of "major" sports coaches who get constant support, the media and the community do not seem to give much attention to "minor" sports coaches. So their families do not read about them in the newspaper, hear about them on the radio, or see them on television. Families are not invited to banquets and social gatherings. In other words, the support system that motivates the spouses and families to encourage coaching efforts is missing. Family and marriage problems may occur. Single coaches may lose themselves in their coaching and find that they lack the time to find or go out on dates. Box 9.1 presents the story of a coach who burned out.

The Effects of Burn-out

The impact of burn-out for coaches is most clearly seen in the coach's relationships with team members. The impact may also affect interpersonal relationships at home, which can destroy marriages, which, in turn, can cause further deterioration in player-coach interaction or increased dedication to athletes and improved player-coach relationships. Often, the time demands and lack of support will cause coaches to move from a concern for athletes (identification) to a complete lack of concern for them (alienation).

These differing levels of concern can be viewed on a continuum with identification at one end and alienation at the other. Typically,

Box 9.1 A Burn-out Scenario

Coach Charlie T. used to be enthusiastic and excited about fulfilling his lifelong dream of coaching high school basketball. "I can't believe I'm finally a coach. I can't wait to teach and develop athletes. Coaching will be much more than my job—it will be my life."

For his first 10 years in coaching his teams were highly successful. Athletes, sports journalists, parents, and teachers marveled at his leadership abilities. Ex-athletes frequently returned and thanked him for his help. Coach Charlie T. was often asked to speak at coaching conferences and community gatherings. His love for coaching was unsurpassed.

Most waking hours were spent thinking about coaching, talking about coaching, scouting games, studying game films, and preparing for competition. Coach Charlie T. always stayed around late after practice working with his athletes. Parents frequently wrote and called to tell him he was just what their children needed. Promotions and advancements came rapidly. His teams were highly admired.

With time, Coach Charlie T. developed a strong commitment to certain values. Persistence and dedication were of crucial importance, even more highly valued than winning. Eventually, he began to perceive that he was the only person who really cared about the athletes as persons, the adults of tomorrow. Others seemed to treat their coaching as just another job. They had little time for their players. They hid in their offices and alienated themselves as much as possible. Even other coaches' athletes came to Coach Charlie T. for help. Their coaches didn't seem to care.

Eventually, Coach Charlie T. began to realize his meager financial situation. Other teachers and coaches were doing better. They had been supplementing their income with other jobs while he was attending to his athletes.

Administrators knew what was going on, but they did not seem to care. They told him not to take his work so seriously. Coach Charlie T. began to notice that even his athletes did not appreciate his concern the way they used to. He began to question his values and become concerned that he couldn't meet his family's financial needs. For the first time, Coach Charlie T. questioned his commitment to coaching. Even his family urged him to get out. Younger coaches didn't understand his lack of enthusiasm. They wouldn't even listen when he tried to explain. They thought Coach Charlie T. was old, lazy, and just didn't care. Soon after Coach Charlie T. decided to get out of coaching. He no longer found it satisfying.

coaches who are approaching burn-out move from close identification with athletes to alienation. Early in their careers, identification comes quite naturally. It has not been long since coaches were athletes. Coaches are quite sensitive to the personal needs and problems of athletes and believe that meeting them is crucial to success. But as coaches' careers advance and bosses give increased attention and rewards to other matters, alienation can set in.

Alienation is often accompanied by a perception that athletes do not really appreciate coaches' efforts to develop good interpersonal relations. Although it is impossible to know for certain, it is likely that this perception is formed by coaches to support their desire to escape. Whatever the reason, coaches in this situation actively seek out experiences in their environment that support their new belief.

As coaches become alienated, one of three nonproductive blaming strategies may surface. In the first, blame for failure and/or alienation is placed *on athletes*. The coach perceives that the athletes did not appreciate the coach when identification was high. In this case, the *athletes caused the problem*. The coach was well-intentioned and free of blame. When this situation is accompanied by failure, blame may be attached to the lack of dedication on the part of the athletes and/or their lack of ability.

The second blaming response of alienated coaches is to accept *self-blame*. This response may cause a coach to become dejected and depressed. At first, the coach may perceive that he/she was not cut out for coaching because the coaching ability was lacking. This response may cause the coach to burn-out and quit. But if the response does not lead to quitting, the coach may become quite dejected and ineffective. This situation occurs frequently at the high school, small college, or major university–"minor" sports level. In these situations, coaches may be allowed to continue coaching despite their ineffectiveness. In addition, such coaches may not have readily available career alternatives. Oftentimes, if coach-teachers quit coaching they may also lose their teaching position.

A third and final blaming strategy occurs when coaches *blame the situation*. The coach has full confidence that he/she would be successful if administrative support was given. When the situation is considered impossible to correct, the coach may quit and find another coaching position or become totally frustrated. This blaming strategy may cause athlete-coach alienation. But it may additionally cause coach-administrator alienation. Failure is attributed to lack of support rather than to the coach or the athletes. Often, an abundance of time and energy is spent complaining about the administration. Jealousies for the support given to other sports is frequently expressed. The eventual result is burn-out.

Preventing and Coping with Burn-out

Burn-out must be prevented if one aspires to happiness and success. The best approach to preventing burn-out begins with increased understanding of the scenario that burn-out is likely to follow.

This understanding must then be followed by *self-awareness* of personal values and behaviors. Coaches must learn to read and interpret their personal experiences and needs in coaching. Recognizing high personal needs for success, combined with enthusiastic concern and commitment to athletes, should be a sign to coaches that they are potential burn-out victims. With this awareness, coaches can begin to use these strengths to their advantage while keeping their needs and behaviors in perspective and balance. Finding a healthy balance among athlete, administrator, family, and personal needs is a highly desired step in the right direction for coping with burn-out.

Making Choices

Some coaches take an approach that is very different than that recommended in the previous paragraph. They recognize that they will only be content if they are totally committed to their coaching and are more than happy to let other concerns suffer. Often, coaches with this view simply accept that they cannot continue with this attitude forever. So they plan an alternate career and decide to spend only a set number of years in coaching and quit at a predetermined time or when they first experience burn-out.

For many coaches, however, it is not so easy to quit and begin another career. They must learn to cope with the chronic stress involved in coaching. For coaches in this situation, a good beginning is recognition of an appreciation of the transition process that coaches naturally go through from their first years to their later years. Reducing the number of sports coached and taking a summer off from coaching are also quite helpful.

Many coaches allow sports to consume their lives. Coaches must learn to leave their work at the office on a daily basis or at least occasionally. Some coaches reject this suggestion owing to a somewhat accurate perception that success also requires an unending dedication. However, time off is important if long-term success is desired.

Blowing Out

Occasionally "blowing out" to colleagues, friends, and assistants may be an effective way of coping. Again, the extremes should be avoided. Excessive and daily complaining can be as motivationally debilitating as keeping all stress and frustration inside. So coaches must learn when open discussions and complaining are appropriate, needed, and useful. Sometimes, complaining is positive and productive.

Keeping It in Perspective

Maintaining an accurate perspective is also helpful. When stress becomes overwhelming there is an inclination to focus on the negative aspects of work. There is a tendency to think about the time demands, the energy consumed, the problems with athletes, the complaints from parents, and the hassles with administrators. Consciously focusing attention on the problems encountered in many other less desirable careers is often quite beneficial.

A New Environment

Another approach to coping is to find a new job. In doing so, coaches must carefully identify the strengths and the *weaknesses* of new positions. They should be certain that they will be more, rather than less, happy. Sometimes, just a new environment will be useful.

Utilize Assistant Coaches

Many successful and happy coaches manage and prevent burn-out by surrounding themselves with quality assistant coaches who possess very different talents. This allows assistant coaches to fill roles not easily filled by head coaches.

Great coaches realize that young assistant coaches can easily identify with athletes. They use the strength of these assistant coaches to maintain interpersonal relationships and feedback information that head coaches need to know.

But great coaches also recognize that putting assistants in this role can potentially cause problems. So they anticipate that many athletes will complain to assistant coaches about injustices by other coaches. They also anticipate that athletes will tell assistants they should be the head coach. Head coaches should tell their assistants to expect such feedback and stress the importance of always supporting other coaches in an enthusiastic manner.

Assistant coaches can be most useful, but head coaches must be willing to give them real responsibilities so that assistants perceive themselves as valued and important. Assistants must understand what is expected and then be trusted to execute the job properly.

Family Support

Many coaches have survived the constant stress of coaching through the unending support of their spouse, family, and close friends. Often, a spouse has become involved in some aspect of the sport in order to avoid constant loneliness. Sometimes, a spouse functions as a sports photographer, a record keeper, or a public relations director. The close interaction with the team can enable the spouse to be interested in and be capable of talking about topics that most interest the coach.

Single coaches often get a great amount of support from their family. A family that is available to listen and share in the problems faced by coaches can effectively counter the pressures involved in coaching.

Be Happy with Who You Are

Healthy and successful coaches know and accept who they are. Although constantly striving for improvement and growth they are proud of what they represent. The ego demands of coaches who are happy with themselves exert a positive rather than a negative influence.

Be Proud of Yourself

Coaches who are proud of themselves do not try to be someone they are not. When their athletes question their coaching strategies they do not get mad and yell in order to defend and protect themselves; rather they confidently explain and defend their practices. They put their energy into mastering the execution of their strategies, knowing full well that execution will lead to success.

Coaches who are comfortable with who they are are happy people and are enjoyable to be with. As a result their players are usually highly motivated. They enjoy playing for coaches who are confident in themselves. Athletes who play for these coaches often model their coaches and become happy and comfortable with who they are. Such athletes are far easier and more enjoyable to coach.

Laugh at Yourself

Because great coaches are comfortable and confident with who they are and what they represent they are able to laugh at themselves. Their sense of humor allows them and their athletes to maintain a realistic perspective on the importance of sports.

Lefty Driesell, a highly successful basketball coach at the University of Maryland, has learned to laugh at himself in order to manage the constant abuse directed at his coaching strategies. Prior to the start of the 1980–81 basketball season, in which his team was picked fifth in the preseason AP and UPI polls, Driesell was quoted as saying, "Everybody thinks I'm stupid, so nobody listens to me anyway. They got all those signs down at Virginia with an empty gas tank on my head. A girl at the 'Diamondback' [Maryland student newspaper] wrote that I was stupid the other day. I am going to write her and tell her that I'm not stupid; I just talk stupid."

At the same preseason press conference, Jim Valvano, who was about to begin his first season as head basketball coach at North Carolina State University, found a sense of humor helpful in managing the pressure involved in following in the footsteps of his highly successful predecessor, Norm Sloan, who had recently resigned. Valvano stated, "My wife doesn't sing the national anthem [Sloan's wife used to perform that chore before each State home game], but she does a very clever tap dance routine to the music." In talking about personnel, which was considered suspect because two recently graduated seniors were both selected high in the National Basketball League draft, Valvano quipped, "When I came down here people told me that I had no problems at center, that I had a 7'5" kid [Chuck Nevitt]. He [Nevitt] came walking towards me, turned sideways and he was gone. He's a human tongue depresser." Asked whether N.C. State would be a physical team or more of a finesse group, Valvano said, "I'm pretty close to being a sissy myself. Before my wife and I came down here we had our house broken into. I happened to walk into the house while they [the intruders] were still there. I yelled out, "If you're still in the house, I'm going to leave; don't show yourself and don't panic."

Mimi Murray, one of the most highly successful gymnastic coaches in collegiate history, while coaching at Springfield College travels the country from coast-to-coast giving coaching seminars. Her introductions always seem to be aimed at one point—trying to convince her audience that she is the dumbest coach and the worst gymnast on record.

These coaches are obviously quite content with who they are. They often use humor and self-beration to relieve pressure and to show others that it's okay to laugh at oneself. It is helpful for coaches to remember that sports is not the most important or the only thing in life.

Humor certainly is not a cure-all for the pressures involved in sports, but it is often a sign of a happy and competent coach. It usually sends a positive and motivationally enhancing signal to athletes. The result is often increased motivation and happiness by players and coaches. Great coaches often fall in love with a community and the community falls in love with them. So they build a program and stay in the same coaching position for an extended time period. Legendary coaches like Knute Rockne and Casey Stengel, college coaching greats such as John Wooden and Dean Smith, and Alphonso Cioffi, the 1979 High School Football Coach of the Year from Rutland, Vermont, all share the common bond of staying at one place for many years. These coaches recognize the value of building interest, trust, involvement, and tradition in one place and maintaining it. They realize that despite the appeal of moving to a "better" situation they will have to begin all over again. To do so will take immense time and energy.

Summary

Great coaches understand themselves well enough to know what they really want out of coaching and out of life. By understanding themselves they do what is best for their success and happiness rather than irrationally responding to their ego demands.

Coaching can be a very stressful occupation and many coaches have experienced burn-out.

Consequently, it is important that coaches recognize the personal traits that predispose one to burn-out. Also, coaches should understand the series of events that may lead to burn-out.

Various strategies can be employed to prevent coaching burn-out. Coaches may decide to limit the length of their coaching careers, may occasionally relieve stress through constructive complaining, may focus on benefits of the coaching career, and may make optimal use of assistant coaches. Family support can be a key ingredient in avoidance of burn-out.

As a result of their perceptions and behaviors, great coaches remain open to innovation while maintaining a consistency in their lives inside and outside of coaching from the beginning to the end of their careers. As a result they remain happy and successful throughout their lives.

Recommended Readings

Akin, G., Hunger J.D., and Yates, J. Burn-out in academia exchange. *The Organizational Behavior Teaching Journal,* May 1980.

Edelwich, J., and Brodsky, A. *Burn-out Stages of Disillusionment in the Helping Professions.* New York: Human Sciences Press, 1980.

Freudenberger, H.J. Staff burn-out. *Journal of Social Issues,* 30(1):159–165, 1974.

Hendrickson, B. Teacher burn-out: How to recognize it, what to do about it. *Learning,* (Jan.): 37–39, 1979.

Maslach, C. Burned-out. *Human Behavior,* (Sept.): 16–22, 1976.

Credit: University of Virginia Sports Information.

Anatomical Basis of Athletic Performance

10

Athletes continually strive to enhance their performance by acquiring and mastering skilled movements. In order to assist athletes in this process coaches must possess a basic understanding of human motion and the structural influences that govern movement. Such knowledges are essential in providing athletes with appropriate activities for refinement of sports skills. This chapter provides a summary of the anatomical factors that govern human movement. Particular emphasis is placed on the skeletal and muscular systems.

Human Movement

Efficient movement is the foundation that underlies successful sport performance. The refinement of sophisticated sports skills is frequently dependent upon the ability of coaches and athletes to apply the principles of human anatomy, biomechanics, and kinesiology. The ability to modify movements and meet the changing requirements of the game often make the difference between success and failure.

Study of Human Movement

The human organism and its ability to move to meet environmental demands has been of interest to scientists in various disciplines. Consequently, different terms have been utilized to describe the varying approaches to the study of human movement. An individual entering the coaching profession must understand the fundamentals of human movement and, thus, should be familiar with some of the terminology employed in this field. The study of human movement as it relates to sports skill performance can be divided into two major categories, *kinesiology* and *biomechanics*.

Kinesiology (the study of movement), emphasizes *the study of the skeletal and muscular systems and the movements that are possible at the numerous articulations of the body.* A thorough understanding of the structural limitations of the human body will assist the coach in designing activities that are developmentally appropriate for the athlete and that avoid excessive strain to any body segment.

Biomechanics is rapidly becoming accepted as an integral area of study for the coach. Hay (1978) has defined biomechanics and its relationship to the analysis of sports techniques as "... *The science that examines the internal and external forces acting on a human body and the effects produced by these forces."* The study of biomechanics traditionally has been divided into two major content areas: *Statics*—the study of the body at rest or in equilibrium; and *dynamics*—the study of the body while moving and the forces that produce motion. Both areas of study are important for the coach and athlete. Skill performance frequently relies upon one's ability to keep the body in a state of equilibrium while periodically shifting body weight to disturb stability and cause motion. For example, the sprinter in starting blocks must balance all the forces acting upon the body in such a manner that movement can be quickly initiated in a horizontal direction. Once the body is moving, the sprinter must maintain dynamic stability through the application of force until the movement is slowed and finally stopped. In studying any sports skill it is important to consider the principles of both static and dynamic movement.

The study of dynamic human motion can be divided into two major subdivisions. *Kinematics* involves the study of the time and space factors in movement, while *kinetics* is the study of the forces that create and modify human motion. Coaches must develop a basic understanding of the kinematic and kinetic foundations of motion in order to qualitatively analyze an athlete's skill performance. Coaches armed with this information can readily provide the performer with relevant feedback intended to refine the motor skill. Kreighbaum and Barthels (1981) have noted that if mechanical information is provided to athletes at their level of comprehension they may develop the ability to

analyze their own performance and initiate self-corrective changes in their movement.

As athletes become more sophisticated and performances improve coaches must rely upon more scientifically based methods of skill instruction. No longer will athletes accept generalized statements regarding their performance. Coaches who are limited to telling their athletes to "keep your eye on the ball" because they are unprepared to analyze the qualitative aspects of movement can no longer survive in sports. Principles of biomechanics and kinesiology allow the coach to explain how and why the human body moves in the manner it does. Evaluating sports skills is a difficult task that requires practice. Once mastered, however, it can be one of the coach's most valuable tools.

Human Movement Defined

Movement provides an individual with the ability to interact and learn from the environment. Numerous authors have attempted to define human movement and these definitions may be summarized as: *The act of changing position in space in relation to some reference point.*

An individual's unique movement ability is the result of a complex interaction of genetic and environmental influences (Smith 1968). Success in many sports requires a specific potential and properly planned practice experiences. Environmental conditions can be easily modified, but genetic make-up is not changeable. In many sports, an individual athlete may have the skills necessary for successful participation, but may lack sufficient body size. Sports such as soccer are currently experiencing rapid increases in participation because they tend to emphasize skilled movement rather than body size.

All movement is designed to achieve a specific purpose. Newborns react to various stimuli with reflexive movements intended to protect the child from injury or to assist in survival. As the neurological system matures the child begins to explore the surrounding environment and gradually gains control over the musculature. The child's first attempts at movement are often uncoordinated and uncontrolled. With time and development the child begins to refine these early movements into more complex movement patterns. By combining the individual movements of several body segments the child finds that complex movements can be utilized to achieve various purposes, including the development of sports-related skills.

Movements of Body Segments

The skeletal system has over 200 articulations (joints) that allow for various degrees of movement. The range of motion of any particular joint is dictated by numerous factors, including: The classification of the joint, the physical structure of the articulating bones, the width of the joint cavity, and the musculature surrounding the joint capsule.

All movements are defined from the standard *anatomical or neutral position* (see Figure 10.1). Although few individuals ever assume this position when performing a movement, it does provide a reference point from which movements can easily be described. Movement at any joint can be performed through a number of planes around an axis that is centered at the joint. It is frequently helpful for individuals who are attempting to understand how the body moves to become familiar with various planes and axes of human motion.

There are three primary planes of motion with corresponding axes. Each plane passes through the body and divides it into equally distributed (mass) segments. The primary planes of movement may be defined as:

Sagittal Plane/Lateral Axis. Divides the body into right and left segments with an axis that passes horizontally through the joint from side to side (Figure 10.2).

Frontal Plane/Anteriorposterior Axis. A plane that divides the body into front and back segments with an axis that passes front to back.

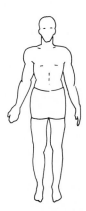

Figure 10.1 The anatomical position provides a reference for describing movements of the human body.

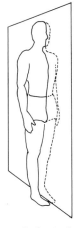

Figure 10.2 The sagittal plane divides the body into right and left halves. Rotations in the sagittal plane occur about the lateral axis.

Transverse Plane/Vertical Axis. Divides the body into upper and lower halves with an axis that passes through a joint vertically.

Movement occurs in a plane of motion around an axis that passes through a joint. For example, flexion of the elbow (as in performing an arm curl) occurs in the sagittal plane around the lateral axis of the elbow. Obviously, movements that are as complex as sports skills rarely occur in any one plane, but rather in some combination of the three primary planes. Logan and McKinney (1977) introduced the concept of diagonal planes and movement of the ball-and-socket joints of the hip and shoulder. They contend that the physical structure of the joint, muscular structure relative to the line of pull, and the increased utilization of angular momentum made it more efficient to utilize a diagonal joint movement, especially when performing ballistic movements. Soccer-style place kicking provides an excellent example of this concept. Traditional flexion-extension–style place kickers in football are usually physically large with heavy musculature in the thigh. In contrast, many of today's soccer-style kickers are smaller, but they utilize trunk rotation and angular momentum to impart a greater force to the ball. The traditional kicker must rely solely on the strength of the upper leg. Although it can easily be shown that movement in a diagonal plane can impart a greater force to an object, there is some evidence that beginning learners cannot successfully produce this motion. Thus, the coach who works with novice performers should concentrate on developing and refining movement in the diagonal plane. This can frequently be accomplished by providing the athlete with numerous opportunities to practice this motion.

Coaches should be familiar with the commonly utilized terminology to describe human motion so they may effectively communicate with the athlete and professionals in related disciplines. The motions of body segments are described from the anatomical position. Table 10.1 presents a summary of the frequently utilized descriptions of human motion.

Structural Influences on Movement

The human body contains a total of 206 bones that articulate at over 200 joints and allow the 656 skeletal muscles to move the body segments in numerous patterns. In performing a sport skill the athlete must precisely sequence the actions of many of body structures so that a highly coordinated movement results.

A fundamental knowledge of the anatomy of the musculoskeletal system is an initial step in understanding human motion and the refinement of sports related skills. Athletes frequently place excessive demands and stress upon the skeletal and muscular systems. Injuries result when these anatomical structures are forced beyond normal levels of stress. Coaches must possess an awareness of the musculoskeletal systems of the human body and accept the responsibility of providing activities and equipment that afford the athlete with a maximal degree of safety.

This section is intended to provide basic anatomical information that may be utilized in conducting a structural analysis of sports skills. This information is particularly important when attempting to determine the conditions that contribute to injury or in developing exercise programs designed to increase muscular strength/flexibility in specific body segments. Structural analysis is the initial step in gaining an increased insight into analyzing and refining skill performance.

Skeletal System

The skeletal system serves five important functions, including: (1) providing form and structure to the human body, (2) protection of vital organs, (3) storage of minerals, (4) production of blood cells, and (5) providing for the attachments of muscles in a system of levers that allow movement. Although each function is im-

Table 10.1: Movement Description

Descriptor		Example	Common Prefixes and Adjectives	
FLEXION	Movement of body segment(s) that results in the *decrease* in the *angle* of the articulating bones (see fig.).		Hyper	Beyond the normal range of motion
			Dorsi	Movement of the foot at the ankle that results in the toes being lifted toward tibia (shin)
EXTENSION	Opposite of flexion—movement of body segment so joint *angle increases* (see fig.).		Plantar	Opposite of dorsiflexion, movement of the foot at the ankle causing the toes to point toward the ground.
ROTATION	Movement of a body segment around its own axis.			
CIRCUMDUCTION	Movement of a body segment that combines flexion, extension, abduction, and adduction, causing a conial-shaped path.		Horizontal	Abduction or adduction of the shoulder across the front of the body.
ABDUCTION	Movement of a body segment *away* from midline of body (see fig.).		Medial	Rotation toward the midline of the body
ADDUCTION	The opposite of abduction—movement of a body segment *toward* the midline of the body (see last fig.).		Lateral	Rotation away from the midline of the body.
INVERSION	Turning the sole of the foot inward. Placing weight on outside of border of foot.			
EVERSION	Turning the sole of the foot outward. Placing weight on inside border of foot.			
SUPINATION	Outward rotation of forearm. Thumb upward.			
PRONATION	Inward rotation of forearm. Thumb downward.			

portant for survival, coaches are particularly interested in the skeletal system's role in the production of efficient movement.

Structure of Bones. The physical structure of bone is frequently considered as nonessential information for the coach. However, this information becomes important when attempting to understand structural limitations or in communicating with an athletic trainer or physician regarding an athlete's injury. Bone is composed of approximately 50% water and 50% organic and inorganic solids, including calcium, phosphorus, and smaller amounts of magnesium, fluorine, chlorine, and iron. Bone is a living tissue that changes in chemical composition with age. The very flexible bones of a youngster become fragile and brittle in the senior citizen.

The skeleton is frequently divided into two major sections. The *axial skeleton* includes the bones of the skull and trunk. The *appendicular skeleton* consists of bones found in the limbs. Each component of the skeletal system plays a distinct role in the performance of efficient movement. The axial skeleton is utilized as a base from which the appendages are moved at a high velocity. For example, in throwing and striking patterns rotational torque is generated in the axial skeleton and is transferred to the rapidly moving limb. In such instances, the velocity of movement is greatest at the end of the long limb.

Bone shape plays an important role in dictating the motion possible in a particular body segment. Often, bones are classified and identified according to their shape and function.

Long Bones. Predominant bones of the upper and lower extremities. Characterized by a long cylindrical shaft (diaphysis) and broad ends specifically shaped to form a stable articulation (epiphysis).

Flat Bones. Bones with characteristic large smooth surfaces designed to provide muscular attachment and protection for underlying organs.

Short Bones. Small compact bones, primarily located in the wrist and ankle, designed to assist in the absorption of forces and to increase the range of motion at the joint.

Irregular Bones. Bone of irregular shapes that provide numerous projections for muscular attachments and protection.

Long bones found in the extremities are of special significance to the coach. Segments of long bones are identified with respect to their position relative to the trunk of the body. The *proximal* end of a long bone is closest to the midline of the body, whereas the *distal* end is furthest from the trunk. *Medial* refers to the inside border of the bone, while *lateral* denotes the outside edge of the segment. The structural arrangement of the extremities provides the athlete with a system of levers that assists in the production of high-velocity movements. However, their speed of movement, unprotected position, and their developmental characteristics make them susceptible to injury.

The epiphyseal ends of long bones are of particular importance to the coach who works with adolescent athletes (Figure 10.3). Located just inside the articulating surface of each long bone of the adolescent is a disk of cartilage called the *epiphyseal plate* (Kreighbaum and Barthels 1981). These plates act as centers where longitudinal growth of the bone takes place and are usually ossified (i.e., hardened) by 20 years of age.

Epiphyseal plates are less strong than surrounding bone tissue, making them susceptible to injury in young athletes. Adolescents are es-

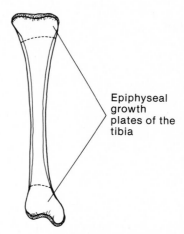

Epiphyseal growth plates of the tibia

Figure 10.3 The epiphyseal growth plates of long bones are structurally weaker than the surrounding ossified bone tissue.

pecially prone to trauma at the epiphyseal plates because of their: (1) physical awkwardness caused by accelerated skeletal growth, (2) active and frequently careless attitude to safety, and (3) increased participation in athletic skills (Salter 1979).

Excessive trauma to the ends of long bones can negatively influence the longitudinal growth of that bone. The epiphysis of the distal end of the femur (thigh bone) and proximal end of the tibia (shin bone, the major bone of lower leg) are very vulnerable to shearing, splitting, or crushing forces. Common injuries to the growth plates include separation of the epiphysis through the epiphyseal cartilage, fractures across the growth plate, and actual crushing of the bone ends. Salter (1979) noted that 70% of longitudinal growth takes place at the distal epiphysis of the femur, while 55% of the tibia's lengthening occurs at its proximal end. Extreme care must be taken to protect the adolescent's knee from excessive trauma. Approximately 59% of all injuries to the epiphyseal plate of the distal end of the femur are the result of athletic participation (Salter 1979). Kennedy (1979) noted another frequent injury to the skeletal structure in athletes. Fractures of the articulating surfaces of long bones are the result of a combination of rotational and compressive forces acting upon the joint structure. The adolescent football player who plants his foot and suddenly turns or the young pitcher who throws hard can cause injury to the articulating surfaces of the long bones.

The developing nature of the adolescent's skeletal structure demands that coaches take great care to select appropriate activities for the young athlete. The majority of injuries to growing bones can be avoided by ensuring that coaches use properly designed and fitted protective equipment, adhere rigidly to the rules of the game and structure teams on the basis of physical size rather than on chronological age (Salter 1979).

Structure of Joints. Rarely does an articulation perform only one movement during the execu-

tion of a high-level athletic skill. Usually, the joint is involved in a series of coordinated actions that combine into a total sports skill. The degree of movement possible in a joint is dependent to a large degree upon its physical structure. The unique structural design of the various joints allows for characteristic differences in function. Joints of the human body are normally classified according to the types of movements permitted and further defined by their physical characteristics. Articulations can be classified as *synarthrodial, amphiarthrodial,* or *diarthrodial,* depending upon the movement characteristics of the articulating bones.

Synarthrodial joints allow only restricted movement and primarily assist in the absorption of forces that are exerted on the skeletal system. The fibrous sutures of the skull allow for the absorption of the numerous internal and external forces exerted on the head during athletic participation.

Amphiarthrodial articulations permit a moderate degree of movement that is allowed by the connective tissue surrounding and located between the adjoining bones. The movement of the vertebrae provides the dual purpose of absorbing forces while allowing for valuable motion. The lateral and rotational movements of the vertebrae are important contributors to efficient movement and sports skill success. Most skills involving a throwing or striking pattern depend upon complete trunk rotation. Although both synarthrodial and amphiarthrodial articulations are important contributors to efficient movement, the diarthrodial joints of the extremities are of primary interest for the coach.

Diarthrodial articulations possess several physical characteristics that allow for high degrees of flexibility, including: (1) a joint cavity separating the bones, (2) smooth hyaline cartilage covering the bone ends, and (3) a synovial membrane that secretes a thick, synovial fluid that provides lubrication for the joint. Diarthrodial joints are subclassified according to physical structure of the bone ends and the movement potential of the joint. Figure 10.4 is a summary of the subclassifications of diarthrodial joints. A joint's physical structure dictates its movement potential. The hinge joint of the elbow is so constricted that it allows only flexion and extension movements, while the ball

Joint Classification	Illustration	Movement Potential of Joint
A Irregular		Gliding-Sliding Movement
B Hinge		Flexion-Extension
C Pivot		Rotation-Circumduction Flexion-Extension Abduction-Adduction
D Condyloid	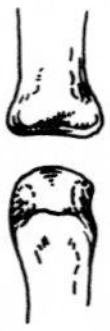	Flexion-Extension Abduction-Adduction Circumduction
E Ball and Socket	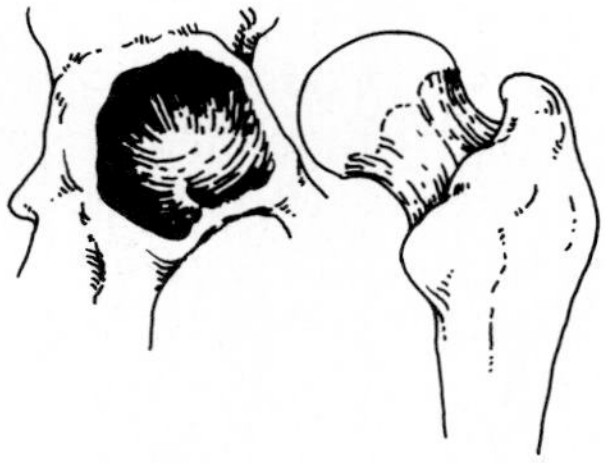	Flexion-Extension Abduction-Adduction Circumduction-Rotation (limited)
F Saddle		Flexion-Extension Abduction-Adduction Circumduction

Figure 10.4 Classifications of diarthrodial joints. (*A*) Irregular (intercarpal). (*B*) Hinge (elbow or humeroulnar). (*C*) Pivot (atlantoaxial). (*D*) Condyloid. (*E*) Ball-and Socket (shoulder). (*F*) Saddle (thumb or carpometacarpal). (Adapted from Hollinshead, W.H., and Jenkins, D.B.: *Functional Anatomy of the Limbs and Back.* 5th ed. Philadelphia: W.B. Saunders Co., 1981.)

and socket structure of the hip joint provides for far greater range of movement.

Muscular System

Movement of body segments is made possible through the contraction of skeletal muscles. The manner in which the muscles contract is a prime determinant of the type of movement and work that results. Coaches are particularly interested in a muscle's ability to produce force for the purpose of generating strength, power, and endurance. *Muscular strength* may be defined as the maximum force that can be applied with one maximal contraction; *endurance* refers to submaximal contractions performed over a sustained period; *power* reflects the individual's ability to produce a force and perform work rapidly.

Organization of Skeletal Muscles in the Body. Perhaps the most basic characteristic of skeletal muscles is that they are attached to bones; hence the term *skeletal* muscle. In general, each skeletal muscle is attached to two bones such that contraction (shortening) of the muscle draws the two bony attachments closer to one another (Figure 10.5). Also, the skeletal muscles are said to be "voluntary," indicating that they are subject to our conscious control. Usually, they contract when we want them to, with the level of force that we desire.

The many skeletal muscles in the body can be organized into several major groups. Each group of muscles works as a unit to produce a certain movement or set of movements. If the coach is to truly understand how athletic skills are performed he or she must develop a familiarity with the ways in which the various muscle groups function to produce basic movements. Figures 10.6 and 10.7 graphically present the major muscle groups of the upper and lower extremities, trunk, head, and neck.

Most skeletal muscles are under voluntary control of the athlete's central nervous system. Each major joint of the human body is moved by the combined action of many muscles. The muscle directly involved in causing a motion is called the *primary mover*, whereas the muscle that causes the opposite movement is referred to as the *antagonist*. During the contraction of a primary mover the nervous system inhibits (relaxes) the antagonist, allowing a smooth and controlled movement.

Structure of Skeletal Muscles. Most tissues in the body are composed of individual living cells that have a structure that is adapted for the function of a specific tissue. In this regard, skeletal muscle is typical. The basic cellular unit in muscle tissue is the muscle fiber. The fibers are long and thin and are embedded in a matrix of connective tissue called *endomysium*. The fibers lie in parallel and are arranged in bundles. Each bundle is surrounded by a second layer of connective tissue, the *perimysium*. These bundles are encapsuled within the *epimysium*, a connective sheath that covers the entire muscle (Figure 10.8).

The layers of connective tissue in a skeletal muscle provide it with structural integrity and serve as a link between the muscle fibers and bone. At the extremities of the muscle the connective tissue layers merge with tendons that are directly attached to the bones. Connective tissue endows muscle with elasticity, a physical characteristic that determines the extent to which the muscle can be stretched. Since skeletal muscles often run across joints, the elastic component of muscle is a major limiting factor in joint flexibility, which, in turn, is an important determinant of performance in many athletic activities. An example of this principle is presented in Figure 10.9.

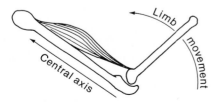

Figure 10.5 Shortening (contraction) of a skeletal muscle causes movement of a limb.

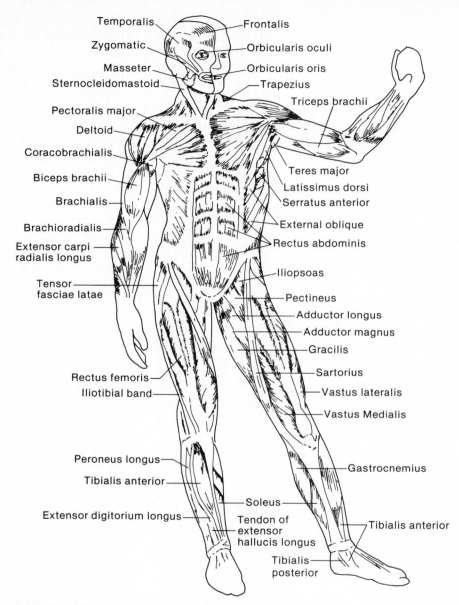

Figure 10.6 Muscles of the human body, anterior view. (From Millard, N.D., King, B.G., and Showers, M.J.: Human Anatomy and Physiology. Philadelphia: W.B. Saunders Co., 1956.)

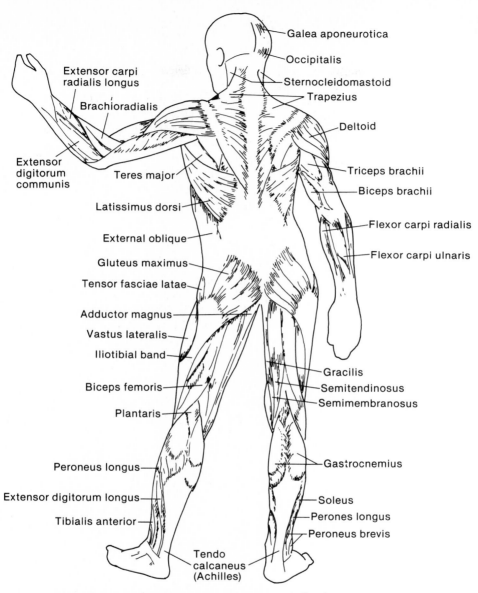

Figure 10.7 Muscles of the human body, posterior view. (From Millard, N.D., King, B.G., and Showers, M.J.: Human Anatomy and Physiology. Philadelphia: W.B. Saunders Co., 1956).

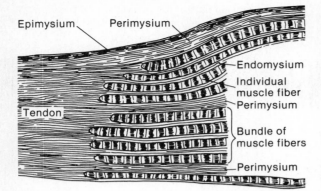

Figure 10.8 Muscle fibers are surrounded by three layers of connective tissue: endomysium, perimysium, and epimysium.

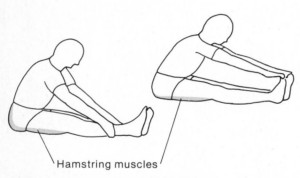

Figure 10.9 Range of motion (flexibility) of the hip joint is determined in part by the extensibility of the connective tissues in the hamstring muscles.

Muscle Shapes. Skeletal muscles have different shapes and vary greatly in size. Muscular tissue is classified according to the arrangement of its muscle fibers in relation to its connective tissue. The size of a muscle and the arrangement of its fibers are important determinants of its abilities to contract quickly and to produce a sufficient force to overcome a resistance.

Fusiform muscles have fibers that run parallel with the line of contraction. This structure allows for a maximum degree of contraction and facilitates rapid shortening. However, fusiform muscles are restricted in the degree of force that they can apply to a bone segment. The parallel nature of the fiber structure of these muscles limits the number of muscle fibers that may be actively involved in a contraction.

Penniform muscles have fibers that radiate from a central tendon, which gives the fiber pattern a feather-like appearance. This unique arrangement allows many more muscle fibers to contribute to a movement, thereby making it more forceful. Although these muscles can generate great force, the range of contraction of penniform muscles is restricted.

Each classification of muscle tissue has subclasses that describe unique structural characteristics (see Figure 10.10).

Types of Muscle Contraction. The type of movement that results from muscular action is dependent upon the location of the muscular attachment, momentum of the moving segments, pull of gravity, and types of joints in-

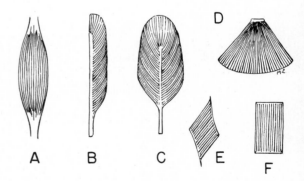

Figure 10.10 Muscles may be classified as fusiform (*A*) or penniform (*B*) according to the alignment of the muscle fibers. (*C*) Bipennate: a series of short muscle fibers that radiate from both sides of a long central tendon. (*D*) Triangular: a relatively large, flat muscle whose fibers radiate from a small tendon to a larger tendon resembling the shape of a fan. (*E*) Rhomboidal. (*F*) Quadrate: a small, flat, four-sided muscle having parallel fibers.

volved in the movement. Some muscles cross over two or more joints and, therefore, cause movement of all these joints at the same time. These multijoint muscles tend to be located in the lower extremity and are utilized primarily for locomotion. During body movements the muscles function to: (1) move a body segment by decreasing muscle length, (2) resist the motion of a body segment caused by some external force, and (3) stabilize an articulation.

Muscular Shortening. When a muscle contracts it exerts a force upon both bone segments to which it is attached. If the force generated exceeds a resisting force a *concentric (shortening) contraction* results. This usually causes one or both of the body segments to move.

Muscular Resisting. At times, muscles are utilized to prevent or restrict external or other muscular forces from moving a body segment. *Eccentric contraction* is the controlled elongation of a muscle under tension. The individual who holds an object in one hand and slowly extends the elbow from a flexed position generates force with the biceps so that the arm can be lowered slowly in a controlled manner. The force causing the extension of the forearm in this case is not the shortening of the triceps, but rather the pull of gravity upon the object held in the hand. Without the action of the biceps the arm would fall in an uncontrolled manner. The ability to control the action of external forces upon individual body segments is necessary in any movement that resists the pull of gravity.

Muscular Stabilization. A muscle that generates force without a change in length is considered to be in static or *isometric contraction*. This type of contraction occurs when an opposing resistance is greater than the muscle's contractile force or when it is necessary to stabilize one or more joints to assist in performing a movement.

Muscles are frequently involved in all three types of contraction during the same movement. This changing role makes it impossible to study muscle action solely with respect to its concentric contraction. Rather it is more beneficial to study the musculature of a joint in relation to all the possible movements of that joint.

Nervous Control of Muscular Activity. Performance of a sports skill is the result of numerous muscles working in a coordinated manner to produce the desired motion. This process depends greatly upon the ability of the nervous system to efficiently grade and sequence the actions of many skeletal muscles. The slightest hesitation or incorrect response to a stimulus can cause the resulting movement to be unsuccessful.

Muscles are controlled by the central nervous system, which delivers an activating stimulus to individual muscle fibers. The nature of this stimulus and the manner in which it functions is discussed in more detail in Chapter 15.

Although the performance of a sports skill is voluntary, the required patterns of muscle contraction are complex and depend upon numerous automatic neural responses. Gowitzke and Milner (1980) have indicated that in the performance of a complex movement the neural control of muscles is mostly involuntary. They further have noted that, although the basic pattern of muscle action is unconsciously set, the performer does control the initiation of the motion, regulation of speed, force, range, and direction of the movement, and the termination of the movement.

The athlete depends upon past experiences in similar environmental situations when activating the musculature in response to a stimulus. Thus, it is important that the coach provide the athlete with practice sessions that simulate the actual environmental demands of the contest. Care, however, must be taken when designing activities for young performers. For example, the eight-year-old basketball player who attempts to shoot a regulation ball into a 10-foot-high goal frequently utilizes whatever style of movement that achieves the desired end. This can lead to the adoption of incorrect mechanical patterns.

Summary

The ability to move efficiently is a fundamental prerequisite to skillful athletic performance. The human skeleton contains numerous articulations that allow for a wide variety of movements that result from muscular action. Performance of an athletic skill is the result of muscles working in a highly coordinated manner to produce a desired motion. The ability of the athlete to coordinate the skeletal and neuromuscular systems is the primary component in determining the quality of a performance. A coach with a basic understanding of the anatomical bases of athletic performance will be better able to assist the athlete in improving performance and experiencing success.

References

Gowitzke, B.A., and Milner, M. *Understanding the Scientific Bases of Human Movement.* Baltimore: Williams and Wilkins Co., 1980.

Hay, J. *The Biomechanics of Sports Techniques.* Englewood Cliffs, New Jersey: Prentice-Hall, Inc., 1978.

Kennedy, J.C. (Ed.) Ligamentous injuries in the adolescent. In *The Injured Adolescent Knee.* Baltimore: Williams and Wilkins Co., 1979.

Kreighbaum, E., and Barthels, K.M. *Biomechanics: A Qualitative Approach for Studying Human Movement.* Minneapolis: Burgess Publishing Co., 1981.

Logan, G.A., and McKinney, W.C. *Anatomic Kinesiology.* Dubuque, Iowa: William C. Brown Co., 1977.

Salter, R.B. Epiphyseal plate injuries in the adolescent knee. In *The Injured Adolescent Knee.* Edited by J.C. Kennedy. Baltimore: Williams and Wilkins Co., 1979.

Smith, H.M. (Ed.). *Introduction to Human Movement.* Reading, Massachusetts: Addison-Wesley Publishing Co., Inc., 1968.

Recommended Readings

Kerr, R. *Psychomotor Learning.* Philadelphia: Saunders College Publishing, 1982.

Kennedy, J.C. (Ed.). *The Injured Adolescent Knee.* Baltimore: Williams and Wilkins Co., 1979, Chap. 4.

Kreighbaum, E., and Barthels, K.M. *Biomechanics: A Qualitative Approach for Studying Human Movement.* Minneapolis: Burgess Publishing Co., 1981.

Luttgens, R. and Wells, K.F., *Kinesiology: Scientific Basis of Human Motion.* Philadelphia: Saunders College Publishing, 1982, Chaps. 1, 2.

Piscopo, J., and Baley, J.A. *Kinesiology: The Science of Movement.* New York: John Wiley and Sons, 1981, Chaps. 2, 4.

Credit: From Sabock, R. J. *The Coach*, 2nd ed. Philadelphia: Saunders College Publishing, 1979.

Musculoskeletal Actions

11

The skeletal and musculature systems work together to produce human movement. In order to positively influence athletic skill performance coaches must understand how the bones and muscles interact during physical activity. For example, the athlete who develops a weight-training program must be able to identify those muscles that significantly contribute to successful participation in a sport and select exercises to increase strength in those muscle groups. Gymnasts must understand the musculoskeletal structure of the body so maximum flexibility can be obtained at each joint. All coaches must be able to relate to athletes and to other professionals regarding injuries associated with the musculoskeletal system.

This chapter is intended to provide the reader with a guide to studying movements at the major joints of the human body. Although there are numerous articulations that allow for various degrees of movement, emphasis in this chapter will be placed on the major joints that contribute to the performance of sports skills. This material is not intended to be a comprehensive review of the musculoskeletal system, but rather to provide the minimum information that an individual entering the coaching profession should possess. It is suggested that as individuals become more comfortable with the general information presented in this chapter they progress to the texts in the bibliography for a more detailed review of human anatomy.

The remainder of this chapter provides a brief introduction to the major joints of the axial and upper and lower appendicular skeleton. Emphasis is placed upon reviewing the physical structure of each joint and identifying the primary contributors to the various movements possible at the joint. It is suggested that when progressing through the various joints of the human body the reader work with a partner so that body segments and movements may be studied through manual manipulation and palpation. Emphasis should be placed upon studying: (1) the muscles in relation to the articulating bones, and (2) the movements that result from both concentric and eccentric contractions of the muscles.

Axial Skeleton

The axial skeleton plays an important role in the performance of sports skills. Although the axial skeleton contains numerous articulations (joints), movement is usually restricted by the physical structure of the joint. Often, flexibility of the vertebral column is an important factor in performing complex sports movements.

Structure of the Vertebral Column

A total of 24 individual vertebrae articulate to form the vertebral column. This column is designed to provide support and shape to the human body, to allow for rotation of the axial skeleton, to protect the delicate spinal cord, and to assist in absorbing gravitational forces exerted upon the body. Vertebrae become increasingly larger toward the lower end of the vertebral column, since each segment must support progressively more body weight. As viewed from the side, the adult vertebral column has four curvatures that act to assist in the absorption of the vertical forces commonly encountered during movement. These curves and the vertebrae that form them are commonly referred to as cervical, thoracic, lumbar, and sacral (Figure 11.1).

Among the many movements possible in the vertebral column are flexion-extension, adduction-abduction, and rotation. These actions are made possible by the unique physical structure of the vertebral column. Although each articulation allows for only a limited range of motion, the summation of these movements across the entire column results in a total movement that is significant. An intervertebral disk of cartilage lies between the segments and provides an articulating surface and assists in the absorption of forces exerted upon the vertebrae. Excessive stress applied to these cartilagenous disks, as frequently encountered in contact sports, can

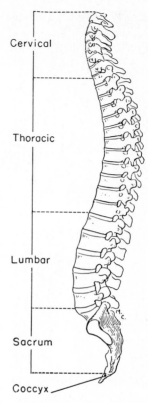

Figure 11.1 Lateral view of spinal column showing four curves.

result in crushing or slippage injuries that require medical care.

Stability in the vertebral column is maintained by strong ligaments and muscles. Boney projections called *spinous* and *transverse processes* provide sites for attachment of muscles and ligaments. These boney processes can be fractured by a forceful blow to the back, as may occur when football players are "speared" with an opponent's helmet.

Injuries to the Vertebral Column

An important balance exists between the antagonist muscle groups that surround the vertebral column. Weakness of any muscle frequently results in a skeletal asymmetry. Such an "unnatural" posture places excessive strain upon the supporting ligaments and can result in a permanent impairment. Although the vertebral column can absorb tremendous force, it can easily be injured. Injury to the vertebrae must be handled with great care because of the location of the spinal cord. Sports that require the athlete to absorb multidirectional forces tend to cause injuries to the vertebral column. Athletes must be taught to avoid placing excessive strain on the back. For example, in baseball, the base runner who indiscriminately performs a head-first slide into second base increases the risk of back injury.

Damage to the vertebral column may also be caused in less obvious athletic situations. Young female gymnasts commonly exhibit an exaggerated lumbar curvature resulting from overdevelopment of the back musculature and underdevelopment of the antagonist abdominal muscles. Such an excessive lumbar curvature may result in problems in later life. Similarly, the performance of a simple exercise, if performed in a mechanically incorrect manner, can result in excessive back strain. Straight leg sit-ups, leg lifts, and bench pressing a weight with the feet on the floor are all examples of exercises that result in an exaggerated arching and straining of the lower back.

Movements in the Vertebral Column

Movement of the trunk is an important contributor to the efficient performance of sports skills. Flexion and extension of the vertebral column assist in the production and transfer of forces and allows the athlete to make significant changes in the position of the center of gravity. Trunk rotation is an important contributor to the production of force and the performance of throwing and striking skills. The baseball pitcher, tennis server, and discus thrower all rely upon the rotational forces generated by contraction of the muscles surrounding the vertebral column.

Vertebral Flexion. Flexion of the trunk results from contraction of the rectus abdominis muscle, which is located on the anterior surface of the trunk. Two sets of fibers extend longitudinally and may contract together (flexion) or singularly (lateral flexion) (see Figure 11.2).

To observe the action of the rectus abdominis have your partner assume a supine position

Trunk	Movement	Primary movers	Muscle location
Flexion		1. Rectus abdominis	

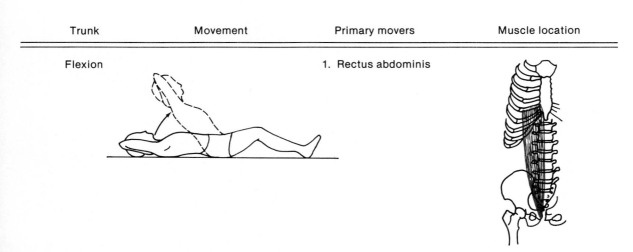

Figure 11.2

with the hands placed behind the head. Stabilize the lower legs while performer slowly lifts the trunk from the floor. Palpate the rectus abdominis as it contracts concentricly during the upward movement and contracts eccentricly as the back is lowered to the floor.

Vertebral Extension. Extension of the vertebral column (Figure 11.3) is the result of contraction of the erector spinae muscles. This group of longitudinal fibers extends up the back, and is characterized by multiple attachments. This muscle is frequently utilized in an eccentric contraction when the trunk flexes against gravity. Because of its symmetrical structure on both sides of the vertebral column the two erector spinae groups may be contracted together (extension) or singularly in an eccentric contraction to assist in lateral flexion.

To observe the action of this muscle group have your partner assume a prone position with the hands placed behind the head. The performer should attempt to elevate the shoulders from the floor. Palpate the contraction of the muscle in the lower back region.

Vertebral Rotation. Fibers of the internal and external obliquus abdominis muscle extends diagonally across the abdomen, allowing for rotation of the vertebral column. The attachment of the external obliquus is such that it rotates the spine toward the opposite side of the body, while contraction of the internal obliquus results in trunk rotation toward the muscle (Figure 11.4).

To observe the action of these muscles have your partner assume a supine position with the arms placed behind the head. Stabilize the upper legs as the performer slowly rotates the trunk to one side. Palpate the external obliquus abdominis on the side opposite the rotation while noting the contraction of the external obliquus on the rotated side.

Upper Appendicular Skeleton

The primary joints of the upper extremity are the shoulder, elbow, and wrist. This series of skeletal articulations provides the athlete with a wide range of motion and the ability to generate movements of high velocity.

Structure of the Shoulder Joint

The large hemispherical head of the humerus and the glenoid fossa of the scapula ar-

Trunk	Movement	Primary movers	Muscle location
Extension	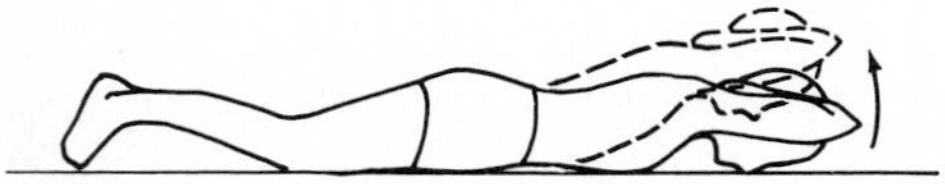	1. Erector spinae	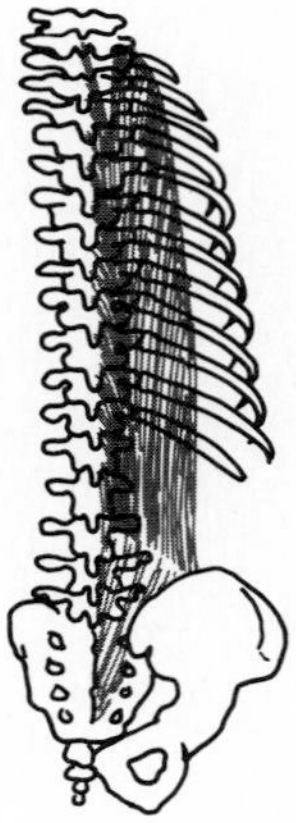

Figure 11.3

Trunk	Movement	Primary movers	Muscle location
Rotation	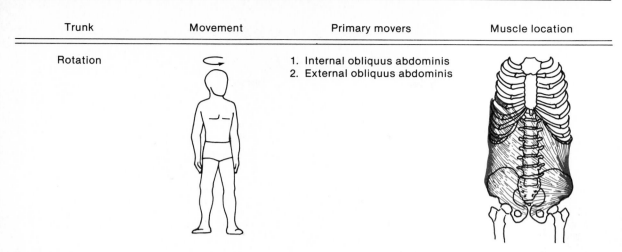	1. Internal obliquus abdominis 2. External obliquus abdominis	

Figure 11.4

ticulate to form the multiaxial joint of the shoulder (Figure 11.5). Skeletal structure of the joint, including its large joint cavity and shallow glenoid fossa, allows a wide range of motion, but contributes to a relatively unstable structure. Strength and stability of the joint is provided by heavy ligamentous and muscular attachments surrounding the joint. Because of the structural characteristics of the shoulder it is prone to dislocation. A dislocation normally results when

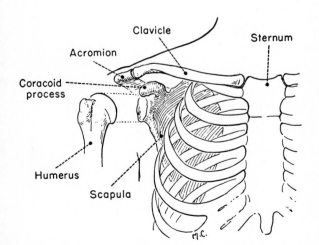

Figure 11.5 Anterior view of the shoulder joint.

the arm is in a position of abduction and a force is applied through a locked elbow, such as when attempting to break a fall with an outreached arm.

The shoulder joint and its associated movements are extremely complex and involve movement of the scapula. Action of the scapula is controlled by a set of individual muscles that can contract to elevate-depress, move laterally or medially, and/or rotate the scapula. The contribution of the scapula in extending the range of motion of the shoulder can easily be observed by raising the arm over the head. An individual's reach can be increased by rotating the scapula outward and upward. This increase in range of motion contributes significantly to all performances that require shoulder movement. Thus, it is important to appreciate that movements of the arm at the shoulder involve the combined action of the shoulder joint and the scapula. However, to simplify learning the actions of the shoulder this presentation will concentrate only upon movements at the glenohumeral joint.

Shoulder Flexion. Flexion of the upper arm involves bringing the humerus forward and upward at the shoulder joint. This action is the result of the concentric contraction of the anterior

Shoulder	Movement	Primary movers	Muscle location
Flexion	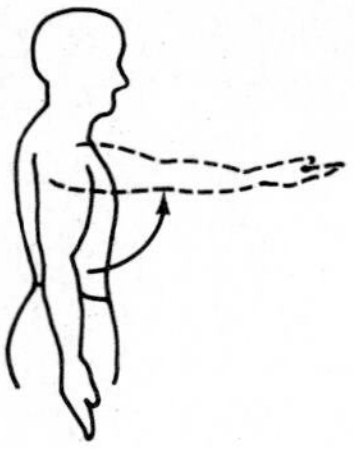	1. Deltoid (anterior fibers) 2. Coracobrachialis	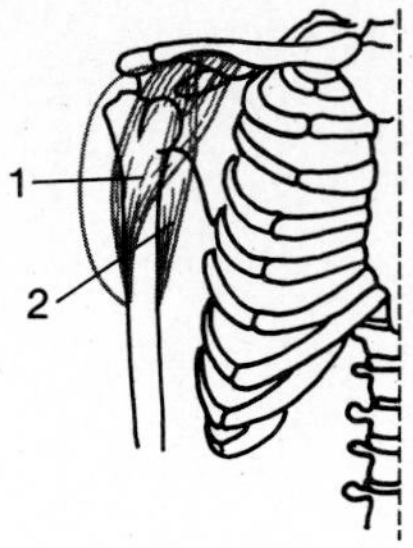

Figure 11.6

fibers of the deltoid and coracobrachialis muscles. Lowering of the arm slowly occurs with the eccentric contraction of the same muscles (see Figure 11.6).

To observe contraction of the anterior fibers of the deltoid, have your partner face you and lift a book with an extended arm. Palpate the deltoid and note the crease that separates the fibers of the deltoid muscle.

Shoulder Extension. Pulling the arm rearward from the shoulder is the result of the action of the latissimus dorsi, teres major, and posterior fibers of the deltoid muscle (see Figure 11.7). The action of these muscles can be observed by standing behind your partner and grasping his/her wrist. The performer should attempt to push the arm rearward against resistance. Palpate the large sheetlike latissimus dorsi and posterior fibers of the deltoid.

Shoulder Abduction. The deltoid muscle is a strong abductor of the arm at the shoulder (Figure 11.8). Multipenniform muscle structures surround the joint capsule, assisting in stabilization. Muscular action can be readily ob-

Shoulder	Movement	Primary movers	Muscle location
Extension	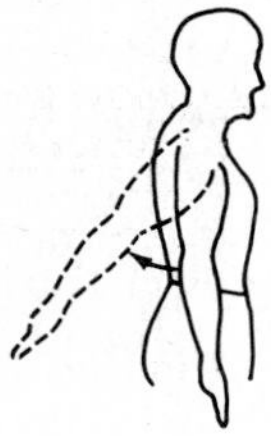	1. Latissimus dorsi 2. Teres major	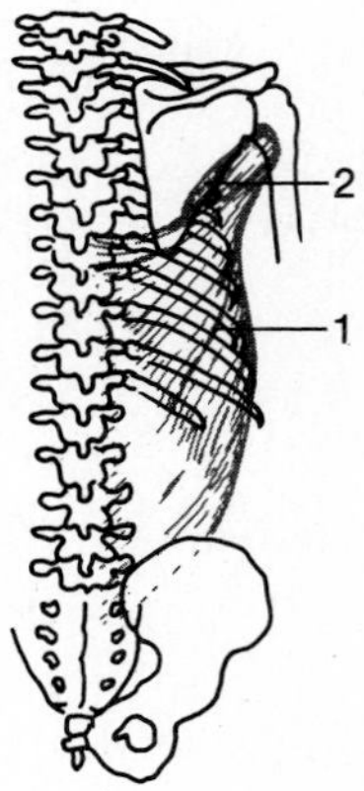

Figure 11.7

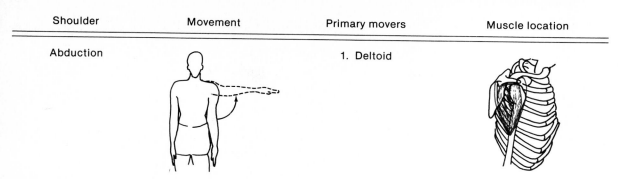

Shoulder	Movement	Primary movers	Muscle location
Abduction		1. Deltoid	

Figure 11.8

served by abducting the arm while holding a weighted object in the hand. The deltoid muscle works during both abduction (concentric) and adduction (eccentric) of the arm in the sagittal plane.

Horizontal Abduction. Abduction of the upper arm when the shoulder is in flexion is called horizontal abduction of the shoulder (Figure 11.9). This motion is frequently encountered during the preparatory phase of sports skills that require rapid arm movements. Horizontal abduction results from contraction of the posterior fibers of the deltoid muscle. The remaining segments of the deltoid act to stabilize the upper arm in a position of flexion.

Palpation of this muscle can be easily accomplished by resisting the motion of the upper arm as it is horizontally abducted. The performer should interlock his/her hands in front of the chest and attempt to pull them apart by moving the upper arm rearward.

Horizontal Adduction. Adduction of the upper arm in the transverse plane is known as horizontal adduction. The pectoralis major, a large fan-shaped muscle covering the anterior chest, is primarily responsible for this movement (Figure 11.10).

The action of the pectoralis major may be observed by placing the palms of the hands together at chest level and pushing with an iso-

Shoulder	Movement	Primary movers	Muscle location
Horizontal abduction	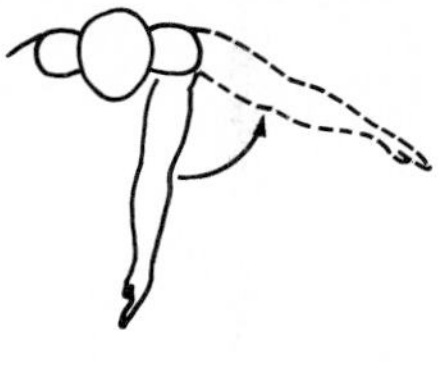	1. Deltoid (posterior fiber)	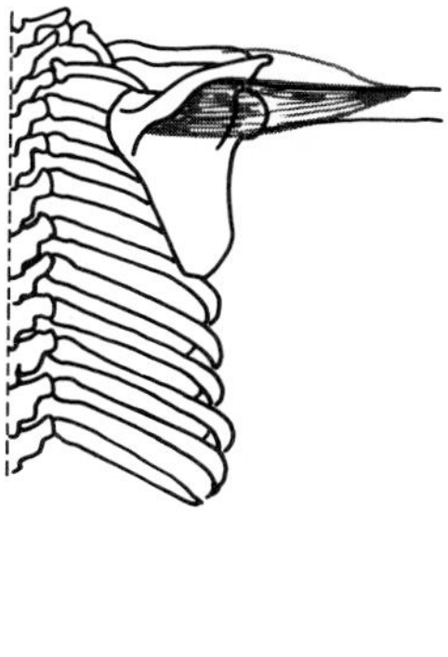

Figure 11.9

Shoulder	Movement	Primary movers	Muscle location
Horizontal adduction		1. Pectoralis major	

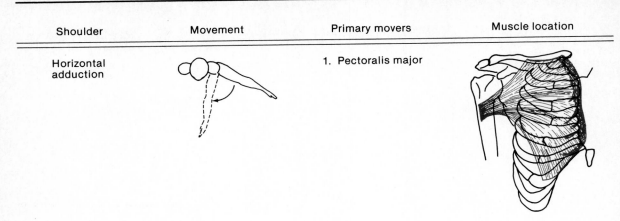

Figure 11.10

metric contraction. Palpate the performer's muscle near the joint and across the anterior chest.

Shoulder Rotation. Lateral rotation (outward) of the humerus is the result of the combined ac- tion of the infraspinatus and teres minor mus- cles (see Figure 11.11). Medial rotation (inward) of the arm results from contraction of the sub- scapularis, which also assists in stabilization of the shoulder joint (Figure 11.12). The muscles

Shoulder	Movement	Primary movers	Muscle location
Lateral rotation		1. Infraspinatus 2. Teres minor	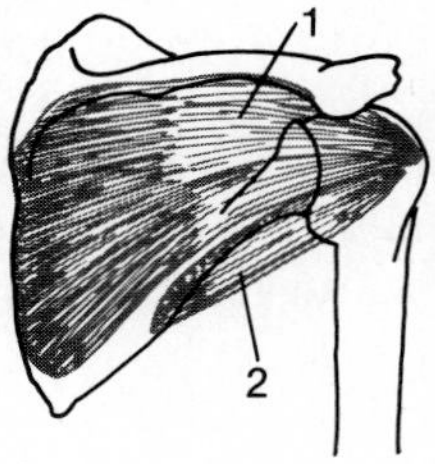

Figure 11.11

Shoulder	Movement	Primary movers	Muscle location
Medial rotation	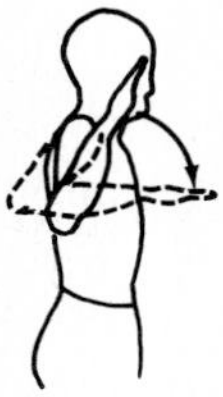	1. Subscapularis	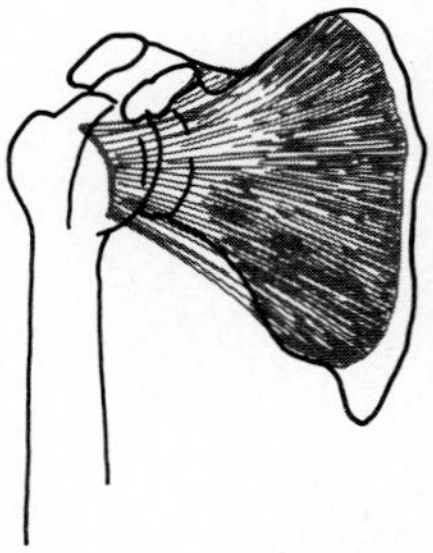

Figure 11.12

that cause lateral and medial rotation of the arm are difficult to observe and palpate during performance of the movements.

Structure of the Elbow Joint

The elbow joint consists of two articulations that allow distinctly different movements. Flexion and extension of the arm occurs at the hinge joint between the humerus and ulna (see Figure 11.13). Pronation and supination of the forearm is possible at the pivot joint between the humerus and radius (proximal radioulnar joint). Both articulations are encased in a common

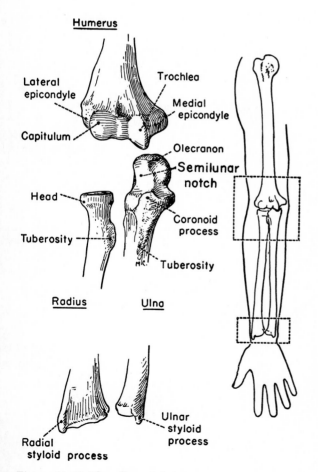

Figure 11.13 The elbow joint.

joint cavity and are surrounded by a strong ligamentous structure. Rotational movements of the forearm also occur at the distal radioulnar joint located at the wrist.

The hinge joint of the elbow allows only flexion and extension, and is frequently injured by excessive stresses resulting from rapid arm movements. Baseball pitchers and tennis players frequently experience stress-related injuries to the elbow. During performance of the overhand throw the elbow is exposed to rotational forces that may cause ligament tears or irritation. An implement such as a tennis racquet increases the lever arm of the forearm and multiplies the stress absorbed by the elbow.

Coaches must carefully consider the single axis of the motion of the elbow when working with the youthful athlete whose skeletal epiphyses have not yet ossified. The young pitcher should be carefully limited in the frequency, duration, and intensity of throwing. Similarly, youthful tennis players should be allowed to utilize a shortened or lightweight racquet so as to reduce stress to the elbow.

Fractures of the bones of the forearm are frequently encountered during athletic participation. These fractures usually result from the extensor thrust reflex that results in the involuntary extension of the arm while falling.

Movements at the Elbow Joint

Elbow Flexion. Decreasing the angle of the elbow joint results from contraction of the biceps brachii and brachialis muscles (Figure 11.14). Located on the surface of the humerus, these muscles are strong flexors of the elbow. The biceps brachii can easily be palpated during resisted flexion of the elbow. The brachialis is hidden beneath the biceps.

Elbow Extension. Straightening of the elbow is accomplished by the contraction of the triceps muscle, which is located on the posterior side of the humerus (Figure 11.15). The physical structure of the triceps and the location of its skeletal attachments make it a strong extender of the elbow. Action of this muscle is easy to

Elbow	Movement	Primary movers	Muscle location
Flexion		1. Biceps brachii 2. Brachialis	

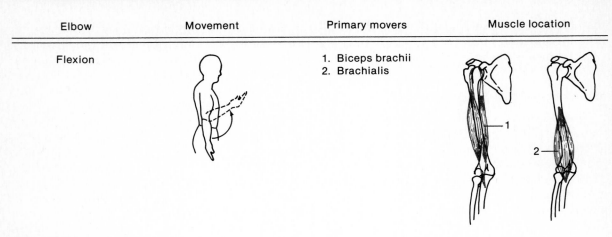

Figure 11.14

Elbow	Movement	Primary movers	Muscle location
Extension		1. Triceps	

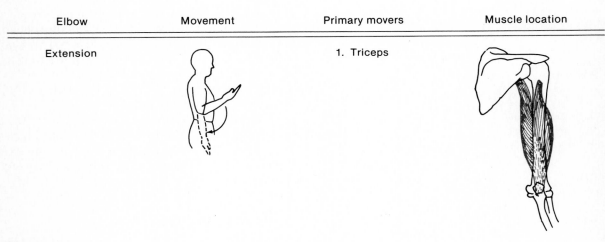

Figure 11.15

identify by providing resistance to your partner's wrist and stabilizing the elbow during elbow extension. Palpate the posterior arm and attempt to locate the various heads of the triceps. The long head is inserted to the lateral border of the scapula and the lateral head is inserted to the upper humerus.

Forearm (Radoulnar Joints) Supination and Pronation. Supination of the forearm involves rotating the radius and ulna so that the palm of the hand faces up. Pronation rotates the forearm so that the palm faces down (Figures 11.16 and 11.17). Muscles involved in supinating and pronating the forearm are difficult to identify by palpation. With your partner's elbow flexed, grasp his/her hand as an attempt is made to supinate (thumb lateral) and pronate (thumb medial) the forearm. Note the actions of the biceps brachii as a supinator and the pronator teres as a pronator of the forearm.

Elbow	Movement	Primary movers	Muscle location
Supination	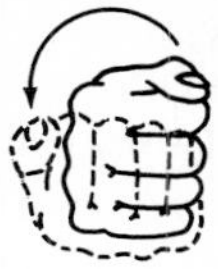	1. Biceps brachii 2. Supinator	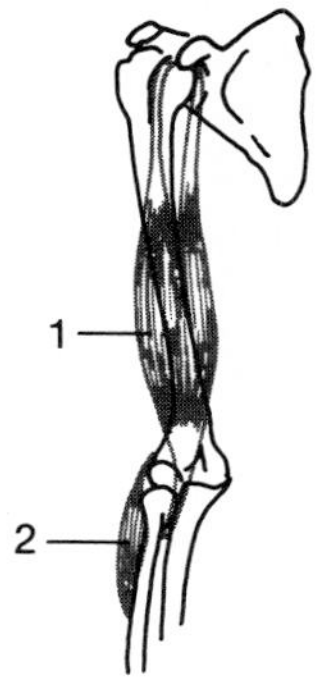

Figure 11.16

Elbow	Movement	Primary movers	Muscle location
Pronation		1. Pronator teres 2. Pronator quadratus	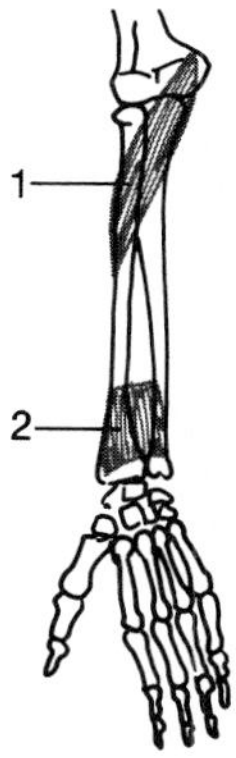

Figure 11.17

Structure of the Wrist Joint

The wrist consists of several articulations that function to allow a wide range of motion. The distal radioulnar joint, which allows for the complete pronation and supination of the hand, articulates with the proximal row of carpal bones. The carpals of the wrist are arranged in two rows of four and the spaces between these bones allow for added range of motion (see Figure 11.18).

The wrist joint is encased in a synovial membrane and is reinforced by a strong ligamentous structure. Injuries to the wrist are frequently associated with strains from overextension of the radiocarpal joint. Fractures often occur across the lower border of both the radius and the ulna when force is applied to a flexed wrist. When the injurious forces are sufficiently great and center at the wrist the carpals may be crushed, fractured, or chipped. This is a painful injury that may require surgical correction.

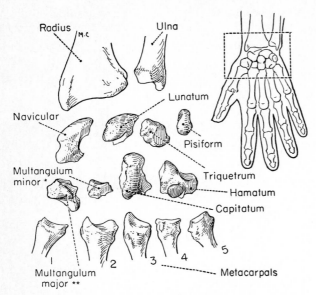

Figure 11.18 Structural components of wrist joint.
*Also called trapezoid. **Also called trapezium.

Movements at the Wrist Joint

The wrist and its multiple articulations allow for a variety of movements, including flexion-extension, abduction-adduction, and circum-duction. The muscles involved in flexion-extension of the wrist also act to assist in producing the other movements of the wrist.

Wrist Flexion. Wrist flexion is caused by contraction of two muscles located on the anterior side of the forearm. The flexor carpi radialis and flexor carpi ulnaris may be palpated when flexing the wrist while applying resistance of the palm of the hand (see Figure 11.19).

Wrist Extension. Wrist extension is produced by the action of the three individual muscles that contract to lift a hand that is in the palm-down position. Located on the lateral border of the forearm, these muscles can be identified as a group, but they are difficult to isolate (see Figure 11.20).

Lower Appendicular Skeleton

The lower extremity is structurally similar to the upper appendicular skeleton. However, articulations of the leg tend to be more stable because of the heavy skeletal structure and the need to absorb the forces encountered during locomotion. The major joints are those at the hip, knee, and ankle.

Wrist joint	Movement	Primary movers	Muscle location
Flexion	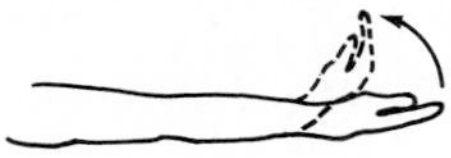	Flexor group 1. Flexor carpi radialis 2. Flexor carpi ulnaris	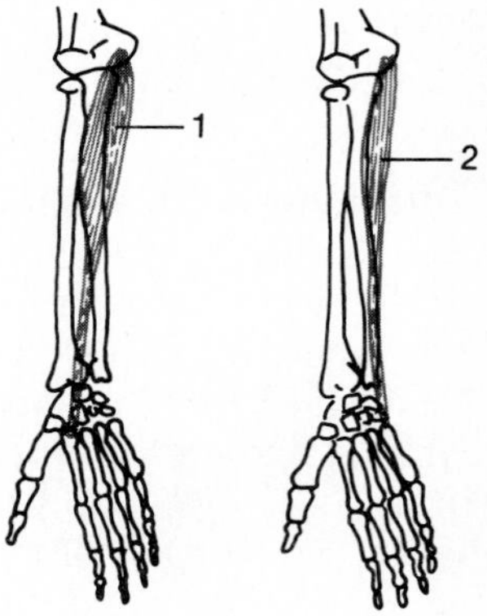

Figure 11.19

Wrist joint	Movement	Primary movers	Muscle location
Extension		Extension group 1. Extensor carpi radialis longus 2. Extensor carpi radialis brevis 3. Extensor carpi ulnaris	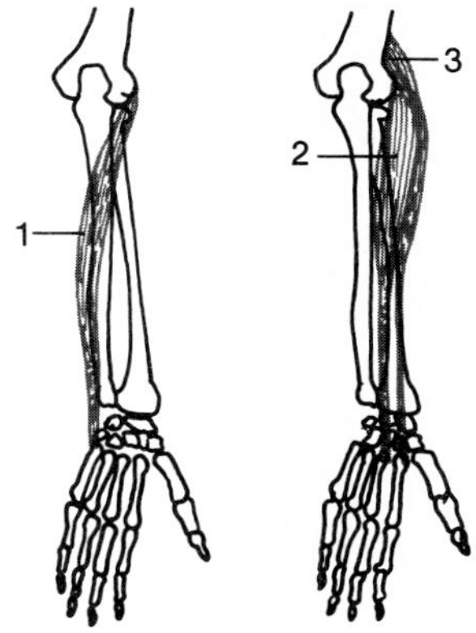

Figure 11.20

Structure of the Hip Joint

The hip is a ball-and-socket joint formed by the semispherical head of the femur and the cup-shaped acetabulum of the pelvis (see Figure 11.21). Although the structure of the hip is very similar to that of the shoulder, its range of movement is somewhat limited. Because of the need to handle the forces of locomotion the socket of the acetabulum is deeper, adding to the structural stability of the joint. Five strong ligaments provide additional support and stability for the hip.

Cartilaginous tissue covers the articulating surfaces of the hip and is most prominent in areas that receive the majority of the pressure of locomotor activities. A synovial capsule encloses the total joint and provides the lubrication needed during joint movements.

The physical relationship between the femur and the pelvis is important during locomotor patterns such as running. Piscopo and Baley (1981) noted that the female's genetically wider pelvic girdle causes a slightly increased inward slant to the femur. This factor may contribute to the difficulty that some female athletes experience when swinging the non–weight-bearing

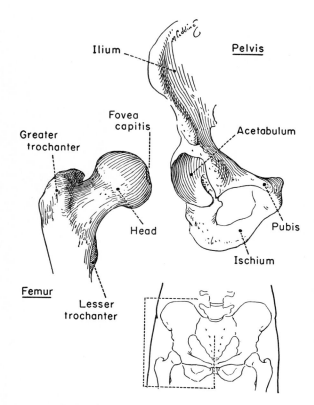

Figure 11.21 Skeletal structure of the hip joint.

leg through while running. Other structural deviations of the hip joint can cause difficulty for athletes. The angle of the neck of the femur in relation to its head and shaft varies and may result in excessive rotary action of the lower leg while running. Also, congenital dislocation at the hip joint can result from an underdeveloped upper rim of the acetabulum that allows slippage of the femoral head while in a weight-bearing position.

Movements at the Hip Joint

Complete range of motion at the hip is an important factor in performance of many sports skills. The movements of the hip are similar to the shoulder and include flexion-extension, abduction-adduction, rotation, and circumduction.

Hip Flexion. Flexion at the hip (see Figure 11.22) occurs in the sagittal plane by contraction of the iliacus and psoas major muscles (commonly referred to as the iliopsoas group). The action of the iliopsoas is difficult to palpate, although the tightness of the contracting muscle can be readily felt. It is suggested that the performer assume a supine position and flex one hip joint. The observer should apply gentle

pressure on the thigh and palpate the contracting iliopsoas.

Hip Extension. Extension of the hip results when the femur is moved rearward in the sagittal plane (Figure 11.23). Frequently, extension of the hip to the neutral position results from the pull of gravity and is controlled by the eccentric contraction of the iliopsoas. Hip extension to the rear results from concentric contraction of the gluteus maximus and hamstring muscle group. The action of the extensors of the hip may be easily palpated. Assume a prone position and lift a straight leg upward. By applying gentle pressure downward on the thigh the action of the muscles may easily be observed.

Hip Abduction. Movement of the leg away from the midline of the body is the result of the contraction of the gluteus medius muscle (Figure 11.24). The gluteus medius is located on the lateral side of the joint, and may be palpated by having the performer lie on his/her side and elevate the upper leg. Slight resistance will require a more forceful contraction and allow for easier identification.

Hip Adduction. Adduction at the hip involves inward movement of the thigh in a frontal plane (Figure 11.25). Adduction results from contraction of three muscles: adductor brevis, adductor longus, and adductor magnus. These

Hip joint	Movement	Primary movers	Muscle location
Flexion (sagittal plane/ lateral axis)	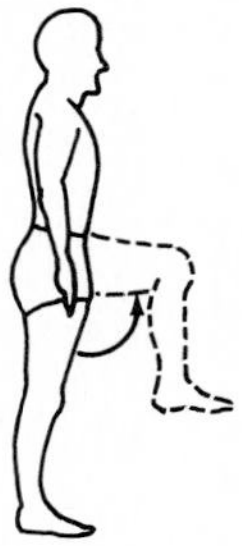	1. Psoas major 2. Iliacus	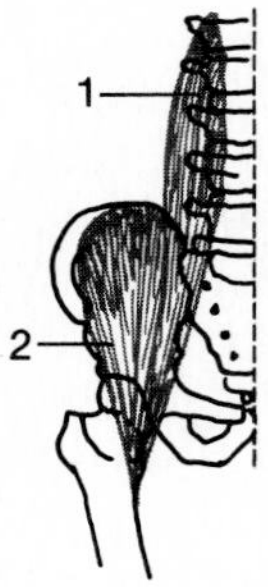

Figure 11.22

Hip joint	Movement	Primary movers	Muscle location

Extension (sagittal plane/ lateral axis)	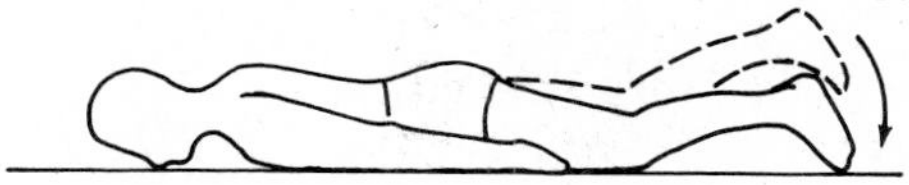	1. Gluteus maximus
		2. Hamstring group
		  A. Biceps femoris
		  B. Semitendinosus
		  C. Semimembranosus
			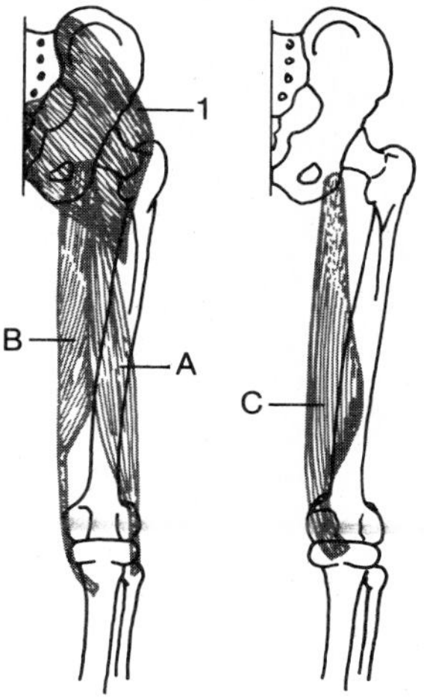

Figure 11.23

Hip joint	Movement	Primary movers	Muscle location
Abduction (frontal plane/ anterior posterior axis)	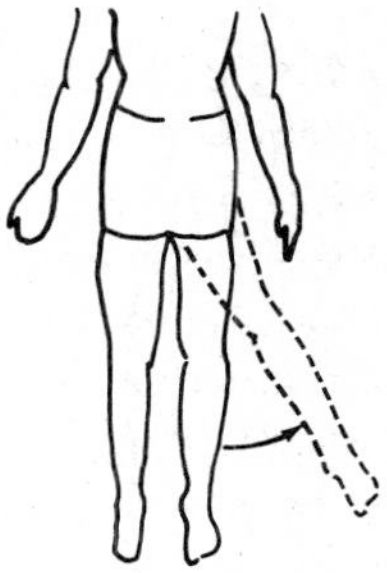	1. Gluteus medius	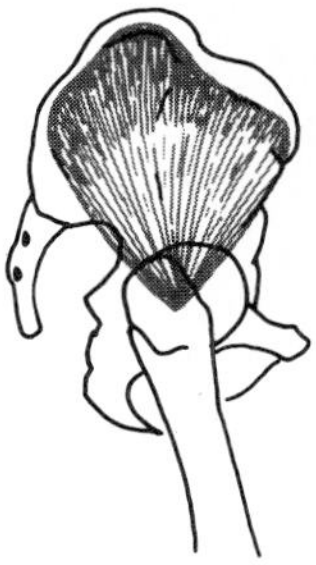

Figure 11.24

muscles work together as the adductor group. Action of the adductor group may be observed by resisting the adduction movement of the thigh.

Structure of the Knee Joint.

The articulating bones of the femur, patella, and tibia form the modified hinge joint of the knee (see Figure 11.26). The knee is the largest joint of the human body and, although relatively strong, it is commonly injured because of its unstable structure.

Coaches should understand the complex physical structure of the knee because this joint is frequently exposed to excessive stress during sports participation. The proximal end of the tibia presents a slightly concave articular surface. Two large condyles of the femur articulate

Hip joint	Movement	Primary movers	Muscle location

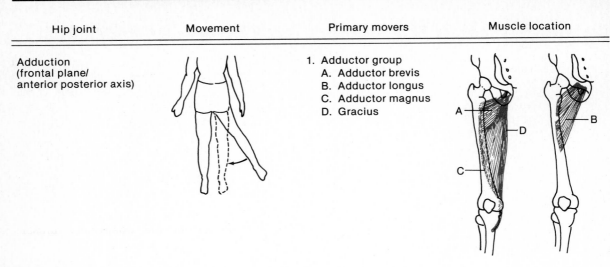

Adduction
(frontal plane/
anterior posterior axis)

1. Adductor group
   A. Adductor brevis
   B. Adductor longus
   C. Adductor magnus
   D. Gracius

Figure 11.25

with the tibia and patella and are surrounded by a strong ligamentous and muscular structure that assists the bones in absorbing the forces encountered during running and jumping. The patella is a floating bone that is suspended in the tendon of the quadriceps muscle. This bone plays a key role in the function of the knee joint. It protects the joint cavity and acts as a fulcrum that increases the mechanical efficiency of the contracting quadriceps muscle.

Located between the articulating surfaces of the knee is a tough cartilage (meniscus) that assists in absorbing the forces exerted upon the joint. Injuries to this crescent-shaped cartilage are relatively common, frequently resulting from excessive rotational forces applied to the joint while it is flexed or from sharp blows to the lateral side of the leg. If the meniscus is split, crushed, or torn it rarely heals and often must be surgically repaired or removed.

The ligamentous structure of the knee is vital to maintenance of joint stability. Cruciate ligaments cross within the joint cavity and function to connect the tibia and femur and to prevent undesired forward and rearward displacements. Sideward stability is provided by collateral ligaments that are located on the medial and lateral aspects of the knee. The anterior and posterior aspects of the joint capsule are stabilized by the popliteal ligament and patellar ligament, respectively.

As the knee moves through its range of motion its stability changes. A completely ex-

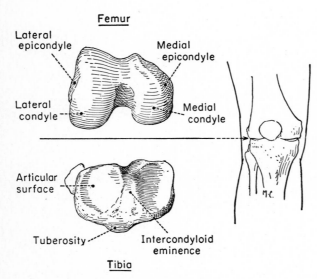

Figure 11.26 Bones of the knee joint.

tended knee is relatively stable because its supporting ligaments are tight. Flexing the knee slackens this ligamentous structure and reduces joint stability.

Injury to the ligamentous structure of the knee can occur even when the joint is in a stable position if the external forces are of sufficient magnitude. The halfback who plants his weight-bearing leg with the knee in the extended position is susceptible to ligament injury because the joint structure may not withstand a powerful lateral blow. Damage can also occur when excessive stress is applied to a knee that is in an unstable position. Although able to absorb great forces while in a flexed position, the knee joint may move beyond its normal range of motion. Swimmers' knee provides an excellent example of such an injury. The breast stroker who applies excessive stress to the knee while kicking with the knee in a flexed position may strain the ligamentous structures of the joint.

Movements of the Knee Joint

Knee Flexion. Decreasing the angle of the knee by pulling the lower leg rearward in the sagittal plane is termed knee flexion (Figure 11.27). Three muscles, biceps femoris, semitendinosus, and semimembranosus, located on the posterior femur, are the primary movers during knee flexion. Referred to as the hamstring muscles, these muscles cross both the hip and knee, but function primarily to flex the knee. Contraction of the hamstrings can be palpated in an individual who flexes one knee while in a prone position. Resistance may be applied behind the ankle to facilitate observation of the hamstring muscle group.

Knee Extension. Extension of the knee results from contraction of the quadriceps muscle group. The quadriceps group includes the rectus femoris, vastus intermedius, vastus medialis, and vastus lateralis. This muscle group is located on the anterior femur and crosses the knee to attach on the tibia (see Figure 11.28). The action of this muscle group may be observed, although it is difficult to isolate the actions of individual muscles. Have your partner sit on a table with the legs hanging over the table edge and the knees flexed. Palpate the quadriceps muscles while the performer extends the knee as resistance is applied to the shin.

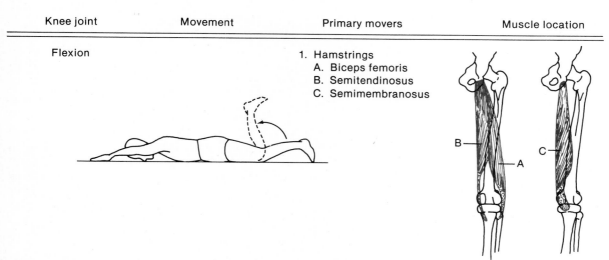

Knee joint	Movement	Primary movers	Muscle location
Flexion		1. Hamstrings A. Biceps femoris B. Semitendinosus C. Semimembranosus	

Figure 11.27

Knee joint	Movement	Primary movers	Muscle location
Extension		1. Quadriceps A. Rectus femoris B. Vastus intermedius C. Vastus medialis D. Vastus lateralis	

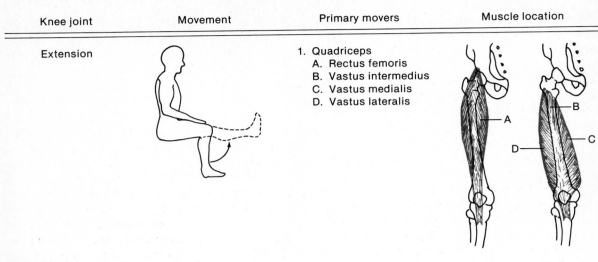

Figure 11.28

Structure of the Ankle Joint

The ankle and foot are important components of the force-delivery system that allows athletes to perform running and jumping movements. The articulating bones of the tibia, fibula, and talus form the hinge joint of the ankle (see Figure 11.29). Articular surfaces are covered with hyaline cartilage and are surrounded by a fibrous capsule.

Because of the extreme forces that are exerted upon the ankle during walking, running and jumping a strong ligamentous structure is important for joint stability. Numerous ligaments support the arches of the foot and reinforce the medial and lateral aspects of the ankle joint.

The anatomy of the ankle joint is relatively strong and rarely is the joint dislocated. Nonetheless, the ankle is very susceptible to athletic injury. An injury that receives considerable attention is spraining or tearing of the achilles tendon. This tendon, which attaches the gastrocnemius and soleus muscles to the heel, is frequently injured by sudden stretching actions. Inflammation of the tendons of the ankle is often encountered during the early stages of training. Specifically, running without proper warm-up and stretching frequently causes irritation to the tendons of the ankle joint.

Sprains of the ankle are usually caused by overinversion of the foot, resulting in a tearing or irritation of the ligaments on the lateral side of the ankle. Fractures of the ankle often result from excessive eversion of the foot, which causes breaks in the proximal ends of the tibia and fibula.

Movements at the Ankle Joint

Ankle Plantar Flexion. Pointing of the toes downward by movement at the ankle joint is termed plantar flexion and results from contraction of two strong muscles that are located on the posterior aspect of the lower leg. These muscles, the gastrocnemius and soleus, can be observed by standing with the feet plantar flexed and the weight on the balls of the feet. The gastrocnemius can be readily observed, but the soleus is somewhat hidden (see Figure 11.30).

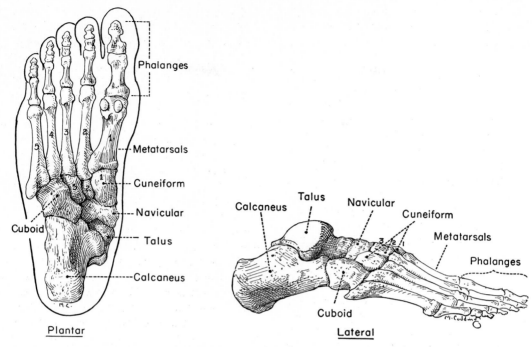

Figure 11.29 Plantar and lateral views of skeletal structure of the ankle joint and foot.

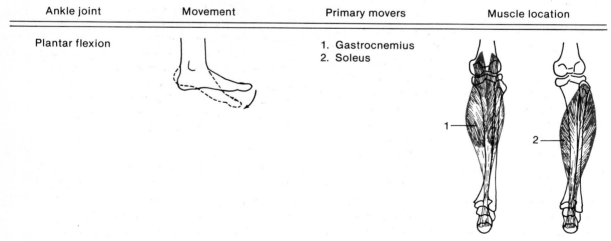

Ankle joint	Movement	Primary movers	Muscle location
Plantar flexion		1. Gastrocnemius 2. Soleus	

Figure 11.30

Ankle Dorsiflexion. Dorsiflexion of the foot lifts the toes toward the anterior aspect of the lower leg, and is caused by contraction of the tibialis anterior muscle (Figure 11.31). Located on the anterior surface of the tibia, the action of this muscle is easily identified by elevating the foot against resistance while palpating the surface of the shin.

Ankle Inversion-Eversion. Inversion and eversion of the ankle involve movements of the sole of the foot inward and outward, respectively (see Figures 11.32 and 11.33). The tibialis posterior muscle inverts the foot and is difficult to palpate because of its location under the gastrocnemius and soleus. Everters of the foot, the peroneus longus and peroneus brevis, are lo-

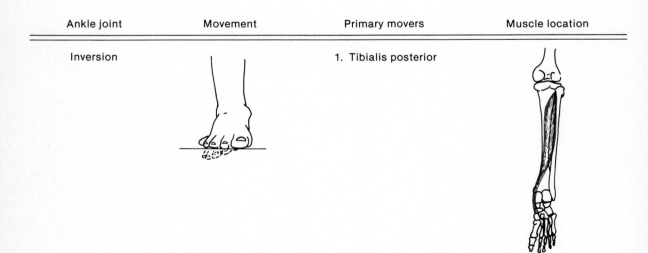

Ankle joint	Movement	Primary movers	Muscle location
Dorsiflexion	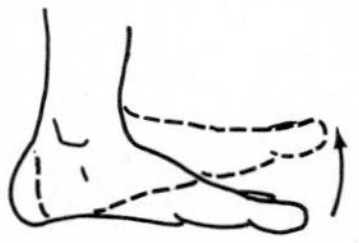	1. Tibialis anterior	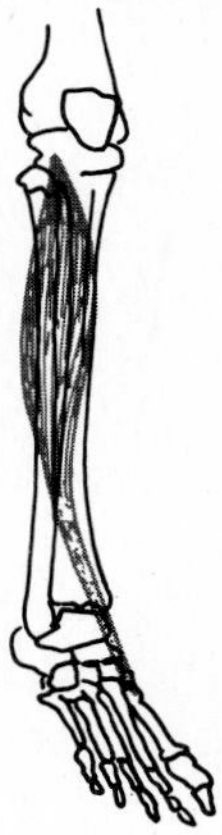

Figure 11.31

Ankle joint	Movement	Primary movers	Muscle location
Inversion		1. Tibialis posterior	

Figure 11.32

Ankle joint	Movement	Primary movers	Muscle location
Eversion		1. Peroneus longus 2. Peroneus brevis	

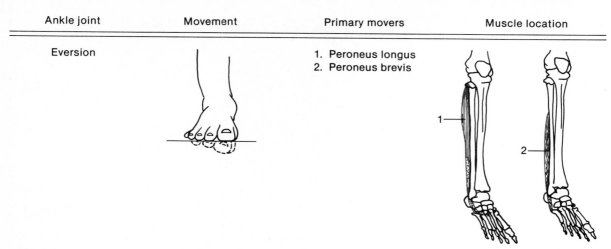

Figure 11.33

cated on the lateral aspect of the leg, and may be palpated when the foot is everted.

Summary

Sports skills involve complex movements of the musculoskeletal structures in the human body. Athletes' levels of performance are frequently restricted by the mechanical limitations of their muscular and skeletal systems. Thus, coaches must possess a fundamental understanding of the anatomical and kinesiological principles that govern human motion. This knowledge allows the coach to provide the athlete with activities that can enhance movement efficiency.

After completing this chapter, the reader should be able to observe the movement of a body segment and understand the skeletal and muscular contributions to that action. This information, if mastered and internalized, can be used by the coach on a daily basis, and can provide a foundation on which many coaching decisions are made.

References

Growitzke, B.A., and Milner, M. *Understanding the Scientific Bases of Human Movement*. Baltimore: Williams and Wilkins Co., 1980, Chap. 4.

Piscopo, J. and Baley, J. A. *Kinesiology*. The Science of Movement. New York: John Wiley and Sons, 1981.

Recommended Readings

Logan, G.A., and McKinney, W.C. *Anatomic Kinesiology*. Dubuque, Iowa: William C. Brown Co. Publishers, 1977, Chap. 5–10.

Luttgens, R., and Wells, K. F. *Kinesiology: Scientific Basis of Human Motion*. Philadelphia: W.B. Saunders Co., 1979, Chaps. 4–6.

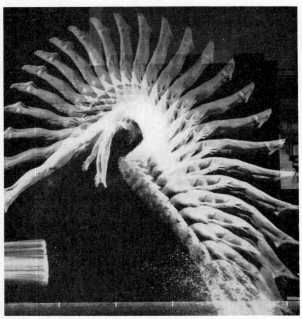

Credit: From Nixon, J. E., and Jewett, A. E. *An Introduction to Physical Education*, 9th ed. Philadelphia: Saunders College Publishing, 1980.

Mechanical Influences on Athletic Performance

12

All human movements are performed in a manner dictated by the principles of physics. Thus, it is essential that coaches become thoroughly familiar with the mechanical factors that influence athletic performance. A mastery of mechanical principles can aid the coach in developing a comprehensive understanding of athletic skills and in designing appropriate and efficient practice techniques for athletes.

Numerous biomechanical studies have been conducted on the major sports skills. Many of these studies have provided knowledge that can improve sports performance if it is applied by coaches and athletes. Unfortunately, far too often research findings have not been effectively communicated to or applied by coaches. The fault for this deficiency lies with both the researcher and the practitioner. In the future it is hoped that researchers will be more willing to interpret their findings for coaches. Likewise, coaches should be more receptive to change and should be better prepared to understand the results of biomechanical research. The purpose of this chapter is to provide the reader with an introduction to the basic principles of biomechanics. A working knowledge of biomechanics is essential to coaching success in the modern sports world.

Laws of Motion

Human motion may be classified as *linear*, when all segments of the body move simultaneously in the same direction, or *angular*, when movement takes place around an axis. As one observes various athletic skills it becomes evident that seldom can a skill be classified as solely linear or angular. Usually, athletic skills involve both linear and angular movements. This combination allows the body to generate increased force. For example, in striking skills (e.g., swinging a baseball bat) the angular motion of trunk rotation (the swing) is combined with the forward horizontal displacement of the body to produce an efficient force generation system. Such combinations of linear and angular actions are common in athletics and make the analysis of sports skills rather complex. The initial step in understanding human movement is to review the laws that govern all motion.

Newton's Laws

During the seventeenth century Isaac Newton formulated three basic laws of motion that explain the principles of why objects move in the manner they do. These laws stand today as the principles that govern human movement and athletic skill performance. Following are summaries of each law of motion and examples of how each law applies to sports skills.

Law of Inertia—A body at rest tends to remain at rest, while a body in motion will tend to remain in motion in a straight line and at a constant rate unless acted upon by an outside force.

Numerous sports require the athlete to start a movement quickly, make changes in direction and speed, and/or stop efficiently. In each instance, the performer must utilize the law of inertia to alter the movement. The sprinter leans forward at the start of a race to overcome the body's tendency to remain stationary. The baseball batter must apply sufficient force to the pitched ball to change its direction, and the runner must slow when changing direction around the bases.

The athlete can overcome inertia more effectively if the skills are performed in a manner consistent with several principles derived from Newton's first law of motion.

Sequential Motion. Sports skills consist of a series of individual body actions that are coordinated to effect a purposeful movement. This combining of actions must be continuous and fluid so that momentum from one body segment can be transferred to the performance of the total movement. A pause between segmental actions decreases efficiency on account of the

loss of momentum generated by the other body segments.

Controlled Action. In any activity in which the individual must alter the direction of movement speed must be controlled. The high jumper must convert horizontal momentum generated in the run-up to vertical movement in order to clear the bar. If the approach is too fast change of momentum will be inadequate and the individual will jump into the bar. The running long jump, however, does not require a change of direction, so the approach can remain fast without negatively influencing performance. In skills that require a rapid change in direction the movement must be performed in a controlled manner.

Momentum. The momentum of an object is a product of its mass and velocity (see Figure 12.1). The football lineman needs a great deal of momentum in order to perform his tasks successfully. It is advantageous, therefore, for a lineman to weigh a great deal (large body mass) and be extremely fast (high velocity). The coach often must determine the specific mass with which individual athletes can perform at their maximum level. For example, each baseball player must determine the bat weight that is optimal for him/her. A bat that is too heavy slows the speed of the swing appreciably; one that is too light lacks sufficient mass to develop optimal momentum.

Law of Acceleration—The velocity of an object is changed (accelerated) at a rate that is directly proportional to the force causing it, in the same direction, and is inversely proportional to the object's mass.

Figure 12.1 Once moving, the momentum of the shot put is greater than the soccer ball because of its greater mass.

In most sports the athlete with the ability to accelerate quickly has an advantage over a slower opponent. The ability to change velocity is dependent upon numerous factors, including the strength and mass of the performer. The ability to accelerate one's body or an object can be improved by considering these principles.

Line of Motion. When attempting to change an object's velocity, force should be applied in the same direction as movement is desired. The sprinter's feet should be placed directly in line with the desired direction of movement (see Figure 12.2). The force generated by the legs should be applied directly rearward. Any misapplication of force causes wasted motion and decreases the rate of acceleration.

Increased Strength. The athlete generates force by contraction of muscles. As an individual's muscle strength increases, the ability to apply force to external objects is enhanced. Coaches should devote considerable effort toward the development of strength in their athletes, particularly those who participate in sports that require rapid acceleration.

Reduced Mass. As the mass of an object decreases, the amount of force necessary to accel-

erate it is reduced. Thus, the athlete who is overweight loses acceleration and speed.

Law of Action-Reaction—For every application of force against a surface there is an equal and opposite reaction.

Sports skills often require the performer to apply a force against a surface. The runner must push against the ground, the batter must have a solid footing and a firm grip, and the basketball player must be able to move quickly down the floor and retain control of the ball. With a basic understanding of the Law of Action-Reaction, the athlete and coach can utilize reaction efforts to their advantage.

Surface. The density of two surfaces plays an important role in the type of reaction that can be expected. The surface to which force is being applied must be firm if the reaction is to be of similar intensity. A soft surface absorbs some force and an equal counter force is not produced. Joggers who run on soft sand find that they must work harder to produce a momentum similar to that which is achieved when running on a firm surface (see Figure 12.3).

Grip. The athlete often finds that grip can play an important role in the type of reaction that

Figure 12.2 In running, the force should be applied directly downward and rearward.

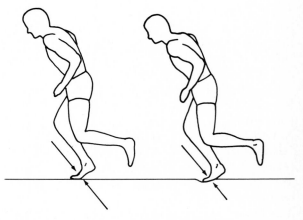

Figure 12.3 Reduced reaction caused by unstable running surface results in decreased efficiency of the run.

can be expected from an object. It is often desirable to use a firm grip when striking an object with an implement so that the momentum of the body can be completely transferred to the object. In other instances, the grip is loosened to produce a "dead" shot, as in the tennis drop shot or when bunting a baseball.

Direction. Reaction occurs in a direction that is opposite to the initial application of force. The athlete desiring to move in one direction must apply sufficient force in the opposing direction. To move forward, force must be applied directly backward. Thus, the golfer must strike the ball in the intended line of flight.

There is no necessity for a coach to memorize these basic laws of motion. Far more useful is a fundamental understanding or "feel" for how these laws apply to specific sports skills. Table 12.1 provides an application of the basic laws of motion to the various phases of the running long jump.

Characteristics of Human Motion

The moving body possesses three general characteristics that exert a profound affect on athletic performance. These factors are velocity, acceleration, and momentum. The relationships between these factors must be considered whenever sports skills are evaluated.

Velocity. The velocity of an object refers to the distance that it moves in a designated period of time. Average velocity is obtained by dividing the distance moved by the time required to perform that action ($\bar{V} = d/t$). When discussing sports performances average velocity has limited value. For example, in track, knowing a runner's average velocity for a mile race provides the coach with little information that can be utilized to guide the athlete in increasing performance. More valuable would be knowledge of velocities taken periodically throughout the race. These "split-times" allow the coach to

Table 12.1: Application of Newton's Laws Through the Phases of the Running Long Jump

	Law of Inertia	*Law of Acceleration*	*Action-Reaction*
Preparatory Phase (Initial run)	The stationary body tends to resist change. Sufficient force must be applied to get the body moving in a forward direction.	The legs should supply sufficient force directly rearward to increase velocity throughout the approach run.	During the approach the jumper applies a force directly rearward. The arms move in opposition of the legs to counteract the rotary action of the legs.
Action Phase (Takeoff and flight)	The horizontal momentum of the body must be converted to an upward direction at takeoff. The speed of the approach run must be sufficient to propel the body in a horizontal direction, yet controlled to allow an appropriate takeoff angle.	The heavier jumper must apply a proportionally greater force than one with a lighter body to propel the body a similar distance.	The takeoff foot should apply a downward force on the takeoff board, propelling the body in an upward direction.
Follow-through Phase (Landing)	The legs extend prior to landing to aid the absorption of the downward momentum of the body.	The body is placed in a position in which the downward force can be absorbed through the joints of the lower extremities, causing a rapid deceleration.	At contact, the ground applies an equal reaction that must be absorbed by the jumpers. The give of the sand aids in absorbing the downward momentum of the body.

interpret the manner in which segments of the race were performed.

Acceleration. Frequently, sports skills require the athlete to make rapid changes in velocity. The sprinter must rapidly increase velocity at the sound of the gun, attempt to maintain a constant velocity throughout the duration of the race, and finally slow the velocity of the run once the finish line is crossed. Acceleration may be defined as the increase in velocity over a given period of time; deceleration denotes the rate at which velocity decreases. In this example, the sprinter accelerates during the initial segment of the race, progresses through a period of no acceleration (no change in velocity), and usually decelerates somewhat prior to the finish. Some sprinters may appear to accelerate near the finish, but this actually is an optical illusion. In fact, such sprinters are simply decelerating less rapidly than their competitors.

Acceleration results from the application of force. Similarly, a counter force must be exerted to decrease velocity. The human body accelerates and decelerates primarily through the forces generated through muscular contraction. Coaches can usually increase the athlete's ability to accelerate by increasing muscular strength, improving body mechanics, and sometimes by reducing body weight.

Momentum. Momentum is defined as the product of an object's mass and its velocity. This property of motion is particularly important when considering participation in contact sports or activities that involve striking an external object. The football lineman's ability to resist the forces of an opponent is a major determinant of the lineman's performance. Thus, football players often increase body mass so as to increase momentum. Excessive weight, however, can negatively influence velocity and thereby reduce momentum. The coach must attempt to balance this weight-velocity figure and estimate an individual's optimal "playing weight."

The "follow-through" phase of many sports skills is important since it aids absorption of the angular momentum of the extremities. A volleyball server continues the downward action of the arm after spiking a ball, and the golfer must continue the path of the club upward after a powerful drive. These follow-through actions allow the performer to decelerate rapidly, moving the limbs without injuring the body tissues.

Force

Force is the energy that is utilized to change the state of motion or shape of an object. This pushing or pulling action can result in an object starting, stopping, or changing direction, depending upon the physical characteristics of the object and the magnitude, point of application, and direction of the force. Most sports skill performances involve movements caused by forces generated by muscle contraction, force of gravity, and/or forces applied by external objects or other individuals.

Gravity acts upon all objects located on the surface of the earth. *Weight* is the measure of this gravitational force. The term *mass* is frequently and incorrectly taken to be synonymous with weight. Mass represents the total amount of matter within an object and its resistance to change (inertia). Although weight and mass represent two different concepts, the coach does not often have to differentiate between the two terms. Since most sports skills are performed upon the surface of the earth, the relationship between mass and weight is consistent; that is, an object that weighs more will have a greater mass (Northrip, Logan, and McKinney 1979).

Muscular contractions are utilized to produce internal forces that control the movements of the body segments. Most movements result from action of numerous muscles, each of which plays one or more of the following roles:

Primary Mover. A muscle whose main function is to cause the desired action.
Antagonist. A muscle that is responsible for the movement opposite to that caused by the pri-

mary mover. For efficient movement when the primary mover contracts, the antagonist must relax.

Fixator. A muscle that contracts to stabilize a joint so a desired movement may be efficiently performed.

Neutralizer. A muscle whose contraction tends to neutralize the action of another.

Lever Systems

The musculoskeletal structure of the human body provides the athlete with a complex system of levers that function importantly in the performance of sports skills. These boney levers are utilized to overcome a resistance or increase the velocity of a body segment.

A simple lever system consists of several components, and the physical arrangement of these components determines a lever's function. A knowledge of levers is essential in understanding the mechanics of human movement. The components of a lever are the following:

Lever Segment. A rigid shaft that transfers a force to a resistance. The lever segment may be divided into two component arms. The portion of the lever between the effort point and the fulcrum is identified as the effort arm, while the resistance arm lies between the fulcrum and resistance point. These lever arms may overlap one another particularly in second and third class levers. In the body, bones serve as lever segments.

Fulcrum. The pivot point around which a lever segment rotates when a force is applied. The joints of the body are fulcrums.

Effort Point. The point on the lever segment at which a force is applied. The sites of muscle attachment are effort points.

Resistance Point. The point at which the line of gravity of the resistance intersects the lever segment.

Levers are classified according to the arrangement of the component parts (see Figure 12.4). The first class lever is characterized by the fulcrum being centered between the effort and resistance. Second and third class levers have the fulcrum located at the end of the lever segment with the effort and resistance interchanged.

A lever is a simple machine that is utilized to gain a mechanical advantage in performing work. Depending upon the type of lever and the arrangement and length of the lever arms, the mechanical advantage of a lever may be increased application of force or increased velocity of a segment. Levers that possess a predominant effort arm allow for the application of increased force, while lengthening the resistance arm results in generating a greater segment velocity.

The human skeletal system consists primarily of third class levers, which are designed for speed. Additionally, many sports skills require the application of force utilizing an implement that lengthens the resistance arm, thereby generating high velocities. The baseball bat, tennis racket, and golf club are all examples of implements that lengthen the resistance arm.

Coaches must be aware that when the resistance arm is lengthened additional application of force is required. Frequently, this results in decreased control and less accuracy. There is little value in placing a long implement in the hands of a weak athlete. A batter with two

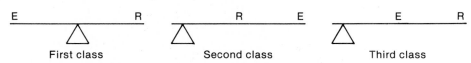

Figure 12.4 Simple lever classification.

quick strikes should shorten the resistance arm by "choking up" to increase accuracy of the swing, although limiting the velocity and force generated by the bat. Similarly, when working with children who do not have sufficient muscular strength to control a regulation implement, smaller and/or lighter implements should be employed. This allows the younger performer to utilize the correct mechanical pattern and aids in the development of proper motor patterns. Additionally, successful experiences encountered with a shortened implement can act as a powerful motivator for continued performance.

Properties of Forces

Forces have certain properties that directly influence human movement. All forces have magnitude, direction, and are applied at a specific point. Optimal performance of sports skills requires that the athlete properly control each of these force characteristics.

Magnitude of a Force. The magnitude of a force exerted by the body depends upon the number, size, and frequency of stimulation of the muscle fibers that are utilized to generate that force. Body segments that are controlled by large muscles (e.g., the legs) can generate and apply greater force than those controlled by smaller muscle groups.

Forces generated by one body segment can be transferred to other segments if the movement is highly coordinated. This transfer of force is an important determinant of skill level in many sports. For example, the baseball pitcher must effectively transfer forces generated by the legs and trunk to the arm during the throwing motion.

Point of Application. The point at which a force is applied to an object is an important determinant of the manner in which the object will move. A force that is applied directly through an object's center of gravity causes the object to move in a line corresponding to the direction of the force. The force of gravity always pulls through the center of gravity of an object toward the center of the earth. Thus, a dropped object falls directly to the ground.

Many athletic skills require the performer to apply a force to an object with a body part or implement. The greatest force can be transferred from one object to another if the impact is concentrated near the object's center of gravity. If the force is applied "off center" the object will tend to spin and change directions.

In some events the application of spin on an object is an important consideration in successful performance. The player of racquet sports can utilize spin to cause the ball to accelerate, decelerate, and change directions in an attempt to deceive the opponent. The defensive football player attempting to tackle a running back may try to hit above or below the ball carrier's center of gravity, causing the ball carrier to rotate to the ground.

Direction. The direction of a force has a major impact on the movement of an object. Movement is usually the result of many forces acting upon a body. The golfer standing on the fairway must consider how all the impinging forces will act on his shot. Factors such as the ball's lie, the wind speed and direction, and the golfer's strength are important considerations in selecting an appropriate club. The direction of the ball's movement reflects the net effect of several forces applied in various directions.

Forces that are applied in the same direction and that have a similar point of application usually produce a resultant force that is equal to the magnitude of the combined forces. Forces that are applied at the same point but in opposite directions have a canceling effect upon each other with movement occurring in the direction of the larger force. For example, a running back who is tackled "head on" will fall forward or backward, depending upon whether the running back or the defensive player applied greater force.

Friction

Friction is the force that opposes the sliding of one surface over another. Frictional forces affect sports skill performances in various ways. The bowler throwing a hooking ball requires sufficient friction between the ball and alley to generate the desired action, while special shoes are worn to reduce friction during the approach. Many athletes utilize special adhesive preparations designed to increase their grip on an implement. Likewise, runners require high degrees of friction between their shoe and the running surface when starting and finishing a race.

The magnitude of the frictional force generated by two surfaces is dependent upon several factors, including the nature of the materials, the shape of the opposing surfaces, the magnitude and direction of the forces causing the surfaces to contact, and the inertia (resistance to movement) of each surface. A basketball coach is particularly interested in the ability of a shoe to grip the court surface, but it must also have sufficient sliding potential to avoid excessively hard stops that may result in injury. Proper material in the sole of the shoe and appropriate surface design can assist in meeting these objectives.

Friction may be classified according to the type of movement that generates the frictional force. *Starting friction* is that force that must be overcome when attempting to displace an object from a static position. This force is particularly important to athletes because it represents the force that allows for a quick change of direction or the ability to initially start the body moving from a stationary position. *Sliding friction* is the force that attempts to stop the sliding action of a moving surface against another. Athletes readily become aware that more force must be generated to overcome starting friction than to keep two similar surfaces moving once started. At times, it is more advantageous to the athlete to keep moving slowly than to completely stop and restart the motion. Frequently, we refer to the individual who momentarily stops as being caught "flat footed" and unable to react to a rapid change of direction.

Two additional classifications of frictional forces directly influence athletic performance.

Rolling friction is a force encountered when a ball moves over a surface. Similar to all other types of friction, the magnitude of the force generated is dependent upon the characteristics of the contacting surfaces. A golfer must adjust the putting force to match the surface of the green, while the soccer player must adjust playing style to meet the characteristics of the turf. *Fluid friction* is encountered when an object moves through air or water. The swimmer wears a special suit and "shaves down" in an attempt to reduce fluid friction. Curve ball pitchers, on the other hand, depend upon friction to assist in forcing a ball to follow a curved path. Fluid dynamics is a complex subject that should be explored in depth by the coach and athlete participating in swimming or in track events that involve throwing for distance.

Pressure

Pressure represents the distribution of a force over a surface area, and is commonly expressed in units such as pounds per square inch (lb/in^2) or kilograms per square meter (kg/m^2). Pressure is a particularly important concept for athletes in contact sports that involve the application of high-intensity forces to an opponent. During participation in a contest an athlete frequently encounters situations in which a force must be efficiently dissipated to prevent injury. Several techniques are commonly utilized by athletes to absorb external forces.

Distribution of Force. An attempt should be made to dissipate a force over a large surface area. The pressure exerted upon the body is directly related to the size of the area of application. A force that is exerted upon a small area is intensified and can easily result in injury to the skeletal and muscular tissues.

Angle Point Collision. Risk of injury from a force can be reduced if the point of application is angled, resulting in a glancing impact. This technique can be best illustrated by the performer that rolls through a fall rather than concentrating the force of impact upon one extended arm.

Dissipate Force Through Joints. Excessive pressure can best be distributed through the joints of the body when these articulations are kept slightly flexed and not locked in position. This allows the force to travel through these joints and be absorbed through the eccentric contraction of the musculature.

Utilize Correct Equipment. Properly designed and fitted athletic equipment can significantly reduce the pressure encountered during participation in contact-related sports.

Projectiles

Numerous athletic contests require performers to project either their body or an object into space. The optimal technique for accomplishing this skill is dependent upon the specific objective of the performance and the rules that govern the contest. Although the motor patterns vary greatly between sports and even between athletes performing the same skill, similar principles govern the trajectory of all projectiles. A basic understanding of the forces that influence nonsupported movement will aid the coach in designing and implementing effective teaching strategies for movements of projectiles.

Four major factors govern the path of a projected object: (1) the speed at which the object is projected, (2) the angle at which the projecting force is applied, (3) gravitational forces influencing the projected object, and (4) the effects of aerodynamic resistance. The athlete must attempt to manipulate the speed and angle of release of an object to compensate for the rather fixed gravitational and aerodynamic forces. Each of these influences must be evaluated when an athlete projects an object into space. The basketball player who pulls up for a jump shot must consider the effects of each of these forces and interpret them into the correct motor response. Similarly, the shot putter must determine which action will result in optimal performance by applying the basic principles that govern nonsupported flight.

Speed of Projection

The speed at which an object is projected, when considered independent of the angle of release, directly influences the distance that the object will cover. Objects that are projected with a greater horizontal force will travel a greater distance before gravity pulls them to the ground. Similarly, the height attained by vertically projected objects is determined largely by the vertical force applied (which establishes the initial speed of movement). The principles are depicted in Figure 12.5.

Force appears to influence both horizontally and vertically projected objects similarly. There is, however, one important difference between the two types of projection. Increased velocity of vertically projected objects not only influences the ultimate height of the projectile but also the amount of time that the object remains in the air. Objects that are projected horizontally are not similarly influenced. Flight time of horizontally projected objects is determined by height at the time of release, but not by speed of projection. Luttgens and Wells (1982) noted that the vertical velocity should, therefore, be emphasized in activities that require maximal time in the air for the performance of intricate stunt patterns. For example, gymnasts and divers benefit from generation of maximal vertical velocity at take-off. Thus, gymnastics and diving coaches frequently cue their athletes to "get good height" in the performance of aerial stunts.

Angle of Release

The horizontal distance that a projectile travels is equal to the product of its horizontal velocity and the time of flight. Only rarely would an athlete have occasion to project an object in exactly a vertical or horizontal direction. Rather, in most instances, the athlete pro-

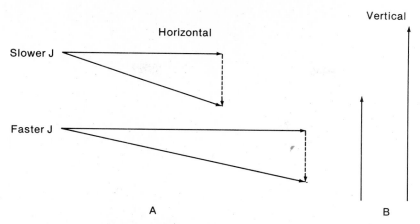

Figure 12.5 Influence of force applied to horizontally and vertically projected objects. (A) Distance increases; time in flight remains the same. (B) Height increases; time in flight increases.

jects an object at an intermediate angle in an attempt to benefit from increased time of flight. The length of time that an object remains in the air is related to the vertical component of the projecting force, while the horizontal force component determines horizontal velocity. Horizontal distance results from a precise balancing of vertical and horizontal force components. Too great a force applied in either direction negatively affects the distance of projection.

The optimum angle of release is dependent upon numerous factors, including the objective of the projection. However, most studies support projecting an object at close to a 45° angle to achieve maximum distance. For example, in many sports accuracy and projectile velocity are of great importance, and in such activities emphasis must be placed upon the horizontal force applied to the object. The athlete must assess the characteristics of flight when aiming a projectile so as to insure that the object will remain in the air for a sufficient period of time to reach its target. Thus, baseball infielders must practice throwing to first base from all locations surrounding their position in order to become

accustomed to the differing force requirements of each throw.

Gravitational Forces

Gravity causes an equal downward acceleration in all projectiles regardless of their mass (32 ft/sec²). This downward pull on an object is a major factor affecting the optimal trajectory of a projectile.

Gravitational force influences all projectiles regardless of their horizontal or vertical velocity. When projected vertically an object continues to travel upward until gravity slows its flight and begins to accelerate it downward. The greater the initial vertical force, the higher an object will travel before being overcome by the gravitational pull. Similarly, the greater its maximum height, the faster its terminal velocity when it reaches the ground.

Objects that are projected horizontally begin to drop the moment support is withdrawn. The projectile's flight time depends only upon the height of release and is independent of horizontal velocity. Therefore, if two objects are released at the same height but with differing horizontal velocities the faster object will travel the greater distance, although both projectiles will remain in the air the same period of time. A baseball pitcher must consider this influence of gravity when throwing pitches of differing velocities. The point and/or angle of release must be adjusted to account for the differing horizontal forces applied to each pitch.

Aerodynamic Resistance and Spin

Many sports require the projection of an object into the air and depend upon the application of spin to add stability to the object's flight or to influence its path. The effects of spin result from the aerodynamic friction of the projectile or the frictional forces resulting from the contact of the projectile with a surface.

As a pitcher releases a curve ball the action of the fingers, wrist, and arm cause a high-velocity spin on the ball. As the ball travels through the air frictional forces are generated between the surface of the ball and the air surrounding the object. Air passes around the ball and is affected by the rotating surface. Figure 12.6 depicts a ball thrown with top spin: Note the air striking the ball below its center makes contact and is quickly accelerated around the object assisted by the spin. Air striking the upper segment of the ball is slowed, disturbed by the spin, and results in increased pressure, causing the ball to accelerate downward at a faster rate than it would be moved by gravity alone.

Spinning objects that strike a surface are affected by forces generated by the rotational

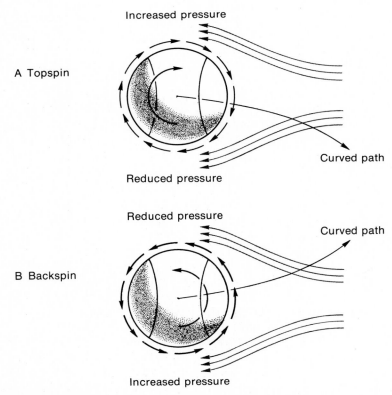

Figure 12.6 Effects of spin and air pressure on the path of a thrown ball.

friction of the object. Tennis players impart various degrees of spin during the serve and ground strokes in an effort to make the ball's path more difficult to follow for the receiving player. An elastic object that strikes a surface at an angle will tend to rebound at a similar angle. Under ideal conditions, the angle of incidence (strike) equals the angle of reflection (rebound). But ideal conditions are rarely encountered, and spin is one factor that influences the manner in which a ball will rebound from a surface. A ball with top spin will tend to rebound with a lower angle and pick up speed; back spin has the opposite effect. The basketball player, golfer, discus thrower, and baseball player all utilize spin in attempting to achieve optimal performance.

Stability

Maintaining a controlled state of equilibrium, regardless of the various internal and external forces acting upon the body, is a fundamental prerequisite to successful athletic skill performance. Stability may be defined as the act of keeping all the forces influencing the human structure balanced. This state of equilibrium is frequently classified as static or dynamic, depending upon whether the individual remains stationary or is moving. Many athletic skills require the performer to momentarily hold a static position prior to initiating movement.

Athletes maintain balance by utilizing the musculature to change the position of body segments so as to keep the center of gravity within the boundaries of the base of support. Maintenance of balance relies upon the positional feedback obtained from the sensory receptors of the nervous system. Numerous proprioceptors provide the athlete with information regarding the position of the body's segments. This process is frequently referred to as *kinesthetic perception*. This valuable feedback is transmitted to the brain, where it is interpreted

and an appropriate movement response is transmitted to the musculature.

Athletes utilize the concept of stability in resisting external forces acting upon the body and in shifting the weight in such a manner to allow for a rapid movement or change of direction. The wrestler concentrates on maintaining a stable posture designed to resist the forces exerted by the opponent, while the gymnast on the balance beam attempts to counter the force of gravity. Each athlete positions the segments of the body in such a manner to resist the external forces and to maintain balance.

Many sports require the athlete to accelerate quickly from a stationary position. When this is required, the performer places the body in an unstable position so that it may easily be thrown off balance, thus initiating the movement. Although allowing for the rapid transfer of weight in one direction, such unstable positions determine movement in other directions. For example, the defender who anticipates the direction of movement of an opponent frequently is caught "flat-footed" when the movement occurs in an unanticipated direction. Athletes must frequently weigh the advantages and disadvantages of placing the body in an unstable position versus the slower more stable posture. The athlete and coach must understand those factors that directly influence stability in order to be able to determine which body position will be most effective.

Center of Gravity

Numerous segmental links are connected together at the joints to form the physical structure of the human body. Each of these segments is affected by the pull of gravity and influences the stability of the total structure. The summation of these gravitational forces is referred to as the mass of an object.

The center of gravity has been frequently defined as the point of an object where the surrounding mass is equally distributed. Locating the center of gravity of the human body is difficult because of its irregular and constantly changing shape. As individual body segments move their relationship to the total body mass changes and modifies the position of the center of gravity.

When the standard anatomical position is assumed the location of the center of gravity is centered within the body at approximately the level of the lumbar vertebrae. The exact position of the center of gravity varies according to body build, age, and gender. Females tend to have a slightly lower center of gravity than males as a result of their wider pelvic structure. Some authors have suggested that this lower center of gravity tends to slow the female performer, making her less able to compete with male counterparts in sports that require speed. Broer and Zernicke (1979), however, noted that the actual difference in the height of the center of gravity is only slight and should represent no significant difference between male and female performers. Children tend to have a proportionately higher center of gravity because of the larger percentage of body weight concentrated in the head. With maturity, the child's body size rapidly increases, while the head size develops at a much slower rate, lowering the center of gravity. Young children frequently experience difficulty with sports such as gymnastics that rely heavily upon stability.

The ability to change the position of the center of gravity relative to the position of the body segments is an important factor in successful athletic skill performance. In many sports success depends on adjustment of stability to meet rapidly changing environmental demands. The skilled running back in football must change from a very stable posture when entering the line to an unstable but rapidly accelerating one once in the defensive backfield. Likewise, the volleyball player who sets the ball on one volley and dives for a dig on the next set possesses the ability to change stability in accordance with the demands of the contest. Optimal performance requires that such athletes anticipate needed shifts in body weight so as to allow suf-

ficient time to perform the muscular adjustments necessary. Frequently, we refer to these athletes as possessing a good "sense" or "feel" for the game.

In some athletic skills the center of gravity must be shifted consistently in a closed movement pattern. For example, the tennis server must shift the weight forward in order to generate the required force necessary to complete a good service. Similarly, the golf drive demands a transfer of the center of gravity forward as the club head begins to move forward.

Changing the position of the center of gravity during the performance of sports skills frequently contributes to the effectiveness of the action. Thus, coaches of developing athletes are well advised to provide these young performers with a sound background in the principles of stability.

Principles Governing Stability

Several fundamental principles govern the maintenance of stable body positions. The following basic concepts will be helpful in mastering these principles:

Line of Gravity. An imaginary line that represents the vertical pull of gravity. This force vector passes through the center of gravity and is an important determinant of stability.

Base of Support. An area representing the surface over which the total body weight is distributed. It is important to note that when supported by more than one segment, this area not only includes the points of contact with the surface but all the area enclosed within these supporting surfaces. The size and shape of the base of support are important variables in maintaining stability.

Stable/Unstable/Neutral Stability. Stability of the human body is frequently classified according to its ability to resist forces intended to upset balance. The individual who assumes a very stable position must actually be lifted to be thrown off balance, but an athlete with an unstable posture may easily be disturbed by a small external force. The primary difference between these classifications of stability is noted in the action of the center of gravity when a force is applied to the object. A stable object's center of gravity must be lifted, while an unstable object's center of gravity immediately begins to fall when stability is disturbed. Rarely does the body assume a position of neutral stability when a force causes no vertical displacement of the center of gravity.

Numerous factors influence the static and dynamic stability of the athlete. Coaches should carefully analyze the stability skills necessary for successful competition in their sport. Frequently, small changes in body position can assist the athlete in gaining an advantage over an opponent. Following is a discussion of the key factors that affect body stability.

Location of the Center of Gravity. The position of the center of gravity in relation to an object's base of support is an important variable in maintaining stability. Greatest stability exists in all directions when the line of gravity passes through the center of the base of support.

The line of gravity must pass within the boundaries of the base of support for an object to be balanced. As this line moves closer to the edge of the base the object becomes increasingly less stable in that direction while increasing stability in the opposite direction. In the performance of athletic skills an individual often requires greater stability in one particular direction. This may easily be attained by shifting the body weight (center of gravity) toward that direction and/or by modifying the size and shape of the base of support. Thus, a football player who prepares to tackle a runner must shift the body weight and foot position to successfully counter the oncoming force.

The position of the line of gravity within the base of support also directly affects an individual's ability to move from a static position. An athlete who desires to move in a given direction

should shift body weight in that direction. A defensive basketball player learns to anticipate another player's action and may lean in an attempt to intercept a pass. It is important for the coach to understand that although an athlete can initiate movements more quickly and absorb greater forces simply by shifting the body weight, there are some disadvantages to this stability. Increasing stability in one direction decreases stability in the opposite direction, making the athlete vulnerable to unexpected forces. Similarly, leaning forward makes it difficult to move rearward. An athlete who makes a commitment to move in one direction will find it difficult to change direction. Successful faking relies upon the athlete's ability to force an opponent to lean in one direction and then to move in the opposite direction. The defensive player who is caught with the center of gravity shifted in the wrong direction loses valuable time in repositioning the body mass. This repositioning of the center of gravity often results in the offensive player gaining the important "step" on an opponent.

Lower the Center of Gravity. Stability of an object increases as the center of gravity is lowered toward the base of support. As the height of the center of gravity increases, the stability of an object decreases proportionally. The greater the distance between the center of gravity and the base of support, the less an object must be displaced before balance is disturbed. Individuals who participate in contact sports must quickly learn that increased external forces can be absorbed without loss of stability if the body weight is lowered prior to contact.

When rugby players form a scrum they attempt to get their body weight as low as possible while still allowing for efficient leg action. This example highlights an important disadvantage to lowering body mass; namely, loss of mobility. As the center of gravity is lowered it becomes increasingly difficult to shift body weight quickly and to initiate movement. In sports that require relatively fast actions there is only a limited advantage to lowering body mass. Coaches frequently must determine which component, stability or mobility, should be most emphasized by an athlete.

Size and Shape of the Base of Support. Stability of an object is dependent upon the size and shape of its base of support. Stability of an individual can be increased by modifying the size and shape of the supporting base. When the athlete is supported by two or more segments the base of support is defined as the area enclosed by those points of contact. Increasing the distance from the line of gravity to the outside border of the base of support in a given direction will increase stability in that direction. For example, the baseball player who prepares to receive a ball thrown at high velocity should move the feet in such a manner as to lengthen the base of support in the direction of the throw. There are several disadvantages to gaining stability by modifying the base of support. These may include decreased mobility and reduced stability in other directions.

Increased Weight. Other factors being equal, the object with a larger mass has greater stability than an object of similar size that weighs less. Heavy objects are more resistant to the influence of outside forces than lighter counterparts. Thus, in athletic events that require stability weight is an important consideration. A large increase in weight, however, is often followed by a decrease in an individual's ability to accelerate the body. The coach often has to weigh the advantages of increased stability against a loss of speed. Selection of a correct "playing weight" is important to successful performance in many athletic events.

Increased Friction. The greater the friction between an object and its supporting surface, the greater its stability. In many sports athletes can improve stability and performance by increasing friction with the surface that supports the body. The basketball player wears specially designed shoes and the golfer utilizes spiked shoes to promote maintenance of stability. This improved contact with the surface makes body adjustments easier, thereby aiding in the maintenance of equilibrium. The athlete without adequate "footing" often must change the mechanics of skill performance, thereby decreasing accuracy and efficiency.

Summary

Principles governing human motion, force, and stability directly influence the manner in which we move. A coach with a basic understanding of these concepts can assist the athlete in making changes in performance designed to increase success. Athletes should be provided with the reasons for performing a skill in a particular manner so they may further understand the mechanical factors influencing a movement. Armed with this understanding, the athlete will better be able to modify a performance to meet the changing environmental demands of the sport.

References

Broer, M.R., and Zernicke, R.F. *Efficiency of Human Movement*. Philadelphia, W. B. Saunders Co., 1979.

Luttgens, K., and Wells, K.F. *Kinesiology: Scientific Basis of Human Motion*. Philadelphia: W.B. Saunders Co., 1982.

Northip, J.W., Logan, G.A., and McKinney, W.C. *An Introduction to Biomechanic Activity of Sport*. Dubuque, Iowa: William C. Brown Co. Publishers, 1979.

Recommended Readings

Gowitzke, B.A., and Milner, M. *Understanding the Scientific Bases of Human Movement*. Baltimore: The Williams and Wilkins Co., 1980.

Hay, J. *The Biomechanics of Sport Techniques*. Englewood Cliffs, New Jersey: Prentice-Hall, Inc., 1978.

Kreighbaum, E., and Barthels, K. M. *Biomechanics: A Qualitative Approach for Studying Human Movement*. Minneapolis: Burgess Publishing Co., 1981.

Piscopo, J., and Baley, J.A. *Kinesiology: The Science of Human Movement*. New York: John Wiley and Sons, 1981.

Developmental Influences on Athletic Skill Performance

13

An individual's ability to successfully perform complex athletic skills is determined by an intricate interaction between genetic and environmental influences. *Physical growth* involves increases in body size and corresponding changes in the various systems of the body. Rate of growth is dependent upon two main factors: (1) increase in the total number of cells, and (2) enlargement of individual cell size by the addition of intracellular materials. Environmental factors influencing an individual are numerous. From early intrauterine life to old age, the human organism learns by exploring and interacting with the environment.

Development is a process that results from anatomical changes associated with maturation. It is generally accepted that a person inherits many genetic traits that, *in toto,* establish potential for athletic performance. The extent to which this potential is realized, however, is strongly influenced by the developmental process. The tall basketball player and 98-pound wrestler both are able to participate successfully in their respective sports partially as a result of genetic endowment. The success of each athlete, however, depends upon the skill level that has been attained through learning. Genetic endowment alone rarely results in athletic success.

Knowledge of human growth and development is utilized by professionals in many fields to evaluate an individual's maturational level and ensure that learning experiences are developmentally appropriate. Coaches at all levels can utilize developmental information to design practices that are maturationally appropriate and to guide in the selection of proper competitive experiences. Information obtained from cross sectional and longitudinal studies also provides the coach with valuable information on the acquisition of sports-related skills.

The Developmental Process

Human development has frequently been divided into several developmental stages.

Likewise, developmental phenomena have been categorized into behavioral domains. Although this approach is helpful in conceptualizing the developmental process, it fails to accurately represent the complex and integrated nature of human behavior. It is important that the coach consider the "whole" athlete when designing and implementing an individual's sports program.

Stages of Development

Most developmental theories are based on the premise that with aging an individual progresses through a series of sequential stages in which physical characteristics change and new skills are learned and refined. Maturation results in increasingly complex behavior as individuals broaden their abilities, increase their level of function, and become more skilled.

At a particular stage of development all children exhibit similar generalized behaviors, although each child represents a unique genetic endowment and set of experiences. These common characteristics allow the coach to become familiar with the sequence in which an athlete's abilities are refined and developed. Table 13.1 lists the stages commonly utilized to classify development and indicates the approximate age range of each stage.

Prenatal Period. Growth and development during the prenatal period is generally divided into three major stages: pre-embryonic (conception to two weeks), embryonic (two to eight weeks), and fetal (eight weeks to birth). The fertilized ovum requires approximately 38 weeks to grow from microscopic size into a newborn infant with an average weight of 6½ to 8 pounds and length of 19 to 21 inches.

During the prenatal period the developing organism is highly dependent upon and affected by the maternal and intrauterine environment. Although a coach has no influence during this period, the genetic traits established and the numerous environmental influences encountered during intrauterine life have a far-reaching influence upon the total individual, including the ability to perform athletic skills. The effects of maternal age, nutrition, and general health are factors that can directly or indirectly influence the developmental process. Also, various drugs taken by the mother can cause adverse effects in the developing fetus. Similarly, numerous birth-related traumas can damage the neurological system of the developing child and negatively affect the acquisition of motor skills.

The initial two weeks of prenatal growth are characterized by rapid cell division as the zygote travels down the fallopian tube and becomes implanted in the uterine wall. As early as the fourth week, cells begin to differentiate into the various organs, systems, and specialized tissues of the body. In the midfetal stage the fetus lengthens and gains weight at an accelerated pace in preparation for birth.

Infancy. The period of infancy begins with the violent and frequently traumatic experience of birth. A fetus is forced from a stable, fluid intrauterine life into the cold, harsh external environment. There the newborn must make a rapid physiological adaptation to an extrauterine existence.

The next two years are characterized by rapid physical growth, increased behavioral development, and a newly acquired social responsiveness. Systems of the body mature and readily adapt to new environmental demands. Over a two-year period an infant gains approximately 20 pounds of weight and increases 13 inches in length. The rate of physical growth is not equal in all body segments, and thus phys-

Table 13.1: Stages of Human Development

Stage	Approximate Age Range
Prenatal	Conception to birth
Infant	Birth to 2 years
Childhood	2 to 10 years
Adolescence	10 to 18 years
Adulthood	18 to death

ical proportions tend to change. The extremities tend to grow more rapidly than the trunk and head.

As the child progressively gains voluntary control over the musculature and is able to move freely within the environment his social world expands. No longer is the mother the only individual in a child's life. Interactions with peers become increasingly significant.

Childhood. Physical growth slows as the proportions of the body continue to change during the childhood period. The extremities lengthen in relation to the trunk and the head reaches its mature size. Frequently, the child's walking pattern is irregular and posture is poor. Height and weight measurements vary among children of similar age as the physiological systems of the body continue to develop. Social and emotional skills are refined as the child acquires expressive language and places value on interactions with others. Moral judgment and behavior are frequently guided by the consequences of the action.

Adolescence. The adolescent period is marked by the onset of puberty and the resulting growth spurt. Females reach puberty younger than males and achieve their maximum rate of growth approximately two years earlier. Although delayed, in males the peak growth rate is higher than for females. Hormonal influences increase the physical differentiation between the sexes as males increase in muscle mass and females tend to accumulate additional fat. These changes can dramatically affect performance in certain sports.

The rapid change in physical size and proportions of the body often results in difficulty with coordinating the actions of the extremities. Changes in height and weight may upset stability and cause a previously skilled child to appear clumsy.

Socialization is centered upon independence and exploration of sexual identity. The need to be associated with peers becomes increasingly important as the child conforms to the group for acceptance.

Adulthood. Physical growth slows and the mature adult achieves peak physical prowess and then gradually loses functional capacity. Body weight frequently increases and compounds the degeneration of the musculoskeletal system. The individual's life centers around a job and family, while recreation is concentrated on several selected activities.

Behavioral Classifications of Development

Human behavior has been traditionally subdivided into three major classifications, termed the cognitive, affective, and psychomotor domains. Successful athletic performance depends upon achieving competence in each behavioral domain. Not only must motor skills be efficiently performed (psychomotor), but the athlete must have a thorough knowledge of the game (cognitive), and possess the ability to effectively control emotions and interact with teammates (affective). Following are more detailed descriptions of the three behavioral domains:

Cognitive Behavior. The behavior domain that includes activities that require the athlete to utilize intellectual abilities. The learning of rules, development of game strategy, planning motor acts, and efficient utilization of learned information are examples of cognitive behaviors associated with athletics. Cognitive activities may range from the simple recall of information to highly organized interpretation and the synthesis of information.

Affective Behavior. The behavior domain that includes the feelings and emotions of the athlete, including the individual's ability to socially interact with teammates. Affective skills can range from simple emotions to complex social interactions.

Psychomotor Behavior. The behavior domain that is associated with the receipt of perceptual information and the ability to initiate an appropriate motor response resulting in a movement. Psychomotor skills range from involuntary reflexive actions to performance of highly coordinated sports skills.

It is important to reinforce the concept that the performance of motor skills is an integrated process requiring behaviors in each developmental domain. The athletes' developmental levels and the particular sport dictate the emphasis that should be placed upon practicing skills in each behavioral classification. Youth sports require that concentrated effort be directed toward refinement of motor skills, while college athletes should place greater emphasis upon the refinement of cognitive strategies. Affective behavior is similarly influenced by the type of sport in which the athlete is engaged. Team sports involve different emotions, attitudes, and feelings than are encountered when participating in an individual sport such as wrestling or tennis. Coaches must evaluate the behavioral demands of a sport and attempt to provide the athlete with developmentally appropriate activities designed to assist in the acquisition of the skills necessary to experience success.

Principles Governing Growth and Development

Numerous principles govern the manner in which an individual grows and develops. Although most of these principles relate directly to the early stages of development, they often indirectly influence the acquisition of new or unique motor skills later in life. These principles can aid the coach in understanding how skills are refined from simple involuntary actions to highly coordinated sports skills.

Developmental Direction. Motor skills are acquired in a progressive and orderly manner. The newborn's movements are stimulated by the child's environment and are primarily reflexive in nature. As the child ages and the neu-

rological system matures progressive voluntary control over the musculature is developed. Perceptual information is integrated into the motor system as additional body actions are refined into complex movement patterns.

Control over the neuromuscular system is refined from the head toward the feet (cephalocaudal) and from the center of the body outward toward the extremeties (proximodistal). Some evidence suggests that movements in certain planes (directions) require higher levels of motor control. For example, shifting of body weight forward and rearward appears to be a relatively easy task when compared with a twisting action of the trunk.

The principle of developmental direction can be readily demonstrated when observing a young child throw and catch a ball. Early attempts at throwing are performed with little trunk rotation, while the skillful pitcher utilizes this action to contribute significantly to the generation of force. Similarly, first efforts at catching usually utilize the arms to surround the ball because the child has not developed the fine motor control needed to use the hands in catching.

Even the coach who works with highly skilled athletes can utilize the principle of developmental direction to design an observational strategy to evaluate the qualitative aspects of a skill performance. The coach attempting to determine why a batter has fallen into a slump should initially concentrate on the more complex actions of twisting the trunk and movements of the hands and feet prior to observing other aspects of the skill. Frequently, the difficulty can be quickly identified by a skillful observer and corrective strategies can be implemented.

An additional concept frequently classified under the principle of developmental direction indicates neuromuscular control over the large muscle masses precedes the acquisition of fine motor control. It is generally accepted that during the beginning phases of learning sports skills emphasis should be directed toward mastering gross actions prior to refining more specific movements.

Individual Differences. As previously mentioned, both physical growth and development are influenced by numerous factors that differ from one individual to another. It must be expected, therefore, that the rate of maturation will be unique for each individual. Although many authors have attempted to identify ages at which specific motor behaviors should be observed, these efforts, at best, provide the observer with a generalized guide to the sequential pattern of development.

A coach must be careful not to make the assumption that all athletes are developmentally capable of executing a complex motor skill based on the performance of their peers. A group of adolescents may have members that represent a wide variance in maturational readiness and skill ability. It is important for the coach to ensure that expectations for each athlete are developmentally obtainable and based upon a realistic perception of the child's level of ability.

Critical Periods. An early study by McGraw (1935) supported the theory that the maturing child passes through *critical periods*. During these periods specific behaviors are most susceptible to change through experience. There appears to be no one optimal age for learning, but rather there are numerous periods when certain behaviors can be easily acquired. Learning experiences provided to the child prior to such a period of development or significantly after its onset tend to have a reduced influence upon learning.

Studies conducted on the acquisition of motor skills reinforce the premise of critical periods. The developmental stage of childhood appears to be an important time for refining and coordinating the foundational movements necessary for later sports skill development. Children whose opportunity to participate in early play experiences is limited will tend to

have difficulty acquiring higher levels of motor performance. The recent improvement in the level of skill of female athletes can be attributed to some degree to the increased opportunity for girls to participate in play-related experiences that promote development of fundamental motor skills.

The theory of critical periods reinforces the value of a well-designed elementary physical education program to the interscholastic athletic program. Increased numbers of children from these programs will possess a foundational skill level on which to develop the sports skills necessary to successfully participate in higher level competitions. Early experiences in movement should be general in nature and should be presented in a play environment. These early activities should not be directed to one sport. Inappropriate competition introduced into the learning of early movements can cause many children to withdraw from the activity.

Maturation Versus Experience. As previously mentioned, a child's growth and development are subject to the combined influences of maturation and environmental experiences. Early developmental patterns result from a process that is primarily genetically determined. Later skills, however, tend to be the result of a child's experiences, although the child must possess the fundamental skills necessary to acquire the more advanced behavior.

Motor skills are frequently classified according to their dependence upon genetic or environmental factors. *Phylogenetic* skills tend to appear automatically and result primarily from the aging process. A coach has little influence over the acquisition of phylogenetic skills, since they appear early during the developmental process and are not directly influenced by instruction.

Ontogenetic skills, however, are those behaviors that are strongly influenced by experience. Sports skills, regardless of level, are ontogenetic in nature. It is important to note that although ontogenetic skills are acquired through environmental influences, the acquisition of these skills is still heavily dependent upon the maturation readiness of the learner. Frequently, our desire to have children play within "regulation" rules results in learning experiences that are not developmentally appropriate. For example, having eight-year-old children play basketball on a full-sized court with a regulation ball and a 10-foot basket causes the performer to distort the motor patterns associated with the game. The outcomes of this practice may be: (1) the performer becomes frustrated by continued failure and ultimately loses interest in the sport, or (2) incorrect movement patterns are reinforced and negatively influence later skill development.

Coaches working with athletes at all developmental stages need to ensure that the experiences that they provide are appropriate. Concentration upon advanced skill development or high-level competition too early will result in many children withdrawing from the sport because of a fear of failure. Emphasis must be placed on experiences that are designed in accordance with the readiness of each athlete.

Genetic and Environmental Factors Influencing Growth and Development

Rarely can an aspect of human behavior be directly attributed to one factor. To the contrary, human behaviors result from the interaction between various influences. The complexity of the maturational process makes the task of predicting athletic success exceedingly difficult. Often, the preadolescent with apparently athletic potential matures into a skilled performer. The numerous factors that influence an individual's growth and development can be classified as genetic or experiential in nature.

Genetic Endowment. At the moment of conception the human organism receives a total of 23 chromosomes from each parent. The genes located on each chromosome determine many of the individual's characteristics. Among these inherited characteristics are numerous factors (e.g., height, body type) that can influence an athlete's ability in specific sports. Although an individual's genetic characteristics play only a limited role in determining whether he/she participates in sports, they are a major influence on the types of activities in which success can be achieved.

It is a common belief among many coaches that some children inherit a "natural ability" for participation in athletics. Also, many believe that these gifted athletes have an advantage over other children in learning motor skills and obtaining a high level of skill proficiency. So-called "general motor ability tests" were designed and utilized by physical educators and coaches in an attempt to identify children who possess this natural ability for athletic performance. However, the theory of general motor ability has not stood the test of time. Numerous studies conducted on the topic have concluded that sports performance is highly specific and that there is no such thing as an all-around, "natural athlete." This conclusion, however, does not mean that individuals do not inherit a predisposition toward success in a *particular* sporting activity. Certainly, this can be the case.

A child's ultimate physical size and growth rate are directly influenced by genetic endowment, although the exact extent of this influence has not yet been determined. It is generally accepted that an individual's physical size is the result of two factors: (1) genetically determined growth potential, and (2) rate of maturation. Therefore, a slowly developing child may remain short during the preadolescent period and experience an intensified growth spurt at puberty.

Studies comparing physical growth of children with height of parents provides some insight into the influence of genetic factors on the growth process. This research has supported the premise that tall parents tend to have children who will be tall. A similar trend exists for individuals of short stature (Malina 1975). Although linear growth appears to be strongly genetically controlled, body weight tends to be more environmentally influenced. An individual can readily change the breadth and circumference of various body segments by controlling nutritional intake and by participating in exercise training programs. Body type, however, also appears to be somewhat genetically determined and can only be modified by long-term manipulation of the athlete's environment.

Female newborns tend to be more developmentally advanced than their male counterparts during infancy, and this trend continues until puberty. Hormones that are secreted directly into the bloodstream control the child's rate of growth. At puberty several of these hormones cause the adolescent "growth spurt." During puberty increased production of the hormone testosterone by males tends to increase muscle mass and strength. In contrast, the adolescent female tends to accumulate additional adipose tissue. Females enter their period of rapid growth earlier than males, but they are usually ultimately surpassed by males in body size.

Environmental Influences. As previously mentioned, a child's motor ability is directly influenced by the nature and quality of movement experiences that are provided during various critical periods. Many sports have seen a dramatic decline in the mean age of advanced level performers. This trend has led many to believe that the earlier a child can specialize, the greater the opportunity for success.

Specialization at too early an age tends to result in the development of "splinter skills." These skills are highly specialized and are not easily transferred between sports. This highly specialized approach can actually retard an individual who does not find success within that sport and desires to change activities. These performers have passed the critical period for development of motor skills without acquiring a strong, varied movement foundation. Although early specialization can result in a few children obtaining superior levels of performance, the majority of children do not benefit from this approach. Emphasis upon early specialization is inappropriate for children who do not possess the genetic endowment or the desire to become an advanced athletic performer. The early developmental years should emphasize a wide variety of experiences and should provide the child with a broad movement background.

Coaches must always remember that only a small percentage of young children possess the potential to compete at the intercollegiate or professional level. We should not forget that a major interest should be the large numbers of athletes who will utilize the skills we teach during their daily lives beyond the athletic field.

One environmental factor that can influence athletic performance potential is nutrition. Numerous studies have compared malnourished children with their normal peers and demonstrated the negative influence of poor eating upon physical growth. Nutritional deprivation appears to be most detrimental to a child's physical growth during a period of rapid growth. Extreme care must be taken when coaching young adolescents in sports that sometimes involve crash dieting for the purpose of "making weight." Wrestlers are notorious for attempting to lose weight by high-energy output and frequent starvation diets. The combined effects of a restricted diet, rapid period of physical growth, and high physical demands of training can have a profoundly negative effect on the developmental process.

Care must be taken to ensure that an athlete's diet is nutritionally sound and that caloric intake is sufficient to meet the energy demands of the sport. The short-term benefits of excessive dieting should never be selected over the nutritional health of the athlete. A more detailed discussion of the athlete's nutritional needs is provided in Chapter 18.

Developmental Acquisition of Athletic Skills

Developmental acquisition of sophisticated movement abilities is a complex phenomena that begins during the prenatal period and continues through adulthood. The ability to successfully move within one's environment is dependent upon the efficient integration of the sensory and motor aspects of the neurological system. The infant and young child spend considerable time and effort learning to coordinate sensory input with appropriate motor responses. This early development of foundational abilities appears to be vital to the later acquisition of highly skilled movements.

Prior to proceeding with the discussion of refinement of advanced sports skills, it is important to discuss how individuals acquire the ability to move in a complex manner. Without this basic information it would be difficult for the coach to understand why some performers have greater difficulty mastering skillful movements.

Developmental stages in the acquisition of motor abilities have been described by numerous authors. Regardless of the specific theory, one concept appears to be consistently held: Motor skills are refined from early, gross actions to highly coordinated and complex movements. This developmental trend of simple to complex and gross to fine is the basis of all motor development theory.

Sequential acquisition of motor abilities can best be understood utilizing a "stage" model. As a child matures the neuromuscular system becomes capable of increasingly complex movements (see Figure 13.1). Motor development can be divided into two main periods: the *preskill* and *skill refinement* phases. Within each phase there are sequential stages that are utilized to assist in describing the observed motor behavior during each period. Behavioral characteristics from one level are utilized to build more advanced skills later in the continuum. It is important to note that a deficit in one stage of the developmental process will tend to influence acquisition of more complex skills.

Preskill Phase

Early motor behavior begins approximately six months into the prenatal period and continues throughout one's life. The refinement of movement abilities during the infancy and early childhood periods focuses on the acquisition of abilities that provide the foundation for all later skill development. Although the coach rarely has a direct influence upon these early stages of development, a knowledge of these periods provides important insights into why some children experience difficulty in acquiring competitive levels of athletic skill.

During the preskill phase of motor development the infant's movements are refined from early reflexive actions into highly coordinated fundamental patterns. Emphasis during this period should be given to the quality and quantity of the child's experiences. There is some evidence to suggest that this phase of development represents a "critical period" in the acquisition of movement abilities.

Three stages of development can be readily identified within the preskill phase. These have been termed the reflexive, sensory integrative, and fundamental movement pattern stages. During each developmental stage movement abilities are refined and become more individualized. Behaviors tend to overlap and, frequently, there is no definite beginning or end to each period.

Reflexive Stage. Reflexive activity is considered the simplest unit of neuromuscular functioning (Sage 1977). Reflexive actions result from stimulation of a sensory receptor that transmits a signal along a reflexive nerve pathway back to the muscle fibers. Typically, these movements are controlled at the level of the

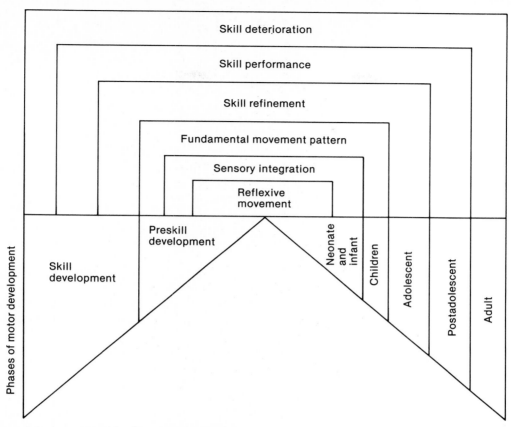

Figure 13.1 Stages in the acquisition of motor behavior.

spinal cord and are not subject to voluntary control.

Although reflexes influence movements at all phases of development, the newborn's first actions are primarily reflexive and involuntary. From these actions the infant gains important information regarding his/her environment. As the child develops and the neurological system matures these early, involuntary movements are repressed and replaced by other reflex actions and by simple, voluntary movements. This developmental phenomenon is frequently utilized by physicians to evaluate neurological maturation. Failure of a reflex to appear or the prolonged continuation of a reflex beyond its

normal period may indicate a neurological impairment. Numerous reflexive actions resemble later forms of voluntary movement. Although the exact role of these early reflexive actions is not clearly understood, it is widely accepted that these experiences with involuntary movements aid in the maturation of neurological centers in the brain.

Reflexive actions also may play a role in the performance of athletic skills. The performer who breaks a fall with an outstretched arm is utilizing a reflex mechanism to improve performance. Frequently, the athlete must exert conscious control over a reflex to inhibit its action. For example, a baseball catcher must watch the ball into his glove even though the natural instinct is to blink; similarly, a gymnast must overcome some reflex actions that tend to cause a loss of equilibrium while balancing on a beam. At times, the athlete must be taught to overcome a natural, reflex action.

Sensory Integration Stage. Early voluntary movements tend to be gross and uncoordinated in nature. Acquisition of these movements is maturationally based and occurs in a predictable sequence based upon developmental principles. The infant gains increasing voluntary control over the larger skeletal muscles and soon acquires the strength to perform simple postural adjustments.

This progression in neuromuscular control tends to inhibit reflexive actions as higher brain centers influence voluntary movement. During the performance of these simple isolated actions the child begins to integrate the input of the numerous sensory receptors with the performance of motor actions. This perceptual process is vital to the acquisition of efficient motor behaviors.

Children soon learn through experience to utilize sensory input to make appropriate decisions that result in a motor response. As the child moves new sensory input is supplied, and through cognitive processes the child makes appropriate adjustments so as to obtain the desired objective. This "feedback loop" can be readily observed in young children. First attempts at reaching for an object are characterized by repeated trials and errors. Slowly, the infant zeros in on the object and makes contact. A similar process can be readily observed in watching a skilled basketball player at the foul line. Frequently, the initial shot is missed but is followed by an accurate attempt. Various sources of sensory input are instantly interpreted and minute modifications are made in the motor patterns so as to attain success. The early integration of sensory and motor systems is vital to all athletic performance. A breakdown in any sensory receptor, neural pathway, or cognitive process can severely limit the child's athletic potential.

Fundamental Movement Pattern Development. Early childhood (ages two to eight years) is characterized by the rapid acquisition and expansion of increasingly complex motor abilities. The isolated movements observed during the integration stage are slowly synchronized into purposeful movement patterns. Young children become actively involved in exploring their environment and in learning about their capabilities and limitations.

The initiation of an upright gait pattern marks the beginning of the development of fundamental movement patterns. Patterns of running, jumping, throwing, catching, and kicking are refined from early uncoordinated movements into highly integrated and skillful patterns. Within the early childhood period children pass through several readily observable stages in acquiring mature and efficient motor patterns. Several authors have summarized this research into systems that can be utilized to observe the quality of a child's motor development (McClenaghan and Gallahue 1978; Wickstrom 1977).

Motor development during the initial two stages is heavily dependent upon the maturational process. Progress is made primarily as a result of aging and does not rely heavily on the youngster's experiences. However, the fundamental movement pattern stage marks a rapid transition from maturationally based development to a process that relies heavily upon cognition and learning.

Movement experiences during the early childhood period appear to influence strongly the quality of development. It is during this time that children should be provided with a broad spectrum of activities. A wide variety of experiences assists the child in developing a strong foundation on which to refine later athletic skills. As emphasized previously, early specialization during this period frequently results in the development of abilities that are unique to only that activity at the expense of all other skills. This approach has a negative influence on the development of a well-rounded performer.

A coach working with young athletes should attempt to provide many quality movement experiences in a nonthreatening or carefully controlled competitive environment. Females particularly need to be provided more opportunities during this period than have been provided previously. Past procedures have allowed many females to mature without developing the basic abilities to perform more advanced motor skills.

Parents and youth sports coaches have a unique opportunity to teach movement to children. Emphasis must be placed on the quality of performance rather than its quantitative results. Highly organized activities should be avoided unless there is careful control. Females should be provided the same opportunities to play and develop as males.

The foundational phase of motor development is a period of rapid growth and emerging abilities. Although the coach rarely has a direct influence upon this developmental phase, the abilities learned during this period directly influence a child's later skill development. Frequently children's play experiences have been restricted during these developmental stages. The results of this systematic limitation is clearly observable in the later performance levels of these children. Parents should be encouraged to play with their children and teach them to enjoy physical activity.

Skill Development Phase

The term "skilled" has been utilized by different authors to describe widely varying levels of ability. Although this term has many different connotations, it generally refers to a higher level of motor performance. Skilled performance is frequently characterized by an appearance of ease, smoothness, and the ability to cope with changing environmental conditions (Sage 1977).

Athletic skills are those movements that are associated with the performance of sports-related activities. Early during the preadolescent period children begin to place considerable importance upon successful participation in athletics. Emphasis is directed toward the refinement of motor skills as adolescents limit their choices and concentrate on those activities in which participation is reinforced.

Athletic skills are refined as the opportunity to participate in appropriate activities increases. Stages in the acquisition of athletic skills include the *refinement*, *performance*, and *deterioration* periods of development. It is important to emphasize that the manner in which one progresses through this developmental sequence is dependent upon his/her inclination to participate in athletic-orientated activities.

Skill Refinement Stage. As motor skills become more complex and the speed at which they are performed dramatically increases new neurological strategies must be developed to efficiently control these actions. No longer can the neurological system consciously coordinate all the individual muscular actions needed to perform even the simplest sports-related skill.

Late in the fundamental movement pattern stage of development and early in the skill refinement stage the child begins to coordinate continuously performed patterns into complex motor programs. These motor programs are defined as a set of preestablished motor commands that assist in performing complex skill patterns with limited conscious neurological involvement. Continual practice during this developmental stage is important to developing these control mechanisms.

The preadolescent period is highly significant in the learning of increasingly complex motor skills. Schmidt (1982) has utilized a cognitive based "schema theory" to help explain this acquisition of skilled performance. He contends that motor programs that are stored in the cerebral cortex are not specific records of movements, but rather they are more generalized rules that assist in governing performance. Therefore, practice is important to the refinement and reinforcement of an athlete's schema.

Several authors (Fitts 1965; Adams 1971) have identified three steps in the acquisition of skilled performance. It appears that all performers, regardless of age, progress through these developmental steps.

Step 1. Cognitive Level. Characterized by a performer's initial attempts at a new skill, which are slow and inconstant. Considerable cognitive attention is needed to perform the skill. Concentration is directed toward establishing a motor program and early motor schema.

Step 2. Associative Level. The second step in sports skill refinement is characterized by increased levels of performance as the motor program is established. Less emphasis must be directed toward attending to the skill as the performer's schema is increased through practice.

Step 3. Autonomous Phase. Continued practice results in further refining of a motor skill to an automatic level. Little cognitive attention is required during the action, allowing the performer to concentrate on environmental factors influencing the performance and strategy.

Experienced coaches can readily identify numerous children and/or adults with whom they have worked who have passed through these phases of skill refinement. The teaching implications of these phases are obvious. Early learning experiences must allow sufficient time for cognitive processing within a controlled environment. As skill is improved practice sessions should be designed in a manner that allows the participant to perform the activity in varying environmental settings.

For example, the early stages of teaching golf should focus on the fundamentals of the strokes as the student cognitively concentrates on the tasks. As these patterns are refined and integrated the student progresses from the driving range to the course. Effort should be placed upon practicing specific situations in which golfers may find themselves when playing. The ultimate goal of practice is to be able to efficiently perform any skill that may be required by the contest. This requires that the performer possess an adequate repertoire of past experiences on which to base motor responses to a specific task. The autonomous phase of motor skill acquisition continues throughout life as the purposes of practice become increasingly specific and level of skill increases.

Skill Performance Stage. As skill performance increases and the adolescent enters the autonomous step of skill refinement interests begin to narrow to those activities that are reinforced. Reinforcement frequently results from successful participation. However, parents and peers have considerable influence in directing an adolescent's athletic interests. Participation narrows to those activities, competitive or recreational, in which success is valued.

The athlete often begins to seek highly competitive environments in which to participate. Although this desire for competition is strong, continued unsuccessful performance can cause the athlete to give up the sport prematurely unless there is proper motivation (see Chapters 3 and 4).

Concentrated practice results in minor changes that can result in increased success. The athlete experiments with numerous variables in an attempt to refine motor skills. Often, changes in one aspect of a movement influence numerous additional factors that govern the level of performance. For example, increased speed is often developed at the expense of control, while attempts at accuracy result in slowed action.

Skill refinement during this time becomes extremely complex. Schmidt (1969) showed how changing one variable, speed of swing, can influence a baseball hitter's overall ability. He found that increasing the speed of the bat allowed for more time to monitor the flight of the ball visually prior to initiating the action. This allowed the performer to make better decisions (see Figure 13.2).

During the skill performance stage, as the athlete begins to feel comfortable with his/her performance, making changes in a skill pattern becomes increasingly difficult. Vic Braden (Braden and Burns 1976), a noted tennis instructor, relates a common experience that supports this premise. He has noted that when a player whose stroke contains numerous extraneous actions is instructed to reduce these movements the response is usually, "Boy, this is really awkward." This is despite the fact that the new stroke is more efficient. Frequently, changes in skill patterns result in decreased levels of performance while the new action is being perfected. During this period an athlete will tend to revert to the old skill pattern, particularly when placed in a competitive situation.

The coach plays an important role in providing the athlete with appropriate feedback regarding the qualitative aspects of performance. This requires a thorough knowledge of the various skills that are necessary to perform a sport. This advanced insight into sports skills is obtained only with a knowledge of motor control and with study of specific sports skills.

Skill Deterioration Phase. As the aging process continues the focus of skill performance

changes from a highly competitive environment to a more recreational orientation. Those individuals who have participated in highly competitive athletics must now direct their energies into other activities. Individuals who participated in team-oriented activities may find it difficult to transfer their skills to individualized, recreational sports.

A successful transition between competitive sports and recreational activities is dependent upon a number of factors, including the athlete's desire to remain active, the types of recreational opportunities available, and the nature of the sport in which they participated. Individuals who have participated in highly organized athletics may experience a sense of loss at the conclusion of their playing eligibility. Few individuals possess the ability to extend their careers through the college and professional levels. This loss of structure frequently results in development of an inactive lifestyle. Another factor influencing skill deterioration is the type of sport in which the athlete participated. Some sports place tremendous time and/or physiological demands upon the participant. This association of extreme effort with athletic training may be generalized to all physical activities. This negative association can reduce the likelihood of later participation in recreational/fitness activities.

It is generally believed that an athlete's peak performance age depends upon the physical

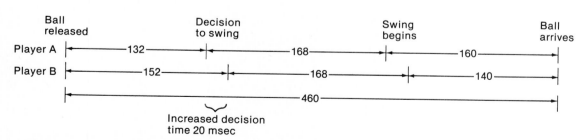

Figure 13.2 A time line showing how speed of swing influences decision time (times in msec). (Adapted from Schmidt, R. A. Consistency of response components as a function of selected motor variables. *Research Quarterly*, 40:561–566, 1969).

demands of the sport, maturational rate, and lifestyle of the athlete. A simple generalization is that after the age of 25 years there is a progressive decline across all aspects of motor performance (Schmidt 1982). Optimal performance is usually attained at an earlier age in sports requiring speed and strength, whereas activities emphasizing cognitive abilities, such as strategy, may mature later in life.

Numerous studies have been conducted attempting to identify the changes in the various systems of the body with age. It may be summarized that after 30 years of age there is a linear decrease in the functional capacity of most physiological systems, resulting in a decreased work capacity. In addition, changes in the neurological system slow the individual's reaction time (Hodgkins 1963). This slowed response time can be attributed to longer nerve conduction times and decreased processing abilities. Although there is some evidence to suggest that regular exercise will help maintain one's physical abilities, the effects of exercise on the deterioration of motor functions with aging are largely unexplored.

Summary

Human maturation can be categorized into developmental stages. Within each stage the individual exhibits a set of generalized characteristics that may be utilized to evaluate development and to assist in providing a set of appropriate learning experiences.

Numerous principles govern the manner in which an individual grows and develops. These developmental principles can assist the coach in better understanding how motor skills are refined from simple involuntary actions to highly coordinated sports-related skills. The acquisition of movement abilities is a complex phenomenon that begins during the prenatal period and continues through adulthood.

Coaches should have a basic understanding of how motor skills are refined so that they may better understand their athletes' needs and abilities. Without this information coaches may fail to recognize the far reaching, developmental implications of their actions.

References

Adams, J.A. A closed-loop theory of motor learning. *Journal of Motor Behavior*. 3:111–150, 1971.

Braden, V., and Burns, B. *Vic Braden's Tennis for the Future*. Boston: Little, Brown and Co., 1977.

Fitts, P.M., and Posner, M.I. Factors in complex skill training. In *Training Research and Education*. Edited by R. Glasser. New York: John Wiley and Sons, 1965.

Hodgkins, J. Reaction time and speed of movement in males and females of various ages. *Research Quarterly*, 34:335–343, 1963.

Malina, R.M. *Growth and Development: The First Twenty Years*. Minneapolis: Burgess Publishing Co., 1975.

McClenaghan, B.A., and Gallahue, D. L. *Fundamental Movement: A Developmental and Remedial Approach*. Philadelphia: W. B. Saunders Co., 1978.

McGraw, M.B. *Growth: A Study of Johnny and Jimmy*. New York: Appleton-Century, 1935.

Sage, G.H. *Introduction to Motor Behavior: A Neuropsychological Approach*. Reading, Massachusetts: Addison-Wesley Publishing Co., Inc., 1977.

Schmidt, R.A. Consistency of response components as a function of selected motor variables. *Research Quarterly*, 40:561–566, 1969.

Schmidt, R.A. *Motor Control and Learning: A Behavioral Emphasis*. Champaign, Illinois: Human Kinetics Publishers, 1982.

Wickstrom, R.L. *Fundamental Motor Patterns*. Philadelphia: Lea & Febiger, 1977.

Recommended Readings

Corbin, C. *A Textbook of Motor Development*. Dubuque, Iowa: William C. Brown Co. Publishers, 1980.

Schmidt, R. A. *Motor Control and Learning: A Behavioral Emphasis*. Champaign, Illinois: Human Kinetics Publishers, 1982.

Williams, H. G. *Perceptual and Motor Development*. Englewood Cliffs, New Jersey: Prentice Hall, Inc., 1983.

Zaichkowski, L. D., Zaichkowski, L. B., and Martiner, T. J. *Growth and Development: The Child and Physical Activity*. St. Louis: C. V. Mosby Co., 1980.

Credit: University of South Carolina Sports Information.

Observation and Analysis of Sports Skills

14

The ability to accurately evaluate athletic skills must rank near the top of the list of competencies needed for effective coaching. Although many coaches are knowledgeable in the techniques and strategies of their particular sport, they frequently lack the ability to evaluate skilled performance. Coaches encounter numerous opportunities to assess individual and team performances in their daily activities. Effectiveness in this evaluative process is often a significant determinant of success in coaching.

Although the preferred method of sports skill analysis depends upon the purposes of the assessment, similar techniques may be employed to evaluate both individual and team performances. An important characteristic of all effective types of skill analysis, regardless of the techniques utilized, is *standardization*. The use of preestablished guidelines is particularly important when utilizing informal methods of evaluation.

The coach must dedicate considerable effort in developing procedures to accurately evaluate athletic skills. This chapter is designed to aid the reader in developing those skills needed to accurately and effectively analyze individual and team athletic skills.

Analyzing Individual Skill Performance

The acquisition of a motor skill depends upon a learning process. Coaches make significant contributions to this process by providing athletes with valuable information (i.e., feedback) regarding their performances. In order to provide useful feedback the coach must be able to accurately evaluate an athlete's performance.

Types of Skill Analysis

Athletic performance can be evaluated in either a qualitative or quantitative manner. The method of assessment selected depends upon the nature of the questions asked, purposes of the analysis, and the nature of the information desired (Higgins 1977).

Quantitative Analysis. Quantitative methods of analysis are frequently utilized in the athletic setting. Competitive athletics, by nature, tend to rely upon quantitative measures to determine the winner and loser in a contest. Measurements of distance jumped, time run, and points scored are methods of quantifying a performance. Although the ultimate objective of an athlete may be to improve quantitative performance, quantitative values alone may provide little information that is useful in refining a skill. For quantitative analysis to be effective it must provide *specific* information regarding the athlete's movement technique.

Biomechanical analysis is frequently utilized to assess specific quantitative aspects of sports skills. Various methods of cinematography can be employed to accurately determine joint displacements and accelerations and velocities of the parts of the body. These data can be utilized to evaluate an individual's performance or to determine the most mechanically efficient movement pattern. The development of specially designed equipment and expanded use of the computer to reduce and analyze large sets of data have dramatically improved the accuracy of this science during the past several years.

Biomechanical studies provide the coach with valuable information regarding the mechanical aspects of a specific skill. These studies have often demonstrated that what was commonly regarded as the correct method of performing a skill was actually incorrect. The ability to record film at extremely high rates (64–500 frames per second) allows the investigator to accurately detail the movement pattern most frequently utilized by successful athletes.

Coaches can significantly benefit from the ability to read and interpret the results of biomechanical studies. Specifically, individuals working with advanced performers can gain considerable information regarding the finer aspects of a skill. The reader is referred to an excellent text by Hay (1978). (See Recommended Readings at the end of this chapter.)

Qualitative Analysis. Qualitative analysis concentrates on the more general aspects of a skill performance. Emphasis upon the "process" components of a skill can be a valuable instructional aid for the coach. Qualitative assessment techniques are primarily based upon visual observation and the results are descriptive in nature. Subjective observation allows the coach to provide the athlete with a continual flow of feedback regarding the qualitative aspects of the performance.

We may rely upon various tools to assist in observational analysis. Regardless of the specific method selected, reliable use of qualitative assessment demands that: (1) the observer be knowledgeable of the skill to be evaluated, and (2) the observations be made in a systematic manner.

Most athletic skills are performed at high speeds, or within an environmental framework that is distracting to the observer. Techniques must be employed to focus the observer's attention upon specific components of the action, slow the skill to allow for a more detailed analysis, and/or provide a permanent record of the performance to allow for repeated viewing. Various photographical, cinematographical, and video techniques have been utilized to aid the observer in accurately evaluating movement skills. These techniques will be discussed in later sections of this chapter.

Although these techniques provide useful evaluative and motivational aids to the coach and athlete, they are frequently time consuming and require a rather significant investment in equipment. For these reasons, emphasis will be placed upon developing a visual observational system that can aid the coach in analyzing live performances. It is important to emphasize that these same techniques may be employed when viewing filmed or videotape recorded performances.

Prior to discussing a systematic approach to observation it would be helpful to review guidelines that will assist the coach in accurately evaluating the qualitative aspects of a skill performance. In utilizing observational techniques the coach should:

Be totally familiar with the mechanical aspects of the skill to be observed. It is important to possess a thorough understanding of the skill to be evaluated. Familiarity with the skill will allow the coach to readily identify deviations from the correct form.

Develop a systematic approach to observing skill performance. The reliability of observations dramatically increases when a consistent observational technique is used. Observational skills will be refined when the same format is repeatedly utilized.

Practice observing skills in a variety of settings. Observation, as with any skill, is refined and developed through practice. During the initial stages of learning the observer must be willing to spend time developing and refining the skill.

Numerous authors have developed observational strategies designed to increase the accuracy and reliability of qualitative analysis. Higgins (1977) noted that observation and description of movement skills is a valuable and useful tool because it: (1) focuses attention upon the sequence of the components of the movements, (2) identifies and directs attention to the most significant aspects of the skill, (3) assists in systematizing thinking related to the relationship between the movement and outcome, (4) identifies those aspects of the skill that should be emphasized during instruction, and (5) assists in the evaluation of performance over a period of time.

Logan and McKinney (1977) have suggested observing a skill in phases and concentrating upon the various skeletal segments. They suggest that when an athletic performance is being analyzed the observer's attention should be divided into the following main areas:

Observation of the Total Performance. Develop a general feeling regarding the execution and timing of the overall performance.

Pelvic Area and Rib Cage Observation. Identify the line of thrust of the total movement and the rotational movements of the trunk.

Base of Support Observation. Assess the area of support and shifts in body weight required by the skill.

Head and Cervical Spine Observation. Evaluate the position of the head relative to the remainder of the body. Determine the focus of the eyes.

Arms and Hand Observation. Observe the directions of movements and sequential actions of the arms and hands. Assess the coordinated action of the arms and legs together.

Leg Observation. Determine the contributions of the hip, knee, and ankle joints to the total movement.

Arend and Higgins (1976) developed a strategy for the classification, subjective analysis, and observation of human movement that includes a three-staged observational process (see Figure 14.1). They suggested that prior to observing a performance the coach should identify the goal of the movement and note its critical features. Once the movement has started, an attempt should be made to identify single aspects of the performance that are performed incorrectly. During the postobserva-

Figure 14.1 Stages of observational assessment as described by Arend and Higgins (1976). (Adapted from Arend, S., and Higgins, J. R. A strategy for the classification, subjective analysis and observation of human movement. *Journal of Human Movement Studies*, 2:36–52, 51, 1976.)

tional period the evaluator should assess the critical features of the skill and provide the performer with specific feedback regarding the performance.

Several authors have suggested breaking sports skills into readily observable segments called phases. This allows for a clear understanding of the movements that occur during the various phases of an action. The objective of this approach is to divide the skill into more readily observable component parts. Commonly identified phases follow.

Preparatory Phase. Movements during the preparatory phase of a skill are designed to set the musculoskeletal articulations in a position advantageous for the performance of the movement. Emphasis should be placed upon analyzing the stance of the athlete and identifying any extraneous movements that may result in wasted or improper motion. Inappropriate actions during this early phase of the movement frequently result in poor mechanics during the action phase of the performance. The preparatory phase is usually defined as beginning with a movement in the direction opposite to the intended line of motion and ending with the start of movement toward the objective.

Action Phase. Joint movements during the action phase of skill performance are frequently ballistic in nature and depend considerably upon sequential timing. The force generated during this phase of the skill is critical to the success of the action. Emphasis should be placed upon analyzing the proper joint mechanics and efficient transfer of force between skeletal segments. Inappropriate movements may result in skeletal stress or injury because of the ballistic nature of the joint action during this phase of skill performance.

Follow-through Phase. Most ballistic actions require a follow-through phase to allow for the absorption of the generated force. In throwing movements, this dissipation of force allows the athlete to release the object at peak velocity without fear of injury resulting from abrupt deceleration. The follow-through also allows the

performer to concentrate on the quality of the performance, such as aim and direction. Inappropriate actions of the joints during the follow-through are an indication that the mechanical aspects of the performance are incorrect.

McClenaghan and Gallahue (1978) suggested an observational technique that can be utilized to evaluate basic movement patterns. Although this approach was designed to evaluate children's movements, it may be easily adapted to assessing higher levels of skill performance. Their technique divides the body into readily observable segments that can be followed during skill performance. Beginning coaches are encouraged to review the following steps and practice their application. Is it important to emphasize that observational skills must be practiced until they become accurate and reliable. The recommended steps in observing an athletic skill follow.

Step 1. Analyze the Sport. Analyze the sport involved and identify those skills that are necessary for successful participation. In team-oriented sports each position may require a different set of skills.

Step 2. Identify Critical Features. For each skill identified as important, define its goal and list the critical features of the performance. A critical feature is defined as a movement that significantly contributes to the performance of the skill (e.g., trunk rotation and transfer of body weight during the throwing skill).

Step 3. Divide the Skill into Phases. Define the preparatory, action, and follow-through phases of the skill. Identify those points in the performance that mark the transition from one phase to the next.

Step 4. Determine Major Anatomical Segments. The body should be divided into easily observable anatomical segments. The mechanical actions of these segments should be identified for each phase of the skill. These segments provide the coach with landmarks upon which to concentrate attention.

Step 5. Practice Observing the Skill. Spend some time practicing newly developed observational skills. During the early stage of practice it is beneficial to observe filmed or videotaped performances that can be slowed or repeated.

Step 6. Observe Live Performance. Utilize the technique to evaluate actual performances. Do not attempt to see everything, but rather concentrate attention upon several key factors.

The process described may seem to be lengthy and cumbersome. However, with sufficient practice, this observational technique can become almost automatic. Coaches who learn proper observational skills will benefit throughout their careers. With these strategies in mind the coach can develop an efficient observational technique. This method is by no means the only method to evaluate a performance, but rather a composite of those techniques that have proven effective. Each coach must develop his own approach to evaluating skill. The important point is that some pre-planned method must be utilized.

Providing Appropriate Feedback

Once the observation of a skill is completed the results must be accurately reported to the performer in a form that can be readily utilized to improve skill proficiency. Skill analysis has limited value if the athlete is not provided with readily usable information regarding the performance. The athlete receives feedback from internal sources (intrinsic) and from others who observe the performance (extrinsic).

As a sport is performed the athlete's sensory nervous system provides considerable information regarding the mechanical aspects of the skill. As will be discussed in Chapter 15, various sensory receptors located in the muscles and joints allow us to monitor the position of the body and body segments. Schmidt (1981) noted that every movement generates certain sources of intrinsic feedback that provide a basis for evaluating the movement. This intrinsic ability to evaluate one's own performance is learned during childhood and, consequently,

young athletes may be less adept at using intrinsic feedback than their older counterparts.

Coaches are often the athlete's primary source of feedback, and a basic understanding of what type of information is most valuable to the learner will assist the coach in designing appropriate teaching strategies. Extrinsic feedback provided by the coach is utilized by the athlete to supplement and augment intrinsic sensory information. Additional extrinsic information is provided by the outcome of the skill performance. For example, the success or failure of a free throw in basketball provides feedback regarding that skill.

This externally provided information has been classified into two categories: knowledge of results and knowledge of performance (Gentile 1972). The coach should utilize both these forms of feedback when working with athletes. Knowledge of results provides the performer with information regarding the success of the action in accomplishing its intended objective, whereas knowledge of performance concerns qualitative information regarding the movement. For example, a golf coach might provide an athlete with information on the distance of a drive (knowledge of results) and on the position of the hands during the swing (knowledge of performance). Frequently, athletes can use the visual sense to obtain information on the results of a performance, but they must depend on the coach to provide information regarding the quality of their performances.

A key question concerning the coach's use of extrinsic feedback is, "How much information should I provide to the performer?" Generally, the skill level of the performer should guide the coach in answering this question. Skilled athletes appear to benefit significantly from information that is highly specific. This feedback assists in the refinement of a movement. Unskilled individuals, however, are less able to incorporate this highly specific information into their performance. For example, studies conducted on children have found that they are usually less capable of utilizing highly specific feedback. Beginning learners must spend considerable effort in attending to the general components of skill performance and have not refined the ability to utilize feedback in making subtle changes in the movement. In this situation, highly precise feedback may actually frustrate the athlete and result in a less effective performance.

This is not to suggest that individuals during early stages of skill acquisition should not be provided with extrinsic feedback. To the contrary, coaches should provide information to the beginning learner. The nature of this information, however, appears to be critical. Feedback should be general in nature, relate to gross actions, and be limited in amount. In contrast, skilled performers require highly specific forms of feedback and frequently are able to utilize precise information to refine a movement. Coaches who work with skilled athletes must develop their observational skills to the extent that this highly specific information can be provided.

The timing of feedback is another factor that must be considered when attempting to provide the athlete with valuable information regarding a performance. Generally, feedback during practice should be provided soon after the skill is completed. Time between trials should be sufficient to allow the athlete to process the information provided.

Also, the frequency of feedback appears to influence performance. Performers generally benefit from feedback that is provided quite frequently. The optimal frequency is that greatest rate of feedback at which the athlete can understand, process, and utilize the information in refining a skill. Feedback that is provided too frequently can confuse the athlete and can negatively influence performance.

Schmidt (1981) noted that with the exception of practice time feedback is the single most important determinant of skill learning. He further indicated that feedback provides the learner with guidance, helps establish associations between movements and results, and provides reinforcement and motivation. One of a

coach's principal functions is to provide appropriate feedback to athletes in a manner that will positively modify skill performance. It is important to emphasize that the coach's ability to analyze a skill is an important prerequisite to provision of valuable feedback.

Analyzing Team Performance

The second form of analysis with which coaches must be familiar involves evaluation of teams or individuals within the game situation. This differs from skill analysis in that the major objective is to identify general strengths and weaknesses that must be corrected in a team or exploited in an opposing team. Although many of the basic analysis skills previously mentioned can be utilized to evaluate game performance, certain additional skills are required. Among these are recording team performances and scouting opponents.

Recording Team Performances

Films of a contest provide the most valuable and accurate method of evaluating the strengths and weaknesses of an individual or team. The value of filming increases when the play is continuous and there is limited opportunity to record information. A second benefit of this technique is that athletes are able to observe their own mistakes and the strengths, weaknesses, and tendencies of an opponent.

Motion Picture Filming. Both coaches and biomechanists can utilize cinematography to record a performance for analysis via repeated viewing and slowed motion. However, the cinematographical analysis utilized by the coach usually differs considerably from that conducted by the biomechanist.

The coach is primarily interested in the qualitative aspects of the performance, while the biomechanist is concerned more with quantitative information. Biomechanical analysis may involve a frame-by-frame assessment of the velocity and acceleration of the various joints. Film provides the investigator with a scaled version of the actual performance and allows for direct measurements. The opportunity for a coach to participate in this formal type of analysis usually is limited. Although seldom directly involved in this level of research, a coach at any level can apply the information obtained from these studies in actual coaching situations. For example, the high jump has been extensively studied by biomechanists. It has been found that the Fosbury Flop method of jumping allows the jumper's center of gravity to pass under the bar while he/she passes over it. In contrast, the Western Roll technique does not provide this same advantage. The advantage of the former method is clear to any track coach.

Coaches tend to utilize cinematographical analysis in a different but equally valuable manner. Basic methods of observational skill analysis can be paired with the use of film to increase the effectiveness of the evaluation. The reliability of observational skill analysis is greatly enhanced when it is used in conjunction with cinematographical techniques.

The most commonly utilized method of analysis remains the use of "game films" to evaluate a team's performance. However, this technique is frequently overlooked as a method for assessing an athlete's individual performance. It is important to emphasize that film can be utilized to evaluate a wide range of team and individual skills.

Film Formats. Until approximately 1965 most motion picture production was done on 16mm film. The only other available format was 8mm, which was primarily utilized for home filming. In comparison to 16mm, the older 8mm systems tended to be grainy and to suffer from a loss of image sharpness when projected. In addition, 8mm projectors were relatively crude and had many deficiencies.

In 1965 the Eastman Kodak Company introduced a new 8mm film that had numerous advantages over the older 8mm film. Super 8 film had a 50% larger picture area, and thus a sharper image quality. Because of this new format, increased quality of camera and projection equipment, and an increased film quality Super

8 film is appreciably sharper and brighter than the regular 8mm format. There are definite advantages and disadvantages to the 16mm and Super 8 formats. Coaches should carefully consider equipment needs prior to selecting either format. Table 14.1 summarizes the advantages and disadvantages of 16mm and Super 8 film.

Film. Film for both 16mm and Super 8 formats is currently available in a wide variety of types. The exact film selected should be based upon various factors, including kinds of subjects to be filmed, the lighting conditions, speed of the film, and the acceptable clarity of the projected image.

The most important factor in film selection is the lighting condition in which the film will be exposed. Natural daylight, of course, is preferred, but this is not available indoors or during night contests. The intensity of light necessary to adequately expose a film is determined by its degree of sensitivity to light. This so-called "film speed" or "exposure index" is commonly expressed as the ASA (American Standards Association) number. For example, a film with an ASA rating of 400 requires less light than a film with a lower ASA number. In most cases, film speed is identified on the container in which the film is sold.

Super 8 film is usually available only in color, although it may be specially ordered in black and white. A wider selection of film types is available for 16mm film. Color films tend to require more light than the higher speed black and white formats. Although the projected image of color film may be more appealing, studies have shown that color film does not facilitate learning more than black and white film.

Cameras. Although Super 8 cameras tend to be simpler to operate than 16mm versions, they do not usually provide the same flexibility. Regardless of the film format selected, the better cameras are equipped with the following features:

Interchangeable Lens. The most important feature of the camera, the lens, is the link be-

Table 14.1: Comparison of 16mm and Super 8 Formats

Feature	16mm	Super 8
Film		
1. Size	40 frames/ft, available in various lengths. Open reel requires threading.	72 frames per foot, available only in 50-ft prepackaged cartridges.
2. Speed	18 frames/sec.	18 frames/sec.
3. Type	Wide range of black-white and color films available. Many special application films can be ordered.	Color film is primarily available; some black-white.
4. Processing	Same day available in many locations. Some labs specialize in processing athletic film.	Black-white film difficult to have processed. Color processing readily available.
Camera		
1. Loading	Manual; film must be threaded by hand.	Cartridge loading may be accomplished in seconds.
2. Film Transport	Motor or spring driven; motor often requires additional power source.	Frequently battery operated; transport slows as batteries drain.
3. Exposure	Manually set; requires exposure meter.	Usually automatic under normal conditions; may be manually set.
4. Lens	Wide range of lenses available; some reflex viewing (through the lens).	Typically zoom lens, often motor driven; reflex viewing.
Projector		
1. Types	Regular and analysis projectors available; good reliability.	Regular and analysis projectors available; reliability poor at present.
2. Threading	Manual threading.	Self-loading common.
3. Viewing	Good for large groups.	Individual and small group viewing.
Cost		
Equipment	Super 8 equipment is slightly cheaper, but usually provides less options and poorer quality than 16mm.	
Films	Can vary widely. 16mm black-white film can be cheaper than Super 8 color. 16mm color tends to be more expensive than Super 8.	

tween the subject and the film. Various filming situations require various lenses. A single lens of a "zoom" type is capable of doing the work of many lens and is helpful when filming athletic events.

Reflex Viewing. Reflex viewing allows the photographer to view the intended scene through the lens. This allows for easier focusing and framing of the picture. In addition, reflex viewing is much preferred when telephoto lenses are employed.

Variable Speed Control. The camera that is to be utilized by the coach should have the capability of filming at various frame rates. Increased film speed improves the clarity of the projected image. This is particularly important when attempting to evaluate an individual's performance and/or when utilizing film as an educational aid.

Light Meter. Whether located internally within a camera or used as an independent accessory, this option is particularly important in setting the correct film exposure. Filming of athletic events often requires unique exposure settings because of varying lighting conditions.

Tripod. Commonly sold as an accessory, a tripod is required in most filming situations because it ensures a stable platform for the camera. Characteristics of a good tripod include a center braced bracket (increased stability) and a smooth operating pan and tilt head.

Numerous other optional equipment items can assist in the filming of an athletic event or skill performance. The purchase of a camera is a significant financial commitment and, therefore, selection should be made only after a careful and thorough review of all available models.

Film Projector. Once the film has been processed, it must be projected for analysis. Although regularly manufactured projectors provide good quality viewing, they often are difficult to utilize in conducting mechanical analyses. Usually, the film must be replayed over and over or slowed to identify specific aspects of a performance; this requires a projector that is manufactured or modified to meet these specialized needs. Several manufacturers have developed highly sophisticated projectors to assist in film analysis. Although these cameras tend to be expensive, their options allow for a thorough analysis. It must, however, be remembered that more complex pieces of equipment are more likely to break down. In the athletic situation a projector tends to take considerable abuse, and so it is recommended that a durable and easy-to-service piece of equipment be obtained.

Videotape. In recent years technical advancements have resulted in videotape production becoming an excellent instructional aid. New advances in the quality of cameras, versatility of recorders, and improvements in tape now provide the coach with many of the advantages that once could be obtained only with film. The videotape system contains several components that must be interfaced into a complete package. These components include the camera, recorder, tape, and monitor.

Camera. The ultimate quality of the video image is dependent to a significant extent upon the capabilities of the camera that is utilized. Inexpensive cameras generally produce projected images that are of poorer quality than those provided by more costly cameras. Cameras are available across a wide range of prices. Generally speaking, the more money invested in the camera, the greater the quality and utility of the product.

As with film cameras certain optional features can increase the quality of videotaping in the athletic setting. Monitor viewing with a telephoto lens, a light intensity indicator, and remote record trigger are valuable in producing a quality product. Videocameras tend to be more fragile than movie cameras, but with some care they usually provide long periods of extended service with only periodic maintenance required. In most situations the camera should be mounted on a stable tripod, but a pistol handle may prove helpful when the coach is using the equipment in an informal manner as an educational aid.

Recorder. The videotape recorder must be matched to the output of the camera. In more expensive systems these two items are usually purchased together. The recorder should have a record of reliability and serviceability. Ideally, the system should be purchased from a dealer who also provides service. Nothing can be more frustrating than a piece of equipment that breaks down just when it is most needed.

Recorders come with several options that enhance their utility in an athletic setting. Features such as speed search, slow motion, and the capability to freeze an action all contribute to the usefulness of videotapes in analyzing skill performance. Many new models allow for extended "still frame" viewing, a particularly useful feature.

Videotape recorders/players come in various formats (determined by tape size and packaging). The most usable formats appear to be the smaller tapes that allow for more compact and portable units. These tapes come precartridged in various lengths and eliminate the need to hand thread the equipment. Tape format is an important consideration because all equipment must be compatible with the format selected.

Monitor. The monitor is the final component of

the videotape system. Frequently, a regular television may be modified (special input cable) to meet the needs of the viewer. The size of the viewing screen is important if the monitor is to be utilized in a group setting. Larger screens are often easier to see, but they tend to reduce the quality of the image. Coaches should evaluate these factors and make the most appropriate selection for their individual needs.

Athletic departments often make significant investments in equipment that can be utilized to evaluate skill performance. Both film and videotape offer the coach various advantages and disadvantages. These pros and cons, summarized in Table 14.2, should be carefully assessed before selecting a method of analysis.

Analysis of Films and Tapes. An important factor in successful use of cinematographical techniques is employment of a *systematic approach* to analysis. Countless hours of film viewing will provide only superficial informa-

tion unless the analysis is carefully conducted. The value of the information obtained from game films is not based upon the number of hours spent watching film, but rather on the manner in which the film is analyzed. Observing game performance is similar to evaluating a live performance, but with the added benefit of instant replay. The distinctions between film analysis and observation of live performance are discussed in the following paragraphs.

The initial step in evaluating team performance from a game film involves review of the total contest. The film should be observed in its entirety. Emphasis should be placed on getting a "feel" for the team's performance rather than noting specific aspects of performance. This is best accomplished when several coaches independently evaluate the team's general characteristics. This first viewing of the film should also be used for purposes of identifying players who exhibited particularly remarkable

Table 14.2: Comparison of Film Versus Videotape

	Film	Videotape
Equipment	Good durability and different units are compatible within 16mm or Super 8 format.	Good durability but recorders/players are not compatible.
Expense	Quality equipment expensive. Film and processing is a repeated expense.	Equipment is expensive. Videotapes can be repeatedly utilized.
Clarity of Image	Clarity of reproduced image is good with most cameras. 16mm offers better resolution than Super 8 format.	Clarity of image dependent upon the quality of camera. Inexpensive cameras frequently result in unacceptable results.
Editing	Film easily removed and spliced into segments.	Editing is difficult and requires additional recorder.
Durability	Film is strong and may be repeatedly reviewed. Easily repaired if damaged.	Tape will tend to weaken with continued use. Difficult to repair if damaged.
Processing	Expensive. Takes time to process.	No processing necessary. May be utilized for instant feedback.
Capabilities	Film may be taken at faster than normal rates, thus slowing action. Action may be frozen for long periods of time with special projector.	Slow motion and freeze frame possible but limited.

strengths and to note any unique tendencies of the total team. A coaching staff can begin to assess their team's performance or design an appropriate game plan for an opponent from this information.

Subsequently, the film should be divided into component parts. Offensive, defensive, and speciality plays should be viewed and evaluated as independent sets. During this step in the analysis greater emphasis should be placed on attempting to identify the strengths and weaknesses of each player. Time should be spent in determining how an opposing team's strengths can be neutralized and their weaknesses exploited. When individual athletes utilize film for self-analysis this phase of the assessment should be used to grade and evaluate their performances. Specific criteria should be employed to judge each player's level of performance.

When coaches analyze an opposing team they should try to identify team characteristics such as specific formations and/or plays. An often valuable technique employed in many sports is the development of a tendency chart. Such a chart records the team's response to certain situations (e.g., in football, defensive plays used on third down with 4–5 yards to go for a first down). This information is frequently helpful when attempting to predict an opponent's next move.

The final step in analyzing game films involves the reduction of large quantities of data into a readily usable form. Care must be taken to ensure that players receive only the information that is valuable to them. In sports that have unique positional characteristics, such as football, this is best done in small groups (e.g., offensive linemen, defensive backs, and so forth). Excessive information tends to dilute that which is of greatest importance and results in confusion. As a general rule, the specificity and amount of information provided to an athlete can increase as level of skill and comprehension improve. For example, there is little value in focusing a beginning tennis player's at-

tention on an opponent's weaknesses when all his/her attention should be directed to the production of a consistent stroke pattern.

Many professional and college teams employ computers to store and analyze large volumes of data. With the advent of the microcomputer and commercially available software, it seems certain that computers will have a profound impact upon skill analysis in the coming decade.

Scouting an Opponent

An opponent's strengths and weaknesses may be determined from an analysis of game films (as previously discussed) or from live observation of the opponent during a contest. It is best to obtain information about a future opponent from as many sources as possible.

Scouting of opponents is a process that must be carefully planned. The recommended amount of scouting and the depth of information obtained varies with the level of competition. When working with beginning skill learners, the effort spent evaluating an opponent often would be better directed toward refining basic skills. However, scouting the opponent is a key factor in coaching skilled athletes.

There are three general components of scouting: pregame planning, game analysis, and postgame summary.

Pregame Planning. Coaches should meet prior to each scouting trip. During this meeting the future opponent should be reviewed and areas of special interest identified. Whenever possible, specific athletes should be discussed so that emphasis may be placed upon observing their performances. If this opponent has been previously played or scouted it is beneficial to review past information regarding the team's personnel and tendencies. This preplanned session enables each coach to become familiar with and to narrow the focus of his/her assignment.

Game Analysis. Forms for recording information should be standardized and coaches should practice utilizing the selected observational techniques. One method that has proven helpful is to allow a new coach to "scout" a team by viewing an old game film.

The contest should be divided into segments that may be analyzed separately. For example, a tennis match could be divided into service, ground stroke, and overall strategy components. Grieve (1977) has suggested utilizing various recording forms to increase effectiveness in scouting football.

Postgame Summary. One of the most important phases in the scouting process is summarization of all information into a final report. This composite must provide the coaches and athletes with pertinent information in a clear and concise manner. The final report should be presented to the coaches at a meeting during which appropriate strategies may be designed to counteract an opposing team's strengths and exploit its weaknesses. Finally, the information should be provided to the athlete(s) in a very concise format.

Summary

The ability to analyze both individual and team performance is an important skill for the successful coach. The recommended method of analysis depends upon the objective of the evaluation. Regardless of the techniques utilized, it is suggested that the coach develop a systematic approach to analyzing performance.

Athletic performance can be evaluated utilizing either a qualitative or quantitative emphasis. Both types of analyses provide the coach and athlete with specific information regarding skill performance. Appropriate feedback should be provided to the learner in such a manner that it may be utilized to refine a skill.

Assessment of game performance may be utilized to evaluate one's own team and to scout an opponent. Various filming and videotaping procedures are available for recording game performances. Coaches should employ predetermined and standardized techniques for recording and summarizing team and individual performance characteristics in analyzing game films and in live scouting of opponents.

References

Arend, S., and Higgins, J.R. A strategy for the classification, subjective analysis and observation of human movement. *Journal of Human Movement Studies*, 2:36–52, 1976.

Gentile, A.M. A working model of skill acquisition with application to teaching. *Quest*, 17:3–23, 1972.

Grieve, Andrew. Effective football scouting forms. *Athletic Journal*, 67 (Apr.):56–57, 1977.

Higgins, J.R. *Human Movement: An Integrated Approach.* St. Louis: C.V. Mosby Co., 1977.

Logan, G.A., and McKinney, W.C. *Anatomic Kinesiology.* Dubuque, Iowa: William C. Brown Co., 1970.

McClenaghan, B.A., and Gallahue, D.L. *Fundamental Movement: A Developmental and Remedial Approach.* Philadelphia: W.B. Saunders Co., 1978.

Schmidt, R.A. *Motor Control and Learning.* Champaign, Illinois: Human Kinetics Publishers, 1981.

Recommended Readings

Hay, J.G. *The Biomechanics of Sports Techniques*, 2nd ed. Englewood Cliffs, New Jersey: Prentice-Hall, Inc., 1978.

Kemp, J.E. *Planning and Producing Audiovisual Materials.* New York: Thomas Y. Crowell, 1975.

Kerr, R. *Psychomotor Learning.* Philadelphia: Saunders College Publishing, 1982, 76–85.

Logan, G.A., and McKinney, W. C. *Anatomic Kinesiology.* Dubuque, Iowa: William C. Brown Co., 1977, pp. 224–251.

Simonian, C. *Fundamentals of Sports Biomechanics.* Englewood Cliffs, New Jersey: Prentice-Hall, Inc., 1981, pp. 165–205.

Exercise comes in many forms and with many individual interpretations. Some sports, like football and basketball, require rapid, forceful maneuvers. Other athletic activities, such as long distance running or swimming, involve gentle and repetitive movements. While the many sports present a wide range of movement styles, it is nonetheless true that all human movements result from the same physiological process: the contraction of skeletal muscles.

Since skeletal muscle contraction plays such a central role in the performance of athletic skills, any study of exercise physiology must include a discussion of how the skeletal muscles function to produce movement. This chapter is dedicated to describing the structure and function of human skeletal muscle. Emphasis is given to the mechanism of muscle contraction and to the means by which the nervous system controls the skeletal muscles during exercise. Since coaching involves the design of training techniques and practice strategies that modify the structural and functional characteristics of athletes' muscles, it is essential that coaches master the information presented in this chapter.

Structure of Skeletal Muscle

The human body includes over 200 anatomically distinct skeletal muscles, which together account for roughly 40% of the total body weight. Skeletal muscles come in numerous shapes and sizes. For example, the tiny, ribbon-like muscles that control eye movements are dwarfed by the thick, powerful hamstring muscles of the posterior thigh. However, despite variations in outward appearance all skeletal muscles have many common characteristics. These similarities are emphasized in this chapter.

Gross Structure of Skeletal Muscle Tissue

As was discussed in Chapter 10, skeletal muscle tissue consists of muscle fibers that are

Muscles at Work

15

long, thin cells. These fibers are bound to one another by layers of elastic connective tissue. These connective tissues merge with tendons that are, in turn, attached to bones. Thus, the force that is generated by active contraction of muscle fibers is transmitted to the skeleton through connective tissues and tendons.

As with all living tissues, skeletal muscle must be provided with a constant supply of nutrients and must continually be cleared of waste products. These functions are the responsibility of the circulatory system. Each muscle is pierced by an artery and a vein that, respectively, transport blood to and from the tiny capillaries surrounding each individual muscle fiber. As blood passes through the capillaries nutrients diffuse from the blood into the muscle fiber and wastes move in the opposite direction (see Figure 15.1).

Also represented in each skeletal muscle is the nervous system. Passing into the muscle is a nerve trunk that is a branch of one of the spinal nerves. The nerve trunks contain two types of neurons (nerve cells), both of which carry messages between the muscle tissue and the central nervous system (brain and spinal cord). *Sensory neurons* carry impulses from the muscle to the central nervous system, providing information regarding the muscle's length and level of

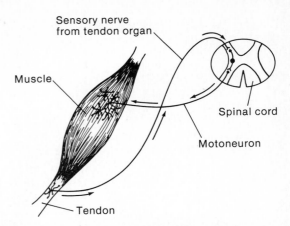

Figure 15.2 Motoneurons transmit nervous impulses to skeletal muscles, while sensory neurons carry impulses from the muscles to the central nervous system.

activity. *Motoneurons* transmit impulses in the opposite direction and carry to the muscle the signals that initiate contraction (see Figure 15.2).

Ultrastructure of the Skeletal Muscle Fiber

One of the basic principles of physiology is: *structure determines function.* In the present context, this principle indicates that an understanding of the function of muscle tissue depends on a knowledge of the structure of the muscle fiber. The muscle fiber is a cell and, as such, has certain characteristics that are common to most cells in the body. However, muscle fibers are very highly organized and specialized cells that possess an ultrastructure that is splendidly adapted for the fiber's function: the generation of force through contraction.

Like all cells, the muscle fiber has a cell membrane, in this case called the *sarcolemma,* which regulates the passage of chemical substances into and out of the cell. Within the sarcolemma is the *sarcoplasm,* a fluid matrix that contains carefully controlled concentrations of

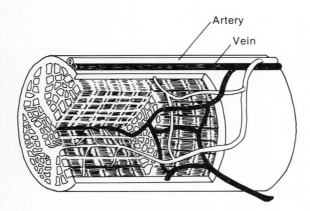

Figure 15.1 Muscle fibers are surrounded by a network of capillaries.

salts and proteins. Suspended in the sarco-plasm are a number of subcellular structures (organelles) that work together during contraction of the muscle fiber.

Perhaps most prominent of the muscle fiber's subcellular structures are the contractile protein filaments. These filaments are linear strands that lie parallel with one another and run longitudinally in the fiber. Two varieties of protein filaments, *actin* and *myosin*, are found in the muscle fiber, and these are arranged in an alternating, overlapping fashion as shown in Figure 15.3A. Sets of these contractile proteins form subunits within the fiber called *myofibrils*. The myofibril is the basic contractile unit in the fiber. Each myofibril consists of numerous sets of actin and myosin filaments, each set being termed a *sarcomere* (Figure 15.3B). The sarco-

meres in a myofibril are arranged in an end-to-end fashion.

Surrounding the myofibrils is a complex set of tiny tubules that form a communication network within the muscle fiber. This network of tubules functions to carry electrical impulses from the surface of the fiber to its interior. As shown in Figure 15.4, one type of tubule, the *T-tubules* carry impulses from the sarcolemma to the center of the fiber. A second set of tubules, the *sarcoplasmic reticulum*, receives impulses from the T-tubules and carries them longitudinally through the fiber. Also, the sarcoplasmic reticulum serves as a storage vessel for calcium ions. As will be discussed later in this chapter, the release of these calcium ions from the sarcoplasmic reticulum is a critical step in the initiation of contraction of the muscle fiber.

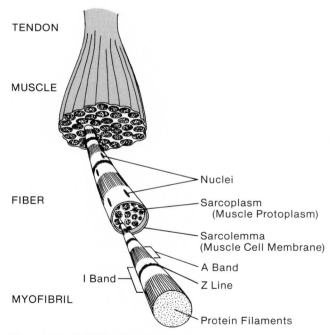

TENDON

MUSCLE

FIBER

MYOFIBRIL

Nuclei
Sarcoplasm (Muscle Protoplasm)
Sarcolemma (Muscle Cell Membrane)
A Band
I Band
Z Line
Protein Filaments

Figure 15.3A Skeletal muscles are composed of muscle fibers (cells) each of which include numerous myofibrils. (From Fox, E.L., and D.K. Mathews. *The Physiological Basis of Physical Education and Athletics*. 3rd ed. Philadelphia: Saunders College Publishing, 1981.)

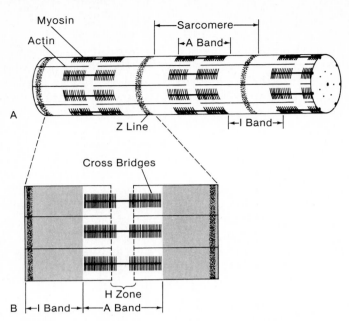

Figure 15.3B Myofibrils consist of actin and myosin protein filaments, which are arranged in sets called sarcomeres. (From Fox, E.L., and D.K. Mathews. *The Physiological Basis of Physical Education and Athletics.* 3rd ed. Philadelphia: Saunders College Publishing, 1981.)

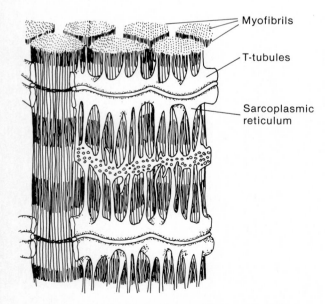

Figure 15.4 T-tubules and sarcoplasmic reticulum surround each myofibril.

Also found in the sarcoplasm are the fuel substances and organelles that are needed to produce the chemical energy used in muscle contraction. The primary raw materials used in energy production are carbohydrates and fats. A specific carbohydrate, glycogen, is stored in the form of granules that are stacked in columns within the myofibrils. Tiny droplets of fat are found around the myofibrils near organelles called *mitochondria*. The mitochondrion is often referred to as the "powerhouse of the cell," since within it are found many of the enzymes that function to release chemical energy from carbohydrates and fats.

Mechanism of Muscle Contraction

A cohesive theory of muscle contraction was presented by the Englishman H. E. Huxley during the 1950's (Huxley and Hanson 1954). Huxley's *sliding filament theory* holds that muscle contraction results from an interaction between the actin and myosin protein filaments in the myofibrils. The nature of this interaction is such that while remaining elongated, the two myofilaments slide past one another, thus reducing the length of the sarcomere. The impetus for this so-called "interdigitation" is provided by the myosin cross bridges that attach to the actin filaments and, in ratchet-like fashion, pull them toward the center of the sarcomere. The simultaneous shortening of many adjacent sarcomeres results in contraction of the entire myofibril. Ordinarily, all the myofibrils in a particular muscle fiber contract simultaneously.

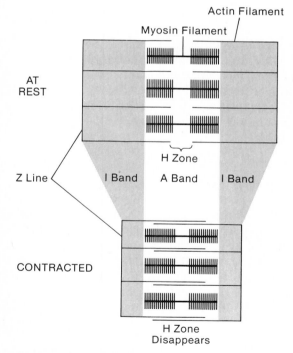

AT REST

Actin Filament
Myosin Filament
H Zone
Z Line
I Band   A Band   I Band

CONTRACTED

H Zone
Disappears

Figure 15.5 The sliding filament theory of muscle contraction—shortening occurs when myosin cross bridges draw actin filaments toward the center of the sarcomere. (From Fox, E.L., and D.K. Mathews. *The Physiological Basis of Physical Education and Athletics.* 3rd ed. Philadelphia: Saunders College Publishing, 1981.)

When many of a muscle's fibers contract in unison, sufficient force is generated to cause a shortening of the muscle as a whole (Figure 15.5).

In order for the actin and myosin to interact to cause muscle contraction, certain chemical substances must be present in the sarcoplasm. One important substance is adenosine triphosphate (ATP). ATP is the immediate source of energy for muscle contraction. During contraction ATP is broken down, and in the process releases a large amount of chemical energy. This chemical energy is utilized to produce the movement in the myosin cross bridges that pulls the actin filaments toward the center of the sarcomere. During a sustained contraction or with repeated contractions a very great number of ATP molecules are utilized. Since only a small amount of ATP is present in the sarcoplasm when work begins, sustained muscular exercise requires a continual and rapid replenishment of the ATP supply. During muscular work the metabolic processes of the cell speed up so that ATP is regenerated at a rate that matches its utilization. A complete discussion of the processes that provide the energy for muscular work will be provided in the next chapter.

Nervous Control of Muscle Contraction

Skeletal muscles are subject to direct, conscious control by the body's central nervous system (brain and spinal cord). In nearly all sporting activities performance depends on the athlete's ability to control the timing and force of muscle contractions with precision. Thus, the degree of coordination between the nervous and muscular systems is an important determinant of athletic performance.

Motor Units

Skeletal muscle fibers are stimulated to contract by specialized nerve cells called *motoneurons.* These motoneurons serve to relay electrical impulses from the brain to the individual muscle fibers. As shown in Figure 15.6, the nervous impulses that result in muscle contraction begin in a specialized area of the brain called the motor cortex. Upper motoneurons descend from the brain and contact lower motoneurons in the spinal cord. Lower motoneurons pass out of the spinal cord in a spinal nerve and terminate in a number of nerve endings; each nerve ending contacts an individual muscle fiber.

All the muscle fibers controlled by a single motoneuron constitute a *motor unit*. The number of fibers in a motor unit varies greatly—the range is from as few as five to as many as several thousand. In general, the larger motor units are found in the larger muscles of the back and limbs, while the smaller muscles of the face and hands are composed of motor units con-

taining relatively few muscle fibers. Regardless of anatomical location, all the muscle fibers in a particular motor unit tend to contract simultaneously, since they are controlled by the same motoneuron.

The stimulus to contract is transmitted from a nerve ending to the muscle fiber through a structure called the *myoneural junction*. When the stimulus reaches a myoneural junction a nerve impulse causes the release from the nerve ending of a chemical substance called acetylcholine. Acetylcholine is a transmitter that allows for the passage of an electrical impulse across the myoneural junction. When the electrical impulse reaches the sarcolemma of the muscle fiber it is carried throughout the fiber by the T-tubules and sarcoplasmic reticulum. Contraction results when the sarcoplasmic reticulum releases calcium ions into the sarcoplasm in response to the electrical impulse. These calcium ions trigger contraction by allowing the interaction of actin and myosin filaments and by facilitating the splitting of ATP. (Hoyle 1970). Thus, the chemical events that result in muscle contraction are initiated by nerve impulses from the brain and spinal cord.

Sensory Receptors

Precise control of muscular activity requires that the central nervous system be provided with a continual flow of information concerning the position of body parts and the contractile state of the muscles. This information is provided to the brain and spinal cord by nerve pathways that originate in various sensory receptors in the muscles, joints, and inner ear. Figure 15.7 presents a diagrammatic representation of the organizational structure of the sensory and motor nervous pathways that influence muscular activity. This so-called *sensory feedback loop* comprises a system in which the brain and/or spinal cord, having received input from the sensory receptors, initiate muscular contractions that alter the state of the sensory receptors.

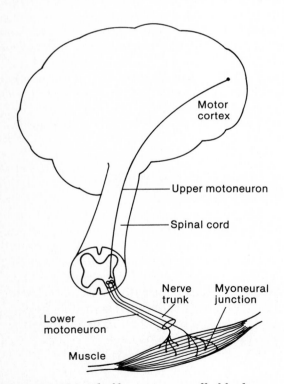

Figure 15.6 Muscle fibers are controlled by lower motoneurons, which are, in turn, stimulated by upper motoneurons descending from the brain.

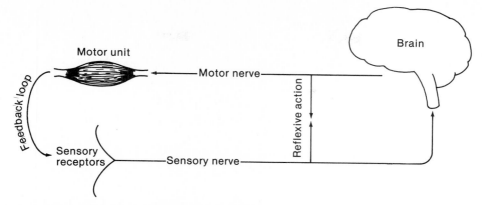

Figure 15.7 Sensory feedback loop. Each movement results in new information being processed by the performer. Note that some responses may be reflexive in nature.

Sensory input to the central nervous system may be transmitted to the brain or may be processed at the level of the spinal cord. If sensory information is relayed to the brain the resulting movement is consciously initiated. However, if sensory stimulation is sufficiently powerful reflexive muscular responses can be initiated by the spinal cord. Such reflex movements occur very rapidly, but the movements often lack precision and control.

Each type of sensory receptor is highly specialized and provides the central nervous system with very specific information. The major sensory receptors that contribute to the control of movement are muscle spindles, Golgi tendon organs, joint receptors, and vestibular receptors.

Muscle Spindles. Muscle spindles are highly specialized sensory receptors that lie in parallel with the fibers of a muscle. The muscle spindles are sensitive to the lengthening of a muscle (stretch) and to the velocity at which the change in length occurs. Muscle spindles function to prevent a muscle from being overstretched. They perform this function by initiating reflexive contraction of the stretched muscle. This is termed the *stretch reflex.*

Muscle spindles play an important and com-plex role in the performance of athletic skills. Stretching exercises to improve flexibility must be performed slowly in order to limit the muscular contraction that results from stimulating the stretch reflex. However, the athlete can utilize the stretch reflex to enhance a ballistic contraction of a muscle. Many preparatory phases in sports skills include an action in the opposite direction of the intended line of motion so as to stretch the active muscles and initiate a reflex contraction.

Golgi Tendon Organs. These sensory receptors are located near the muscle-tendon junction and lie perpendicular to the fibers of the muscle. Golgi tendon organs are sensitive to tension, and thus are stimulated by the contraction of a muscle. When sufficiently stimulated these sensory receptors inhibit the contraction of the muscle in which they are located. This mechanism is designed to protect the muscle from excessive tension and can be observed when a muscle abruptly relaxes during a forceful contraction. Also, Golgi tendon organs may facilitate the complete relaxation of a muscle immediately following a strong contraction. This phenomenon is vital to efficient muscular control and to the performance of skills that require multiple actions of a body segment.

Joint Receptors. Pressure-sensitive receptors located within the joint tissues provide valuable sensory information regarding the position, direction, velocity, and acceleration of movements of a body segment. This information is vital to the maintenance of correct body position or form during the performance of a skill.

Vestibular Mechanisms. Specialized receptors located in the inner ear (labyrinthine receptors) provide the central nervous system with information that aids in the maintenance of balance during movement. The athlete relies significantly upon this sensory information when performing skills that require shifting of the body weight or projection of the body into space.

The information provided by these sensory receptors is necessary for the performance of coordinated sports skills. This kinesthetic information, when combined with the information obtained from other sensory systems, provides the basis on which the athlete selects and initiates correct motor responses to the changing environmental demands encountered on the playing field.

Muscle Fiber Types

The fundamental mechanisms of muscle function are the same in all skeletal muscle fibers. However, it has been known for many years that human muscles are composed of two types of fibers. These have been termed fast-twitch (FT) and slow-twitch (ST) fibers. In recent years much research in exercise physiology has focused on determining the significance of the FT and ST fibers in athletic performance. As indicated by their names, fast-twitch fibers contract more rapidly than do slow-twitch fibers. Figure 15.8 demonstrates that stimulated FT fibers develop their peak tension in about 20 milliseconds, while ST fibers require approximately 60 milliseconds to generate their maximum force. This suggests, of course, that FT fibers should have an advantage over ST fibers

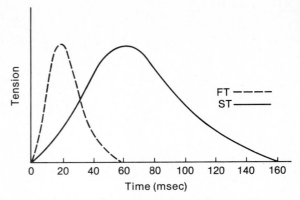

Figure 15.8 Tension curves for fast-twich and slow-twitch skeletal muscles.

whenever maximum speed of muscle contraction is desired.

FT and ST fibers also differ somewhat in their abilities to perform certain types of muscular work. FT fibers are well adapted for high-intensity activity, since they are able to split and regenerate ATP rapidly. However, FT fibers tend to fatigue quickly because they are poorly adapted for the production of energy through aerobic metabolism (see Chapter 16). In contrast, the ST fibers are relatively fatigue resistant owing to their high capacity for aerobic metabolism.

All skeletal muscles include a mixture of FT and ST muscle fibers. However, individual motor units include only FT or ST fibers. As shown in Figure 15.9, the FT and ST fibers are distributed throughout the muscle.

Scientific evidence suggests that the FT and ST motor units are preferentially recruited by the nervous system to perform the types of exercise for which each is best adapted (Gollnick et al. 1973). For example, if an athlete were to perform a low-intensity activity, like jogging, the ST fibers in the leg muscles would be called upon to generate the force needed to perform the movements. However, if the athlete were to begin sprinting, the FT fibers quickly would be called into play.

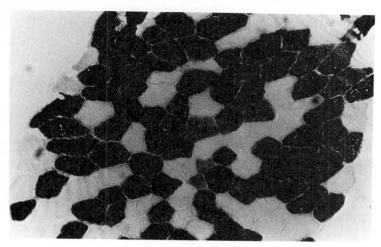

Figure 15.9 Fast-twitch (dark) and slow-twitch (light) fibers distributed in a skeletal muscle. (From Fox, E.L., and D.K. Mathews. *The Physiological Basis of Physical Education and Athletics.* 3rd ed. Philadelphia: (Saunders College Publishing, 1981.)

It now seems clear that an athlete's ability to perform certain types of exercise is determined, in part, by the relative proportion of FT and ST fibers in his/her skeletal muscles. The ratio of FT to ST motor units in a particular skeletal muscle varies tremendously from one person to another. For example, in the gastrocnemius muscle of the calf the percentage of ST fibers has been observed to vary from below 25% to over 75%. Available evidence suggests strongly that the FT/ST muscle fiber ratio is determined genetically and cannot be modified by training. The importance of the FT/ST fiber ratio has been reinforced by studies of world class athletes. Such studies have indicated that successful endurance athletes tend to have a preponderance of ST fibers, while power/speed athletes have a greater proportion of FT fibers (see Figure 15.10).

This information, of course, supports what coaches have known for many years: Athletic performance is determined in part by genetically established inherited traits. But it should be emphasized that muscle fiber type is far from a perfect predictor of athletic potential. Studies have shown that a fairly wide range of muscle fiber types is compatible with high levels of performance in most athletic events. Also, it must be borne in mind that athletic performance is determined by a multiplicity of physical and psychological variables. No single variable establishes one's athletic potential.

Factors Affecting Contraction of Skeletal Muscles

Thus far our discussion of skeletal muscles has focused on processes that operate at the cellular or subcellular level. However, during the performance of sports skills each muscle operates as an intact unit. During physical activity each active muscle's function is to contract with the levels of force and speed needed to perform a particular bodily movement. Following is a discussion of several factors that determine the speed of contraction and force of contraction of skeletal muscles.

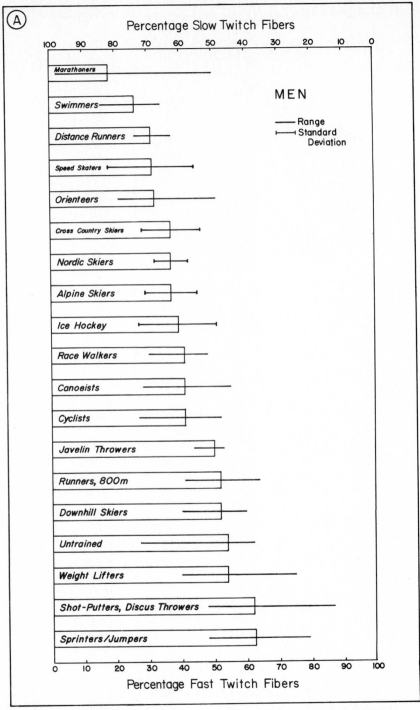

Figure 15.10 Fiber type distributions in male (A) and female (B) athletes. (From Fox, E.L., and D.K. Mathews. *The Physiological Basis of Physical Education and Athletics*. 3rd ed. Philadelphia: Saunders College Publishing, 1981.)

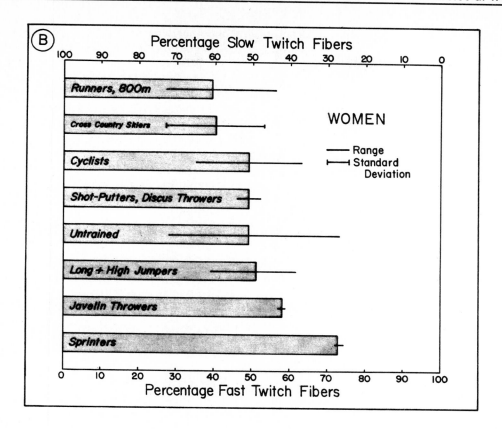

Gradation of Force

Skilled athletes constantly exhibit an ability to control the force generated by the contraction of their skeletal muscles with almost absolute precision. Two physiological functions work together to allow the athlete to vary the force of muscle contraction.

The primary means by which an athlete controls the force of muscle contraction is by *varying the number of motor units recruited.* Each skeletal muscle consists of many motor units, and, theoretically, the nervous system can call on any number of them to contract at a particular time. The greater the number of motor units contracting, the greater the force generated.

A second method for varying a muscle's force of contraction is to *vary the frequency of nervous impulses delivered to the individual motor units.* Whenever a motor unit is stimulated to contract a single time it will generate about the same amount of force. However, if a second stimulus is delivered before complete relaxation of the motor unit occurs its fibers will contract again and with greater force. When very high frequencies of nervous impulses are delivered to a motor unit it can develop three to four times the force generated when contraction results from a single stimulus.

It should be noted that both of the methods for force gradation are executed by the nervous system. Thus mastery of these functions is a matter of "learning." This learning takes place through a lifetime of experiences and, in the case of the athlete, through many hours of specific practice. For example, the golfer who holes a 30-ft putt demonstrates an ability to generate exactly the correct amount of force in the muscles that move the golf club. The golfer, in essence, has recruited, in each active muscle, the correct number of motor units and has stimulated each unit at the proper frequency.

Force of Contraction and Muscle Length

The maximum force that can be generated by a muscle is dependent upon its length. Ordinarily, a muscle can develop its greatest force when it is near its maximum resting length (MRL). This MRL usually corresponds to the length of a muscle when the joint that it crosses is fully extended (but not hyperextended). As shown in Figure 15.11, as the muscle shortens its maximum force of contraction decreases. This observation is particularly important for athletes who seek to generate maximal levels of force. The key principle is: If all other factors are held constant, a muscle will generate its greatest force when contracted at its maximum resting length. However, it must be remembered that the muscles act through the bony lever system of the body. Thus, in applying the length-tension principle the coach must also consider the mechanical factors that may affect force application (see Chapter 12). Often, it is

found that *maximum force application* (as distinct from muscle force generation) is observed at a joint angle that involves an optimal combination of muscle length and mechanical advantage. For example, in performing a forearm curl in weight lifting, maximum force can be applied to the barbell when the angle at the elbow joint is approximately 90°. In this position the elbow flexor muscles are somewhat shortened, but mechanical factors more than overcome this disadvantage.

Force-Velocity Relationship

The velocity with which a muscle is capable of contracting is inversely related to the force that is required to cause the contraction. Thus, as is shown in Figure 15.12, maximum velocity of contraction will occur when the force required is minimal. This phenomenon is commonly encountered in everyday life: We all know that we can lift a relatively light object more rapidly than a heavy object.

The force-velocity relationship in skeletal muscle has important applications in sports performance, particularly in activities that depend on maximal speed. It is known that the maximum velocity of movement is best related to the percentage of the muscle's maximum force required. Thus, we would expect that if the relevant muscle groups became stronger maximum speed of movement at a particular level of force generation should increase. This would be anticipated since, as shown in Figure 15.12, after strength improvement a given amount of force will represent a smaller percentage of the muscle's maximum. Experimental training studies have supported this hypothesis. Consequently, coaches should recognize that speeds of movement can be increased by increasing the strength of the muscles involved in performing that movement. For example, the speed with which a shot putter can move the shot from his shoulder to the release position can be increased by improving the strength of the muscles that extend the elbow joint.

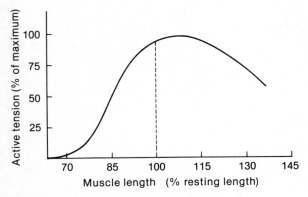

Figure 15.11 A muscle's maximal force of contraction is related to its length.

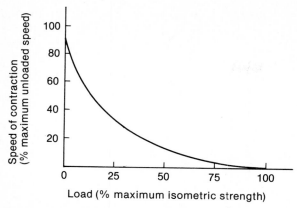

Figure 15.12 A muscle's maximum speed of contraction is inversely related to the load that it must overcome.

Muscle Temperature and Speed of Contraction

Maximum speed of muscle contraction is affected by muscle temperature. Studies on isolated animal muscles have shown that cooling a muscle below its normal temperature markedly reduces its speed of contraction; conversely, warming a muscle can slightly increase its maximum speed of contraction. These observations suggest that warming the important muscle groups should aid performance in speed-related athletic activities. Consequently, one is tempted to conclude that precompetition warm-up should improve speed. While the research data on this issue are conflicting, it does seem reasonable to recommend a thorough warm-up prior to speed-related athletic contests.

Summary

Skilled athletic movements depend upon the precise control of skeletal muscle contractions.

The sliding filament theory of muscle contraction indicates that muscle shortening results from an interaction between the subcellular protein filaments actin and myosin. Contraction and relaxation of muscle is controlled by the central nervous system, which receives sensory input from peripheral receptors such as muscle spindles, Golgi tendon organs, and joint receptors. Human muscle fibers may be categorized as either fast-twitch (FT) or slow-twitch (ST). ST fibers are well adapted to endurance exercise, while FT fibers are preferentially utilized during high-intensity activity. The force generated by a contracting muscle is affected by several factors, including the frequency of nervous stimulation, number of motor units recruited, length of the muscle, speed of contraction, and muscle temperature. An understanding of the fundamentals of muscle physiology is essential to a mastery of exercise physiology and to the design of proper training programs for athletes.

References

Gollnick, P.D., Armstrong, R.B., Sembrowich, W.L., Shephard, R.E., and Saltin, B. Glycogen depletion pattern in human skeletal muscle fibers after heavy exercise. *Journal Applied Physiology*, 34:615–618, 1973.

Hoyle, G. How is muscle turned on and off? *Scientific American*, 222:84–93, 1970.

Huxley, H.E., and Hanson, J. Changes in the cross striations of muscle during contraction and stretch, and their structural interpretation. *Nature*, 173:973–976, 1954.

Recommended Readings

Knuttgen, H.G. (Ed). *Neuromuscular Mechanisms for Therapeutic and Conditioning Exercise*. Baltimore: University Park Press, 1976.

Lamb, D.R. *Physiology of Exercise, Responses and Adaptations*. New York: Macmillan Publishing Co., 1978.

Credit: University of South Carolina Sports Information.

The Energetics of Muscular Activity

16

Athletic activities often provide dramatic demonstrations of human energy expenditure. The basketball player who performs a center jump must expend energy at a very high rate, albeit for only an instant. In contrast, the channel swimmer expends energy at a moderate rate for many hours. This chapter discusses the processes by which the body generates energy for muscular activities. In addition, this chapter provides a description of the patterns of energy expenditure typically observed during exercise and includes an explanation of how athletes' performances are often limited by their energy transfer capabilities.

Energy, Work, and Power

In sports we commonly speak of an athlete as having "lots of *energy*" or as being "out of *energy*." Likewise, we tend to call athletes "hard *workers*" or "*work* horses," and, of course, we often refer to some athletes as "*powerful*." Since common usage can blur the true scientific meanings of certain terms, we should begin our discussion of human energy expenditure by defining *energy*, *work*, and *power*.

Energy

Energy is the capacity to perform work. Although energy is found in many specific forms, it is most often quantified in terms of the universal heat unit, the kilocalorie (kcal).* Energy is found in two primary forms, *potential energy* and *kinetic energy*.

Sources of potential energy are found all around us. For example, the body of the diver who had ascended to a high platform possesses considerable potential energy. That potential for work performance is dramatically demonstrated as the diver leaps off the platform and descends rapidly to the pool below. Potential

---

*One kcal is that amount of heat required to increase the temperature of 1 liter (L) of water 1° Celsius (C).

energy also is stored in such forms as electricity and heat and within the structure of chemical substances such as foodstuffs.

Kinetic energy is the energy of movement and, as such, is commonly observed in sporting activities. In athletics we often see rapid transformations of potential energy to kinetic energy. In the example cited previously, the diver's potential energy is quickly converted to kinetic energy as descent occurs. Likewise, the football halfback who sprints downfield demonstrates a high level of kinetic energy. The potential energy source of this football player's kinetic energy will be discussed in later sections of this chapter.

A key concept regarding energy is summarized in the following fundamental law of physics: *Energy is neither created nor destroyed; however, it can change form.* Thus, athletes do not create energy, nor do they destroy or eliminate it. However, athletes do continuously transform potential, chemical energy to kinetic, mechanical energy. This energy transformation is the foundation on which muscular activity is based.

Work

Work is a demonstration of kinetic energy. Work involves movement and is quantitatively equal to the product of force and the distance through which the force is applied ($W = F \times D$). Since energy is the capacity to do work, energy and work are terms that can be used interchangeably, and that can be expressed in the same units (i.e., calories, foot-pounds [ft-lb], kilogram-meters [kg·m]). Thus, a certain amount of muscular work can be thought of as equivalent to a matching quantity of potential energy. For example, the 140-lb cross country runner who runs up a hill that is 200 feet high performs 28,000 ft-lb of work and this is equivalent to about 9 kcal of energy (Figure 16.1).

Power

Power is work expressed per unit time:

$$P = \frac{\text{work}}{\text{time}}$$

Power is an extremely important concept in athletics since it designates the rate at which work is performed. Usually, in sports we are less concerned with the amount of work that athletes perform than with the rate at which they perform it. In sports higher levels of performance are usually associated with higher rates of work; that is, greater power.

Since work is an expression of kinetic energy, power can be expressed in units of either work or energy per unit time. Continuing with the example of the cross country runner (Figure 16.1), if the uphill run was completed in two minutes, the power output would be 14,000 ft-lb per minute. This is equivalent to a rate of energy expenditure of 4.5 kcal per minute.

Energy Transformation by Skeletal Muscles

As discussed in Chapter 15, muscle contraction is accompanied by the breakdown of aden-

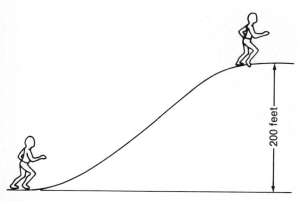

Figure 16.1 Computation of work and power. When a 140-lb runner runs up a 200-ft hill, 28,000 ft-lb of work have been performed. Runner's body weight = 140 lb. Time to climb hill = 2 min. Work = force × distance = 140 lb × 200 ft = 28,000 ft-lb.

$$\text{Power} = \frac{\text{work}}{\text{time}} = \frac{28,000 \text{ ft-lb}}{2 \text{ min}} = 14,000 \text{ ft-lb/min.}$$

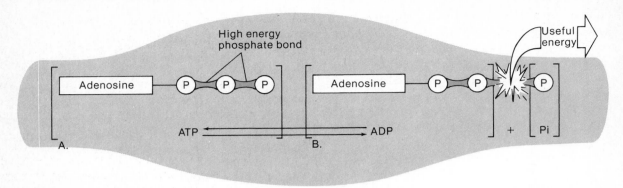

Figure 16.2 (A) The ATP molecule contains two high-energy phosphate bonds. (B) During muscle contraction ATP is broken down to ADP, releasing the energy that is used to fuel the contractile process. (From Fox, E. L., and D. K. Mathews. *The Physiological Basis of Physical Education and Athletics.* 3rd ed. Philadelphia: Saunders College Publishing, 1981.)

osine triphosphate (ATP). ATP, sometimes called the "energy currency" of the cell, is found in the muscle fibers and is the immediate source of energy for muscle activity. As demonstrated in Figure 16.2, each ATP molecule contains two high-energy phosphate bonds. These chemical bonds represent a pool of potential energy that can be transformed to mechanical energy under the proper circumstances.

During contraction of a muscle fiber the high-energy bonds of many ATP molecules are broken. The rupture of these bonds is facilitated by the action of an enzyme that is located at the tip of the myosin cross bridges. When ATP is broken the energy stored in its chemical bonds is used to cause movement in the myosin cross bridges. It is the movement of these myosin cross bridges that causes the fibers to generate tension and to shorten. Thus, muscle contraction involves a transformation of chemical energy to mechanical energy; that is, ATP bond energy is used to fuel the movements of the human body (Huxley 1969).

Muscular activity can continue only as long as the muscle fibers contain a ready supply of ATP. However, the muscle fibers maintain a very limited amount of ATP and this store, conceivably, could be depleted with only a very few contractions. Thus, it is clear that sustained muscular activity requires that the ATP supply be continuously and rapidly refilled. The maintenance of the ATP supply in skeletal muscle is so important to normal functioning that the muscle fibers have evolved a very elaborate and effective system for generating ATP.

The metabolic pathways that maintain the ATP stores of the muscle fibers do so by regenerating ATP from the products of its degradation. As shown in Figure 16.2, during contraction ATP is broken down to ADP (adenosine diphosphate). The regeneration of ATP is accomplished by reattaching a phosphate group to ADP. Since the breakdown of ATP releases energy for use in muscle contraction, it is clear that regenerating ATP must require the input of energy. The metabolic processes of the muscle fiber are dedicated to providing the chemical energy needed to regenerate ATP. The metabolic pathways accomplish this task by releasing chemical energy from the foodstuffs we eat. This release of energy usually occurs *aerobically* (i.e., with the use of oxygen), but it can take place *anaerobically* (without oxygen) for brief periods of time.

Anaerobic Muscle Metabolism

Ultimately, all the energy for muscular activity is provided by aerobic metabolic processes.

However, certain forms of physical activity require that the immediate sources of energy for ATP regeneration of skeletal muscles be anaerobic. The muscle fibers possess two energy-yielding systems that can function in the absence of oxygen (Gollnick and Hermansen 1973).

Creatine Phosphate System

Creatine phosphate (CP) is a chemical substance that, like ATP, contains a high-energy phosphate bond (see Figure 16.3). But, unlike ATP, CP cannot be used directly to provide the energy for muscle contraction. Rather, as shown in Figure 16.3, CP is utilized to regenerate ATP.

Since CP is found in the muscle fibers and since only a single chemical reaction is needed to transfer its bond energy to ATP, the CP system can function very rapidly. Thus, the power (rate of energy yield) of the CP system is quite high. In contrast though, this system's capacity (total amount of energy) is relatively low. This is true because muscle fibers maintain only a modest store of CP. Thus, the CP system is very useful in providing the energy for very high-intensity, short-duration physical activities. For example, the energy required to perform a 40-yd sprint can be provided entirely by: (1) using that ATP available in the muscle fibers at the onset of exercise, and (2) regenerating ATP at the expense of the muscle's CP stores.

Anaerobic Glycolysis

In sporting activities athletes are frequently called upon to perform high-intensity exercise

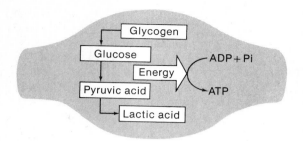

Figure 16.4 Anaerobic glycolysis is a series of chemical reactions that result in the breakdown of glycogen to lactic acid. In the process, energy is released and used to regenerate ATP. (From Fox, E.L., and D.K. Mathews. *The Physiological Basis of Physical Education and Athletics*. 3rd ed. Philadelphia: Saunders College Publishing, 1981.)

that continues for more than a few seconds (e.g., for 400-m dash). In such circumstances, a metabolic pathway called anaerobic glycolysis assumes considerable importance. This pathway uses the stored carbohydrate, glycogen, as its raw material. Anaerobic glycolysis involves a series of chemical reactions that release energy from the glycogen molecule. This energy is utilized to regenerate ATP, which, in turn, is used in muscle contraction (see Figure 16.4).

Anaerobic glycolysis is a great benefit to athletes since it provides a means by which substantial amounts of ATP energy can be provided without the utilization of oxygen. (As will be discussed later in this chapter, the muscles' supply of oxygen is often limited.) However, anaerobic glycolysis has one major disadvantage and that is its end-product, lactic acid. It has long been known that lactic acid is associated with muscle fatigue. When large amounts

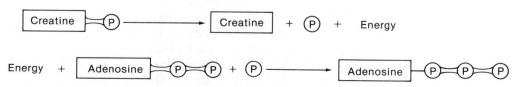

Figure 16.3 Creatine phosphate (CP) contains a high-energy phosphate bond, which when broken can provide energy to regenerate ATP from ATP and inorganic phosphate.

of lactic acid accumulate in a muscle its function is impaired and the result is fatigue (Tesch et al. 1978). Consequently, the capacity of the glycolytic system is limited by the individual athlete's tolerance for lactic acid. The typical athlete's lactic acid tolerance limit is attained with about one minute of sustained, "all out" exercise.

Aerobic Muscle Metabolism

The body's primary energy system is aerobic metabolism. This system provides energy for regeneration of ATP by oxidizing the carbohydrates, fats, and proteins that are stored in the cells. Unlike the anaerobic system, aerobic metabolism is highly efficient and produces no fatigue-generating end-product. Thus, the body prefers to utilize the aerobic pathway, and during exercise always uses it to the greatest extent possible (Holloszy 1973).

As shown in Figure 16.5, the raw materials for aerobic metabolism are oxygen and one of the three primary foodstuffs: carbohydrates, fats, or proteins. Under normal circumstances, very little protein is utilized for energy expenditure. However, both fats and carbohydrates are important energy sources during muscular activities. Since substantial amounts of glycogen (a carbohydrate) and triglyceride (a fat) are typically stored in muscle fibers, the availability of these substances seldom poses a limitation during exercise. However, the muscle fibers are capable of storing only a small amount of oxygen and, therefore, oxygen must be continually delivered to the muscle fibers.

Aerobic metabolism causes a complete breakdown of the foodstuffs that are used as raw materials. This contributes to the relatively high efficiency of the aerobic system, since nearly all of the energy stored in the foodstuff molecule is used to regenerate ATP. For example, aerobic metabolism of one unit of glycogen results in a regeneration of 38 units of ATP. In contrast, anaerobic metabolism of a unit of glycogen regenerates only two units of ATP. Also, it should be noted that the end-products of aerobic metabolism are water and carbon dioxide. Both of these substances can easily be disposed of by the body and, consequently, their production poses no limitation to the athlete's work capacity. This, of course, is in contrast to anaerobic glycolysis, which produces lactic acid.

Since the aerobic system is efficient and produces no fatiguing end-product, it is the muscle's preferred energy source. During low- and moderate-intensity exercise, aerobic metabolism provides virtually all the ATP energy needed by the muscles. This can occur because, under such circumstances, the cardiorespiratory system is able to transport oxygen to the muscles at an adequate rate. Thus, athletic activities that involve sustained, moderate-intensity exertion are particularly dependent on the aerobic metabolic system.

The role of oxygen in aerobic metabolism cannot be overemphasized. Stated simply, in the absence of oxygen aerobic metabolism cannot occur. Oxygen is plentiful in the atmosphere. However, the principal site of aerobic metabolism during exercise is the mitochondria in the muscle fibers. Thus, in order for oxygen to participate in metabolism it must be transported from the atmospheric air to the muscle mitochondria. This task is accomplished by the cardiorespiratory system (lungs, heart, blood vessels, and blood). Since this system provides such crucial support for active muscles, cardiorespiratory functions during exercise will be discussed in considerable detail in the next chapter.

Power and Capacity of the Energy Systems

Each of the three energy systems makes an important contribution to the athlete's ability to perform vigorous exercise. The three systems complement one another, but each possesses unique characteristics that cause it to be the dominant energy source during a certain type

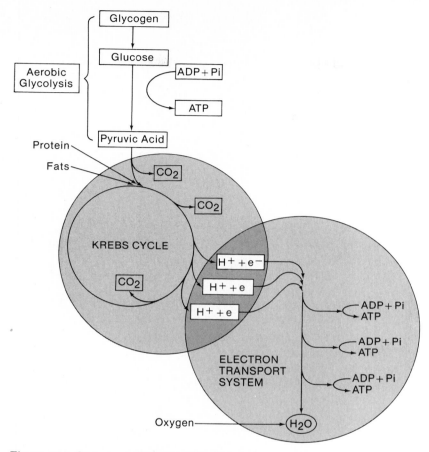

Figure 16.5 Summary of the aerobic (oxygen) system. Glycogen is oxidized in three major series of chemical reactions, aerobic glycolysis in which pyruvic acid is formed and some ATP resynthesized; the Krebs cycle in which CO_2 is produced, and H+ and e− are removed; and the electron transport system in which H_2O is formed from H+, e−, and oxygen, and more ATP is resynthesized. Fats and proteins, when used as fuels for ATP resynthesis, also go through the Krebs cycle and the electron transport system. (From Fox, E.L., and Mathews, D.K. *The Physiological Basis of Physical Education and Athletics.* 3rd ed. Philadelphia: Saunders College Publishing, 1981.)

of exertion. It is particularly significant that the three systems differ in maximal power and maximal capacity.

Power, as discussed earlier in the chapter, refers to the rate at which work is performed.

Thus, with reference to an energy system, *maximal power* refers to the greatest rate at which the system can provide energy for muscular work. The *maximal capacity* of a system is the total amount of energy available for muscular

Table 16.1: Maximal Powers and Capacities of the Three Energy Systems*

System	Maximal Power (Units of ATP Provided per Min)	Maximal Capacity (Total ATP Units Available)
ATP-CP	3.6	0.7
Anaerobic Glycolysis	1.6	1.2
Aerobic	1.0	unlimited

*From Fox, E. L., and Mathews, D. K. *The Physiological Basis of Physical Education and Athletics.* 3rd ed. Philadelphia: Saunders College Publishing, 1981.

work through that system. Table 16.1 presents typical maximal powers and capacities for the three energy systems.

The maximal power of the CP system is very high and, consequently, it is the muscle's primary energy source during very high-intensity activity (e.g., jumping, sprinting). However, since the muscle fibers store only small amounts of CP, the capacity of this system is low and alone it can support only a few seconds of intense activity. At the opposite end of the range, the aerobic system possesses a virtually infinite capacity, but it has a very limited maximal power. The capacity of the aerobic system is considered unlimited because its raw materials, oxygen and either carbohydrate or fat, are usually available in far larger amounts than would be needed during a single exercise bout. However, the maximal rate of energy expenditure through the aerobic system, the *maximal aerobic power,* is limited by the maximal rate at which the cardiorespiratory system can transport oxygen to the muscles. As will be discussed in the next chapter, this rate of oxygen transportation is often quite limited.

The maximal power and capacity of the anaerobic glycolysis system falls between those of the CP and aerobic systems. The capacity of the anaerobic glycolysis system, though greater than that of CP, is limited by the accumulation of its fatiguing end-product, lactic acid. The maximal power of the glycolytic system is quite

great, and, thus, it can provide the ATP needed for relatively high-intensity activity.

The Energy Continuum

While the three energy systems are unique, they often work together in providing energy for muscular work (Fox and Mathews 1981). Under resting conditions virtually all of the body's ATP energy is provided through aerobic metabolism. During exercise aerobic metabolism always provides as great a fraction of the muscle's total energy requirement as possible. The magnitude of this fraction depends on the rate at which oxygen is delivered to the active muscles. During many forms of exercise aerobic metabolism cannot meet the total energy requirements because of limitations posed by the oxygen transport system (i.e., cardiorespiratory functions). In such instances, anaerobic processes complement aerobic metabolism so that the muscle's energy requirement is satisfied.

The relative contributions of the aerobic and anaerobic systems to total energy expenditure depend largely on the intensity and duration of the exercise bout. As shown in Figure 16.6, during very short-duration, high-intensity exercise the anaerobic systems dominate. This is required because the muscle's supply of oxygen falls short of its oxygen demand under such circumstances. With exercise of only a few seconds duration the CP system is able to provide

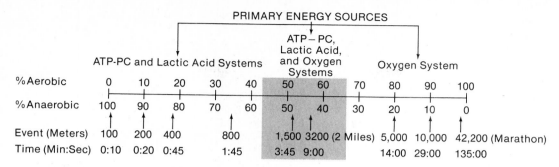

Figure 16.6 The approximate percentage of contribution of aerobic and anaerobic energy sources in selected track events. Nonshaded areas represent predominance of either anaerobic (left) or aerobic (right) metabolism. The shaded area represents events in which anaerobic and aerobic systems are of nearly equal importance. (From Fox, E.L., and Mathews, D.K. *The Physiological Basis of Physical Education and Athletics.* 3rd ed. Philadelphia: Saunders College Publishing, 1981.)

essentially all the needed ATP energy. However, as the duration of high-intensity exercise increases beyond a few seconds anaerobic glycolysis becomes an increasingly important energy provider. Athletes who perform exhaustive exercise of 15 seconds to two minutes duration derive much of their muscular energy from glycolysis and, therefore, may experience fatigue on account of lactic acid accumulation.

Aerobic metabolism functions during all forms of exercise and, consequently, always makes some contribution to the athlete's total energy requirement. This contribution becomes increasingly significant as the duration of activity increases. As demonstrated in Figure 16.6, during an "all out" work bout of two minutes duration approximately one half of the body's energy is supplied aerobically. Longer duration activities rely to an even greater extent on the aerobic system. Muscular activities of greater than three to four minutes duration depend almost entirely on the aerobic system for their energy supply.

per unit time). The work involved in human movement occurs through the transformation of potential, chemical energy to kinetic, mechanical energy. This transformation is accomplished by skeletal muscle fibers that convert the chemical energy of ATP to the mechanical energy of muscle contraction. The anaerobic and aerobic metabolic systems function to maintain adequate levels of ATP in the muscle cells. The anaerobic systems, which include the creatine phosphate and glycolytic pathways, do not require oxygen, can function at high rates of power, but manifest very limited capacities. In contrast, the aerobic system requires oxygen, functions at moderate levels of power, and has a virtually unlimited capacity. The aerobic system provides most of the energy for low- and moderate-intensity activity, while the anaerobic systems predominate during very high-intensity activities. During many activities the aerobic and anaerobic systems work together to meet the muscles' demand for ATP energy.

Summary

Athletic activities involve performance of work, which frequently must be performed rapidly; that is, at a high level of power (work

References

Fox, E.L., and Mathews, D.K. *The Physiological Basis of Physical Education and Athletics.* 3rd ed. Philadelphia: Saunders College Publishing, 1981.

Gollnick, P.D., and Hermansen, L. Biochemical adaptations to exercise: Anaerobic metabolism. In *Exercise and Sport Sciences Reviews*. Vol. 1. Edited by J. Wilmore. New York: Academic Press, 1973.

Holloszy, J.O. Biochemical adaptations to exercise: Aerobic metabolism. In *Exercise and Sport Sciences Reviews*. Vol. 1. Edited by J. Wilmore. New York: Academic Press, 1973.

Huxley, H. The mechanism of muscular contraction. *Science*, 164:1356–1366, 1969.

Tesch, P., Sjodin, B., Thorstensson, A., and Karlsson, J. Muscle fatigue and its relation to lactate accumulation and LDH activity in man. *Acta Physiologica Scandinavica*, 103:413–420, 1978.

Recommended Readings

Astrand, P.-O., and Rodahl, K. *Textbook of Work Physiology*. 2nd ed. New York: McGraw-Hill, 1977.

Lehninger, A.L. *Bioenergetics*. 2nd ed. Menlo Park, California: W.A. Benjamin, Inc., 1973.

Margaria, R. The sources of muscular energy. *Scientific American*, 226:84, 1972.

Credit: University of Virginia Sports Information.

Oxygen Transportation and Oxygen Consumption

17

Oxygen is transported from atmospheric air to the cells of the body by the cardiorespiratory system. During exercise this system functions to support aerobic metabolism by increasing the rate at which oxygen is delivered to the active muscles. The cardiorespiratory system consists of four components: the lungs, heart, blood vessels, and blood. As shown in Figure 17.1, these components are organized into a closed system of vessels and organs that provides for a constant circulation of blood to the lungs and to all the other tissues of the body. The cardiorespiratory system plays a key role in the body's overall response to exercise and, consequently, a description of the basic functioning of each of its components follows.

The Cardiorespiratory System and Gas Transportation
The Heart

The heart is a four-chambered, muscular organ that functions to pump blood through the cardiovascular system. The heart moves blood by forceful, rhythmical contractions of the muscle fibers that compose the walls of its chambers. Figure 17.2 shows the direction of blood flow through the heart's chambers. The heart's contractile pattern is such that the two atria contract simultaneously and approximately $\frac{1}{10}$ of a second later the two ventricles contract together.

From the standpoint of exercise performance, the most important chamber of the heart is the left ventricle. This chamber pumps oxygenated blood to all the organs and tissues of the body, including the skeletal muscles. The volume of blood pumped by the left ventricle with each contraction is termed the *stroke volume*. Under resting conditions the stroke volume ranges from 70 to 120 milliliters (mL) of blood. The frequency of the heart's contractions is called the *heart rate*. The resting heart rate typically varies from 50 to 80 beats per minute in different individuals. The product of the heart rate and stroke volume is *cardiac out-*

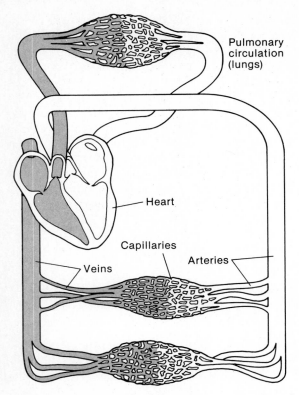

Pulmonary circulation (lungs)

Heart

Capillaries

Arteries

Veins

Figure 17.1 The cardiorespiratory system consists of a closed system of vessels and organs through which the blood is circulated.

Arteries carry blood away from the heart. The arteries possess relatively thick, muscular walls that enable them to withstand the high pressure generated by the pumping action of the cardiac ventricles as the blood is forced into the arteries.

Capillaries are thin-walled vessels that surround the cells of the body. The walls of capillaries act as a semipermeable membrane for exchange of various substances between the blood in the capillaries and the extracellular fluids that bathe the cells.

Veins return blood from the capillaries to the right side of the heart. The walls of the veins are much thinner than those of the arteries because the blood loses much of its pressure as it passes through the capillaries, causing the venous pressure to be quite low.

Blood vessels are not rigid, static structures. Rather they are flexible tubes that can vary considerably in diameter. Blood vessels can be constricted (narrowed) through contraction of muscle cells that line the vessel walls. Relaxation of these muscle cells allows a vessel to dilate (open).

Constriction and dilation of blood vessels is an important determinant of blood flow distribution to various tissues of the body. For example, dilation of the arterioles (i.e., small arteries) in a particular muscle tends to increase blood flow to that muscle. Constriction of those vessels has the opposite effect.

put, the volume of blood pumped by the heart per minute. A normal resting cardiac output in an adult of average size is 5 liters (L) per minute. Cardiac output is a crucial variable during exercise and its magnitude is a major determinant of the rate at which oxygen is delivered to the active muscles. As might be expected, cardiac output increases markedly during exercise.

Vessels

Blood is carried throughout the body by the blood vessels. There are three fundamental types of blood vessels:

Blood

The blood that circulates through the vascular system is composed primarily of *plasma* and *red blood cells*. Plasma is a watery fluid that contains controlled concentrations of salts, proteins, and nutrients such as glucose. Suspended in the plasma are the red blood cells, which constitute approximately 40% of the total blood volume. It is these red blood cells that allow the blood to effectively transport oxygen.

The red blood cells contain a high concen-

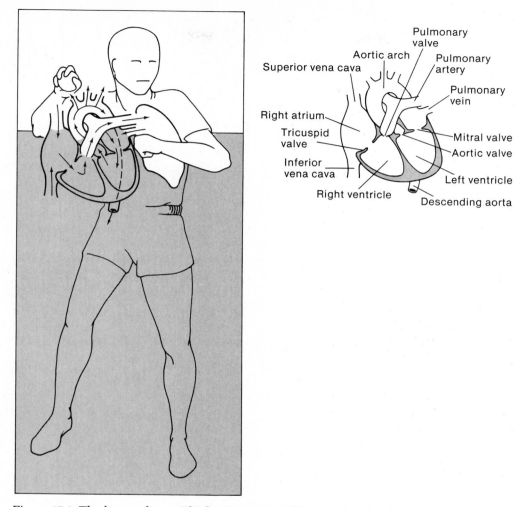

Figure 17.2 The human heart. The heart consists of four main chambers: the left atrium, left ventricle, right atrium, and right ventricle. The direction of blood flow is indicated by arrows. (From Fox E.L., and Mathews, D.K. *The Physiological Basis of Physical Education and Athletics.* 3rd ed. Philadelphia: Saunders College Publishing, 1981.)

tration of a red-pigmented protein called *hemoglobin*. Hemoglobin plays a critical role in oxygen transportation since it is capable of reversibly binding oxygen. As shown in Figure 17.3, hemoglobin tends to bind oxygen when its environment is oxygen rich, and it releases oxygen to environments that are relatively low in oxygen. This means that hemoglobin takes up oxygen in the lungs and releases it to tissues such as active muscles.

In individuals whose blood contains normal amounts of hemoglobin (12–17 grams [g] of hemoglobin per 100 mL of blood), the oxygen-carrying capacity of the blood approximates 20 mL

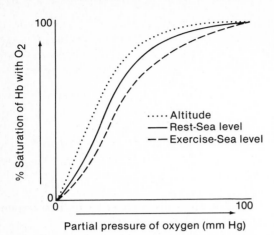

Figure 17.3 The oxygen-hemoglobin binding curve describes the relationship between the oxygen content of the environment (PO_2) and the saturation of hemoglobin with oxygen (% Hb saturation). Hemoglobin tends to bind oxygen in the lungs and release it to other body tissues. (From Fox, E.L. *Sports Physiology*. Philadelphia: W.B. Saunders Co., 1979.)

of oxygen per 100 mL of blood. Under almost all circumstances, blood becomes fully oxygenated as it circulates through the lungs. Thus, the arterial blood that is pumped by the left ventri-

cle leaves the heart and reaches the tissues in a fully oxygenated state.

When arterial blood reaches capillaries in oxygen-consuming tissues it encounters an environment that is relatively low in oxygen concentration. Under such circumstances, some oxygen is released from the blood's hemoglobin and diffuses into the tissue cells, where it can be used in aerobic metabolism. It is important to note that the fraction of the blood's oxygen that is released to the tissues is determined by the oxygen concentration of those tissues. In tissues that consume oxygen at a slow rate, relatively little oxygen is released from the red blood cells; however, in tissues that utilize the oxygen at a higher rate, a greater fraction of the blood's oxygen is unloaded. Thus, the red blood cells' release of oxygen to tissues increases with the rate of oxygen consumption by those tissues.

Ventilation

Ventilation is the movement of air into and out of the lungs. This process occurs through the rhythmic contraction and relaxation of the ventilatory muscles. As shown in Figure 17.4, inspiration occurs when contraction of the dia-

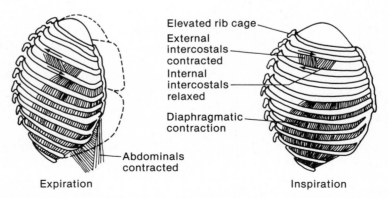

Figure 17.4 Ventilation results from alternating contraction and relaxation of the diaphragm and intercostal muscles. During exercise forced expirations are enhanced by contraction of the abdominal muscles.

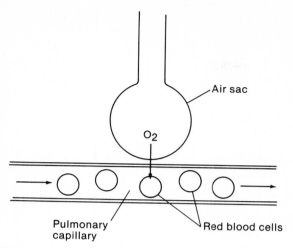

Figure 17.5 As blood circulates through the lung oxygen diffuses from air in the air sacs across the respiratory membrane into the red blood cells.

phragm and intercostal muscles expands the chest cavity. Expiration results from compression of the chest cavity, which takes place automatically with relaxation of the inspiratory muscles during rest. Forced expirations, such as those that occur with exercise, are enhanced by contraction of the abdominal muscles.

Ventilation is a crucial component of the oxygen transport process. Since oxygenation of the blood occurs as the red blood cells circulate through capillaries in the lungs, exchange of oxygen between the air in the lungs and the red blood cells depends on a continual diffusion of oxygen across the respiratory membrane (see Figure 17.5). Such diffusion can occur only so long as the concentration of oxygen in the air in the air sacs of the lungs (i.e., alveoli) is higher than that in the blood pumped to the lungs.* Thus, ventilation must take place at a rate that is sufficient to maintain a relatively high oxygen

*Gases and other substances in solution always tend to diffuse (move) from an area of high concentration to an area of lower concentration.

concentration in the alveolar air. Under normal circumstances, the ventilatory process is quite effective and, consequently, the blood's hemoglobin becomes almost fully oxygenated as it circulates through the lungs.

Carbon Dioxide Transportation

This chapter deals primarily with oxygen transportation and consumption. However, just as important to proper functioning of aerobic metabolism is elimination of its gaseous end-product, carbon dioxide (CO_2). CO_2 is produced in the mitochondria of the cells; it is cleared from the body by ventilation of the lungs. Thus, CO_2 must be transported from the tissue cells to the lungs.

Like oxygen, CO_2 is transported by the cardiorespiratory system. However, the exact manner of its transport by the red blood cells is unique. As shown in Figure 17.6, CO_2 enters the blood by diffusing from the cells into tissue capillaries. Once in the blood, CO_2 diffuses through the plasma and into the red blood cells. When CO_2 enters the red blood cells it rapidly undergoes a series of chemical reactions that ultimately produce the charged particle bicarbonate. Thus, CO_2 is carried through the bloodstream in the form of bicarbonate ions. After taking up CO_2 in the tissue capillaries, blood returns to the right side of the heart and is pumped to the lungs. Upon reaching the lung capillaries the chemical reactions that produced bicarbonate quickly reverse to yield CO_2. Gaseous CO_2 then diffuses from the blood into the air sacs of the lungs and subsequent ventilations expire the CO_2 into the atmosphere.

Cardiorespiratory Responses to Exercise

Vigorous exercise is accompanied by marked adjustments in the cardiorespiratory functions. These responses are necessitated by the increased demand for oxygen by the working skeletal muscles. As discussed in Chapter 16,

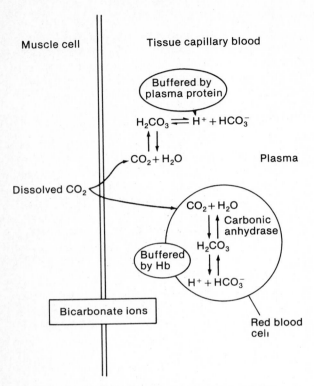

Figure 17.6 Carbon dioxide is transported in the blood largely in the form of bicarbonate ions.

active muscles seek to support their elevated adenosine triphosphate (ATP) requirements by aerobic metabolism. Since the muscles' rate of aerobic metabolism is limited by their oxygen supply, it is clear that the cardiorespiratory system plays a crucial role in supporting the athlete's exercise performance.

A discussion of the four fundamental adjustments made by the cardiorespiratory system during exercise follows.

Increased Cardiac Output

Perhaps the most fundamental cardiorespiratory response to exercise is increased cardiac output. This increase results from increases in both the stroke volume and heart rate (remember, cardiac output = stroke volume × heart rate) as shown in Figure 17.7; both the heart rate and stroke volume increase in proportion to the intensity of exercise. In an untrained individual the stroke volume can increase to about twice its resting level; the heart rate can increase to approximately three times its level at rest. These maximum values determine the individual's maximum cardiac output, which in the untrained person typically approximates five to six times the resting value. This, of course, results in a marked increase in the rate of oxygen delivery to tissues such as the skeletal muscles.

Diversion of Blood Flow to Working Muscles

During exercise it is primarily the active skeletal muscles that require increased blood flow and oxygen delivery. Other tissues, such as the digestive organs, require no increase in blood flow during exercise. This differential blood flow requirement is recognized by the cardiorespiratory system, which responds by diverting a greater fraction of the cardiac output to the working skeletal muscles. This is accomplished through dilation of arterioles in active muscles and constriction of arterioles in other tissues.

As shown in Figure 17.8, the shift of blood flow to active muscles can become quite extreme. Indeed, during very intense exercise as much as 90% of the cardiac output may be diverted to the skeletal muscles. This adjustment of the blood flow pattern complements the increased cardiac output so that increased oxygen delivery is focused largely on the tissues in greatest need, the active skeletal muscles.

Increased Arteriovenous Oxygen Difference

The difference between the oxygen content of arterial and venous blood is termed the arteriovenous oxygen difference (A-$\dot{V}$ O$_2$). As dis-

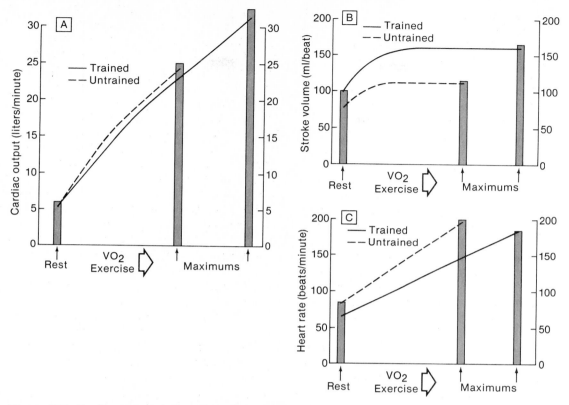

Figure 17.7 Cardiac output (A), stroke volume (B), and heart rate (C) increase as exercise intensity increases. Cardiac output is equal to the product of the heart rate and stroke volume. (From Fox, E.L., and Mathews, D.K. *The Physiological Basis of Physical Education and Athletics.* 3rd ed. Philadelphia: Saunders College Publishing, 1981.)

cussed earlier in this chapter, arterial blood is almost always fully saturated with oxygen and, thus, contains about 20 mL of oxygen per 100 mL of blood. Venous blood is always relatively deoxygenated. However, its oxygen content varies across a wide range (5–15 mL oxygen/100 mL blood). As compared with resting conditions, during exercise more of the blood's oxygen is released to the working muscles; consequently, venous blood oxygen levels are decreased. As shown in Figure 17.9, venous oxygen content decreases as intensity of exercise increases. This reduction in venous oxygen reflects greater oxygen delivery to the tissues; that

is, a greater A-$\dot{V}$ O_2. During very strenuous exercise A-$\dot{V}$ O_2 can increase from about 5 mL to about 15 mL of oxygen per 100 mL of blood and, thus, increases oxygen delivery to the tissues to three times the resting level.

Increased Ventilation

During exercise elevated cardiac output increases blood flow through the lungs as well as through the peripheral tissues. Thus, to ensure a complete oxygenation of the blood, ventilation must increase in proportion to the increase in cardiac output. As shown in Figure 17.10,

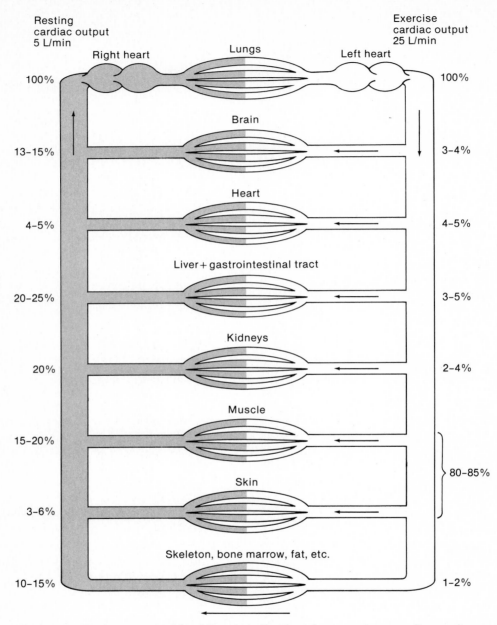

Figure 17.8 During exercise blood flow is redistributed so as to increase flow to the active muscles. The redistribution is accomplished by selective constriction and dilation of arterioles.

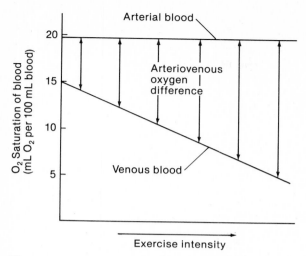

Figure 17.9 Arteriovenous oxygen difference increases with exercise owing to greater unloading of oxygen to the active muscles. This is reflected as a reduced venous blood oxygen content; arterial blood remains fully oxygenated across the entire range of exercise intensities.

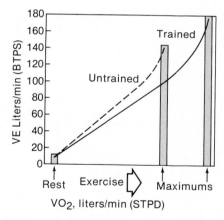

Figure 17.10 Ventilation increases linearly with exercise intensity up to the anaerobic threshold (AT). At intensities above the AT ventilation increases rapidly. (From Fox, E.L., and Mathews, D.K. *The Physiological Basis of Physical Education and Athletics.* 3rd ed. Philadelphia: Saunders College Publishing, 1981.)

ventilation of the lungs increases linearly with work intensity up to a level called the anaerobic threshold. Above this level, ventilation increases rapidly and the exerciser may experience ventilatory stress (dyspnea) or breathlessness. The significance of anaerobic threshold will be discussed later in this chapter.

Ventilation must increase during exercise so that a normal alveolar air composition is maintained. Specifically, it is crucial that relatively high oxygen levels and relatively low CO_2 levels be maintained in the alveolar air. Such conditions are required to ensure a steady diffusion of oxygen into the blood and constant diffusion of CO_2 out of the blood. In normal, healthy individuals (i.e., those not afflicted with pulmonary diseases) the ventilatory process is very effective and, indeed, arterial blood becomes fully oxygenated and adequately cleared of CO_2 during even the most exhaustive exercise. Consequently, ventilation is not normally a limiting factor in the athlete's oxygen transport system (Shepard 1969).

These four fundamental cardiorespiratory responses to exercise work in synchrony to meet the skeletal muscles' increased demand for oxygen. As demonstrated in Figures 17.7 to 17.10, each component of the cardiorespiratory system responds in proportion to the intensity of exercise. In general, the system adjusts only to the extent needed to insure adequate oxygen delivery to the muscles. Thus, the cardiorespiratory system maintains maximum efficiency by doing the least work necessary to accomplish its gas transport task.

The efficiency and effectiveness of the cardiorespiratory functions are ensured by an elaborate and fully integrated set of nervous and chemical control factors. These factors are summarized in Figure 17.11, which demonstrates that the focal point for cardiorespiratory control is a nerve center in the brain called the cardiorespiratory center. This center is the origin of nerve pathways that travel to the heart, blood vessels, and ventilatory muscles. By varying its output of nerve impulses the cardiores-

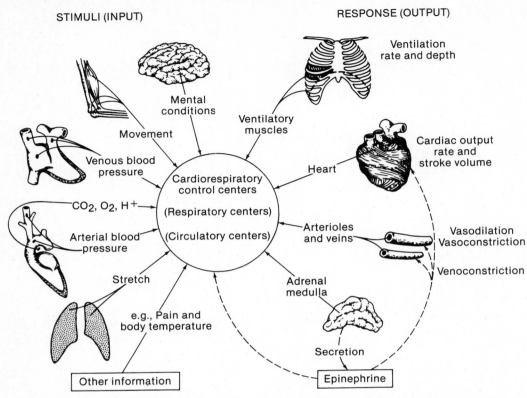

STIMULI (INPUT)

RESPONSE (OUTPUT)

Figure 17.11 The cardiorespiratory system is controlled by the cardiorespiratory center, a nerve center located in the brain. The cardiorespiratory center integrates various forms of stimuli and in response elicits appropriate modifications in ventilation and blood flow. (From Fox, E.L., and Mathews, D.K. *The Physiological Basis of Physical Education and Athletics.* 3rd ed. Philadelphia: Saunders College Publishing, 1981.)

piratory center can increase or decrease the heart rate and stroke volume, constrict or dilate blood vessels, and alter the rate and depth of breathing. The center's nervous output is influenced by various forms of nervous and chemical input that it receives by way of nerve pathways from sensory receptors throughout the body. In particular, the system is sensitive to changes in: (1) the oxygen, carbon dioxide, and acid-base levels of the blood, (2) blood pressure, (3) mechanical stimuli from moving limbs and muscles, and (4) input from conscious levels of the brain.

Oxygen Consumption During Exercise

As discussed in Chapter 16, a fundamental physiological response to exercise is an increased rate of ATP utilization in the active muscle fibers. Because of its efficiency and great capacity the aerobic metabolic system is the muscle's preferred source of ATP. However, the rate at which ATP can be regenerated aerobically is limited by the rate at which oxygen can be delivered by the cardiorespiratory system to the active muscles. In the following paragraphs we describe the typically observed responses of aerobic metabolism to various forms of exercise.

Since aerobic muscle metabolism can occur only with the utilization of oxygen, the body's rate of oxygen consumption is an absolute reflection of its *aerobic* metabolic rate. Oxygen consumption can be readily measured by collecting and analyzing an individual's expired air. Many studies of oxygen consumption during exercise have been performed over the years, and consequently we know a great deal about the response of aerobic metabolism during exercise.

An individual's rate of oxygen consumption ($\dot{V}O_2$) is quantified in liters of oxygen consumed per minute (L/min). Such values are greatly affected by body size, since a larger person possesses more metabolically active tissue and larger organs in the cardiorespiratory system. In exercise physiology we are frequently interested in comparing the rates of oxygen consumption among athletes who differ in body size. In such comparisons it is necessary to control for these variations in body size, which is most commonly accomplished by expressing $\dot{V}O_2$ relative to body weight—that is, milliliters of oxygen consumed per kilogram of body weight per minute (mL/kg/min).

Oxygen Consumption at the Onset of Exercise

Figure 17.12 demonstrates the response of oxygen consumption at the beginning of a constant intensity, submaximal work bout. At the start of exercise the rate of oxygen consumption begins to increase immediately, but it typically requires two to three minutes to attain the level demanded by moderately strenuous work. This "lag" in the $\dot{V}O_2$ response indicates that aerobic metabolism cannot respond rapidly enough to meet the body's entire energy requirement during the transition from rest to exercise. During this transition period the body is said to accumulate an oxygen deficit. *Oxygen deficit is de-*

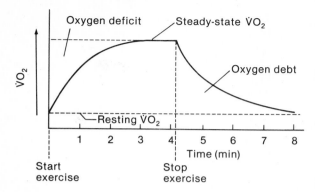

Figure 17.12 At the onset of submaximal, constant-intensity exercise the rate of oxygen consumption ($\dot{V}O_2$) increases to a steady state in two to three minutes. The delayed response in $\dot{V}O_2$ results in accumulation of an oxygen deficit. During recovery the oxygen debt is repaid as $\dot{V}O_2$ gradually returns to resting level.

fined as the difference between the body's oxygen demand and the volume of oxygen actually consumed at the onset of exercise.

Since aerobic metabolism cannot provide all the required energy at the start of vigorous exercise, it is clear that the anaerobic metabolic processes must be utilized. Indeed, the oxygen deficit is an indication of an anaerobic metabolic contribution to the total energy demand. The higher the intensity of exercise, the greater is the oxygen deficit and the contribution of the anaerobic systems. For example, a middle-distance runner tends to accumulate a substantial oxygen deficit at the start of a race, since the total rate of energy expenditure far exceeds the aerobic system's ability to provide ATP energy. In contrast, a golfer who walks down a fairway accumulates a very small oxygen deficit because walking involves a relatively moderate and gradual increase in the rate of energy expenditure.

The pattern of the oxygen consumption response at the onset of exercise is probably related to the cardiorespiratory adjustments that take place at that time. Oxygen consumption can increase no more rapidly than the rate of oxygen delivery to the working muscles. Thus, it seems likely that the accumulation of an oxygen deficit at the onset of vigorous exercise is dictated by the gradual adjustments in cardiorespiratory variables such as cardiac output. It is known, for instance, that heart rate requires two to three minutes to attain a steady state level.

Oxygen Consumption Following Vigorous Exercise

Upon termination of vigorous exercise the body's rate of oxygen consumption remains at an elevated level for several minutes. As shown in Figure 17.12, over a period of 20 to 30 minutes $\dot{V}O_2$ gradually declines back to its normal resting level. The "excess" oxygen consumed following exercise is termed the oxygen debt. *Oxygen debt is defined as the difference between oxygen consumed following exercise and that which would be consumed during a comparable period of rest.*

The oxygen debt represents an amount of energy that the body must expend in recovering from an exercise bout. Several specific factors contribute to the oxygen debt: (1) some of this energy is used to restore the muscle cells' supplies of ATP and phosphocreatine, (2) some energy must be expended in clearing the blood and other tissues of lactic acid, (3) some oxygen is utilized following exercise to replenish the body's modest oxygen stores (e.g., oxygen in solution in body fluids and bound to muscle myoglobin), and (4) after exercise the body's temperature, heart rate, and ventilation, which have been elevated by exertion, decline gradually to resting levels and while elevated these processes must be supported by oxygen consumption.

Oxygen Consumption in Relation to Work Intensity

As emphasized in Chapter 16, aerobic metabolism is the body's preferred energy system.

Thus, it should not be surprising that as exercise intensity increases, the rate of oxygen consumption increases proportionally. Figure 17.13 demonstrates this principle and shows that, for a given athlete, oxygen consumption and exercise intensity are linearly related up to a point beyond which oxygen consumption can no longer increase despite further increases in work intensity. The exercise intensity at which oxygen consumption plateaus varies greatly among different individuals. The factors that determine an athlete's maximum rate of oxygen consumption will be discussed in the next section.

Since oxygen consumption and aerobic metabolism are dependent upon transportation of oxygen to the active muscles, cardiorespiratory functions play a key role in an athlete's response to exercise of increasing intensity. As with oxygen consumption, cardiac output, ventilation, and arteriovenuous oxygen difference all increase in proportion to exercise intensity. These responses can have great practical significance for the athlete. Variables such as the heart rate and ventilation are relatively easy for the athlete to monitor. Since these functions in-

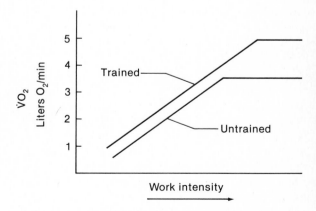

Figure 17.13 Rate of oxygen consumption ($\dot{V}O_2$) increases with increasing work intensity up to some maximum level. Maximal oxygen consumption or maximal aerobic power varies widely among different individuals and is increased by appropriate training.

crease in direct proportion to both exercise intensity and oxygen consumption, the athlete or coach can use the heart rate and/or ventilation as practical, on-the-field measures of exercise intensity. For example, swimmers can learn to accurately judge their pace by becoming familiar with their individual ventilatory responses to exercise at various intensities.

Oxygen Consumption and Performance of Endurance Exercise

Since the capacities of the anaerobic metabolic systems are extremely limited, the energy for long-duration exercise must be provided primarily by aerobic metabolism. As discussed previously, the aerobic system functions only with the consumption of oxygen. Consequently, an athlete's ability to consume oxygen is a key determinant of his/her ability to perform endurance exercise. Indeed, it has long been known that successful endurance athletes consistently demonstrate an ability to consume oxygen at high rates for extended periods of time. In recent years we have learned a great deal about the factors that determine an athlete's level of performance in endurance activities. In this section we shall discuss three factors that are particularly important for endurance athletes. These are *maximal aerobic power, anaerobic threshold,* and *oxygen cost of activity* (i.e., efficiency).

Maximal Aerobic Power

Maximal aerobic power, frequently called maximal oxygen consumption, is the greatest rate at which an individual is capable of consuming oxygen during exercise. In the physiological literature maximal aerobic power is abbreviated $\dot{V}O_2$max. It is important to emphasize that $\dot{V}O_2$max refers to a *rate* of oxygen consumption, not simply an amount of oxygen consumed. For example, virtually anyone is capable of consuming 5 L of oxygen if given long enough to do it. However, very few individuals, most of whom are highly trained endurance athletes, are able to consume 5 L of oxygen in one minute.

Maximal aerobic power is best measured by observing the rate of oxygen consumption as an individual performs an exercise bout in which intensity is gradually increased until exhaustion occurs. A common laboratory method for assessment of $\dot{V}O_2$max involves analyzing expired air samples collected from a subject who performs a graded treadmill run to exhaustion. As was shown in Figure 17.13, the rate of oxygen consumption is expected to increase in proportion to exercise intensity. However, each athlete eventually reaches a point at which his/her rate of oxygen consumption can increase no more despite further increases in work intensity. This greatest rate of oxygen consumption is the athlete's $\dot{V}O_2$max and is an absolute measure of the greatest rate at which the individual can provide ATP energy by aerobic metabolism. Nonlaboratory field methods for estimation of $\dot{V}O_2$max will be discussed in Chapter 21.

Maximal aerobic power is known to vary greatly among individuals. If $\dot{V}O_2$max values are expressed relative to body weight, as they should be when comparing individuals, scores ranging from less than 6 to over 80 mL/kg/min have been reported for various types of persons. At the high end of the scale are world class endurance athletes such as distance runners and cross-country skiers, whereas severely incapacitated heart patients are found at the low end of the range. For many years much research has been directed toward identifying the physiological factors that determine and limit an individual's $\dot{V}O_2$max. Although this issue has not been completely settled, some of the factors that affect $\dot{V}O_2$max are as follows:

Cardiorespiratory Function. An individual can consume oxygen no more rapidly than the cardiorespiratory system can transport oxygen to the active tissues. Thus, the functional capacity of an athlete's cardiorespiratory system is probably a key determinant of his/her

$\dot{V}O_2$max. Most exercise physiologists tend to agree that the maximum pumping capacity of the heart (maximal cardiac output) is the most important of the cardiorespiratory variables. However, other cardiorespiratory factors such as ventilatory capacity and blood hemoglobin levels may limit $\dot{V}O_2$max in some persons.

Aerobic Muscle Metabolism. During exercise oxygen is literally *consumed* in the muscle fibers that are actively contracting. Thus, $\dot{V}O_2$max is a reflection of the skeletal muscles' ability to extract oxygen from the blood and use it in aerobic metabolism. While physiologists disagree as to the importance of muscle metabolic capacity in determining $\dot{V}O_2$max, it is clear that athletes can have high $\dot{V}O_2$max values only if their active skeletal muscles are able to use oxygen rapidly in aerobic metabolism.

Body Fatness. Fat tissue adds to the total body weight, but it does not contribute directly to the athlete's ability to consume oxygen during vigorous exercise. Thus, if $\dot{V}O_2$max is expressed relative to body weight, fat weight tends to increase the denominator without affecting the numerator of the $\dot{V}O_2$ expression:

$$\dot{V}O_2(mL/kg/min) = \frac{\dot{V}O_2 \text{ (L of } O_2) \times 1000}{\text{body weight (kg)}}$$

Thus, excessive body fatness tends to decrease weight-relative $\dot{V}O_2$max and functional capacity by increasing body weight.

Training State. The activity habits and training background of athletes can substantially affect $\dot{V}O_2$max scores. It is now well documented that both cardiorespiratory and muscle metabolic functions adapt to endurance training and contribute to increases in $\dot{V}O_2$max (Ekblom et al. 1968). In Chapter 22 we will discuss training for improved cardiorespiratory endurance in much more detail.

Genetic Endowment. Although $\dot{V}O_2$max can be increased through appropriate training, most training studies show that the magnitude of such increases is limited to 10 to 20%. These figures may underestimate the increases that occur with long-term, high-intensity training programs; but nonetheless, it seems clear that an individual athlete's $\dot{V}O_2$max can vary only within some genetically determined range (Klissouras 1972). This same principle probably applies to all other biological factors that effect human performance.

There is no doubt that maximal aerobic power is an important determinant of endurance exercise performance. Support for this conclusion comes from several lines of research. Descriptive studies have shown that highly successful athletes in endurance events consistently show high $\dot{V}O_2$max values. Table 17.1 lists previously recorded $\dot{V}O_2$max values for successful athletes in various sports. The reader will note that the highest values were reported for sports that require relatively high rates of energy expenditure for extended time periods (i.e., distance running, cross-country skiing). Other studies have observed high correlations between $\dot{V}O_2$max and performance in endurance sports such as distance running, swimming, and cycling (Costill 1967). Also, it is well documented that appropriate training tends to simultaneously increase $\dot{V}O_2$max and endurance performance (Ekblom et al. 1968).

Table 17.1: Maximal Aerobic Power ($\dot{V}O_2$ in mL/kg/min) in Highly Competitive Male and Female Athletes

Sport	Males	Females
Cross country skiing	84	73
Distance running	83	62
Orienteering	80	62
Badminton	66	56
Swimming	70	55
Fencing	61	45
Archery	58	40
Untrained	44	37

*Data from Astrand, P.-O., and Rodahl, K. *Textbook of Work Physiology.* 2nd ed. New York: McGraw-Hill Book Co., 1977.

Thus, it seems clear that a high maximal aerobic power is a prime prerequisite to a high level of performance in endurance activities.

Anaerobic Threshold

During exercise of relatively low intensity the body's entire energy requirement is met by aerobic metabolism. However, as exercise intensity increases to higher levels anaerobic glycolysis begins to work in combination with the aerobic system. *The exercise intensity at which the by-product of anaerobic glycolysis, lactic acid, begins to accumulate in the muscle tissue or blood is called the anaerobic threshold* (AT). The work intensity at which the anaerobic threshold occurs is typically expressed as a percentage of the $\dot{V}O_2$max. Values as high as 90% of $\dot{V}O_2$max have been reported in some highly successful endurance athletes.

In recent years exercise physiologists have come to recognize that AT is an extremely important determinant of endurance performance (Costill et al. 1973). This variable is so important because studies have shown that athletes are unable to work for more than a few minutes at exercise intensities that exceed the AT; that is, fatigue sets in rapidly when the lactic acid concentration in the muscles reaches high levels. Thus, experience shows that in long-duration activities, such as marathon running or long-distance cycling, athletes should select an exercise intensity that approaches but does not exceed AT.

Since AT only recently has come under close scientific scrutiny, its determinants are not fully understood. However, it does seem clear that AT is affected by training (Davis et al. 1979). In beginners both $\dot{V}O_2$max and AT (expressed as a percentage of $\dot{V}O_2$max) increase substantially during the initial months of training. Thus, the athlete's ability to sustain moderately intense exercise may increase with training much more than would be predicted from the increases in $\dot{V}O_2$max alone. Although AT is altered by training, available evidence suggests that it is also a

function of genetic endowment. For example, persons with a higher percentage of slow-twitch muscle fibers (which are less inclined to produce lactic acid) are expected to show higher ATs.

Measurement of AT tends to be rather imprecise even when sophisticated laboratory equipment is employed. Nonetheless, athletes can learn to identify their own AT with reasonable accuracy. It is known that at work intensities near AT hyperventilation begins to occur. Thus, athletes who show very heavy, labored breathing are probably working at intensities above their AT. Also, an athlete's perception of fatigue is highly related to work intensity, and with experience athletes can learn to identify the intensity of work at which they begin producing lactic acid. Many athletes would describe this as the lowest intensity that "I know I could not sustain for more than 8 to 10 minutes."

Oxygen Cost of Activity (Efficiency)

A third factor that profoundly affects endurance performance is the oxygen cost of activity for the individual athlete. This variable is sometimes called *efficiency*. To the physicist efficiency is the ratio between the work output and energy input of a machine. That is,

$$\text{efficiency} = \frac{\text{work or energy output}}{\text{energy input}}$$

With human movement we might consider work output to be the amount of physical work accomplished in some period of time. Measurement of total human work output is extremely difficult in complex sporting events and, thus, is seldom attempted. More frequently, work output is operationally defined using terms that can more easily be measured. For example, we might consider "running at 6 miles per hour" or "freestyle swimming at 75 yards per minute" to be expressions of work output. Energy input can be directly measured by monitoring the athlete's rate of oxygen consumption while exercise is performed at a certain level of work output.

Studies have shown that for familiar activities such as running most individuals consume oxygen at *approximately* the same rate. For example, running at 6 mph requires oxygen to be consumed at about 35 mL/kg/min. However, it is important to note that there is significant variability in the oxygen cost of activity even for common movements like running. Oxygen consumption during running at 6 mph may vary from 30 to 40 mL/kg/min. Using the term *efficiency* as defined in the preceding paragraph, athletes who consume less oxygen when performing submaximal intensity activity are said to be more efficient—that is, they expend less energy in order to accomplish a given work output. The variability in oxygen cost of activity is greater for more complex and less familiar activities. For example, a novice swimmer is expected to be considerably less efficient (higher oxygen cost) than an experienced swimmer when the two swim at a designated pace.

As suggested previously, for oxygen cost of activity, the lower the better. Athletes who are more efficient consume oxygen at a lower rate while exercising at a given level and, consequently, place less stress on the cardiorespiratory and aerobic metabolic systems. Also, efficient performers, as compared with the less efficient, are able to work at higher levels of work output before reaching AT or $\dot{V}O_2$max. We might, for example, consider two runners who have the same $\dot{V}O_2$max and AT values but substantially different oxygen costs of running. The more efficient runner would be able to run at a faster absolute pace before reaching AT and $\dot{V}O_2$max. Clearly, efficiency is an advantage for the endurance athlete.

It is known that efficiency of movement varies among individuals, but the reasons for this variability are not fully understood. One factor that is presumed to be important is *mechanical efficiency*. This refers to the amount of mechanical work performed by persons as they execute a particular athletic skill. For example, hurdlers in track and field perform work against gravity as they leap over the hurdle. Skillful hurdlers are able to clear a hurdle with minimal vertical movement, whereas novice hurdlers are frequently observed to jump high over each barrier. Obviously, more vertical movement involves more work, greater energy expenditure, and lower overall efficiency. Similar examples could be drawn from each specific sport and, thus, it is important that coaches become familiar with the mechanical factors that affect efficiency of human movement (see Chapter 12).

A Physiological Model of Endurance Performance

In order to perform endurance exercise athletes must consume oxygen at elevated levels for extended time periods. The maximum work rate that an athlete can sustain for long periods is determined by the combined effects of maximal aerobic power, AT, and oxygen cost of activity. The ideal endurance athlete would have a very high maximal aerobic power (70–80 mL/kg/min), a very high AT (80–90% $\dot{V}O_2$max), and a very low oxygen cost of activity (or high efficiency). Studies have shown that world class performers in sports such as long-distance running, swimming, and cycling do show these characteristics. Frequently, however, endurance athletes achieve high levels of success despite having only moderately favorable values for one of the three important variables. One notable example is Frank Shorter, the 1972 Olympic marathon champion. Shorter's maximal aerobic power has been measured at approximately 70 mL/kg/min, certainly a high value, but not particularly high for a distance runner. Additional studies showed that Shorter has a very high AT and a very low oxygen cost of running (i.e., high efficiency). Thus, it is important to note that endurance performance depends on a combination of variables related to aerobic metabolism.

Summary

Performance of endurance exercise depends on: (1) transportation of oxygen from the atmosphere to active muscles, and (2) utilization of this oxygen by the muscles in aerobic metabolism. The process of oxygen transport is performed by the cardiorespiratory system, which consists of four components: lungs, heart, blood vessels, and blood. During exercise each component of the cardiorespiratory system responds in such a way as to increase the overall rate of oxygen transport to active muscles. The principal adjustments are: (1) increased cardiac output, (2) diversion of blood flow to working muscles, (3) increased arteriovenous oxygen difference, and (4) increased ventilation.

At the onset of exercise the body's rate of oxygen consumption rapidly increases to a level that is proportional to the exercise intensity. Though rapid, this adjustment is not immediate and, consequently, an oxygen deficit is accumulated. Following exercise the body's oxygen debt is repaid as oxygen consumption falls gradually to its resting level.

Performance capacity for endurance activities is determined by three factors related to oxygen consumption: maximal aerobic power, anaerobic threshold, and oxygen cost of activity (efficiency). These factors combine to determine the greatest exercise intensity that the athlete can sustain for an extended period of time.

References

Astrand, P.-O., and Rodahl, K. *Textbook of Work Physiology.* 2nd ed. New York: McGraw-Hill Book Co., 1977.

Costill, D.L. The relationship between selected physiological variables and distance running performance. *Journal of Sports Medicine,* 7:61–66, 1967.

Costill, D.L., Thomason, H., and Roberts, E. Fractional utilization of the aerobic capacity during distance running. *Medicine and Science in Sports,* 5:248–252, 1973.

Davis, J.A., Frank, M. H., Whipp, B. J., and Wasserman, K. Anaerobic threshold alterations caused by endurance training in middle-aged men. *Journal of Applied Physiology,* 46:1039–1046, 1979.

Ekblom, B., Astrand, P., Saltin, B., Stenberg, J., and Wallstrom, B. Effect of training on circulatory response to exercise. *Journal of Applied Physiology,* 24:518–528, 1968.

Klissouras, V. Genetic limit of functional adaptability. *Internationale Zeitschrift fur Angewandte Physiologie Einschlesslich Arbeitsphysiologie,* 30:85–94, 1972.

Shephard, R.J. The validity of the oxygen conductance equation. *Internationale Zeitschrift fur Angewandte Physiologie Einschlesslich Arbeitsphysiologie,* 28:61–75, 1969.

Recommended Readings

DeVries, H.A. *Physiology of Exercise for Physical Education and Athletics.* 3rd ed. Dubuque, Iowa: W. C. Brown, 1980.

Fox, E.L. *Sports Physiology.* Philadelphia: W. B. Saunders Co., 1979.

Shephard, R.J. *Endurance Fitness.* 2nd ed. Toronto: University of Toronto Press, 1977.

Nutrition for the Athlete

18

Throughout the history of sports the athlete's diet has been a particular concern. Since the time of the ancient Greeks, who believed that athletes should consume large amounts of meat, it has been a common perception that athletic performance can be enhanced by manipulation of the diet. Research conducted in recent years has tended to reinforce the conclusion that athletic performance can be altered by some dietary practices. However, this research has shown that many of the most commonly held beliefs regarding the athlete's diet are in fact incorrect. In this chapter we provide a review of the fundamental principles of human nutrition and summarize current knowledge of the impact that diet can have on athletic performance. In the course of this discussion we shall endeavor to dispel some of the misconceptions that have plagued the field of athletic nutrition for many years.

Sources of Energy for Muscular Work

One of the most important purposes of any person's diet is provision of adequate food energy. For athletes, many of whom expend large amounts of energy in training and competition, the energy content of the diet is particularly critical. In this initial section we shall: (1) describe the dietary nutrients that provide energy, and (2) discuss the factors that affect the sources of energy during exercise. In a later section of this chapter we shall discuss the concept of energy balance and its impact on body weight and body composition.

Carbohydrates, Fats, and Proteins

The energy value of food is expressed as *kilocalories* (kcal). Three basic foodstuffs contribute to an individual's total caloric intake. These nutrients are carbohydrates, fats, and proteins. The three differ in chemical structure, metabolic role, and caloric value. Carbohydrates and proteins provide about 4 kcal of energy per gram (g), whereas fats yield approximately 9 kcal of energy per gram. Table 18.1 provides a listing of important food sources of the three energy-yielding nutrients. The foods listed in each category are those that consist primarily of the designated energy nutrients. However, it should be noted that many food items include combinations of the three primary food stuffs. For example, most breakfast cereals consist primarily of carbohydrates, but they do include small proportions of protein and fat.

The energy-yielding nutrients enter the athlete's system in the form of food. As the food passes through the digestive system enzymes act to break down each of the primary foodstuffs into small chemical units that can be absorbed into the bloodstream (see Figure 18.1). For example, a complex carbohydrate such as starch is broken down as it passes through the mouth and stomach. The product of this digestive process is a simple carbohydrate, glucose, which can be absorbed into the bloodstream from the small intestine. Once the energy nutrients enter the bloodstream they may be transported to the liver for storage or further chemical processing or they may be carried directly to the cells of the body for use in metabolism.

Nutrients entering the cells of the body may be utilized immediately in one of the many metabolic pathways. Frequently, however, nutrients are incorporated into the cell's storage pool and saved for use at a later time. Two nutrient stores are particularly important to the exerciser. *Glycogen* is a storage form of carbo-

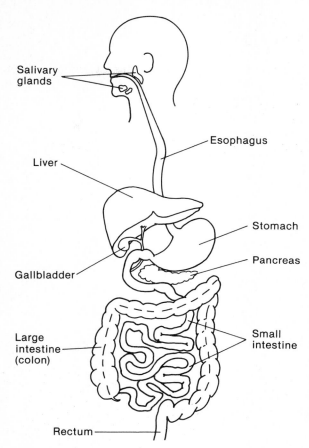

Figure 18.1 Digestion involves a series of physical and chemical actions that break down food so that nutrients can be absorbed from the intestinal tract into the blood stream. Mouth: (1) Food is physically broken into small particles by the teeth; (2) saliva lubricates food and begins the enzymatic break down of carbohydrate. Stomach: (1) Food is liquified by gastric juices; (2) enzymes and hydrochloric acid begin the chemical break down of proteins and fats and continue digestion of carbohydrates. Small intestine: (1) Enzymes secreted by liver and pancreas complete digestion of carbohydrates, fats, and proteins; (2) nutrients are absorbed into the bloodstream.

Table 18.1: Important Food Sources of the Energy-Providing Nutrients: Carbohydrate, Fat, and Protein

Nutrient	Food Sources
Carbohydrate	Cereals, grains, bread, pasta, sugar, honey, dried fruit
Fat	Oils, margarine, butter, nuts, peanut butter, salad dressing, marbled meats
Protein	Meat, fish, eggs, nuts, legumes, cereals

hydrate that can be used as fuel for either aerobic or anaerobic metabolism (see Chapter 16). The glycogen storage capacity of the muscle cells is quite limited and with long-duration exercise it is possible to virtually deplete the glycogen store of the active muscles. *Triglycerides are a form of fat that can be stored within the cells.* The total pool of triglycerides stored within a muscle cell can be substantial and sufficient to provide much of the energy for very long exercise bouts.

The primary bodily function of both carbohydrates and fats is provision of energy for cellular work. This includes the contractile work of muscle fibers; therefore, carbohydrates and fats are the principal sources of energy for exercise. Carbohydrates are particularly efficient sources of energy for muscular activity, since about 10% less oxygen is required to yield a calorie of energy using carbohydrates as compared with fats. However, fats are an excellent storage form of energy, since each gram of fat yields over twice as much energy as a gram of carbohydrate (9 cal vs. 4 cal). Thus, both carbohydrates and fats play key roles in providing the energy needed for muscular activity.

In contrast, protein does not ordinarily serve as an important source of energy. Rather, proteins are used primarily in growth, repair of tissues, and synthesis of cellular products such as enzymes and hormones. Protein is a key component of most body tissues and, thus, adequate dietary protein is important so that the structural integrity of tissues, including muscle, can be maintained. Proteins can serve as fuel for energy metabolism, but under normal circumstances, protein provides only a negligible fraction of the body's total energy requirement. *Thus, it is a misconception that protein is a primary source of energy for muscular exertion.*

Factors Affecting the Sources of Energy During Exercise

As mentioned previously, carbohydrates and fats both represent sources of food energy that can be utilized during exercise. Under most circumstances, a combination of fats and carbohydrates are used. The relative proportion of fat and carbohydrate metabolized in skeletal muscles during exercise is determined by the nature of the exercise and the athlete's diet prior to the exercise bout.

One factor affecting the muscles' source of energy is intensity of exercise. During rest and relatively low-intensity exercise most of the body's energy is provided through metabolism of fats. However, as intensity of exercise increases, carbohydrate becomes an increasingly important energy source. This conversion to carbohydrate usage at higher work intensities is useful, since carbohydrate metabolism requires less oxygen than fat metabolism and, thus, is somewhat less stressful for the cardiorespiratory system.

Duration of exercise is another factor that affects the proportions of fat and carbohydrate used for muscle metabolism. As duration of exercise increases the muscle cells gradually decrease their use of carbohydrate and proportionately increase utilization of fat. This changeover is dictated by a gradual depletion of the muscle's supply of glycogen. During very long-duration exercise, such as marathon running, cycling, or swimming, the glycogen concentration of the active muscles may approach zero, leaving fats as the principal source of energy. In such circumstances, athletes normally experience a sensation of fatigue that requires a reduction of work intensity. This phenomenon, sometimes called "hitting the wall" by marathon competitors, is probably related to the relative inefficiency of fat as a source of energy for high-intensity exercise.

The athlete's diet can profoundly alter the magnitude of the muscle glycogen store and can thereby affect the proportions of fat and carbohydrate used during subsequent exercise. A diet high in carbohydrate can help to elevate glycogen stores, whereas a low carbohydrate diet may allow muscle glycogen levels to drop. When the muscles have plenty of glycogen available they tend to use more carbohydrate than when glycogen stores are depressed. As will be discussed in a later section of this chapter, it is important that the endurance athlete enter competition with the muscle glycogen stores at a relatively high level.

Basic Nutritional Requirements

A proper diet provides an individual with: (1) sufficient calories to maintain energy balance, (2) adequate amounts of vitamins and minerals to support body metabolism, and (3) enough water to maintain fluid balance. In this section we describe nutritional practices that can ensure that the athlete's diet meets these fundamental criteria.

Caloric Needs

As a general principle, the athlete's diet should provide adequate food energy to maintain *caloric balance*. Caloric balance refers to a state in which the number of calories taken in food exactly balances the calories expended. As depicted in Figure 18.2, three major factors determine an individual's caloric expenditure. Calories expended in supporting metabolism and calories lost in excrement vary somewhat among individuals, but are not profoundly affected by exercise. Of course, calories expended in physical activity tend to be higher in habitual exercisers than in sedentary persons. Thus, the caloric expenditure of athletes tends to vary in proportion to the amount of activity involved in their sport. However, sports differ

greatly in the intensity and duration of exercise that they demand. Consequently, it is impossible to generalize about the caloric expenditure of athletes as a group. However, the data in Table 18.2 do provide some guidance regarding the energy demands of participation in selected sports.

Over a period of time an athlete's caloric expenditure should be balanced by caloric intake. If caloric intake exceeds caloric expenditure a weight gain occurs, since the excess calories are stored in the form of body tissue. Such a state of *positive caloric balance* is appropriate in young persons who are growing and in athletes who are attempting to add muscle tissue via a weight-training program (see Chapter 22). A *negative caloric balance* results when caloric expenditure exceeds caloric intake. This condition requires that calories be mobilized from existing tissues and, thus, causes a weight loss. Such a weight loss may be appropriate in athletes who need to lose fat tissue. However, a chronic weight loss may indicate that an athlete's diet is not providing adequate food energy. Because of the high energy demands of their sport some athletes may have difficulty in

Table 18.2: Caloric Requirements of Selected Sports Activities*

Sport	Kilocalories Expended per Minute of Activity
Cycling (13.1 mph)	11.1
Dancing	3.3 –7.7
Football	8.9
Golf	5.0
Gymnastics	2.5 –6.5
Rowing (87 strokes/min)	7.0
Running	10.0–17.0
Tennis	7.1
Skating (fast)	11.5
Skiing	10.0–15.0
Squash	10.2
Swimming	11.0–14.0
Wrestling	14.2

*From *Nutrition for Athletes*. Washington, D.C.: AAHPERD Publications, 1971.

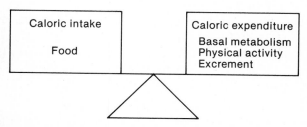

Figure 18.2 Caloric balance is a state in which the calories ingested in food are equal to the calories expended by or eliminated from the body.

maintaining their body weight and may require close supervision of their dietary practices.

Vitamins and Minerals

Vitamins are organic compounds that are needed in very small amounts in the diet but that are essential to normal cellular metabolism. Vitamins do not provide calories, but they are required for the proper utilization of food energy by the body. Approximately 10 vitamins have been identified as *essential nutrients*— that is, substances that the body must have but that it cannot synthesize. Consequently, vitamins must be included in the diet.

Table 18.3 lists the vitamins and the food sources and functions of each vitamin.

It should be noted that the vitamins may be classified as either fat soluble or water soluble.

The water-soluble vitamins cannot be stored in appreciable amounts in the body and can be lost in the urine. Consequently, a daily dietary supply of these vitamins is recommended. The fat-soluble vitamins are typically found in foods that contain fats and can be stored in the body in significant amounts. Since the body can store the fat-soluble vitamins, excessive intake of these vitamins, as may occur with "mega-vitamin" dosages, can result in overstorage and vitamin toxicity.

A recommended daily allowance (RDA) has been established for each vitamin. It certainly seems appropriate to recommend that the athlete's diet should provide the RDA for each vitamin, since many vitamin deficiencies are associated with impaired physical performance capacities. In another section of this chapter we shall discuss the issue of vitamin supplemen-

Table 18.3: Vitamins: Food Sources and Functions*

Vitamin	Sources	Functions
Fat-soluble Vitamins		
A	Liver, eggs, milk, butter, yellow vegetables	Adaptation to dim light; resistance to infection
D	Sunlight, fish, eggs, dairy products	Aids absorption of calcium
E	Green vegetables, vegetable oils	Prevents oxidation of essential vitamins and fatty acids
K	Green vegetables, liver	Blood clotting
Water-soluble Vitamins		
Thiamine (B_1)	Meat, cereals, milk, legumes	Energy metabolism
Riboflavin (B_2)	Milk, fish, eggs, meat, green vegetables	Energy metabolism
Niacin	Cereals, peanut butter, green vegetables, meat, fish, poultry	Energy metabolism, fatty acid synthesis
Pyridoxine (B_6)	Cereals, bananas, meats, spinach, cabbage, lima beans	Protein and glycogen metabolism; hemoglobin synthesis
Folic Acid	Green vegetables, mushrooms, liver	Blood cell synthesis
Cobalamin (B_{12})	Meat, poultry, fish	Blood cell synthesis; energy metabolism; nervous system function
C	Citrus fruits, tomatoes, potatoes, broccoli, cabbage	Formation of connective tissue; metabolism of vitamins

*From Smith, N. J. *Food for Sport.* Palo Alto, California: Bull Publishing Co., 1976.

tation and its relationship to exercise performance.

Minerals are elements in their simple, inorganic form. Over 20 minerals are found in the human body and, like vitamins, these substances are considered essential nutrients. Table 18.4 lists those minerals that are of particular concern in human nutrition and indicate the respective food sources, physiological functions, and RDAs. Minerals are often classified as either *macronutrients*, those that are needed in substantial amounts, or *micronutrients* of which only trace amounts are required in the diet.

As with the vitamins, an adequate dietary intake of the essential minerals is needed to maintain good health and normal function. Thus, athletes should take care to ensure that their diet provides the RDA for each mineral. In certain cases, mineral supplementation may be appropriate for some athletes and this issue will be discussed later in this chapter.

Water

Perhaps the most essential of all nutrients is water. The body fluids consist primarily of water and, as such, it is crucial to normal functioning that water intake be sufficient to balance the daily water loss. Even sedentary persons lose substantial amounts of water each day through sweating, respiration, production of urine, and elimination of feces. For athletes the loss of water, particularly through sweating, can be massive.

Maintenance of body water balance is of particular concern for athletes who train and/or compete in hot, humid environmental conditions. In such circumstances, dehydration can occur, resulting in impaired metabolic functioning and increased risk of heat illness. In Chapter 19 we shall discuss in more detail the role of water in regulation of the athlete's body temperature and shall recommend procedures by which the active athlete can maintain fluid balance.

Proportions of Basic Foodstuffs in the Athlete's Diet

As discussed previously, the total amount of food required by athletes is determined by body size and physical activity level. From the standpoint of maintaining caloric balance food sources of calories are not particularly important. However, the composition of the diet *is* a critical factor in health maintenance and athletic performance. Thus, the athlete's diet should reflect a proper blend of carbohydrates, proteins, and fats.

Most nutritionists recommend that about 55 to 60% of the diet's calories come in the form of

Table 18.4: Minerals: Food Sources, Functions and Recommended Daily Allowances (RDA)*

Mineral	Sources	Functions
Calcium	Dairy products, green vegetables, legumes	Bone formation; enzyme reactions; blood clotting
Iron	Liver, meats, soybeans, dried fruits	Hemoglobin formation, muscle growth; enzyme synthesis
Zinc	Shellfish, grains, meats	Growth; blood cell production; healing; enzyme reactions
Fluorides	Water supplies	Formation of teeth and bones
Iodine	Seafood, water supplies, iodized salt	Synthesis of thyroxine

*From Smith, N. J. *Food for Sport*. Palo Alto, California: Bull Publishing Co., 1976.

carbohydrates. Within the carbohydrate category about 90% of the calories should be derived from "complex carbohydrates" such as fruits, vegetables, cereals, and grains. The remaining carbohydrate calories may be consumed as simple sugars (e.g., pastry, candy, and refined sugar products). Carbohydrates, particularly those of the complex variety, tend to come in foods that are important sources of potassium, phosphorus, magnesium, zinc, iron, the B vitamins, and Vitamins C and E. Endurance athletes and others in very heavy training may require a diet that provides a higher than normal percentage of carbohydrate calories. A high consumption of carbohydrates may help to replenish the muscle stores of glycogen that tend to become depleted with long-duration exercise.

Protein should provide about 10 to 15% of total calories. This proportion of protein in the diet is sufficient to meet the basic protein needs of even very active athletes. Foods rich in protein include meats, dairy products, and many vegetables. It is possible to meet the body's protein requirement by consuming a vegetarian diet; however, this necessitates consumption of a careful mix of vegetables (see Smith 1976). Protein-rich foods are major sources of iron, zinc, and Vitamins B_6, B_{12}, and D.

Fats should constitute about 25 to 30% of the diet's caloric value. Fats tend to make foods more palatable and are important sources of food energy. Also, fats are often found in foods that include significant concentrations of fat-soluble vitamins (A, D, E, and K).

Energy Balance and Weight Control

In many athletic activities body weight is an important determinant of performance. One is unlikely, for example, to become a great defensive tackle in football or a world class shot putter without maintaining a relatively large body weight. However, across the spectrum of sports an even more important variable is body composition. Body composition refers to the ratio of fat tissue to lean tissue in the body and is most commonly expressed as percentage of body fat (% fat). Percent fat is the percentage of the total body weight that is fat:

$$\% \text{ fat} = \frac{\text{fat weight (kg)}}{\text{total body weight [kg]}}$$

It is important to note that body weight and body composition are not synonymous. It is quite common in sports like football for athletes to be quite heavy and yet very lean (low % fat). Thus, body weight is not an accurate measure of body composition. In Chapter 21 we shall explain measurements of body composition, and Chapter 22 includes a discussion of optimal body composition for various sports. For purposes of health maintenance it is recommended that males maintain a % fat not greater than 15% and females not greater than 25%.

An individual athlete's body composition is determined by a complex set of genetic and environmental factors. Fat, or adipose, tissue consists of fat cells that increase in number throughout childhood. The number of fat cells developed early in life varies considerably among different persons. Fat cell proliferation during childhood may be affected by environmental factors such as dietary and exercise habits; but after the stage of puberty the number of fat cells remains stable. Since fat cell number is a primary determinant of body composition, the normal range for % body fat for a given person is probably firmly established by the teen years. Thereafter, only the most extreme environmental conditions (e.g., starvation) cause % fat to move outside this range. The key point is that not all persons can be 8 to 10% fat, and efforts to bring this about may be harmful to an athlete's health and sports performance.

Although genetic factors may establish the reasonable range for an athlete's body composition, % fat can be substantially affected by personal habits and behavior. Of prime importance are diet and exercise. These two factors combine to determine caloric balance, as was discussed earlier in this chapter. Persons who chronically maintain a positive caloric balance (i.e., caloric intake exceeds caloric expenditure) tend to gain weight by increasing in size of the fat cells. This, of course, results in an increase of % body fat. A decrease in % body fat results from a negative caloric balance. Specific methods for decreasing % fat will be discussed in Chapter 22. It shall suffice to state at this point that the caloric value of the diet is a major determinant of body composition and, therefore, is a matter of concern for all athletes.

Percentage of body fat is an expression of fat weight relative to total body weight. Since total body weight is equal to the sum of fat weight and lean body weight (LBW), it is clear that LBW is an important determinant of overall % fat. For a given fat weight, the greater the LBW the lower the % body fat. Lean weight, like fat weight, is determined by both genetic and environmental factors. Changes in muscle mass, a major component of lean weight, can be quite substantial with activities such as weight training. Thus, it should be noted that overall % fat may be significantly altered by changing LBW independent of changes in fat weight.

Nutritional Supplements and Athletic Performance

Over the years the public and many coaches have come to believe that optimal sports performance requires that athletes consume a special diet. In certain restricted ways this perception is correct. As discussed earlier in this chapter, many athletes require a greater than normal volume of food in order to maintain caloric balance. In the next chapter we will emphasize the importance of fluid replacement for athletes who train in hot environmental conditions. But with very few exceptions, dietary supplements are unneeded and may even be harmful. Regrettably, misinformed individuals and various commercial interests continue to propagate the myth that athletic performance

can be promoted by ingestion of a multitude of dietary supplements. In the following paragraphs we will present scientific conclusions regarding the value of various diet supplements and modifications.

Protein Supplements

Protein is one of the three basic foodstuffs and, as previously discussed, should constitute about 10 to 15% of the caloric intake. This basic guideline applies equally to athletes and nonathletes, since exercise training does not increase the body's need for protein (Consolazio et al. 1975). Regrettably, protein supplementation has become extremely common among certain groups of athletes, particularly those engaged in weight training. The assumption seems to be that ingestion of a high protein diet will in some manner facilitate increased development of muscle mass. Research has shown that this assumption is incorrect (Rasch and Pierson 1962). Protein powders, drinks, and pills are a waste of money, and athletes should be informed of this fact. Also, athletes should know that excessive protein consumption can cause loss of appetite, diarrhea, and dehydration (Smith 1976).

The protein component of an athlete's diet should meet the following criteria:

1. Protein should be obtained from the normal food sources (e.g., meat, fish, nuts, and cereals).
2. Protein intake should constitute about 10 to 15% of total calories, a proportion typically found in a normal, well-balanced diet.

Vitamins

Vitamins are the most commonly utilized dietary supplement in contemporary society. Thus, it is not surprising that many athletes supplement their normal diet with various vitamin pills and preparations. At one time or another claims have been made for the beneficial effects on athletic performance of virtually every vitamin. Most frequently, these claims have been made by the commercial interests that sell vitamin supplements. *Controlled scientific studies have shown with remarkable consistency that vitamin supplements do not enhance exercise performance.*

The recommendations for dietary supplementation of two vitamins, C and E, have been particularly persistent and widespread in the athletic community. Proponents of Vitamin C supplementation say it reduces the frequency and severity of common colds. Controlled scientific studies have failed to reinforce this conclusion (Mayer 1975). Vitamin E supplements have been widely utilized by athletes for presumed benefits to performance of endurance exercise. This presumption is incorrect and the practice of Vitamin E supplementation is useless. In the words of Nathan J. Smith, M.D., author of *Food for Sport*, "Supplements of Vitamin E do not increase stamina, do not increase circulation or delivery of oxygen to muscles, do not lower blood cholesterol, do not prevent graying of hair, and perhaps of most interest, do not enhance sexual potency or cure infertility" (Smith 1976).

In summary, vitamins are key nutrients and athletes should receive the RDA of each. Since athletes typically ingest more food than sedentary persons, the risk of vitamin deficiency is miniscule in athletes who eat a well-balanced diet. As such, vitamin supplements are rarely needed, almost always wasteful, and if taken in extreme dosages may be harmful to health.

Minerals

Dietary supplementation of various minerals occasionally has been recommended for athletes. However, such supplementation is rarely needed, since most of the minerals that are essential in the diet are abundant in many common foods. An exception for some athletes is iron. Iron is a key component of hemoglobin, the protein that carries oxygen in the blood-

stream, and of several cellular enzymes. Iron deficiency can lead to anemia (low hemoglobin concentration in the blood), a condition associated with impairment of aerobic metabolism and endurance exercise performance.

In recent years a condition called "sports anemia" has been described (Williamson 1981). This condition is characterized by a lower than average blood hemoglobin concentration and is most commonly observed in endurance athletes such as distance runners. Causes of sports anemia are not fully understood; however, it seems clear that dietary iron deficiency can be a contributing factor. Also, heavy training may increase the rate of destruction of red blood cells and may cause significant iron loss through profuse sweating (Pate 1983).

Female athletes are at particularly high risk of developing anemia because menstrual bleeding results in a substantial loss of iron. Available studies indicate that many female athletes fail to obtain the RDA of iron in their diet (Clement and Admundson 1982). These observations indicate that female athletes should be routinely screened for anemia and iron deficiency. Those who are proven to be iron deficient should increase their intake of iron-rich foods (e.g., liver, dates, kidney beans, beef) and may benefit from dietary iron supplements.

Glycogen Loading

In recent years a dietary manipulation technique called "glycogen loading" has become very popular among endurance athletes. This procedure is based on two well-documented phenomena: (1) depletion of muscle glycogen is associated with fatigue in long-duration exercise, and (2) the muscle glycogen level can be altered by manipulation of an athlete's dietary and exercise patterns.

Studies of muscle glycogen in athletes have been conducted using a muscle biopsy procedure that involves surgically removing a small piece of muscle for chemical analysis. In the 1960's two Swedish physiologists, Jonas Bergstrom and Erik Hultman, used muscle biopsy procedures to observe the response of muscle glycogen to various diets and exercise treatments (Bergstrom et al 1967). They found that following exhaustive long-duration exercise 24 to 48 hours are required for muscle glycogen stores to be replenished. Furthermore, they found that the levels to which muscle glycogen returned depended on the athlete's diet during the recovery period. Highest levels of muscle glycogen were obtained with a diet very high in carbohydrates. In addition, it was found that even greater glycogen levels could be achieved if a low glycogen concentration was maintained for 24 to 48 hours following the exhaustive exercise bout. This can be achieved by ingesting a low carbohydrate diet. These observations led to the popularization of the so-called "glycogen loading" procedure.

Many different approaches to glycogen loading have been utilized by different athletes and there is no consensus as to the specific procedure that is best. The regimen outlined in Table 18.5 is consistent with available research findings and with the experiences of many endurance athletes.

It is important to note that glycogen loading is not recommended as a precompetition protocol for all athletes. Since glycogen depletion is a factor only in very long-duration and intense exercise, glycogen loading is expected to be beneficial to performance only in sports that involve over an hour of continuous, high-intensity activity. Glycogen loading is *not* likely to benefit athletes in the most common team sports such as basketball, football, volleyball, and baseball. Also, glycogen loading is not recommended for athletes who have metabolic diseases such as diabetes or hypoglycemia.

Although the glycogen loading procedure is apparently safe (Blair et al. 1982), coaches and trainers should recognize the technique is a stressful one and that during the low carbohydrate "depletion phase" athletes may experience considerable fatigue. This suggests that the complete glycogen loading procedure should be used sparingly. A less stressful but nonetheless quite useful technique involves reduced activity and ingestion of a high carbohydrate diet for the 24 to 48 hours prior to competition. This technique elevates muscle glycogen stores substantially, but it avoids the stress associated with maintaining a low glycogen level for an extended time period.

The Precompetition Meal

In many sports the precompetition meal has taken on mythical proportions. Many coaches and athletes have come to believe that ingestion of certain foods can lead to an immediate enhancement of performance. The facts do not support this belief. The pregame meal is notable more for the problems it can cause than for the benefits it can provide. Thus, the principal goal should be to design a pregame meal that does not prevent athletes from performing up to their potential. Prime considerations are timing of the meal, mix of basic foodstuffs, digestibility and palatability.

The precompetition meal should be scheduled so that the stomach is empty by the time of

Table 18.5: Glycogen Loading Regimen

Day	Exercise	Diet
Day 1	Long-duration activity to deplete muscle glycogen	Begin low carbohydrate diet
Day 2	Moderate-duration activity to maintain depletion of glycogen	Low carbohydrate until after training session; begin high carbohydrate after training
Day 3	Minimal activity	High carbohydrate
Day 4	Minimal activity	High carbohydrate
Day 5	Competition	High carbohydrate 2½–3 hours before competition; mixed diet after competition

the competition. For most athletes 2½ to 3 hours is an adequate time for food to clear the stomach, but not so long as to allow hunger to set in. The rate at which food is digested is a function of its mix of basic foodstuffs. Carbohydrates are digested much more rapidly than fats or proteins; it is therefore recommended that the pregame meal consist primarily of carbohydrates to speed digestion.

A precompetition meal comprised primarily of carbohydrates can help to maintain blood glucose levels and thereby ward off the perception of fatigue. While emphasizing carbohydrates, priorities should be given to the attractiveness and palatability of the meal. For these purposes, modest amounts of proteins and fats can be included in the meal. Also, care should be taken to accommodate individual preferences of athletes. Athletes should never be forced to consume foods that do not "agree with them."

A final concern is the fluid content of the pregame meal. In sports that involve heavy sweating and the possibility of significant dehydration, the pregame meal should include plenty of water. Pre-event hydration can, in a sense, initiate the fluid replacement process before fluid loss even begins. Of course, beverages are a major source of water, but so too are many foods such as fruits and vegetables.

One common pre-event dietary practice that is specifically *not* recommended is ingestion of a sugary solution (e.g., honey, soft drink, glucose solution) within one hour of competition. The disadvantages associated with this practice are described in more detail in Chapter 20.

Nutrition and the Athlete's Health

In concluding this chapter, it seems appropriate to focus on the role of the diet and maintenance of good health. Certainly, a principal goal of sports participation, particularly for children, is promotion of good health. Thus, the dietary practices recommended by coaches should promote the long-term well-being of their athletes.

In recent years scientific investigations have identified a number of disease problems that are associated with certain dietary practices. Of particular concern is the link between cardiovascular disease and consumption of a diet that is high in saturated fats and cholesterol. Cardiovascular diseases are the most frequent causes of death in the United States and most cardiovascular disease deaths result from a disease process called *atherosclerosis*. This disease involves the deposition of fatty plaques on the inner walls of the arteries. If the plaques become large enough blood flow to vital tissues may become occluded. The result can be development of potentially lethal diseases such as coronary heart disease and stroke. It is important to note that the atherosclerotic process often begins in childhood, although symptoms of atherosclerotic disease are seldom observed until the middle adult years.

Three major factors that are associated with the incidence of atherosclerotic cardiovascular disease are cigarette smoking, high blood pressure, and elevated levels of cholesterol in the blood. The latter factor is related to dietary intake of saturated fats and cholesterol. Over the past century the typical American diet has gradually shifted toward consumption of greater amounts of animal fats, which are particularly high in cholesterol and saturated fat. This unfortunate trend is probably a major explanation for the current high incidence of coronary heart disease in the United States.

In 1977 a United States Senate Select Committee on Nutrition and Human Needs issued a set of dietary goals. These goals, which are presented graphically in Figure 18.3, recommend that Americans should reduce their dietary intake of fat, cholesterol, refined sugar, and salt while increasing consumption of complex carbohydrates. To accomplish these goals Americans should make the following changes in food selection:

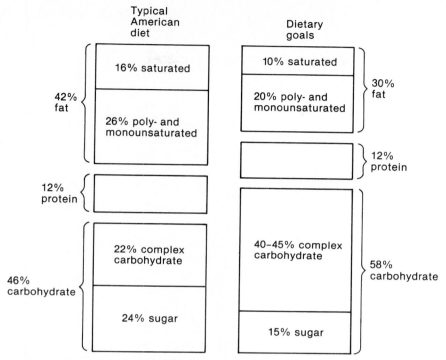

Figure 18.3 The typical American diet is too high in fat and too low in complex carbohydrate. (From *Dietary Goals for the United States*. 2nd ed. Washington: U.S. Government Printing Office, 1977.)

1. Increase consumption of fruits, vegetables, and whole grains.
2. Decrease consumption of red meat and increase consumption of poultry and fish.
3. Decrease consumption of foods high in fat and partially substitute polyunsaturated fat for saturated fat.
4. Substitute nonfat milk for whole milk.
5. Decrease consumption of butter fat, eggs, and other high cholesterol sources.
6. Decrease consumption of sugar and foods high in sugar content.
7. Decrease consumption of salt and foods high in salt content.

In the present context it is important to emphasize that the dietary practices recommended above are perfectly consistent with optimal athletic performance. The healthy diet is also a "high-performance diet." It is recommended that coaches guide their athletes toward the adoption of a diet that will promote good health as well as optimal athletic performance.

Summary

The athlete's diet should provide an adequate intake of food energy to maintain caloric balance and should include adequate amounts of the nutrients required to support body metabolism. Ordinarily, these objectives can be met by ingesting a mixed diet in which approximately 55% of calories are derived from carbohydrates, 15% from protein, and 30% from fat. Although vitamins and minerals are essential nutrients, dietary supplements of these substances are seldom needed. Athletic performance is not enhanced by ingestion of large amounts of nutrients such as protein, Vitamin C, or Vitamin E. However, athletes should take particular care to ensure that their diets provide adequate water, complex carbohydrates, and iron. Endurance athletes may benefit from manipulating the diet to achieve "glycogen loading."

References

Bergstrom, J., Hermansen, L., Hultman, E., and Saltin, B. Diet, muscle glycogen and physical performance. *Acta Physiologica Scandinavica*, 71:140–150, 1967.

Blair, S., Sargent, R., Davidson, D., and Krejci, R. Blood lipid and ECG responses to carbohydrate loading. *Physician and Sportsmedicine*, 8:68–75, 1980.

Clement, D.B., and Admundson, R.C. Nutritional intake and hematological parameters in endurance runners. *Physician and Sportsmedicine*, 10(3):37–43, 1982.

Consolazio, C.F., Johnson, H.L., Nelson, R.Q., Dramise, J. G., and Skala, J.H. Protein metabolism of intensive physical training in the young adult. *American Journal of Clinical Nutrition*, 28:29–35, 1975.

Mayer, J. *A Diet for Living*. New York: David McKay Co., Inc., 1975.

Nutrition for Athletes. Washington, D.C.: AAHPERD Publications, 1971.

Pate, R. R. Sports anemia: a review of the current research literature. *Physician and Sportsmedicine*, 11(2):115–131, 1983.

Rasch, P.J., and Pierson, W.R. Effect of a protein dietary supplement on muscular strength and hypertrophy. *American Journal of Clinical Nutrition*, 11:530–532, 1962.

Select Committee on Nutrition and Human Needs, U.S. Senate. *Dietary Goals for the United States*. 2nd ed. Washington, D.C.: U.S. Government Printing Office, 1977.

Smith, N.J. *Food for Sport*. Palo Alto, California: Bull Publishing Co., 1976.

Williamson, M.R. Anemia in runners and other athletes. *Physician and Sportsmedicine*, 9(8):73–79, 1981.

Recommended Readings

Bogert, J., Briggs, G., and Calloway, D. *Nutrition and Physical Fitness*. 9th ed. Philadelphia: W. B. Saunders Co., 1973.

Costill, D.L. Nutritional requirements for endurance athletes. In *Toward an Understanding of Human Performance*. Edited by E. J. Burke. Ithaca, New York: Mouvement Publications, 1980.

McArdle, W.D., Katch, F.I., and Katch, V.L. *Exercise Physiology: Energy, Nutrition and Human Performance*. Philadelphia: Lea & Febiger, 1981.

Nutrition for Athletes. Washington, D.C.: AAHPERD Publications, 1971.

Pariskova, J., and Rogozkin, V.A. *Nutrition, Physical Fitness and Health*. Baltimore: University Park Press, 1978.

Smith, N.J. *Food for Sport*. Palo Alto, California: Bull Publishing Co., 1976.

The Environment and Human Performance

19

In many sporting activities athletes are called upon to train and compete in extreme environmental conditions. In such circumstances, competitive success can depend largely on the athlete's ability to cope with the environment. The athlete must be prepared to properly adjust his/her training regimen and competitive strategies in accordance with variations in the environmental conditions. Also, it is crucial that the coach fully appreciate that the athlete's safety may be gravely threatened by certain climatic conditions. In this chapter, particular emphasis is given to the limitations and dangers presented by high levels of heat and humidity.

Controlling the Body's Temperature

Human beings are warm-blooded animals; as such, they are faced with the never-ending task of maintaining a relatively constant internal body temperature, normally about 37°C (98.6°F). This constant internal temperature must be maintained despite wide variations in environmental temperature and marked fluctuations in the rate of body heat production. Since effective regulation of temperature is essential to life, the body attaches high priority to maintenance of heat balance.

Heat Balance

The factors that affect body temperature are summarized in the *heat balance equation* (see Figure 19.1), which indicates that five factors interact to determine the body's temperature. These are:

Metabolic heat production takes place continually, since heat is a by-product of cellular metabolism. In fact, about 80% of the chemical energy expended by the body ultimately is transformed into heat. Consequently, the rate of metabolic heat production is linked to the rate of body metabolism. Under normal resting conditions, a steady rate of metabolic

$$+ \text{(Heat gain)}$$
$$M \pm Cd \pm Cv \pm R - E = 0 \text{ (Heat balance)}$$
$$- \text{(Heat loss)}$$

Figure 19.1 The heat balance equation summarizes the physical processes that affect heat gain and loss by the body. M = metabolic heat production; Cd = conductive heat exchange; Cv = convective heat exchange; R = radiant heat exchange; E = evaporative heat loss.

heat production is needed to offset a continual loss of heat to the environment. However, during exercise the body's elevated rate of metabolism results in proportionately higher rates of metabolic heat production.

Conduction involves the direct transfer of heat between two substances that differ in temperature. Heat tends to move from an area of high temperature to an area of lower temperature. In most circumstances, body temperature exceeds the temperature of the air (or water) surrounding it. Thus, we ordinarily expect the body to experience a steady loss of heat through conductive cooling. However, if the environmental temperature exceeds body temperature conduction can result in a gain of heat for the body.

Convection, the transfer of heat through movement of a heated substance (e.g., air, water), can greatly affect the body's rate of conductive heat exchange. For example, if cool air is circulated rapidly past the body's surface heat loss will occur at a higher rate than if already heated air were to remain close to the skin. Clothing tends to reduce conductive heat loss by restricting convective heat transfer.

Radiation is a physical process by which heat is transmitted via electromagnetic waves. These waves are often emitted by an energy source in the form of visible light waves. When these waves strike an object they can be absorbed and transformed into heat. For example, the body tends to gain heat when it is struck by sunlight. In addition, though, the body emits electromagnetic waves and can lose heat through radiation. Thus, depending on environmental conditions, radiation can result in either a net gain or loss of heat for the body.

Evaporation is the physical transformation of a liquid to a gas. Since evaporation is fueled by an absorption of heat by the evaporating liquid, the process tends to cool the environment in which it occurs. Thus, evaporation of water from the body surface results in a transfer of heat from the skin to the environment. As will be discussed later in this chapter, evaporation of sweat is a critical heat loss mechanism for the athlete.

Heat balance and maintenance of normal body temperature occurs when the body's rate of metabolic heat production is exactly offset by its rate of heat loss to the environment. A net heat gain by the body will cause an increase in body temperature, while a heat loss will result in a drop in body temperature. The body can tolerate small fluctuations in its core (central) body temperature. However, deviations of more than 4 to 5°C from the normal 37°C are usually associated with permanent damage to the nervous system, if not death.

Thermal Regulation

Control of body temperature depends on regulation of the factors that determine heat balance. Located in the brain is a set of nerve cells called the *thermoregulatory center*. This nerve center is responsible for monitoring changes in body temperature and for eliciting appropriate responses in the heat exchange process. The thermoregulatory center functions like a thermostat that is almost always set at the same temperature, 37°C.

As depicted in Figure 19.2, the thermoregulatory center receives sensory input from heat- and cold-sensitive neurons located in the skin (peripheral receptors) and from receptors in the brain itself (central receptors). The central tem-

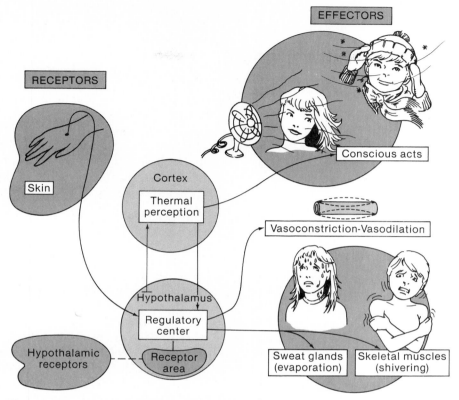

Figure 19.2 The thermoregulatory center receives sensory input from thermal receptors and elicits responses in thermal effectors. (After Fox, E.L., and Mathews, D.K. *The Physiological Basis of Physical Education and Athletics*. 3rd ed. Philadelphia: Saunders College Publishing, 1981.)

perature receptors are particularly important, since they detect the slightest shifts in brain temperature away from the set point, 37°C. The skin temperature receptors are primarily useful in alerting the individual to rapid changes in environmental temperature. Our conscious recognition of these changes in environmental temperature allows us to make appropriate behavioral responses (e.g., adding or removing clothing).

Deviations in brain temperature away from 37°C cause the thermoregulatory center to activate appropriate responses in thermal effector organs. An increase in body temperature requires an increase in the rate of heat loss to the environment. This is accomplished by:

1. *Activation of the sweat glands in the skin.* These glands release sweat onto the body surface from where it can evaporate, thereby cooling the body surface.
2. *Dilation (opening) of blood vessels in the skin.* This action increases blood flow to the body surface and promotes transport of heat from the warmer core of the body to the cooler skin.

These responses work together to increase the rate of heat transfer from the body to the environment. When body temperature returns to normal the responses are "turned off" by the thermoregulatory center.

Exercise in the Heat

Vigorous exercise causes a marked increase in the body's rate of metabolic heat production. For example, a 150-lb track athlete who runs at a six minutes per mile pace expends approximately 20 kilocalories (kcal) of energy per minute. As much as 80% of this energy may eventually be transformed to heat. Thus, our runner produces about 16 kcal of heat per minute. If all of this heat were stored in the body and the activity continued for 30 minutes, the athlete's temperature would soar to 45.5°C—a level far above that consistent with life!

Clearly, the high rate of metabolic heat production that accompanies exercise is potentially dangerous. Therefore, it is imperative that the exerciser's body increase its rate of heat transfer to the surroundings. Ordinarily, this can be accomplished through the two basic processes mentioned previously: sweating and increased blood flow to the skin. When environmental conditions are cool and dry these normal thermoregulatory responses are quite able to control body temperature. In most persons this is true even with the most vigorous and prolonged forms of athletic activity.

However, conditions of high temperature and humidity can represent a formidable challenge for the thermoregulatory process in athletes in certain sports. Under such conditions, the conductive and evaporative avenues of heat loss are severely limited. These limitations may dictate that certain adjustments in exercise intensity be made. For example, consider the cyclist who is called upon to compete for long periods in hot, humid conditions. Such conditions may impair this athlete's performance in several ways:

1. Blood flow to the skin may be elevated to such a level as to necessitate reduced blood flow to the working muscles. This can impair oxygen delivery to these muscles, thereby limiting aerobic metabolism.
2. An extremely high sweat rate may lead to dehydration, which is itself known to impair endurance performance.
3. A limited capacity for heat loss to the environment may require that heat balance be maintained by reducing the rate of metabolic heat production—that is, by reducing the exercise intensity.

These factors usually dictate that the athlete's capacity for long-duration, moderate- to high-intensity exercise will be impaired when conditions are hot and/or humid. Indeed, experience indicates that record performances in endurance activities are virtually never set in hot environments. It is imperative that the coach and athlete recognize these limitations and plan for them accordingly. The coach should not expect top performances from endurance athletes in heat stress conditions. Thus, the athlete should be prepared to adjust the intensity of exercise in proportion to the degree of heat stress. For example, it could well prove foolhardy for our competitive cyclist to set the same pace on a hot day as might be appropriate in cooler conditions.

Assessment of Heat Stress

The degree of heat stress encountered by an athlete is determined largely by the temperature and relative humidity of the environment. High environmental temperature limits the body's rate of conductive heat loss. Elevated relative humidity restricts evaporative cooling. Thus, in assessing overall heat stress it is crucial that both temperature and humidity be considered.

Several methods for measurement of environmental heat stress are available to the coach or trainer. One technique involves the use of a

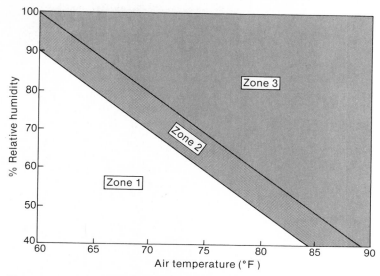

Figure 19.3 A temperature-relative humidity index can be used to assess heat stress. Zone 1 is safe, Zone 2 requires that caution be used, and Zone 3 mandates that extreme care be employed with any vigorous activity programs. (After Fox, E.L., and Mathews, D.K. *The Physiological Basis of Physical Education and Athletics.* 3rd ed. Philadelphia: Saunders College Publishing, 1981.)

temperature/relative humidity table (see Figure 19.3) that identifies "caution" and "danger" zones. Use of this table requires that a measurement of relative humidity be obtained. This can be accomplished by using a sling psychrometer such as that shown in Figure 19.4. This device measures both dry bulb and wet bulb temperatures. Another method for assessment of environmental heat stress involves measurement of only wet bulb temperature. Using the guidelines presented in Table 19.1, the wet bulb temperature can be employed to assess heat stress and to appropriately modify training/exercise programs.

It should be noted that if relative humidity is high the overall environmental heat stress can be very severe when temperatures are rather moderate. Also, it should be remembered that radiative heating by direct sunlight and restric-

Table 19.1: Guidelines for Interpretation of Wet Bulb Temperature (WBT)

WBT	Precautions
Less than (60°F)	No precaution needed.
61–66°F	Carefully monitor all participants.
67–72°F	Ensure that all participants ingest water frequently.
73–77°F	Provide frequent rest breaks in addition to precautions listed above.
78°F or higher	Postpone exercise session or greatly reduce intensity and duration of activity.

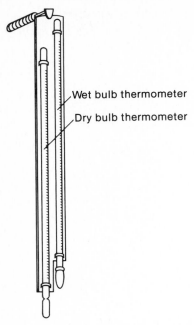

Figure 19.4 A sling psychrometer can be used to measure relative humidity by assessing wet and dry bulb temperatures. (After Fox, E.L., and Mathews, D.K. *The Physiological Basis of Physical Education and Athletics*. 3rd ed. Philadelphia: Saunders College Publishing, 1981.)

tion of convective heat transfer by heavy clothing can contribute to the athlete's heat stress.

Heat Acclimatization

The athlete's physiological responses to exercise in the heat are known to improve with *acclimatization*. Acclimatization is the process of adaptation that occurs with repeated exposures to a particular condition. Heat acclimatization is a well-documented phenomenon and one that can greatly enhance the athlete's performance and safety.

Heat acclimatization results in an increased maximum rate of sweating and improvement in cardiovascular responses. These factors facilitate body cooling and thereby promote comfort and endurance exercise performance. In addition, and perhaps most importantly, acclimatization reduces the athlete's risk of developing a potentially lethal heat illness.

Fortunately, an athlete can attain almost full heat acclimatization with five to eight days of gradually incremented exercise in the heat. Ideally, this should be accomplished by gradually increasing the duration and intensity of exercise and the degree of heat stress. For example, a football team's preseason training program might begin with 15 minutes of moderate-intensity, continuous exercise (i.e., jogging) wearing only shorts. Over the next week, the training sessions could build gradually to 30 minutes of higher intensity exercise in shirts and shorts.

Also, the coach should be aware that training, *per se*, carries a considerable "acclimatizing" effect. A well-trained, physically fit athlete responds more favorably to exercise in the heat than does the low fit person. This is also true of relatively lean individuals as compared with the obese. Thus, athletes should be encouraged to participate in appropriate preseason training programs. Such programs can improve the athlete's heat tolerance as well as benefit performance in other ways.

Prevention and Treatment of Heat Illnesses

Heavy exercise in heat stress conditions can lead to the development of heat illnesses. These illnesses are extremely dangerous and can represent a serious threat to the athlete's health. Regrettably, several heat-related deaths seem to occur every year in athletic and other exercise situations. Consequently, it is absolutely essential that the coach take every precaution to prevent heat illness. Also, coaches must be prepared to recognize the symptoms of the various heat illnesses and, if necessary, to deliver proper first aid treatment.

The symptoms of the various heat illnesses are as follows:

1. *Heat cramps* are painful, involuntary muscle contractions occurring during or after vigorous exercise in hot conditions.
2. *Heat exhaustion* is extreme fatigue associated with heavy exercise in heat stress conditions. Symptoms include cold, clammy skin, rapid sweating, approximately normal body temperature, and possibly nausea or fainting.
3. *Heat stroke* is a failure of the body's thermoregulatory process caused by overexposure to heat stress. Symptoms include high body temperature, hot, dry skin, and disorientation or unconsciousness. Heat stroke can be a fatal condition if not treated promptly and properly.

Prevention of Heat Illnesses

In almost all cases, heat illnesses in athletes are preventable. Proper precautions by the coach, trainer, and team physician can greatly reduce the risks of heat illnesses. Common sense as well as legal liability demand that such precautions be taken. Whenever athletes are called upon to train or compete in hot and/or humid conditions, the following recommendations should be heeded:

1. The intensity and duration of exercise should be adjusted in accordance with the degree of heat stress. Exercise bouts should be substantially curtailed when temperature and/or humidity are significantly elevated (see Figure 19.3).
2. In hotter times of the year, practices and competitions should be scheduled at the coolest time of the day: early morning or evening.
3. The coach should ensure that athletes adequately replace the water lost in sweat by drinking regularly during and after heavy

exercise in the heat. More detailed recommendations on fluid replacement are provided in the following section.
4. Athletes should wear minimal clothing and the clothing that is worn should be designed to maximize heat transfer. White colored materials tend to reflect more of the sun's rays and mesh fabrics optimize convective and evaporative cooling.
5. Athletes should be fully acclimatized to the heat before engaging in heavy training sessions or competitions.
6. Athletes *and* coaches should be fully educated regarding the symptoms of heat illnesses and should be instructed to seek or deliver assistance at the earliest possible time.
7. Since chronic dehydration increases the risk of heat illnesses, coaches should monitor athletes' body weights at the start and finish of practice. A steady day-to-day loss of weight may signal progressive dehydration.
8. Particular care should be taken to monitor the status of low fit, obese, young (prepubertal), and elderly athletes, since these groups are at greater risk of heat illnesses.
9. Athletes should be screened for past history of heat illnesses. Some individuals are particularly intolerant of heat and should be identified prior to initiating athletic activity. Such persons should be monitored very closely during exercise in the heat.

Fluid and Salt Replacement

An important step in preventing heat illnesses involves replacement of the fluids lost through sweating. During heavy exercise in conditions of heat stress the athlete can lose up to 2 liters (L) of sweat per hour. This dehydration not only increases the risk of heat illnesses, but impairs performance in endurance activities. Thus, from the standpoints of both safety and performance, it is to the athlete's advantage to optimize fluid replacement.

Studies have shown that the preferred approach to fluid replacement involves frequent ingestion of small volumes of either water or a very dilute glucose-electrolyte (sugar-salt) beverage. The fluid ingested should be one that will rapidly pass through the stomach and be absorbed from the small intestine. In this regard, no commercial athletic beverage is better than water and, as has been shown by Coyle and coworkers (1978), several are not as good.

A prepared glucose-electrolyte beverage may be of some benefit in very long-duration activities during which blood glucose levels may tend to drop. If a glucose-electrolyte beverage is taken during exercise it should be very dilute, since highly concentrated solutions can retard the rate at which fluid passes through the stomach, thereby reducing fluid absorption.

Sweat contains moderate concentrations of the body salts (sodium, potassium, chloride, and others). While it is not critical that these salts be replaced *during* an exercise bout, in the long term, the salt content of body fluids must be maintained. Usually, the athlete's normal diet contains sufficient salt to balance that lost through sweating. However, when experiencing extreme sweat losses the athlete may require increased dietary salt. In this regard, ingestion of a glucose-electrolyte beverage after exercise may be of benefit. Another approach would involve addition of moderate amounts of extra salt to the athlete's meals. Either of these approaches is preferred to ingestion of salt tablets, which contain so much salt that they can retard the passage of fluid through the stomach.

Treatment of Heat Illnesses

Whenever a heat illness occurs the coach should act quickly to ensure that proper first aid treatment is provided. The first aid treatments recommended by the American National Red Cross are listed in Table 19.2.

Table 19.2: First Aid Treatments for Heat Illnesses (American National Red Cross)

Heat Cramps

1. Apply firm pressure with hands or gently massage the cramped muscle.
2. Give the victim sips of salt water (1 teaspoon of salt per glass), half a glass every 15 minutes for one hour.

Heat Exhaustion

1. Give the victim salt water as described in item 2, under Heat Cramps.
2. Have victim lie down and elevate feet 8–12 inches.
3. Loosen victim's clothing.
4. Apply cool, wet cloths and fan victim or remove to a cool environment.
5. If victim vomits, cease giving fluids and transport to hospital where an intravenous salt solution can be provided.
6. Advise the victim to avoid exercise and heat stress for several days.

Heat Stroke

1. Take immediate action to cool the individual, but take care to prevent chilling once temperature drops below 102°F.
2. Remove clothing and repeatedly sponge skin with cool water or rubbing alcohol; or apply cold packs; or place the victim in a tub of cold water.
3. Use fans or air conditioners to promote cooling.
4. Do not give stimulants.
5. Seek medical assistance immediately.

Special Problems

Environmental heat stress can represent a significant risk for any person who performs vigorous exercise for prolonged periods. However, history indicates that athletes in two sports, football and long-distance running, are at particularly high risk of developing heat illnesses. In recent years, several heat stroke deaths have occurred in these sports and, consequently, particular care should be taken with these activities.

Football. Football presents an almost uniquely stressful situation for the body's thermoregulatory functions. Not only is football often played in conditions of environmental heat stress, but the football uniform greatly impairs heat transfer to the environment. In addition, the weight of the uniform adds to the body's rate of energy expenditure and heat production. Also, many untrained young athletes begin preseason football practice at the warmest time of the year and in an unacclimatized state. These factors combine to place football players in considerable danger of heat stress illnesses.

The extreme degree of heat stress often encountered in football has been evidenced by a high rate of heat stroke death in football players. Between 1959 and 1962 12 football players died of heat stroke (Fox et al. 1966). This rate has dropped significantly in recent years owing to the adoption of proper preventive procedures by coaches and trainers. Football coaches should be particularly attentive to the precautions listed earlier in this chapter. Every effort should be made to guarantee that football players replace fluids during and after practice. In addition, the football uniform should be worn only after heat acclimatization has been attained and after a reasonable level of physical fitness has been developed. In this regard, progressive preseason training programs can be invaluable.

Long-Distance Running. Long-distance runners encounter increased risk of heat illnesses because of their sustained, high rate of metabolic heat production. This prolonged activity can cause significant dehydration, which leaves the athlete vulnerable to heat exhaustion and heat stroke. In recent years, with massive numbers of persons participating in jogging and competitive road racing, a rash of heat stroke deaths have occurred in long-distance running. This prompted the American College of Sports Medicine to issue a position statement on prevention of heat illnesses in long-distance runners. The steps outlined in this position statement (See Table 19.3) should be followed by all who administer or participate in long-distance running competitions.

Table 19.3: The American College of Sports Medicine Position Statement on Prevention of Heat Injuries during Distance Running

Based on research findings and current rules governing distance running competition, it is the position of the American College of Sports Medicine that:

1. Distance races (> 16 km or 10 miles) should *not* be conducted when the wet bulb temperature–globe temperature* exceeds 28°C (82.4°F).
2. During periods of the year when the daylight dry bulb temperature often exceeds 27°C (80°F), distance races should be conducted before 9:00 a.m. or after 4:00 p.m.
3. It is the responsibility of the race sponsors to provide fluids that contain small amounts of sugar (less than 2.5 g glucose per 100 mL of water) and electrolytes (less than 10mEq sodium and 5 mEq potassium per L of solution).
4. Runners should be encouraged to frequently ingest fluids during competition and to consume 400–500 mL (13–17 oz) of fluid 10–15 minutes before competition.
5. Rules prohibiting the administration of fluids during the first 10 km (6.2 miles) of a marathon race should be amended to permit fluid ingestion at frequent intervals along the race course. In light of the high sweat rates and body temperatures during distance running in the heat, race sponsors should provide "water stations" at 3–4 km (2–2.5 mile) intervals for all races of 16 km (10 miles) or more.
6. Runners should be instructed in how to recognize the early warning symptoms that precede heat injury. Recognition of symptoms, cessation of running, and proper treatment can prevent heat injury. Early warning symptoms include the following: piloerection on chest and upper arms, chilling, throbbing pressure in the head, unsteadiness, nausea, and dry skin.
7. Race sponsors should make prior arrangements with medical personnel for the care of cases of heat injury. Responsible and informed personnel should supervise each "feeding station." Organizational personnel should reserve the right to stop runners who exhibit clear signs of heat stroke or heat exhaustion.

It is the position of the American College of Sports Medicine that policies established by local, national, and international sponsors of distance running events should adhere to these guidelines. Failure to adhere to these guidelines may jeopardize the health of competitors through heat injury.

---

*WB–GT = 0.7 (WBT) + 0.2 (GT) + 0.1 (DBT), where WBT = wet bulb temperature, GT = globe temperature, and DBT = dry bulb temperature. (Adapted from Minard, D. Prevention of heat casualties in Marine Corps Recruits. *Military Medicine*, 126:261, 1961.)

Exercise in the Cold

Cold represents far less risk for the athlete than does heat. Nonetheless, cold conditions can affect an athlete's performance and, in extreme situations, can be a health hazard. Consequently, the coach should be aware of the body's responses to cold environmental conditions and should prepare his/her athletes for safe and successful cold weather exercise.

When exposed to the cold the body's rate of heat loss increases markedly and, thus, the core temperature tends to fall below 37°C. To prevent such a drop in body temperature the thermoregulatory center in the brain can elicit two primary responses:

1. *Constriction of blood vessels in the skin.* This action reduces the rate of blood flow to the skin and helps to conserve heat in the body. Reduction of skin blood flow reduces the rate of conductive heat loss.
2. *Initiation of shivering.* Shivering is caused by rapid, tremorous muscle contractions. These contractions require an increase in energy expenditure and metabolic heat production. The heat produced through shivering can help to balance the high rate of heat loss experienced in cold conditions.

As discussed previously, vigorous exercise causes an increase in the body's rate of heat production. When environmental conditions are cold, transfer of metabolic heat to the environment occurs readily. Consequently, during exercise in cool or moderately cold conditions heat balance can be easily maintained and no extreme thermoregulatory responses are required.

Since minimal blood flow is provided to the skin during exercise in the cold, maximal rates of blood flow can be directed to the skeletal muscles. This promotes oxygen delivery and aerobic muscle metabolism. Also, when conditions are cold relatively little fluid is lost through sweating. Consequently, it is not surprising that outstanding performances in endurance activities (e.g., distance running, cycling) are usually recorded in cool or cold conditions. However, this is not the case for athletes in activities that depend on maximal speed and/or power. In such sports cold conditions may impair performance because of difficulties in achieving adequate "warm-up." Thus, speed/power athletes must take particular care to warm-up fully when conditions are cold.

When training or competing in extremely cold conditions, the athlete may be vulnerable to frostbite. Frostbite occurs when a body part freezes or becomes partially frozen. This is most likely to occur in tissues such as fingers, toes, and ears, since cold-induced constriction of blood vessels may markedly reduce blood flow to these areas. Consequently, athletes who participate in winter sports and others who exercise in extremely cold weather should carefully protect the extremities and facial tissues.

Exercise at High Altitude

High altitude can markedly affect performance in many athletic activities. However, experience shows that the impact of altitude on performance is not uniform—some athletic performances tend to be improved, whereas others are adversely affected by high altitude. In this section we shall: (1) discuss the physiological factors that operate when exercise is performed at high altitude, and (2) provide some recommendations for athletes who must compete at high altitude.

Physiology of Exercise at High Altitude

As one ascends to high altitude the air literally becomes "thinner." This derives from the fact that atmospheric pressure is a function of the height of the air column over a particular location on the earth's surface. As depicted in Figure 19.5, a typical sea level atmospheric

Figure 19.5 As one ascends to high altitude atmospheric pressure and the air's partial pressure of oxygen (PO_2) gradually decline. A reduced PO_2 can cause incomplete oxygenation of the blood and impaired endurance exercise performance. (A) At sea level atmospheric pressure = 760 mm Hg; PO_2 = 159 mm Hg. (B) At 5000 ft atmospheric pressure = 630 mm Hg; PO_2 = 132 mm Hg. (C) At 7400 ft atmospheric pressure = 570 mm Hg; PO_2 = 119 mm Hg.

pressure is 760 mm of mercury (Hg). At an altitude of 5000 feet above sea level (comparable to that at Denver, Colorado) atmospheric pressure approximates 630 mm Hg and at 7400 feet (as at Mexico City) atmospheric pressure is further reduced to 570 mm Hg. Since the density of a gas is related to the pressure around it, at high altitudes the air is less dense than at sea level.

The reduced density of gases at high altitude means that air presents less resistance to objects that move through it. For example, in order for a propelled object, such as a football, to move through the air it must overcome "wind resistance." The thinner air at high altitude presents less wind resistance and, thus, it should not be surprising that football kicking records are frequently set at high-altitude locations. This same principle applies when the propelled object is an athlete's body. Sprinters and long jumpers in track and field experience an advantage when competing at high altitude. This generalization was reinforced by experiences at the 1968 Olympic Games at Mexico

City. During that Olympiad Bob Beamon of the United States set his remarkable long jump world record (29′ 2½″) and Jim Hines, also of the United States, established an Olympic record in the 100-meter (m) dash.

Regardless of altitude, the *composition* of atmospheric air remains constant. Thus, the fraction of air that is oxygen is 20.93% at high altitude as well as at sea level. However, since total gas pressure is reduced at high altitude, the *partial pressure* of oxygen decreases as one ascends to high altitude. The partial pressure of a gas is the fraction of the total gas pressure accounted for by that gas. Table 19.4 provides computations of the partial pressures of oxygen (PO_2) at sea level and at an altitude of 10,000 feet.

The reduced PO_2 that prevails at high altitudes has great significance for athletes whose sports demand high rates of aerobic metabolism. Oxygenation of the blood as it circulates through the lungs depends on maintenance of a relatively high PO_2 in the air in the lung's air sacs. If the PO_2 of atmospheric air falls below a critical level oxygenation of blood will be incomplete and the oxygen transportation process will be impaired. Owing to the nature of hemoglobin, the blood's oxygen-carrying protein, oxygen transport is not reduced until atmospheric PO_2 decreases to approximately 120 mm Hg. This corresponds to an altitude of 5000 feet. As altitude increases PO_2 progressively

Table 19.4: Computation of Partial Pressure of Oxygen (PO_2) at Sea Level and at an Altitude of 10,000 feet

Sea Level

PO_2^* = 760 mm Hg × 0.2093
PO_2 = 159 mm Hg

High Altitude (10,000 feet)

PO_2 = 523 mm Hg × 0.2093
PO_2 = 109 mm Hg

$^*PO_2$ = barometric pressure × 20.93%

drops and oxygen transport becomes increasingly impaired. At extremely high altitudes, such as encountered by mountain climbers, even the lowest levels of exercise demand the use of external oxygen supplies.

Since oxygenation of the blood is impaired with high altitude, performance of athletic activities that depend on high rates of aerobic metabolism are negatively affected. For most persons the threshold for this performance decrement occurs at an altitude of about 5000 feet and becomes progressively more severe at higher altitudes. Again, citing experience gained at the 1968 Olympics at Mexico City, performances were markedly reduced in all distance running events longer than 800 m. For example, the winning time in the 10,000-m run was over one minute slower than the winning time in the preceding Olympiad in Tokyo.

Acclimatization to Altitude

The impact of high altitude on endurance exercise performance is most adverse during the first day or two following ascent. After this period, a gradual improvement in exercise tolerance is observed in most persons. This adaptive response, called *altitude acclimatization,* involves several physiological mechanisms. An almost immediate response to high altitude is increased ventilation. This aids in oxygenating the blood, but has the potentially adverse side effect of "blowing off" excessive amounts of carbon dioxide. This increased elimination of carbon dioxide tends to make the blood more alkaline, i.e. increases pH, a condition that is ultimately reversed by excretion of bicarbonate in the urine.

Two important acclimatizing factors require significant periods of time to develop. Over the first few weeks of altitude exposure the number of red blood cells and the hemoglobin concentration of the blood increase substantially. These effects increase the oxygen-carrying capacity of the blood and thereby promote oxygen delivery to the muscles during exercise. With extended stays at high altitude the aerobic capacity of skeletal muscle tends to increase. However, this response may require so long to develop as to be of little practical significance for most athletes.

Practical Suggestions

Endurance athletes who compete at high altitude can almost certainly expect their performances to be impaired. The degree of impairment will be determined by the elevation, the athlete's degree of acclimatization, and the athlete's ability to appropriately adjust his/her activity to the physiological limitations imposed by high altitude. It is suggested that endurance athletes heed the following recommendations when competing at high altitude:

1. If possible, altitude acclimatization should be effected by ascending to altitude three or more weeks prior to competition.
2. If a lengthy acclimatization period is impossible, athletes should ascend to high altitude immediately prior to competition.
3. Intensity of exercise should be adjusted in relation to the elevation. A performance decrement should be anticipated and athletes should "pace" themselves accordingly. For example, a distance swimmer should set a slower pace at high altitude than at sea level.

Summary

Varying environmental conditions can profoundly affect athletic performance and threaten the athlete's safety. Of particular concern is environmental heat stress, which markedly impairs endurance exercise performance and presents a substantial risk of heat illnesses. The negative impact of heat stress can be reduced through gradual acclimatization to exercise in the heat and by properly attending to dietary replacement of fluid. Cold environmental conditions can negatively affect performance in speed/power activities and, in extreme circumstances, can present a risk of frostbite. High altitude is associated with reduced oxygenation of the blood and a consequent impairment of aerobic metabolism and endurance exercise performance. Sustained exposure to high altitude results in an acclimatization that improves substantially the capacity for endurance exercise at high altitude.

References

Coyle, E.F., Costill, D.L., Fink, W.J., and Hoopes, D.G. Gastric emptying rates for selected athletic drinks. *Research Quarterly (Washington)* 49:119–124, 1978.

Fox, E.L., Mathews, D., Kaufman, W., and Bowers, R. Effects of football equipment on thermal balance and energy cost during exercise. *Research Quarterly (Washington)*, 37:332–339, 1966.

Recommended Readings

Buskirk, E.R., and Bass, D.E. Climate and exercise. In *Structural and Physiological Aspects of Exercise and Sport*. Edited by W.R. Johnson and E.R. Buskirk. Princeton, New Jersey: Princeton Book Co., 1980.

Fink, W.J. Fluid intake for maximizing athletic performance. In *Nutrition and Athletic Performance*. Edited by W. Haskell, J. Skala, and J. Whittam. Palo Alto, California: Bull Publishing Co., 1982.

Fox, E.L., and Mathews, D.K. *The Physiological Basis of Physical Education and Athletics*. 3rd ed. Philadelphia: Saunders College Publishing, 1981.

Pugh, L. Athletes at altitude. *Journal of Physiology*, 192:619–646, 1967.

Wyndham, C.H. The physiology of exercise under heat stress. *Annual Reviews of Physiology*, 35:193–220, 1973.

Most experienced coaches and athletes recognize that sports performance depends primarily on two factors: genetic endowment and training (i.e., skill practice, conditioning, and mental preparation). Nonetheless, the highly competitive nature of athletics has motivated some athletes to seek "short cuts" to success. Over the years athletes have attempted to gain competitive advantage by utilizing many different substances and treatments. These so-called *ergogenic aids* have ranged from the relatively harmless ingestion of sugar tablets to the highly risky administration of anabolic steroids. In this chapter we shall discuss several of the treatments that athletes have used for the purpose of promoting performance. In addition, we shall examine the ethical issues that are raised by the use and abuse of drugs and other substances by athletes.

Terminology

An "ergogenic aid" is any substance or treatment that improves, or is thought to improve, physical performance (the term ergogenic means "work producing"). As will be emphasized frequently in this chapter, many of the treatments that have been presumed by athletes to have ergogenic capabilities actually have little or no impact on physical performance. Therefore, the inclusion of a particular treatment under the heading of ergogenic aid should not be interpreted as indicating that the treatment actually does enhance performance. The list of presumed ergogenic aids is quite long and includes many drugs, various dietary supplements, and certain physical and psychological treatments. In this chapter we shall consider only those ergogenic aids that are physiological in nature.

"Doping" is a term that is widely used among international sports medicine authorities. It refers to the use of drugs for the purpose of improving sports performance. Both over-the-counter and prescription drugs can be considered doping agents, although it has been sug-

Drugs and Special Aids to Sports Performance

20

gested the term doping be applied only to "the use of a prescription drug for other than clinically justified purposes" (Clarke 1977). Later in this chapter we shall address the efforts that have been made by regulating bodies of international sports to control the use of drugs by athletes.

Amphetamines

Amphetamine (Benzedrine) is a synthetic central nervous system stimulant that is similar in effect to the natural hormone epinephrine. Amphetamine and its various derivatives are known to increase alertness and to offset drowsiness caused by lack of sleep. Also, amphetamines tend to increase heart rate, blood pressure, and metabolic rate in persons who are at rest.

The effects of amphetamines on exercise tolerance and athletic performance are not entirely clear, since the available research literature contains conflicting reports. However, most studies have found that amphetamine has no significant effect on endurance capacity (Golding and Barnard 1963; Williams and Thompson 1973). In one recently reported study Chandler and Blair (1980) found that amphetamine had no effect on maximal aerobic power, but that work time in an exhaustive treadmill test was increased. This finding was explained by higher postexercise blood lactic acid concentrations, suggesting that the subjects who used amphetamine were able to make more complete use of their anaerobic energy sources. Nonetheless, at present, one must conclude that the ergogenic effects of amphetamine have not been proven. However, athletes who take amphetamine often feel "pepped up" and tend to perceive that their performance is enhanced, even if it is not. This may explain why amphetamine is one of the most commonly used drugs among athletes.

Amphetamines are prescription drugs and should be taken only for medical purposes. Excessive doses of amphetamine can cause insomnia, hyperexcitability, and other serious side effects. Chronic amphetamine use can lead to a psychological addiction. Also, it should be noted that amphetamine usage is banned by most sports-regulating organizations. It will be recalled that in the 1972 Olympic Games Rick Demont, an American swimmer for the United States, was disqualified from competition after having won a gold medal because he had used ephedrine, a drug with amphetamine-like properties, to treat his asthmatic condition.

Anabolic Steroids

In recent years anabolic steroids have come into wide usage by athletes in sports that demand high levels of strength and body weight (e.g., weight lifters, weight throwers in track and field, football linemen, and others). Anabolic steroids are synthetic compounds that are similar in structure and effect to testosterone, the male sex hormone. The term "anabolic" refers to "protein building." Like testosterone, the anabolic steroids tend to be androgenic; that is, they often generate secondary male sex characteristics such as facial hair and deepening of the voice.

Anabolic steroids are produced and marketed under various trademarks, including Dianabol, Deca-Durabolin, and Maxibolin. These drugs have been developed to emphasize the anabolic characteristics of testosterone while minimizing the androgenic effects. They are used medically for the treatment of protein deficiency and to overcome weight loss in bedridden patients. Steroids can be administered either orally or by injection.

Anabolic steroids have been used by many athletes for purposes of promoting muscle building and weight gain. However, controlled scientific studies of steroid use have produced very confusing and conflicting results. Some well-designed studies have found that anabolic steroids had no effect on strength, muscle mass, and body weight, while other, apparently equally well-designed investigations, have reported increases in the same variables (Fahey and Brown 1973; Fowler et al. 1965; Rogozkin 1979; Ward 1973). One must conclude that the effects of anabolic steroids on performance-related variables in athletes are unclear at the present time. Nonetheless, personal testimonies by individuals suggest that a great many athletes believe that steroids can facilitate strength development and deposition of muscle mass. There is at least one point on which all authorities seem to agree: Anabolic steroids, in the absence of vigorous weight training, have no impact on strength or muscle mass in normal, healthy persons.

Also, there is a strong consensus that anabolic steroid utilization carries a substantial health risk. Prolonged use of steroids apparently can cause liver damage. In males, anabolic steroid utilization has been associated with reduced testicular size and decreased sperm production. In females, steroids tend to have a masculinizing effect. Indeed, the health risks associated with steroid use are so severe as to prompt the American College of Sports Medicine (1977) to issue a position statement on this subject. This statement is presented in Box 20.1. Steroid use has been banned by the International Olympic Committee, and in recent years several amateur athletes have been disqualified from international competition after testing revealed that they had utilized anabolic steroids.

Alkalinizers

As was discussed in Chapter 16, anaerobic glycolysis is one of the primary processes by which adenosine triphosphate (ATP) energy can be provided to support muscular activity. A product of anaerobic glycolysis is lactic acid, which if produced in large amounts can impair muscle function and cause fatigue. Lactic acid causes fatigue by lowering the pH of the tissues; that is, the tissues become relatively acidic. The level of fatigue experienced at a specific muscle

---

Box 20.1 American College of Sports Medicine Position Statement on the Use and Abuse on Anabolic-Androgenic Steroids in Sports

Based on a comprehensive survey of the world literature and a careful analysis of the claims made for and against the efficacy of anabolic-androgenic steroids in improving human physical performance, it is the position of the American College of Sports Medicine that:

1. The administration of anabolic-androgenic steroids to healthy humans below age 50 in medically approved therapeutic doses often does not of itself bring about any significant improvements in strength, aerobic endurance, lean body mass, or body weight.

2. There is no conclusive scientific evidence that extremely large doses of anabolic-androgenic steroids either aid or hinder athletic performance.

3. The prolonged use of oral anabolic-androgenic steroids (C_{17}-alkylated derivatives of testosterone) has resulted in liver disorders in some persons. Some of these disorders are apparently reversible with the cessation of drug usage, but others are not.

4. The administration of anabolic-androgenic steroids to male humans may result in a decrease in testicular size and function and a decrease in sperm production. Although these effects appear to be reversible when small doses of steroids are used for short periods of time, the reversibility of the effects of large doses over extended periods of time is unclear.

5. Serious and continuing effort should be made to educate male and female athletes, coaches, physical educators, physicians, trainers, and the general public regarding the inconsistent effects of anabolic-androgenic steroids on improvement of human physical performance, and the potential dangers of taking certain forms of these substances, especially in large doses, for prolonged periods.

lactic acid concentration is related to the body's ability to buffer lactic acid. Buffering refers to the maintenance in a solution of a normal pH (i.e., hydrogen ion concentration). The buffering capacity of body fluids is determined by the so-called "akaline reserve," which is largely a function of bicarbonate concentration. The greater the alkaline reserve, the greater the capacity of the body fluids to maintain a normal pH despite the introduction of an acid such as lactic acid.

Alkalinizers are substances that can temporarily increase alkaline reserve in body fluids. Several studies have observed the effects of orally administered sodium bicarbonate on exercise performance. These studies have observed substantial improvements in tolerance to high-intensity forms of exercise that depend largely on anaerobic glycolysis for ATP energy. In one investigation a total of 0.3 g/kg body weight of bicarbonate was orally ingested in small amounts over a three-hour period (Jones et al. 1977). This procedure resulted in a 62% increase in work time to exhaustion on a high-intensity bicycle ergometer test.

The effects of alkalinizers on exercise performance, as currently documented, certainly are intriguing. However, while most subjects apparently tolerate the procedure well, some individuals may experience digestive upsets. Also, it should be emphasized that alkalinizers are expected to promote exercise performance only in sustained, high-intensity activities that demand a high anaerobic capacity. More study of alkalinizers seems warranted.

Caffeine

Caffeine is probably the most commonly used drug in contemporary society in the United States. It is found in substantial concentrations in coffee, tea, and many soft drinks. Caffeine is a central nervous system stimulant that tends to decrease drowsiness, increase alertness, and mask the sensation of fatigue. In addition, in a resting individual, caffeine tends to alter cardiovascular function by increasing variables such as heart rate and blood pressure.

From the standpoint of exercise performance, the most important effects of caffeine are exerted on two peripheral tissues: adipose (fat) tissues and skeletal muscle. Caffeine has been shown to facilitate mobilization of free fatty acids from adipose tissue and to stimulate use of fat as an energy source by skeletal muscles. Increased utilization of fat for energy production causes a proportional decrease in carbohydrate use. Therefore, caffeine is said to have a "glycogen-sparing" effect on skeletal muscle metabolism. Since fatigue in long-duration exercise is associated with muscle glycogen depletion, an agent that slows glycogen depletion would be expected to delay the onset of fatigue.

In recent years, it has been documented that the glycogen-sparing effect of caffeine can significantly promote performance in long-duration, endurance exercise. For example, Ivy and coworkers (1979) have reported that ingestion of caffeine before and during exercise resulted in a 7.4% increase in work output during two hours of bicycling. This effect was achieved with administration of 500 mg of caffeine before and during exercise. This dose is equivalent to that found in three to five cups of coffee.

Occasional use of caffeine is not known to cause severe health problems. However, it should be noted that caffeine is a diuretic and, as such, may cause frequent urination. This may prove inconvenient to athletes in many sports and could contribute to dehydration. Consequently, it is recommended that caffeine use be curtailed when endurance activity is performed in heat stress conditions (see Chapter 19).

Glucose

Glucose and its intracellular storage form, glycogen, are major sources of energy during high-intensity exercise. As mentioned in the previous section on caffeine, fatigue in endurance exercise has been associated with depletion of muscle glycogen. Also, it has been documented that the perception of fatigue is related to the concentration of glucose in the blood. A low blood glucose level (i.e., hypoglycemia) results in central nervous system depression and a consequent sensation of fatigue. Therefore, it is not surprising that many athletes have utilized glucose and other simple sugars as ergogenic aids.

Although glucose is a commonly used ergogenic aid, the available evidence suggests that its ergogenic effects are quite limited and that, in certain circumstances, glucose ingestion may harm performance. Both glucose and muscle glycogen levels decrease substantially only with very long-duration exercise. Therefore, glucose ingestion is not recommended prior to or during activities that involve less than 90 minutes of sustained, high-intensity exercise. However, glucose ingestion may benefit performance by preventing the hypoglycemia that may develop with prolonged activity such as marathon running, swimming, and cycling. Studies have shown that glucose ingested during sustained exercise can help to maintain blood glucose levels and can contribute to energy metabolism (Ahlborg and Felig 1976).

Orally ingested glucose can benefit performance only if it is absorbed into the bloodstream. Thus, it is crucial that glucose be taken in a readily absorbable form. As was noted in Chapter 19, highly concentrated fluids slow the rate of gastric emptying and impair absorption of water and other nutrients. Available evidence indicates that a relatively dilute 5% glucose solution (5 g of glucose dissolved in 100 mL of water) is optimal. Such a solution allows rapid fluid absorption and contributes to the maintenance of blood glucose levels (Van Handel 1980).

Ingestion of glucose can actually impair endurance performance if it is taken prior to exercise. Under resting conditions glucose intake causes insulin to be released from the pancreas into the bloodstream. A rise in blood insulin promotes carbohydrate metabolism and can lead to premature muscle glycogen depletion (Costill et al. 1977). During exercise the insulin response to glucose ingestion is blunted. Therefore, endurance athletes should not initiate ingestion of glucose until immediately before or during competition.

Oxygen Breathing

Oxygen breathing refers to the practice of breathing a hyperoxic gas mixture; that is, one that contains a greater percentage of oxygen than the 20.93% found in atmospheric air. This, of course, can occur only through use of a specially prepared gas source and breathing system. The effects of oxygen breathing on exercise performance have been studied in several different ways. In this section we shall review the effects of breathing oxygen: (1) prior to exercise, (2) during exercise, and (3) after exercise.

Available evidence suggests that breathing oxygen before exercise can enhance performance only if two criteria are met. First, only a brief period of time (i.e., less than two minutes) can intervene between cessation of oxygen breathing and initiation of exercise. Second, the exercise bout must be of relatively high intensity and short duration (Wilmore 1972). Breathing oxygen prior to exercise has no significant effect on long-duration performance. Thus, it would seem that use of oxygen before exercise is in almost all cases useless or impractical.

Considerable evidence indicates that breathing oxygen *during* exercise does substantially enhance performance (Wilson and Welch 1975). Controlled studies have consistently reported that $\dot{V}O_2$max (maximal aerobic power) and work time to exhaustion are increased by breathing hyperoxic gas mixtures. These effects are presumably due to increases in oxygen transport by the blood. Although oxygen breathing clearly can enhance endurance performance, the procedure is an impractical one in a competitive sports situation. While an athlete could conceivably breathe from an external gas source while performing sports such as rowing or cycling, such a practice would certainly be frowned upon by the opposition!

In recent years oxygen breathing has been widely used by athletes for its presumed benefit in speeding recovery *after* vigorous exercise. It is particularly common in football. This procedure has been studied extensively and the results indicate that the effects are insignificant. For example, the recovery rate for heart rate is unaffected by oxygen breathing (Hagerman et al. 1968). Thus, while there may be some beneficial psychological impact, in physiological terms postexercise oxygen breathing is ineffective.

Blood Doping

In the early 1970's Swedish exercise physiologists touched off a minor controversy by reporting the results of research that was aimed at artificially increasing the blood hemoglobin concentration (Ekblom et al. 1972). This procedure, which came to be known as "blood doping," involved removing and subsequently reinfusing a significant volume of the subject's blood. This procedure increases hemoglobin concentration because during the period between blood removal and reinfusion the body naturally replaces the lost red blood cells and hemoglobin. The infusion of red blood cells, which can be stored indefinitely in a frozen state, causes an increase in hemoglobin concentration that persists for at least several days. Numerous studies have now examined the effects of blood doping on performance of endurance exercise. Some studies indicate that if the particular procedure actually increases hemoglobin concentration, maximal aerobic power and exercise tolerance are increased (Gledhill 1982). However, it should be noted that several other studies of blood doping have found the

procedure to have no effect on exercise performance. In general, these studies have failed to increase hemoglobin concentration because the time period between blood removal and reinfusion was too brief (Williams et al. 1973).

Although some recent evidence suggests that blood doping can improve endurance performance, the procedure is not recommended for use by athletes. Blood reinfusion involves risk of infection and several other health problems. Also, it should be noted that the procedure has been banned by the international sports-regulating bodies.

Drug Abuse in Athletes

In recent years society-at-large has been plagued by a persistent and pervasive drug abuse problem. A number of psychoactive drugs (e.g., marijuana, cocaine, heroin) have come into wide usage. Many other prescription and over-the-counter drugs have been overutilized or employed inappropriately. Indeed, the drug problem in the United States has become so extensive that ours has sometimes been labeled a "drug culture." Against this troubling backdrop, it is not surprising that drug abuse has infected the world of athletics. In this section we shall: (1) address the causes for drug abuse in athletes, (2) describe the efforts that have been made to eliminate or control drug use by athletes, and (3) discuss the role of the coach in dealing with drug-related problems.

Reasons for Drug Use in Athletics

In solving a social problem like drug abuse the first step must be to understand the causes of the problem. Clarke (1977) has suggested that athletes use drugs for one or more of the reasons discussed in the following paragraphs.

To Cure. Medical science has developed a great many drugs that can cure or facilitate recovery from illness. For example, a physician might prescribe an antibiotic drug for an athlete who suffers from influenza. Since the intent in this case is to return the athlete to good health, most would consider such use of drugs appropriate. However, there can be instances in athletics in which curative drugs are used in an unethical manner. Pain-killing agents may, in a short term sense, "cure" a problem and allow an athlete to return to training and/or competition. If the early return to activity is promoted at the expense of the athlete's long-term well-being such drug use would be considered by many to be inappropriate.

To Control. Many drugs function to control diseases for which no cures are available. Diabetics, epileptics, and asthmatics can now function quite normally through the use of appropriate medications. While such use of drugs would seem to pose no ethical problems, the coach should be knowledgeable regarding the interactive effects of the drug and exercise. For example, regular exercise may reduce a diabetic's insulin dosage. In such cases, the coach should consult with the athlete's physician to ensure that an appropriate drug regimen is maintained.

To Comfort. Certain drugs, notably the anti-inflammatory agents, function principally to reduce the discomfort associated with an injury or illness. These drugs may promote curing by reducing swelling or inflammation. However, the comforting drugs carry a rather obvious risk of abuse. Tranquilizers and pain-killing agents can be used to mask problems that require other forms of therapy. They can be used to allow an athlete to perform when his/her interest would be best served by rest. One might also consider the psychoactive "recreational" drugs as falling in this category. To the extent that these drugs allow athletes to cope with or escape from psychological problems, drugs such as marijuana and cocaine might be termed "comforting." The wide availability of comforting drugs demands that coaches develop a personal philosophy regarding the use of such substances by their athletes.

To Improve. As discussed earlier in this chapter, some drugs have been utilized by athletes for the purpose of improving performance. An-

abolic steroids and amphetamines are the drugs most commonly employed for their presumed ergogenic effects. These and other drugs have been widely used despite the lack of convincing evidence that they actually enhance performance. Typically, athletes use drugs for ergogenic purposes because of competitive pressures. The athlete may feel that the only way he/she can obtain a desired goal is by using a doping agent. Very frequently athletes have reported that they use a given drug because the opposition uses it. While these practices may be based on bad science and faulty logic, the fact is that many athletes take drugs for the presumed ergogenic effects. Here again, it is crucial that the coach have a well-developed philosophy concerning drug use. But it is just as important that the coach be technically knowledgeable regarding the real effects of the various drugs.

Prevention of Drug Abuse in Sports

Coaches and athletic administrators have long been concerned about the inappropriate use of drugs by athletes. In recent years this concern has led many sports groups to adopt formal policies and procedures designed to discourage drug abuse by athletes. The International Olympic Committee and its affiliates around the world and numerous other amateur sports-organizing bodies have condemned the use of many specific drugs by athletes. In general, the banned substances have been those that were presumed to provide some advantage to sports performance. This is despite the fact that very few substances or treatments have been proven to provide such advantages.

Condemnation of drug abuse is one thing, but prevention of the problem is quite another. While many sports organizations have banned the use of drugs by their member athletes, few groups have taken effective steps to enforce these regulations. For example, the National Collegiate Athletic Association (NCAA) states the following policy: "The NCAA condemns the employment of nontherapeutic drugs in any of its member institutions or affiliated organizations by staff members who authorize or allow their student-athletes to use such drugs and by student-athletes who do use such drugs.'' However, the NCAA has implemented no specific procedures that could realistically lead to enforcement of this policy.

In recent Olympic Games and in certain other international sports competitions definite steps have been taken to enforce drug regulations. The International Olympic Committee has devised an elaborate testing system to identify athletes who use banned substances prior to international competitions. Nonetheless, the problem of drug abuse persists and it would appear that even the most ambitious testing scheme will not eliminate it (Barnes 1980). This suggests that individual coaches must play active roles in preventing drug abuse among their athletes.

Role of the Coach

If coaches are to prevent drug abuse among their athletes they must begin by thinking through the issue and developing a clear plan for dealing with it. Simply condemning drug abuse is not enough. Rather, the coach must create an atmosphere that discourages inappropriate use of drugs. Creation of such an atmosphere demands that coaches play *active* roles in educating and communicating with their athletes.

Philosophy. Initially, coaches must develop a personal philosophy of coaching that is consistent with prevention of drug abuse. Such a philosophy would adhere to the following tenants:

Sports should be fun.

Sports should contribute to the healthy development and long-term well-being of young athletes.

Athletes should "play to win," but should derive primary satisfaction from the *process* of participation in sports and from attainment of personal goals (which may not involve placing first).

Victory and athletic achievement are meaningful only if attained in a fair, sportsmanlike manner.

Coaches who embrace such a philosophy are unlikely to place excessive "win-at-all-cost" pressure on their athletes. The actions of such coaches nonverbally communicate to athletes that the purposes of sports are enjoyment and self-fulfillment. The true joy of a sport is associated with its "play" component and with the personal satisfaction gained from developing one's *natural* talent to its fullest.

The Coach as Educator. One specific action that coaches can take to discourage drug abuse is to educate athletes regarding the true effects and risks of drug use. Many athletes learn about drugs from peers, and information obtained in this manner may be highly inaccurate. Likewise, many athletes are ignorant of the health risks associated with many drugs. Any athlete who uses drugs has made a decision that the benefits of drug use outweigh the associated hazards. Thus, it is crucial that coaches ensure that athletes know the facts about drugs. Education alone will not eliminate drug abuse, but it can reduce its incidence. At the least, education can guarantee that athletes who choose to use drugs will do so with a knowledge of the risks they are taking.

The Coach as Counselor. The coach-athlete relationship is one of the most intense in our society. Coaches can have a great impact on the development of young athletes. Part of this impact is associated with modeling and, thus, is somewhat independent of the quality of coach-athlete communication. However, coaches can impact optimally on athletes only if open, sincere lines of communication exist. In dealing with the prevention and treatment of drug abuse the coach may need to function as a counselor. This function can be performed only if the coach masters certain basic communication skills. Among these skills are:

Be a good listener. The athlete who uses drugs does so for specific reasons. Frequently, these reasons can be identified and analyzed by listening intently to the athlete (see Chapter 2).

Be nonjudgmental. Athletes know that society-at-large condemns drug abuse and should already know that the coach opposes drug use for nontherapeutic reasons. Thus, there is little to be gained by making the athlete feel guilty. There is some likelihood that the athlete's drug abuse may be linked to a poor self-image and feeling of inadequacy. The coach must strive to understand the situation and to help the athlete weigh the benefits and risks of drug use. Remember, the most important decisions are those that athletes make for themselves.

Be informed. A counseling relationship often provides an opportunity to educate. Coaches should have the facts on drug effects and should be prepared to help the athlete learn about these facts.

Be caring. Perhaps the most essential trait of an effective counselor is sincere concern. The athlete who senses that the coach genuinely cares about his/her welfare is likely to participate with enthusiasm in the counseling process. To be an effective counselor the coach must care more about the well-being of the athlete than winning games.

Thus, in dealing with drug-related problems the coach must assume multiple roles. Coaches should adopt a fundamental philosophy that discourages cheating and that shuns the win-at-all-cost mentality. Also, coaches should educate athletes regarding the risks of drug abuse and should be prepared to counsel athletes who encounter drug abuse problems.

Summary

Ergogenic aids are substances or treatments that improve, or are thought to improve, physical performance. Over the years many special procedures have been used by athletes in an effort to enhance performance beyond the level attainable through normal training. While some of these procedures actually benefit performance, scientific studies have revealed that many of the most widely used techniques have little physiological impact.

Amphetamines and anabolic steroids are two of the most commonly used drugs among athletes. However, research has failed to confirm a consistent ergogenic effect for either substance. In contrast, both drugs carry significant health risks. Alkalinizers may benefit performance in short-duration, high-intensity activity, while properly administered doses of caffeine and glucose apparently provide ergogenic effects for participants in long-duration, moderate-intensity activities. Oxygen breathing before and during exercise can aid performance, but the procedure is lacking in practicality. Blood doping, if accomplished in certain ways, can enhance endurance performance, but carries substantial risks to health.

In striving to prevent drug abuse by athletes the coach must understand the reasons why drugs are used by athletes. In addition, the coach should be cognizant of the doping regulations that have been adopted by the governing bodies of sports. Finally, coaches should develop a personal philosophy of coaching that discourages drug abuse and should develop the teaching and counseling skills needed to deal with drug-related problems.

References

Ahlborg, G. and Felig, P. Influence of glucose ingestion on fuel-hormone response during prolonged exercise. *Journal of Applied Physiology,* 41:683–688, 1976.

American College of Sports Medicine. Position statement on the use and abuse of anabolic-androgenic steroids in sports. *Medicine and Science in Sports,* 9:xi–xiii, 1977.

Barnes, L. Olympic drug testing: improvements without progress. *Physician and Sportsmedicine,* 8:21–24, 1980.

Chandler, J.V., and Blair, S.N. The effect of amphetamines on selected physiological components related to athletic success. *Medicine and Science in Sports and Exercise,* 12:65–69, 1980.

Clarke, K.S. *Drugs and the Coach.* Washington, D.C.: AAHPERD Publications, 1977.

Costill, D.L., Coyle, E., Dalsky, G., Evans, W., Fink, W., and Hoopes, D. Effects of elevated FFA and insulin on muscle glycogen usage during exercise. *Journal of Applied Physiology,* 43:695–699, 1977.

Ekblom, B., Goldbard, A., and Gullbring, B. Response to exercise after blood loss and reinfusion. *Journal of Applied Physiology,* 33:175–180, 1972.

Fahey, T.D., and Brown, C.H. The effects of anabolic steroids on strength, body composition and endurance of college males when accompanied by a weight training program. *Medicine and Science in Sports,* 5:272–276, 1973.

Fowler, W.H., Gardner, G.W., and Egstrom, G.H. Effect of an anabolic steroid on physical performance of young men. *Journal of Applied Physiology,* 20:1038–1040, 1965.

Gledhill, N. Blood doping and related issues: a brief review. *Medicine and Science in Sports and Exercise,* 14:183–189, 1982.

Golding, L.A., and Barnard, R.J. The effects of d-amphetamine sulfate on physical performance. *Journal of Sports Medicine and Physical Fitness,* 3:221–224, 1963.

Hagerman, F., Bowers, R., Fox, E., and Ersing, W. The effects of breathing 100 per cent oxygen during rest, heavy work and recovery. *Research Quarterly,* 39:965–974, 1968.

Ivy, J.L., Costill, D.L., Fink, W.J., and Lower, R.W. Influence of caffeine and carbohydrate feedings on endurance performance. *Medicine and Science in Sports,* 11:6–11, 1979.

Jones, N.L., Sutton, J.R., Taylor, R., and Toews, C.J. Effect of pH on cardiorespiratory and metabolic responses to exercise. *Journal of Applied Physiology,* 43:959–964, 1977.

Rogozkin, V. Metabolic effects of anabolic steroid on skeletal muscle. *Medicine and Science in Sports,* 11:160–163, 1979.

Van Handel, P.J. Glucose utilization during exercise. In *Encyclopedia of Physical Education, Fitness and Sports: Training, Environment, Nutrition and Fitness.* Edited by G.A. Stull. Salt Lake City: Brighton Publishing Co., 1980.

Ward, P. The effect of an anabolic steroid on strength and lean body mass. *Medicine and Science in Sports,* 5:277–282, 1973.

Williams, M.H., and Thompson, J. Effect of variant dosages of amphetamine upon endurance performance. *Research Quarterly,* 44:417–422, 1973.

Williams, M.H., Goodwin, A.R., Perkins, R., and Bocrie, J. Effect of blood reinjection upon endurance capacity and heart rate. *Medicine and Science in Sports,* 5:181–186, 1973.

Wilmore, J.H. Oxygen. In *Ergogenic Aids and Muscular Performance.* Edited by W.P. Morgan. New York: Academic Press, 1972.

Wilson, G.D., and Welch, H.G. Effects of hyperoxic gas mixture on exercise tolerance in man. *Medicine and Science in Sports,* 7:48–52, 1975.

Recommended Readings

Brooks, R.V. Anabolic steroids and athletes. *Physician and Sportsmedicine,* 8:161–163, 1980.

Golding, L.A. Drugs and hormones. In *Ergogenic Aids and Muscular Performance.* Edited by W.P. Morgan. New York: Academic Press, 1972.

Lamb, D.R. *Physiology of Exercise: Responses and Adaptations.* New York: MacMillan Publishing Co., 1978.

Williams, M.H. *Drugs and Athletic Performance.* Springfield, Illinois: Charles C Thomas, 1974.

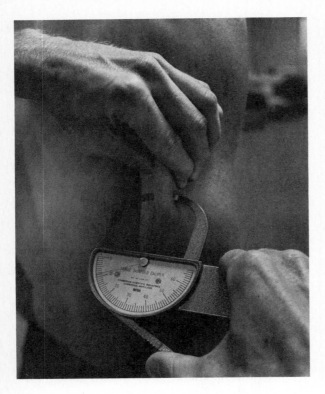

Conditioning Programs: Strategies for Improving Athletic Fitness

21

Successful athletic performances occur when the skillful, knowledgeable, and well-conditioned athlete enters competition with the proper psychological outlook. A basic premise of this book is that sports performance is determined largely by a complex set of mental/psychological, biomechanical, and physiological factors. In the first two sections of this book we addressed the psychological and biomechanical determinants of performance and in the previous chapters in this section we reviewed the fundamental physiological responses to exercise. In this and the following chapter we shall discuss the training process by which the athlete's exercise capacity can be improved. Specifically, in this chapter we shall: (1) identify the physical fitness components that affect athletic performance, (2) provide a method for analyzing the fitness needs of specific athletes, and (3) present techniques that can be used to evaluate physical fitness in athletes.

Components of Athletic Fitness

Coaches and physical educators have long recognized that physical fitness is multifaceted. Therefore, there is no single test of "overall fitness" and no one training technique can be used to generate "overall fitness." Rather, it is well established that physical fitness consists of several components, each of which is unique and physiologically independent of the others. In this section we shall define the various physical fitness components and describe the importance of each in athletic performance.

Muscular Strength

Muscular strength is defined as the force that a muscle group can exert in a single maximal effort. Maximum force exerted by a muscle group depends in part on the type of muscular contraction employed. Muscular contractions can be *isometric, isotonic,* or *isokinetic* in nature. Table 21.1 provides definitions and de-

Table 21.1: Isometric, Isotonic, and Isokinetic Muscle Contractions

---

Isometric. An isometric contraction is one in which force is applied while the length of the muscle remains unchanged.

Example. Pushing against an immovable object.

Isotonic. An isotonic contraction is one in which the length of the muscle changes as force is applied. Isotonic contractions can be either "concentric" (muscle shortens) or "eccentric" (muscle lengthens).

Example. Lifting a barbell (concentric contraction); lowering a barbell (eccentric contraction).

Isokinetic. Isokinetic contractions are performed at constant velocity against an external resistance that varies in proportion to the force applied. Isokinetic contractions are performed only with the use of specially designed equipment.

Example. Maximal knee extension against a Cybex isokinetic dynamometer.

---

scriptions of these three types of muscular contractions.

The strength of a muscle depends largely on its size. Specifically, a muscle's strength is highly correlated with its cross-sectional area that in turn, is a function of the number and diameter of the fibers in the muscle. Also, strength is determined by the ability of the nervous system to recruit motor units. As was discussed in Chapter 15, the force generated by a muscle varies with the number of motor units recruited and with the frequency of their stimulation. Thus, maximum muscular strength is exhibited when the greatest possible number of motor units are stimulated as frequently as possible.

Muscular strength is an important determinant of performance in many athletic activities. Strength is important in sports that demand that high levels of force be applied to an external object (e.g., discus throw), to an opponent (e.g., football), or to the body itself (e.g., sprinting, jumping).

Muscular Endurance

The term muscular endurance refers to the ability to perform repeated isotonic or isokinetic contractions or to sustain an isometric contraction against significant resistance. Muscular endurance tends to be correlated with muscular strength. For example, an athlete whose maximal bench press is 200 pounds is usually able to perform more repetitions with 100 pounds resistance than could the athlete whose maximum is 150 pounds. Although related to strength, muscular endurance is an independent fitness component that is determined by several physiological factors other than strength. Specifically, muscular endurance is probably related to the magnitude of the adenosine triphosphate (ATP) and creatine phosphate (CP) stores in the muscle and to the maximum rate of muscle blood flow during heavy exertion. This latter factor is partly determined by the muscle's degree of capillarization.

Muscular endurance, as differentiated from muscular strength, is important in sports that involve rapidly repeated, forceful isotonic contractions or sustained isometric contractions. Examples would be gymnastics and rock climbing.

Anaerobic Power and Speed

Anaerobic power is the maximum rate at which work can be performed using anaerobic energy sources. An obvious manifestation of an athlete's anaerobic power is his/her maximal speed of movement in an activity such as sprint running. Anaerobic power and speed are determined by the following factors: (1) muscle fiber type (distribution of fast- and slow-twitch muscle fibers), (2) neuromuscular coordination, (3) biomechanical factors (i.e., skill), and (4) muscular strength.

Athletes whose muscles contain relatively large percentages of fast-twitch fibers tend to have high levels of anaerobic power and speed. This results from the fact that fast-twitch muscle fibers contract more rapidly than slow-twitch fibers. As was emphasized in Chapter 15, muscle fiber type is an inherited trait that apparently cannot be altered through training. Neuromuscular coordination refers to the ability of the nervous system to rapidly activate and deactivate muscle groups in a synchronized fashion. As with fiber type, this characteristic is relatively unresponsive to training. In contrast, biomechanical efficiency and muscular strength can be improved through appropriate training. Thus, athletes can improve power and speed by enhancing skill and strength; however such improvements occur within the limitations imposed by genetically established neuromuscular traits (i.e., muscle fiber type and coordination).

Anaerobic Capacity

The maximum amount of work that can be performed using the anaerobic energy system is the anaerobic capacity. Anaerobic capacity is a key determinant of the athlete's ability to perform sustained, very high-intensity activities such as the 400-meter run or 100-meter swim. As was discussed in Chapter 16, energy for muscular work can be provided by the ATP-CP and anaerobic glycolysis systems, neither of which require oxygen. The capacity of the ATP-CP system is very small and is limited to the amount of these substances present in the muscles at the onset of exercise. The capacity of the anaerobic glycolysis system is limited by the athlete's ability to produce and tolerate lactic acid, the fatigue-causing end-product of this system. Therefore, an athlete's anaerobic capacity is determined by: (1) the resting concentration of ATP and CP maintained in the muscle fibers, (2) the activity of the muscle enzymes that produce lactic acid, and (3) the capacity of the body fluids to buffer lactic acid (see the discussion of alkalinizers in Chapter 20). Each of

these factors is apparently somewhat responsive to training.

Cardiorespiratory Endurance

Cardiorespiratory endurance refers to the ability to perform large muscle, whole body, moderate-intensity activity for extended periods of time. Cardiorespiratory endurance determines the athlete's ability to perform activities such as distance running, swimming, and cycling. It also affects the rate of recovery following heavy exercise. Athletes with high levels of cardiorespiratory endurance are able to sustain moderate-intensity exercise for long periods of time and tend to recover quickly following vigorous activity. Cardiorespiratory endurance is a key fitness component for almost all athletes, since training and/or competition in most sports demand sustained exertion at moderate to high intensities.

The physiological determinants of cardiorespiratory endurance were discussed extensively in Chapter 17. To summarize, an athlete's tolerance for whole body endurance exercise is determined by maximal aerobic power ($\dot{V}O_2$max), anaerobic threshold, and efficiency. These factors are affected by inherited characteristics such as heart size, muscle fiber type, and anthropometric traits (i.e., body size). However, substantial evidence indicates that overall cardiorespiratory endurance can be profoundly improved by appropriate training.

Flexibility

Flexibility is the maximum range of motion possible in a joint or a series of joints. Flexibility is of obvious importance in sports that require that athletes assume designated body positions, such as gymnastics and diving. In addition, good flexibility is needed for optimal biomechanical efficiency in many sports. For example, a hurdler in track and field needs excellent hip flexibility in order to clear the hurdle in the fastest, most efficient manner. Also, in recent years sports medicine experts have pointed to the importance of flexibility in preventing both traumatic and overuse injuries. Thus, nearly all athletes should be concerned to some extent about maintenance of good flexibility.

Flexibility is determined by the structure of the specific joint(s) involved and by extensibility of the tissues that cross the joint. In Chapter 10 it was pointed out the ball-and-socket joints (e.g., the shoulder) are innately more flexible than hinge joints (e.g., the knee). Since athletes vary in bone structure, flexibility at a joint such as the hip is partly determined by inherited skeletal characteristics. However, flexibility can be altered through training, since the extensibility of muscle and joint tissues varies with the demands placed upon them. A prime determinant of joint flexibility is the extensibility of the muscles that cross the joint. As was discussed in Chapter 10, muscle fibers are bound together by several layers of connective tissue. This connective tissue is elastic and its degree of elasticity determines the overall extensibility of the muscle. Muscles that are seldom stretched tend to shorten and become "tight" because the connective tissues gradually lose elasticity.

Body Composition

Body composition refers to the ratio between fat weight and total body weight and is usually expressed as percentage of body fat (% fat). Studies of body composition in athletes have led to two important conclusions: (1) excessive body fatness (i.e., obesity) negatively affects exercise tolerance and athletic performance, and (2) successful performers in specific sports tend to manifest characteristic levels of body fatness. Table 21.2 lists the % fat ranges reported for high-level performers in various sports. The data presented in Table 21.2 indicate clearly that sports vary considerably in terms of the body compositions that are associated with suc-

Table 21.2: Body Composition (% fat) of Olympic Athletes (Tokyo, 1964)

Males	
Event	**% Fat**
Track and Field	
Sprinters	10.1
Marathon runners	2.7
Decathlon	18.0
Jumpers	8.2
Weight throwers	29.4
Swimming	12.1
Basketball	13.2
Gymnastics	9.9
Wrestling (light weight)	12.7
Rowing	14.1
Females	
Event	**% Fat**
Track and Field	
Sprinters	12.4
Jumpers	14.1
Weight throwers	33.8
Swimming	16.6
Diving	13.9
Gymnastics	14.7

Adapted from Hirata, K. Physique and age of Tokyo Olympic champions. *Journal of Sports Medicine and Physical Fitness*, 6:207–222, 1966.

cessful performance. However, it should be noted that with the exception of weight throwers in track and field none of the successful athletic groups were obese (% fat > 15% for males or 25% for females).

Body composition is determined by the amounts of fat and lean tissue in the body. Fat tissue consists of fat cells, and is distributed primarily under the skin and around the internal organs. During infancy and childhood both the number and size of the fat cells gradually increase. However, after adolescence the number of fat cells remains constant. Therefore, in mature persons changes in overall fat weight are due entirely to changes in the size of the fat cells. Of course, body composition is also affected by lean weight. The greater the lean weight at a given total body weight, the lower is the % fat. Thus, an athlete who gains lean weight while keeping fat weight constant experiences a decrease in % fat.

An individual's % fat is in large part a reflection of his/her caloric balance. As indicated in Figure 21.1 caloric balance is determined by two factors: caloric intake and caloric expenditure (see Chapter 18). Food energy is our sole source of caloric intake. Energy is expended in body metabolism, the rate of which is markedly increased with exercise. Thus, overall caloric expenditure is determined primarily by the individual's level of physical activity. If caloric intake chronically exceeds caloric expenditure, the excess energy is stored in the body in the form of fat. Body weight and body fat are lost if caloric expenditure exceeds intake over an extended period of time.

Designing Conditioning Programs

One of the most critical functions performed by the coach is the design of conditioning programs. To be effective conditioning programs must be appropriate for the specific athletic activity involved and should be suited to the needs of the individual athlete. Therefore, coaches must be capable of analyzing the physical demands of various sports and must be able to evaluate the fitness status of individual athletes.

Fitness Demands of Specific Sports

The first step in designing conditioning programs is to perform a critical analysis of the specific sport. The purpose of this analysis is to identify and prioritize the fitness components that contribute to success in the athletic activity. It can be assumed that virtually all athletes, regardless of the sport, should manifest adequate levels of fitness in all components. So in a sense, all fitness components are somewhat important for all athletes. But typically, in a given sport certain components are more important to performance than others, and consequently should receive greater attention in the conditioning program. To cite two obvious examples: muscular strength is a key determinant to performance for a lineman in football; in contrast, cardiorespiratory endurance is the most impor-

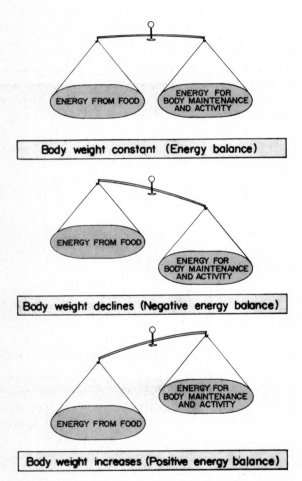

Figure 21.1 Body composition (% fat) and body weight are determined largely by caloric balance. Caloric balance is determined by caloric intake (food energy) and caloric expenditure (energy for body maintenance and activity). (From Fox, E. L., and Mathews, D. K. *The Physiological Basis of Physical Education and Athletics.* 3rd ed. Philadelphia: Saunders College Publishing, 1981.)

tant fitness component for a long distance runner.

As was discussed in Chapter 16, athletic performance is often limited by the athlete's ability to provide energy for muscular work. Conditioning can enhance the athlete's energy transformation capabilities. However, the effects of training are highly specific and it is essential that conditioning activities be focused on the appropriate energy system(s). Therefore, in analyzing sports the coach should first identify the energy system that predominates. Duration of activity can serve as a useful guideline in this analysis. Activities that involve only a few seconds of high-intensity exertion primarily tax the ATP-CP system. High-intensity exercise for 40 to 120 seconds taxes the glycolytic system. Longer duration activity (i.e., greater than two minutes) makes primary use of the aerobic energy system. Therefore, in track and field the 100-meter sprinter requires high levels of anaerobic power (ATP-CP system), the 400-meter sprinter needs a well-developed anaerobic capacity (glycolytic system), and the 10,000-meter runner must have a high maximal aerobic power (aerobic system).

Of course, there are many instances in which more than one energy system is important to performance in a single sport. For example, the soccer player during competition performs one to two hours of moderate-intensity activity during which many very high-intensity sprints are performed. Consequently, soccer players should strive to optimize both anaerobic power and maximal aerobic power. Swimmers who specialize in the 200-meter freestyle event (duration one and half to two minutes) tax both the aerobic and glycolytic energy systems; therefore, in training they should strive to improve anaerobic capacity and maximal aerobic power.

In many sports the energy systems constitute prime determinants of performance. In most sports, however, fitness components other than those directly related to energy transformation are also very important. Components such as

muscular strength, flexibility, and body composition may relate directly to performance or may indirectly affect performance by altering energy demand. For example, flexibility is directly related to performance in sports such as gymnastics and diving. In other sports flexibility may indirectly affect performance by altering efficiency of movement or injury risk. Body composition frequently has an indirect effect on athletic performance. Variations in body composition usually involve change in body mass. In most endurance sports a low body mass is useful in minimizing energy demand. In other sport activities, such as line play in football and heavyweight wrestling, a high body mass may enhance performance. Thus, % fat is usually substantially lower in successful endurance athletes than in football linemen.

A complete discussion of the fitness demands of the many sporting activities is beyond the scope of this book. In Table 21.3 we provide a rating of the importance of the various physical fitness components to performance in the common athletic activities. It is suggested that this table be used as a general guide in identifying the fitness components that should receive primary attention in athletic conditioning programs.

Fitness Needs of Individual Athletes

After identifying the fitness demands of a particular sport, the coach should determine the specific needs of each individual athlete. This should be accomplished by comparing each athlete's current fitness status with established fitness standards for the sport involved. For example, a football coach might assess upper body muscular strength in each athlete by administering a maximal bench press test. After expressing the scores as kilograms lifted per kilogram of body weight, the coach would compare each athlete's results to accepted standards for the various football positions. Athletes found to be lower than the desired standard for their position would be prescribed a

Table 21.3: Relative Importance of the Various Fitness Components to Performance in Selected Sports

Sport	Muscular Strength	Muscular Endurance	Anaerobic Power	Anaerobic Capacity	Cardiorespiratory Endurance	Flexibility	Body Composition
Baseball	1	2	1	3	2	2	2
Basketball	2	2	1	2	2	2	2
Boxing	1	1	1	2	1	2	1
Cross Country	3	2	3	2	1	2	1
Cycling							
Sprints	2	2	1	1	2	2	2
Distances	3	2	2	2	1	2	1
Diving	1	3	1	3	3	1	2
Fencing	2	2	1	3	2	2	2
Field Hockey	2	2	1	2	2	2	2
Football	1	2	1	3	2	1	2
Golf	1	2	1	3	2	1	3
Gymnastics	1	1	1	2	2	1	1
Handball	1	2	1	2	1	2	2
Ice Hockey	1	2	1	2	1	1	2
Ice Skating							
Sprints	1	2	1	1	2	1	2
Distances	2	2	2	1	1		2
Lacrosse	1	2	1	2	1	2	2
Racquetball	1	2	1	2	1	2	2
Rowing	1	1	2	1	1	2	2
Skiing							
Soccer	1	2	1	2	1	1	2
Squash	1	2	1	2	1	2	2
Swimming							
Tennis	1	1	1	2	2	2	2
Track and Field							
Sprints	1	2	1	2	2	1	2
Jumps	1	3	1	3	3	1	2
Weight throws	1	2	1	3	3	1	2
Distance runs	3	2	3	2	1	2	1
Middle distance runs	2	2	2	1	1	2	1
Volleyball	1	2	1	3	2	2	2
Weight Lifting	1	1	1	2	3	1	2
Wrestling	1	1	1	1	1	1	1

1 = Very Important (a key determinant of performance); 2 = Important (should be developed to a high level); 3 = Not Important (not needed at a high level)

conditioning program designed to bring them up to the standard.

As indicated previously, evaluation of fitness is an integral step in the process of determining the fitness needs of individual athletes. However, since the fitness demands of the different sports are highly specific, no single fitness test battery or set of standards can be used to assess "athletic fitness." To the contrary, coaches may need to develop a test battery that is unique to the sport they are coaching. For example, the gymnastics coach might require a test that emphasizes flexibility and upper body strength. On the other hand, a basketball coach would need a test that includes measurements of anaerobic power and cardiorespiratory endurance.

Fitness scores of individual athletes should be compared to standards for successful athletes in the particular sport when possible. However, frequently such standards will be unavailable, particularly for younger athletes. If such is the case, an athlete's fitness can be compared to population standards (i.e., norms) or to standards developed locally by the coach.

Program Design

In designing conditioning programs the coach should select activities that: (1) optimize the athlete's capacities in those fitness components that are most important in the particular sport, and (2) develop to at least an adequate level any relevant fitness components in which the athlete may be deficient.

In accomplishing these objectives the coach must establish priorities. Training time dedicated to a particular fitness component should be allocated in proportion to the importance of that component to performance. For example, a gymnast might reasonably spend 45 minutes per day in flexibility training, but for a tennis player such an investment of time would be excessive. In general, the coach's goal should be to design a training program that effectively and efficiently addresses the fitness demands of

the specific sport and the fitness needs of the individual athlete.

Evaluation of Physical Fitness Components

As emphasized in the preceding sections of this chapter, proper design of conditioning programs requires that coaches be aware of the fitness level of their athletes. Also, a knowledge of individual fitness characteristics can aid the coach in directing athletes to particular sports or positions in which they are most likely to succeed. For these reasons, coaches must know how to measure physical fitness. In this section we shall describe procedures that can be employed to measure physical fitness in athletes. In some cases specialized equipment is required. However, most of the measures included demand relatively inexpensive equipment and can be easily administered in a typical coaching situation.

Anaerobic Power and Speed

Anaerobic power and speed are highly related to one another and, therefore, can be evaluated with similar techniques. All accepted measures of anaerobic power involve maximal whole body exertion for a short period of time.

Sprint Runs. Sprint runs are perhaps the simplest procedures for measurement of anaerobic power and speed. One of the common sprint tests is the 50-yard dash. This test requires that the athlete, beginning from a standing or crouching start, run 50 yards as quickly as possible. Standards for the 50-yard dash are provided in Table 21.4.

Vertical Jump. Leg power can be evaluated by measuring the athlete's vertical jumping ability. As depicted in Figure 21.2, the athlete first stands next to a wall and reaches as high as possible while keeping both feet flat on the floor. Second, the athlete jumps from a crouch and touches the wall while at the peak of the jump. The distance between the height of the jump

Table 21.4: Standards for the 50-Yard Dash (in Seconds)

	Males	Females
Excellent	6.1	7.0
Good	6.4	7.4
Average	6.6	7.9
Fair	7.0	8.3
Low	7.5	8.9

Adapted from *AAHPER Youth Fitness Test Manual.* Washington, D.C.: AAHPER Publications, 1976.

Table 21.5: Standards for the Vertical Jump (in Inches)

	Males	Females
Excellent	25	13
Good	21	11
Average	16	8
Fair	9	3
Low	2	1

Adapted from Johnson, B.L. and Nelson, J.K. *Practical Measurements for Evaluation in Physical Education.* 3rd ed. Minneapolis: Burgess Publishing Co., 1979.

and the standing reach is the vertical jump score. Accuracy of measurement can be enhanced by having the athlete mark the wall with a piece of chalk. Vertical jump standards are presented in Table 21.5. It should be noted

Figure 21.2 The vertical jump test involves measuring the difference between an athlete's standing reach and the height to which he/she can jump.

that performance in the vertical jump is affected by body weight as well as leg power.

Margaria Test of Anaerobic Power. The Italian physiologist Rodolfo Margaria developed a test of anaerobic power that involves sprinting up a short staircase (Margaria et al. 1966). It will be recalled from Chapter 16 that power is equivalent to work performed per unit time. With the Margaria Test (as modified by Kalamen) work is computed as the product of body weight and vertical distance between the third and ninth steps on a staircase (Kalamen 1968). If the time required to sprint between these two steps is measured, anaerobic power can be computed as follows:

$$\text{power (kg-m/sec)} = \frac{\text{body weight (kg)} \times \text{vertical distance (m)}}{\text{time (sec)}}$$

Figure 21.3 presents a more detailed description of the procedure for administration of the Margaria Test and Table 21.6 provides standards for this test.

Anaerobic Capacity

At the present time no entirely satisfactory test exists for measurement of anaerobic capacity outside the laboratory environment. However, tests of middle distance running ability probably provide some information about the athlete's anaerobic capacity. For example, in

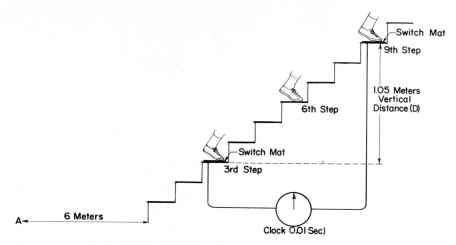

Figure 21.3 The Margaria Test of anaerobic power (as modified by Kalamen). Subject starts at point *A* and runs as rapidly as possible up the flight of stairs, taking them three at a time. The time it takes to traverse the distance between stair 3 and stair 9 is recorded in 0.01 second. The power generated is a product of the subject's weight and the vertical distance (*D*), divided by the time. (From Fox, E. L., and Mathews, D. K. *The Physiological Basis of Physical Education and Athletics.* 3rd ed. Saunders College Publishing, 1981.)

adolescents and young adults the 600-yard run could be used to evaluate anaerobic capacity. However, it should be noted that performance in an activity such as the 600-yard run is affected by anaerobic power and maximal aerobic power as well as anaerobic capacity. There-fore, the results of a running test such as the 600-yard run should be interpreted with caution. Standards for the 600-yard run are pre-sented in Table 21.7.

Several authors have proposed techniques for measurement of anaerobic capacity using high-intensity bicycle ergometer exercise. A

Table 21.6: Standards for the Margaria Test of Anaerobic Power, Kalamen Revision (in Kilogram-Meters per Second)

	Males	*Females*
Excellent	224	182
Good	188	152
Average	150	121
Fair	113	92
Low	< 113	< 92

From Fox, E.L., and Mathews, D.K. *The Physiological Basis of Physical Education and Athletics.* 3rd ed. Philadelphia: Saunders College Publishing, 1981.

Table 21.7: Standards for the 600-Yard Run (in Minutes and Seconds)

	Males	*Females*
Excellent	1:30	2:10
Good	1:45	2:25
Average	1:50	2:40
Fair	2:00	3:00
Low	2:20	3:30

Adapted from *AAHPER Youth Fitness Test Manual.* Washington, D.C.: AAHPER Publications, 1976.

complete description of these procedures is beyond the scope of this book. However, the reader may wish to consult the references listed at the end of this chapter (Bar-Or 1980; Pate et al. 1983).

Muscular Strength

As mentioned previously in this chapter, maximal muscular contractions can be performed isometrically, isotonically, or isokinetically. Therefore, muscular strength can be measured using any of the three types of contractions. Outside the laboratory environment muscular strength is usually evaluated using maximal isotonic contractions. A typical test is the one repetition maximum (1 RM) for the bench press (see Figure 21.4). In this test the

athlete experiments to determine the maximum resistance that can be moved through the full range of motion a single time. Isotonic strength can be tested using either free weights or a supported weight system (e.g., universal gym). Strength is specific to a particular muscle group, and therefore multiple tests are needed to assess "overall strength." Table 21.8 provides standards for the common isotonic strength tests.

Special equipment is needed to evaluate isometric or isokinetic strength. In the laboratory isometric strength is often evaluated with handgrip or back/leg dynamometers and cable tensiometers. Testing procedures using these instruments have been thoroughly described in other publications (Clarke 1966; deVries 1971). With increasing frequency athletic trainers,

A. Bench press   B. Bench squat

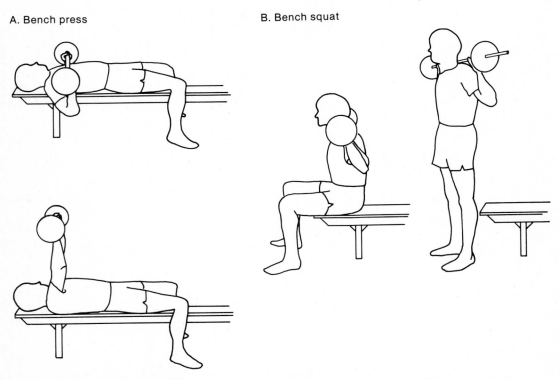

Figure 21.4 Muscular strength (isotonic) can be measured as the one repetition maximum (1 RM) for the common weight training movements.

Table 21.8: Standards for Isotonic Muscular Strength Tests—One Repetition Maximum (1 RM) Relative to Body Weight (1 RM/Body Weight)

	Males		Females	
	Bench press	Bench Squat Test	Bench Press	Bench Squat Test
Excellent	1.3	2.1	0.6	1.5
Good	1.2	1.8	0.5	1.3
Average	1.0	1.2	0.4	0.9
Fair	.8	0.9	0.3	0.7
Low	< .8	< 0.9	< 0.3	< 0.7

Adapted from Johnson, B.L., and Nelson, J.K. *Practical Measurements for Evaluation in Physical Education.* 3rd ed. Minneapolis: Burgess Publishing Co., 1979.

physical therapists, and researchers are measuring strength with isokinetic contractions. The Cybex isokinetic dynamometer provides a measure of "peak torque," which is indicative of muscular strength at controlled rates of movement (e.g., 60° per second or 120° per second). The Cybex apparatus also can be em-ployed to measure torque during an isometric contraction. Testing procedures for the Cybex isokinetic dynamometer are described in the manual that accompanies the apparatus (Cybex 1980).

Muscular Endurance

As with muscular strength, muscular endurance can be measured employing isometric, isotonic, or isokinetic contractions. In the athletic setting muscular endurance is usually measured with isotonic contractions using either the body weight or an external weight for resistance. Calisthenic exercise tests such as the one minute timed sit-up test are easy to administer to large groups of athletes. However, interpretation of these test results is complicated by the fact that resistance is provided by body weight. For example, obese individuals are often unable to perform a single pull-up, but they may perform quite well on muscular endurance tests that involve repeated movement of a standard external resistance (e.g., a 50-lb barbell). Figure 21.5 describes several common

Figure 21.5 Muscular endurance can be measured with calisthenic exercise tests. *(A) Bent-knee Sit-up Test.* The participant performs as many sit-ups as possible in one minute. The feet are stabilized by a partner and the hands are clasped behind the neck. *(B) Push-up Test.* The participant performs as many push-ups as possible before encountering exhaustion. *(C) Flexed-arm Hang.* The participant is assisted into the "up" position (chin above the bar) and maintains this position as long as possible.

Table 21.9: Standards for Calisthenic Tests of Muscular Endurance

	Males		Females	
	Sit-ups	*Push-ups*	*Sit-ups*	*Flexed-arm Hang*
Excellent	50	53	36	34 sec.
Good	42	42	29	17
Average	37	35	24	8
Fair	32	27	19	3
Low	27	21	15	1

Adapted from Hockey, R.V. *Physical Fitness, The Pathway to Healthful Living.* 4th ed. St. Louis: C.V. Mosby Co., 1981.

calisthenic exercise muscular endurance tests and Table 21.9 presents standards for these tests.

A preferable approach to measurement of isotonic muscular endurance involves performance of a maximal number of muscular contractions against an external resistance that represents a standard percentage of the body weight. For example, an athlete might be directed to perform as many repetitions as possible of the two-arm curl with a barbell that weighs 33⅓% of the body weight. Many of the common weight training movements can be employed in measurement of muscular endurance. Table 21.10 provides the percentages of body weight that should be used with the various external resistance muscular endurance tests. Table 21.11 presents standards for these tests.

Muscular endurance can be measured with isokinetic contractions using the Cybex isokinetic dynamometer. The athlete performs repeated, maximal contractions at a designated angular velocity such as 60° per second. The contractions are performed at a set cadence and are continued until fatigue causes torque to decrease to a preselected percentage of peak torque. For example, an athlete might be directed to perform repeated knee extensions against a dynamometer set to move at no more than 60° per second. The score for this test would be the number of repetitions performed before torque decreased to 50% of peak torque.

For details on this testing procedure the reader is directed to the procedures manual for the Cybex dynamometer (Cybex 1980).

Isometric muscular endurance can be measured as the maximum time that a specified

Table 21.10: Recommended Resistances (Percentage of Body Weight) for Isotonic Muscular Endurance Tests

Test	Percentage of Body Weight
Two-arm Curl	33⅓
Bench Press	66⅔
"Lats" Machine Pull Down	66⅔
Quadriceps Lift	66⅔
Leg Curl	33⅓

From Hockey, R.V. *Physical Fitness, the Pathway to Healthful Living.* 4th ed. St. Louis: C.V. Mosby Co., 1981.

Table 21.11: Standards (Repetitions) for the Isotonic Muscular Endurance Tests Described in Table 21.10

	Males	Females
Excellent	17	15
Good	12	11
Average	9	8
Fair	5	4
Low	< 5	< 4

Adapted from Hockey, R.V. *Physical Fitness, the Pathway to Healthful Living.* 4th ed. St. Louis: C.V. Mosby Co., 1981.

level of force generation can be maintained. Typically, isometric muscular endurance is measured using cable tensiometers or isometric dynamometers, as described in the previously cited references (Clarke 1966; deVries 1971).

Cardiorespiratory Endurance

The "gold standard" measurement of cardiorespiratory endurance is the direct observation of maximal aerobic power ($\dot{V}O_2$max). This test can be administered only in the laboratory setting and is quite time consuming and expensive. Consequently, direct measures of $\dot{V}O_2$max are impractical in many sports situations. Fortunately, exercise physiologists have developed several methods by which $\dot{V}O_2$max can be estimated with acceptable accuracy in the field setting.

Valid estimates of $\dot{V}O_2$max can be obtained using either maximal exertion or by observing the heart rate response to standard submaximal exercise. The latter approach is often preferred when subject motivation is questionable or when maximal exertion may involve an excessive health risk. These two conditions seldom exist in the athletic setting, and consequently maximal exertion tests, being easier to administer, are usually preferred.

As with most fitness components cardiorespiratory endurance is somewhat specific to the mode of exercise employed in testing. Therefore, as a general rule, it is preferable that a sport-specific mode of exercise be used in testing cardiorespiratory endurance. For example, in competitive cyclists it is preferred that cardiorespiratory endurance be evaluated with a standardized cycling task. Since many of the most common sporting activities in the United States involve running as a principal mode of movement, distance running tests have been widely used to evaluate cardiorespiratory endurance in athletes. Distance running tests have been shown to be valid estimators of $\dot{V}O_2$max and have the advantage of using a mode of exercise with which most persons are familiar (Cooper 1968; Cureton 1982).

Research has shown that optimal predictions of $\dot{V}O_2$max are obtained with distance runs that last longer than nine minutes (Baumgartner and Jackson 1975). For athletic groups of adolescent age or older it is recommended that either the 12-minute run for distance or 1.5-mile run for time test be employed. With the 12-minute run the athlete is instructed to run and/or walk as far as possible in 12 minutes. The 1.5-mile run test involves running and/or walking 1.5 miles as fast as possible. Both of these tests provide comparably accurate measures of cardiorespiratory endurance and the choice of tests is primarily a matter of individual preference. Distance running tests should be administered on a level, accurately measured course (e.g., track, football field, gymnasium) and participants should be encouraged to run at an even pace. Standards for the 12-minute and the 1.5-mile running tests are presented in Table 21.12.

Assessment of cardiorespiratory endurance by observation of heart rate response to standard submaximal exercise may be applicable in some athletic situations. Procedures for administration of submaximal exercise tests of cardiorespiratory endurance are provided in several other references (Astrand and Ryhming 1954; deVries 1980).

Table 21.12: Standards for the 12-Minute Run and 1.5-Mile Run Tests of Cardiorespiratory Endurance

	12-Min Run (miles)		1.5-Mile Run (min:sec)	
	Males	*Females*	*Males*	*Females*
Excellent	2.00	1.50	9:00	12:00
Good	1.80	1.30	10:15	13:45
Average	1.60	1.20	11:30	15:00
Fair	1.40	1.10	12:45	16:15
Low	1.20	1.00	14:00	17:45

Adapted from Hockey, R.V. *Physical Fitness, the Pathway to Healthful Living.* 4th ed. St. Louis: C.V. Mosby Co., 1981.

Flexibility

Flexibility is highly joint-specific, and therefore there is no single measure of "overall flexibility." To the contrary, specific tests are needed to measure maximal range of motion in each of the major joints in the body. In selecting flexibility tests the coach should identify those joints and muscle groups in which flexibility is most important for the sport involved.

Flexibility can be evaluated with laboratory instruments called flexometers, which measure the degree of rotation possible at a joint (Leighton 1955). However, these devices are not widely available and are seldom used in the athletic setting. More common are maximal static stretching tests, which quantify flexibility in terms of linear units (e.g., centimeters, inches). For example, flexibility of the low back/hamstring region can be assessed with the sit-and-reach test. As depicted in Figure 21.6, this test involves maximal hip flexion and is scored as the distance reached relative to the soles of the feet. The performer should bend slowly forward and hold the position of greatest stretch for a full second. Standards for the sit-and-reach test are presented in Table 21.13. Low back/hamstring flexibility is a matter of concern in many sports, and consequently the sit-and-reach test is widely used in the athletic setting. Other tests of flexibility have been described elsewhere (Hockey 1981).

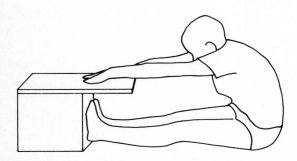

Figure 21.6 The sit-and-reach test of low back/hamstring flexibility.

Table 21.13: Standards for the Sit-and-Reach Test (scores are expressed as centimeters reached relative to the soles of the feet)

	Males	Females
Excellent	+21	+22
Good	+17	+18
Average	+11	+12
Fair	+5	+8
Low	−2	+2

Adapted from *AAHPERD Health Related Physical Fitness Test.* Reston, Virginia: AAHPERD Publications, 1980.

Body Composition

Body composition, quantified as percentage of body fat (% fat) cannot be estimated accurately from measures of height and weight. These measures fail to discriminate adequately between the lean and fat components of the total body weight. In the laboratory % fat can be determined via the underwater weighing technique, which is based on the premise that the buoyancy of the body is related to its fat content. The body of a fatter individual is more buoyant, and therefore tends to weigh less when submerged in water than that of a leaner person of equal body weight on land.

The underwater weighing procedure is being used with increasing frequency at the professional and international amateur levels of sports competition. However, the time and expense associated with underwater weighing precludes its use in mass testing situations. More practical is estimation of % fat from measures of skinfold thickness.

Skinfold estimates of % fat are predicated on the knowledge that much of the body's fat tissue is stored immediately under the skin. As shown in Figure 21.7, a skinfold includes two layers of skin and the underlying subcutaneous fat. The thickness of the skinfold is measured with a specially designed skinfold caliper. Figure 21.8 provides a description of the method

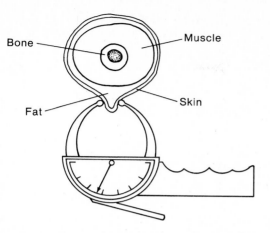

Figure 21.7 A skinfold includes two layers of skin and the underlying subcutaneous fat.

for measuring skinfold thicknesses and Figure 21.9 identifies the sites at which skinfold thicknesses are frequently measured. Research has shown that a single skinfold measure can provide a reasonably accurate estimate of % fat. Greater accuracy is obtained when skinfold thicknesses are measured at several sites on the

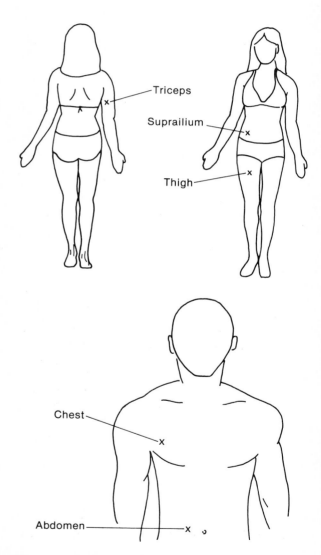

Figure 21.9 Anatomical sites for measurement of skinfold thickness.

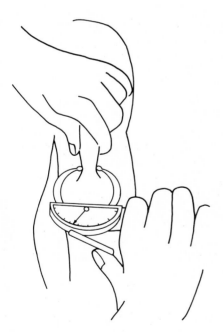

Figure 21.8 Method for measuring a skinfold thickness: All measures should be taken on the right side of the body; caliper jaws should be applied at a depth approximating the thickness of the skinfold; and skinfold should be held firmly between the thumb and forefinger of the left hand while the calipers are applied with the right hand.

body surface and the individual measures are entered into a previously established "prediction equation."

Skinfold prediction equations developed by Jackson and Pollock have come into wide use in recent years (Jackson and Pollock 1978; Jackson et al. 1980). These researchers have presented prediction equations that appear to provide accurate estimates of % fat in athletic groups of widely differing body types and training backgrounds. The prediction equations for males and females are:

Males

$$Body\ Density = 1.1093800 - 0.0008267\ (A) \\ + 0.0000016\ (A)^2 \\ - 0.0002574\ (C)$$

Females

$$Body\ Density = 1.0994921 - 0.0009929\ (B) \\ + 0.0000023\ (B)^2 \\ - 0.0001392\ (C)$$

where, A = sum of chest, abdomen, and thigh skinfolds (mm); B = sum of triceps, thigh, and suprailium skinfolds (mm); C = age (years)

Males and Females

$$\%\ fat = \left[\frac{4.95}{body\ density} \right] - 4.50$$

Numerous other methods for estimation of % fat from anthropometric measures have been developed over the years. The reader is referred to several excellent reference sources for a more thorough treatment of this issue (Lohman 1981; McArdle et al. 1981).

As mentioned earlier in this chapter, standards for body composition (% fat) vary considerably from sport to sport. Table 21.14 provides general standards for body composition in young adults.

Summary

Athletic fitness is a multifaceted characteristic that encompasses several physiologically independent components. Among these components are muscular strength, muscular endurance, anaerobic power (speed), anaerobic capacity, cardiorespiratory endurance, flexibility, and body composition. Fitness status in each component is determined by a set of physiological variables that are influenced by genetic and environmental factors. Training is an environmental factor that can profoundly affect the athlete's overall state of fitness.

Conditioning programs for athletes should focus on those fitness components that are most highly related to performance in the specific sport. The various athletic activities differ markedly in the fitness demands that they place on athletes. Also, athletes show great interindividual variability in fitness level. Optimal conditioning programs take account of this variability and provide a training dose that is appropriate to the needs of the individual athlete.

In designing conditioning programs coaches must be capable of measuring and evaluating fitness in athletes. This chapter provides descriptions of fitness measures that are practical for use in the typical coaching situation. Also provided are fitness standards that can be used to interpret the scores obtained in the measurement process.

Table 21.14: Standards for Body Composition for the General Population of Young Adults

	Males	Females
Very Lean	8	14
Lean	11	20
Average	15	25
Moderately Overfat	20	32
Obese	30	45

Adapted from Falls, H.B., Baylor, A.M., and Dishman, R.K. *Essentials of Fitness.* Philadelphia, Saunders College Publishing, 1980.

References

Astrand, P.O., and Ryhming, I. A nomogram for calculation of aerobic capacity (physical fitness) from pulse rate during submaximal work. *Journal of Applied Physiology*, 7:218–221, 1954.

Bar-Or, O., Anaerobic capacity and fiber distribution in man. *International Journal of Sports Medicine*, 1:82–85, 1980.

Baumgartner, T.A., and Jackson, A.S. *Measurement for Evaluation in Physical Education*. Boston: Houghton Mifflin Co., 1975.

Clarke, H.H. *Muscular Strength and Endurance in Man*. Englewood Cliffs, New Jersey: Prentice-Hall, Inc., 1966.

Cooper, H.K. A means of assessing maximal O_2 intake, *JAMA*, 203:201–204, 1968.

Cureton, K.J. Distance running performance tests in children—What do they mean? *Journal of Physical Education, Recreation, and Dance*, 53(7):64–66, 1982.

Cybex. *Isolated Joint Testing and Exercise*. Bay Shore, New York: Lumex, Inc., 1980.

deVries, H.A. *Laboratory Experiments in Physiology of Exercise*. Dubuque, Iowa: William C. Brown Co., 1971.

deVries, H.A. *Physiology of Exercise for Physical Education and Athletics*. 3rd ed. Dubuque, Iowa: William C. Brown Co., 1980.

Hockey, R.V. *Physical Fitness, the Pathway to Healthful Living*. 4th ed. St. Louis: C.V. Mosby Co., 1981.

Jackson, A.S., and Pollock, M.L. Generalized equations for predicting body density of men. *British Journal of Nutrition*, 40:497–504, 1978.

Jackson, A.S., Pollock, M.L. and Ward, A. Generalized equations for predicting body density of women. *Medicine and Science in Sports*, 12:175–182, 1980.

Kalamen, J. Measurement of Maximal Muscular Power in Man. Doctoral Dissertation, Ohio State University, 1968.

Leighton, J. Instrument and technic for measurement of range of joint motion. *Archives of Physical Medicine and Rehabilitation*, 36:571–578, 1955.

Lohman, T.G. Skinfolds and body density and their relation to body fatness: A review. *Human Biology*, 53:181–225, 1981.

McArdle, W.D., Katch, F.I. and Katch, V.L. *Exercise Physiology: Energy, Nutrition and Human Performance*. Philadelphia: Lea & Febiger, 1981.

Margaria, R., Aghemo, I. and Rovelli, E. Measurement of muscular power (anaerobic) in man. *Journal of Applied Physiology*, 21:1662–1664, 1966.

Pate, R.R., Goodyear, L., Dover, V., Dorociak, J., and McDaniel, J. Maximal oxygen deficit: A test of anaerobic capacity. *Medicine and Science in Sports and Exercise*, 15:121, 1983 (abstract).

Recommended Readings

AAHPER Youth Fitness Test Manual. Washington, D.C.: AAHPER Publications, 1976.

AAHPERD Health Related Physical Fitness Test Manual. Reston, Virginia: AAHPERD Publications, 1980.

Burke, E.J. (Ed.). *Toward an Understanding of Human Performance*. Ithaca, New York: Mouvement Publications, 1980.

Falls, H.B., Baylor A.M., and Dishman, R.K. *Essentials of Fitness*. Philadelphia: Saunders College Publishing, 1980.

Fleishman, E.A. *The Structure and Measurement of Physical Fitness*. Englewood Cliffs, New Jersey: Prentice-Hall, Inc., 1964.

Thomas, V. *Science and Sport*. Boston: Little, Brown and Co., 1970.

Wilmore, J.H. *Training for Sport and Activity*. 2nd ed. Boston: Allyn and Bacon, Inc., 1982.

Training might be defined as systematic participation in exercise for the purpose of increasing physical functional capacity and exercise tolerance. In the athletic setting the ultimate purpose of training is to enhance sports performance. In this chapter we present specific information regarding the techniques that can be used to improve the athlete's status in each of the components of athletic fitness. The major portion of this chapter is dedicated to the description of specific training activities. However, it is crucial that these individual training methods be combined in a complementary fashion so that an optimal overall training regimen results. Consequently, we begin this chapter with a discussion of the general principles upon which all athletic conditioning programs should be based.

Principles of Training

Successful athletic conditioning programs consist of a series of training techniques, each of which has been proven to be physiologically effective. However, in designing training programs the coach must consider the interactions among individual training procedures and must consider the training process in relation to the athlete's overall life situation. Optimal training programs are those that are conducted in accordance with certain general principles. These principles, if applied conscientiously, allow the coach to customize training techniques so as to best meet the needs of individual athletes. Also, these principles serve as guidelines in long-term planning and can provide a basis for modifying training programs when unexpected circumstances arise. The general principles of training discussed in this section constitute the foundation upon which all successful exercise training programs are constructed.

Training Methods: The Tools of the Trade*

22

*Portions of this chapter are adapted from Pate, R.R. Principles of training. In *The Injured Athlete.* Edited by D. Kulund. Philadelphia: J. B. Lipincott Co., 1982.

Overload

The most basic principle of training is *overload*. It is well established that most physiological systems are capable of adapting to functional demands that exceed those encountered in normal, daily life. In large part, training consists of systematically exposing selected physiological systems to intensities of work or function that exceed those to which the system is already adapted. A key, however, is to avoid *excessive* overload, since physiological systems are unable to adapt to stresses that are too extreme. Later in this chapter we describe exercise regimens that appropriately overload the physiological systems that determine athletic fitness.

Consistency

There is no substitute for consistency in a training program. Successful athletes, almost without exception, adhere to a training regimen with extreme regularity for several or more years. Most physiological systems require exposure to overloading activities three or more times per week. However, it should be noted that the preferred frequency of training depends on the season, the individual athlete, the athletic activity, and the specific component of fitness. Thus, a particular athlete might train 12 times per week during certain phases of the year and only three times per week at other stages; and he/she might participate in endurance training six times per week and resistance training (e.g., weight lifting) three times per week.

Specificity

The effects of training are highly specific. They are specific to the particular physiological system overloaded, to the particular muscle groups utilized, and indeed to the particular muscle fibers recruited to perform the work (Fox et al. 1975; Pate et al. 1978). There is no single training technique that can produce any and all desired outcomes; commercial advertizing claims to that effect should be rejected as fallacious.

Since performance in most sports depends on the development of several physical fitness components (see Table 21.3), most training programs should include several types of exercise, and in many cases several modifications of each specific technique. For instance, the swimmer's training program might consist of a complex combination of swimming activities using various strokes, intensities, and durations. In addition, the swimmer might participate in stretching exercises for flexibility and resistance exercises to develop muscular strength and muscular endurance.

Progression

Successful training programs plan for a steady rate of progression over a long period of time. If an athlete is to continue to improve over several years of participation, his/her training program must progress so that the appropriate physiological systems continue to be overloaded. However, at the same time, it is important to note that too rapid an incrementation of the training stress can lead to exhaustion and impaired performance. Coaches must design training programs that continue to challenge the athlete but avoid excessive overload.

Individuality

No two persons look exactly alike and no two persons are exactly alike physiologically. Consequently, no two athletes should be expected to respond in exactly the same fashion to a particular training regimen. Factors such as age, sex, maturity, current fitness level, years of training, body size, body type, and psychological characteristics should be considered by the coach in designing each athlete's training regimen. In many athletic situations absolute individualization of training programs may be impractical. When this is the case, the coach should strive for individualization by homogeneously grouping athletes. Coaches must remember that successful teams are composed of successful individual athletes; therefore the optimal training program is that which best fits the needs of each individual team member.

State of Training

An athlete's response to a training program depends greatly on his/her fitness level at the onset of the program. As a general rule of thumb, beginners respond best to moderate doses of training. These moderate amounts of exercise are sufficient to generate positive physiological adaptations but are not so demanding as to cause long-term fatigue. Athletes who are already well trained usually thrive on an exercise regimen that would exhaust the beginner. Indeed, initially well trained athletes may require very demanding programs in order to overload the physiological systems and attain a higher fitness level. In most athletic settings, coaches are well advised to design separate training programs for "rookies" and "veterans."

Periodization

Periodization refers to the tendency for athletic performance to vary in a cyclic fashion over time. Few athletes are able to sustain a peak performance level for more than a few weeks; thus it is important for training and competitive schedules to be structured so that peak performances are attained at the desired time. Intense training and competition tend to bring athletes to optimal performance levels. The key of course is to avoid attaining this level too early in the competitive season. Ideally, the training program should build to a maximum intensity one half to two thirds of the way through the season, so that peak performances are achieved during the championship competitions at season's end. At the conclusion of a season a recovery phase should be planned.

During this period the athlete should train less frequently and less intensely than during the competitive season. This planned recovery period allows the athlete to enter the next period of heavy training physiologically and psychologically refreshed.

Plateauing

In many athletes performance tends to improve incrementally rather than in a smooth, steady fashion. The athlete may spend weeks, months, or even years in performance plateaus. This can lead to considerable frustration and requires patience on the part of athletes and coaches. If all concerned are certain that the training program has been properly incremented, that illness is not a factor, and that the athlete has not attained his/her ultimate performance potential, the athlete should persevere and maintain confidence that a substantial improvement could occur at any time. In some cases an improvement in performance may require an ideal competitive environment and such situations arise very infrequently.

Stress

Stress has been defined by Hans Selye, the famous stress researcher, as the body's nonspecific response to external stressors (Selye 1956). When the body is exposed to extreme stressors for extended periods of time the so-called "stress syndrome" is elicited, which may lead to a stage of exhaustion that is typified by fatigue, illness, and injury. Coaches must recognize that strenuous training represents a significant stressor that, if combined with other physical or psychological stressors, can induce a stage of exhaustion known as "staleness" or "peaking-out" in the athlete; of course this is not compatible with optimal training or performance. Prevention of stress-induced exhaustion can be accomplished by designing properly individualized training programs, by carefully observing the athlete for signs of fatigue (e.g., upper respiratory illness, bloodshot eyes, loss of concentration), and by reducing the training load if the athlete encounters other unavoidable stressors (e.g., school exams, personal conflicts, change in environment). Sensitive coaches can prevent most stress-related illnesses in their athletes. On the other hand, those programs that adopt a ruthless "survival of the fittest" philosophy can expect to lose many athletes to preventable illness and injury.

Competitive Stress

Competition is physiologically and psychologically more stressful than training and too frequent competitions pose great risk to the athlete. Athletes who compete too frequently are particularly prone to the stress-related difficulties mentioned previously. Since the many sporting activities vary greatly in their physical demands, it is not possible to draw a broad generalization concerning the optimal frequency of competition. However, it does seem fair to conclude that the more physically demanding the activity, the less frequently one should engage in competition. Contrasting examples are baseball players and marathon runners. Baseball players, excepting pitchers, are generally able to function well when competing as frequently as four to five times per week. Marathon runners seldom compete at the full marathon distance (26.2 miles) more than two to three times per year.

Muscular Strength
Principles of Strength Training

All successful approaches to strength training have one key factor in common: They significantly *overload* the active muscle groups. Strength gains result when a muscle is repeatedly stimulated to generate a level of force that exceeds that to which it is well accustomed. Many different techniques can be used to effectively overload muscles. These methods differ principally in the nature of the external resis-

tance against which the muscular force is applied. The external resistance determines the type of muscular contraction that is performed (i.e., isotonic, isometric, or isokinetic). The specific training techniques also vary markedly in the type and expense of equipment required. While there may be benefits associated with some of the more costly types of strength training equipment, coaches should bear in mind that any method that significantly overloads the muscles can be expected to improve muscular strength.

The principles of progression and specificity apply very importantly to strength training. If the goal of a program is development of optimal strength, the external resistances must be regularly incremented so as to ensure that the muscles are continually overloaded. This principle, termed "progressive resistance," is a central feature of strength training programs that experience long-term success (O'Shea 1979). The principle of specificity applies to strength training in several different ways. First, strength improves significantly only in those muscles that are active and overloaded in the training process. Therefore, comprehensive strength training programs must use multiple exercises to ensure that all important muscle groups are trained. Second, research has shown that strength gains are somewhat specific to the type of muscle contraction used in training (Clarke 1973). Thus, for example, isometric training is most effective in improving isometric strength and less effective in improving isotonic and isokinetic strength. This suggests that the athlete should train using a type of contraction that mimics as closely as possible the type of contractions that will be used in competition. Also, strength gains are related to the speed of muscle contraction employed in training. Frequently, in athletics the goal is to apply high levels of force at peak speed (i.e., develop optimal power). Consequently, it is recommended that athletes in power-related activities perform at least some of their strength training using resistances that can be moved rapidly.

Many strength training experts are now recommending that athletes use high resistance-slow speed contractions in the off-season and preseason but employ some lower resistance-high speed contractions immediately prior to and during the competitive season.

Isotonic Training Techniques

The most common approaches to strength training employ isotonic muscle contractions. Isotonic exercises usually involve moving an external resistance, such as a barbell, through a complete joint range of motion. With these exercises the external resistance (i.e., weight of the barbell) remains constant but the force generated by the muscles varies with the angle of the joint(s) that the muscles cross. In general, with isotonic contractions the muscles generate peak force only when the joint angle is in its least mechanically advantageous position. For example, in performing the two-arm curl, the biceps muscles are called upon to generate peak force only when the elbow joints are fully extended. As the elbow is flexed its mechanical advantage increases and the level of force required of the biceps muscles is reduced. Also, with most isotonic exercises the muscles work at peak force only during the concentric (i.e., shortening) phase of the movement. During the eccentric (i.e., lengthening) phase, a smaller percentage of the muscle's peak force is demanded. Thus, with the two-arm curl the biceps muscles generate peak force only when contracting concentrically with the elbow joints extended. Despite these limitations, isotonic exercises do develop strength and have been very successfully implemented in many athletic settings.

Two general approaches to isotonic training are in wide usage. *Free weights* (barbells and dumbbells) are relatively inexpensive and are advocated by those who feel that there are benefits associated with the need to balance the free weight as it is moved. *Supported weight systems* (e.g., Universal Gym) are safer than free weights because the weight is held within a rack that prevents it from falling on the lifter. However, the supported weight systems are significantly more expensive than free weights.

Regardless of the type of weight moved the same fundamental training techniques are recommended for all isotonic strength programs. Figure 22.1 presents isotonic exercises than can be used to train each of the major muscle groups. Extensive research (Clarke 1973) indicates that optimal rates of strength gain result when a particular isotonic exercise is performed as follows:

Establish resistance so that exhaustion occurs with five to six repetitions (five to six repetition maximum).

Three training sessions per week (alternate days).

Perform three sets of each exercise per session.

In each set perform as many repetitions as possible.

Many modifications of this fundamental approach to isotonic training have been used with success. The most important factor seems to be the relative resistance against which the muscles work. Regardless of the specific protocol established, weights should be selected so that exhaustion occurs with a relatively small number of repetitions (i.e., ten or less). Optimal strength gains do not result when relatively light weights are moved a large number of times.

Other Strength Training Techniques

Isokinetic Strength Training. In recent years various isokinetic and quasi-isokinetic training procedures have come into wide usage among athletes. Isokinetic muscle contractions are performed at a constant rate of joint movement and involve work against an external resistance that varies as the joint moves through its range of motion. During an isokinetic contraction the muscle can exert maximal force throughout the movement. Isokinetic strength training requires the use of special devices. The Cybex Isokinetic Dynamometer mentioned in Chapter 21 provides a true isokinetic resistance. However, the Cybex apparatus is used principally for strength testing and for therapeutic exercise in the physical therapy setting. Far more common in the athletic setting are Nautilus machines that allow quasi-isokinetic contractions to be performed. Nautilus machines employ a cam system to vary external resistance as a joint moves through its range of motion.

The principles for isokinetic strength training are essentially the same as for isotonic contractions. That is, it is recommended that a given muscle group be trained three alternating days per week and that resistance be established so that exhaustion occurs with five to six repetitions. The manufacturers of Nautilus equipment suggest that only one set of each exercise should be performed at each training session. However, the validity of this recommendation has not be clearly established.

Isometric Strength Training. Strength can be improved with repeated, forceful isometric contractions. Available research indicates that an optimal approach involves daily performance of eight to ten maximal contractions, each of which is sustained for five to six seconds (Mueller and Rohmert 1963). A major disadvantage of isometric strength training involves joint angle specificity in strength gain. Strength gains occur principally at the position held during the contraction and are substantially less at other joint angles. Consequently, when isometric training is used in the athletic setting it is typically employed in conjunction with isotonic and/or isokinetic procedures.

Calisthenic Exercises. Traditional calisthenic exercises (e.g., push-ups, pull-ups, sit-ups) can be used to develop muscular strength. Calisthenic exercises involve isotonic muscle contractions in which the resistance is provided by all or part of the body weight. In most athletes, calisthenic exercises represent a less than optimal approach to strength training, since body weight may not provide the recommended overloading resistance (i.e., that which causes exhaustion after five to six repetitions). However, calisthenics are very useful with beginners and are easily implemented with large groups of athletes.

Physiological Adaptations to Strength Training

Muscular strength improves in response to resistance exercise owing to adaptations in the trained muscles and in the nervous system that controls the muscles. The primary muscular adaptation is *hypertrophy,* an increase in the size of the muscles. Muscular hypertrophy results from an increased diameter of the muscle fibers (Goldberg et al. 1975). The number of muscle fibers is apparently unaffected by normal training. Development of muscular hypertrophy is associated with maintenance of increased numbers of the contractile protein filaments, actin and myosin (see Chapter 15).

In addition, muscular strength is increased through a nervous system adaptation that allows the athlete to recruit an increased number of motor units at one time. This may result from a "learning" process situated in the motor cortex of the brain or may reflect an increased force threshold for activation of Golgi tendon organs. These sensory receptors initiate the inverse myotatic reflex that limits the muscle's potential for force generation (see Chapter 15). The nervous system adaptations to strength training are at least as important as the muscle-based hypertrophic adaptation. The nervous adaptation helps explain why strength gains are so specific to the type of training that is performed.

Appropriate training can generate rapid and substantial increases in muscular strength. Controlled studies have shown that previously untrained participants can expect a 10 to 25% increase in strength with six to eight weeks of training. Greater gains can be obtained with more prolonged training. Available evidence

Figure 22.1 Isotonic strength training exercises. *(A)* Upright rowing. *(B)* Military press. *(C)* Bench press. *(D)* Leg curl. *(E)* Hack squat. *(F)* Knee extension. *(G)* Heel raise.

suggests that strength gains can be retained with less frequent training than was required to generate the initial gain. However, if training is discontinued substantial strength is lost within four to five weeks. This suggests that athletes should continue to strength train during their competitive season but may do so as infrequently as once per week and effectively retain strength that was developed during a preseason three-day-per-week program.

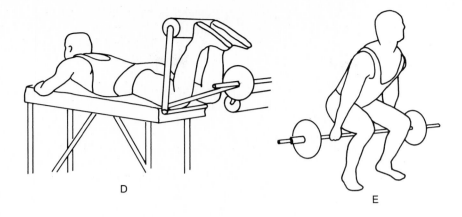

D

E

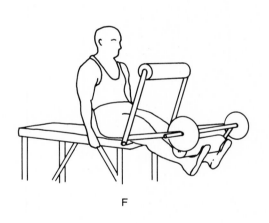

F

G

Muscular Endurance

As was discussed in Chapter 21, muscular endurance is largely determined by and is highly related to muscular strength. Consequently, the techniques for development of muscular endurance are very similar to those used to increase strength. In training for increased muscular endurance resistive exercise should be used in a manner that is fundamentally the same as that described in the previous section of this chapter. However, for isotonic and isokinetic techniques lower resistance and higher numbers of repetitions should be performed. For example, resistance should be set at approximately the ten-RM (repetition maximum) level rather than the five- to six-RM range recommended for development of strength alone. In development of isometric endurance, forceful contractions should be sustained for ten to twenty seconds or longer.

Anaerobic Power and Speed

Anaerobic power and speed are heavily dependent on genetically established factors such as muscle fiber type (see Chapters 15 and 21). However, anaerobic power and speed can be increased by increasing muscular strength and by improving the mechanical efficiency (skill) of movement. The techniques for increasing strength were discussed earlier in this chapter. In striving to increase anaerobic power, strength training should be focused on the muscle groups that are most involved in the particular athletic activity. For example, for power movements such as sprinting and jumping strength should be developed in the propulsive muscles of the lower limb (i.e., extensor muscles of the hip and knee joints and the plantar flexors of the ankle joint).

Principles of athletic skill enhancement were discussed in Chapters 7 and 13. The reader is referred to those chapters for techniques that can be employed in improving the efficiency of power movements. Since sprint running and jumping play key roles in many athletic activities, coaches should become particularly familiar with these movement skills. Extensive discussions of training procedures for improvement of sprint running and jumping are provided in several references (Dintiman 1964; Hay 1978; Luttgens and Wells 1982).

Anaerobic Capacity
Principles of Training for Anaerobic Capacity

Anaerobic capacity is determined by the extent to which an athlete is capable of providing ATP (adenosine triphosphate) energy via the anaerobic glycolytic system (see Chapters 16 and 21). This system is most important and limiting during very high-intensity exercise that lasts for 45 seconds to five minutes. Relatively little controlled research has been directed toward identifying optimal training techniques for enhancement of anaerobic capacity. However, some evidence indicates that anaerobic capacity can be increased with repeated performances of high-intensity exercise (Gollnick et al. 1972).

Logic would suggest that the anaerobic glycolytic system should respond to training that places a high demand on this system. The glycolytic system is utilized whenever energy is expended at a rate that exceeds the aerobic power and in an amount that exceeds the capacity of the ATP-CP (creatine phosphate) system. These conditions are met with exercise bouts that are at least one to two minutes in duration and demand that energy be expended at a rate greater than the maximal aerobic power.

Training Techniques

Although data are lacking, an extensive base of practical experience indicates that anaerobic capacity can be improved with high-intensity interval training. Interval training involves periods of high-intensity exercise that are alternated with active recovery periods. To develop the anaerobic capacity the exercise periods should last at least one minute and should be performed at an intensity that leads to a substantial accumulation of lactic acid in the skeletal muscles and blood. Since a high level of muscle lactic acid is associated with fatigue, the athlete can be certain that the anaerobic capacity has been taxed if he/she is significantly fatigued at the end of each work interval. In this context, the recovery period should be of sufficient length to insure a nearly complete clearance of lactic acid from the muscle. This can usually be accomplished with five to ten minutes of light exercise.

An example of an anaerobic capacity training session for an 800-meter track and field specialist is as follows:

Warm-up. Thirty minutes of light jogging, striding, and stretching.

Training session. Four repetitions of a 600-meter run at a pace moderately slower than race pace (duration = 1:15 to 1:50) with ten minutes of light jogging between repetitions.

Cool-down. Thirty minutes of light jogging and stretching.

Comparable sessions could be designed for middle distance cyclists, ice skaters, and swimmers.

Cardiorespiratory Endurance Principles of Training the Aerobic System

Improvements in cardiorespiratory endurance are obtained primarily through increases in maximal aerobic power ($\dot{V}O_2$max) and anaerobic threshold. However, in some activities, such as swimming, substantial improvements in efficiency are possible. In designing endurance training programs coaches should specify the mode, frequency, duration, and intensity of exercise (Pollock 1978). This section provides guidelines for designating each of these components of a cardiorespiratory endurance training program.

Modes of Exercise. Numerous specific forms of aerobic exercise can be utilized to generate improvements in cardiorespiratory endurance. All proper aerobic training activities increase the body's rate of aerobic metabolism ($\dot{V}O_2$), increase the heart rate, *and* allow these increases to be sustained for extended periods of time. The primary aerobic activities (see Table 22.1) include those that allow the metabolic and cardiorespiratory functions to be increased to a particular predetermined level and maintained at that level throughout the duration of the activity. Secondary aerobic activities, which include many of the popular recreational games

Table 22.1: Modes of Aerobic Exercise

Primary Aerobic Activities	Secondary Aerobic Activities
Running/Jogging	Handball
Swimming	Basketball
Cycling	Racquetball
Ice skating	Rope skipping
Cross country skiing	Aerobic dance

and sports, cause a more intermittent elevation of the cardiorespiratory functions and are less easily regulated in terms of work intensity. Primary aerobic activities generate a training effect in less time than the secondary activities and are preferred when very high levels of cardiorespiratory endurance are sought. However, many persons find the secondary aerobic activities to be more enjoyable, and of course enjoyment can promote adherence to an exercise regimen. Also, secondary aerobic activities may be useful in maintaining aerobic fitness during the off-season. For a given athlete, the ideal aerobic activity is one that: (1) provides appropriate intensity, (2) is most similar to the activity for which he/she is training (principle of specificity), and (3) he/she is most likely to adhere to.

Frequency. Research has shown that in previously sedentary beginners improvements in cardiorespiratory fitness can be generated with as few as two training sessions per week. Beginners improve at close to the optimal rate with three sessions per week (nonconsecutive days). However, in some athletes daily training sessions may be required just to maintain an already high capacity for endurance work. In activities such as distance running and swimming many athletes train twice per day. While the advantages of twice-per-day training sessions have not been clearly documented, it is apparent that a high frequency of training contributes to a high exercise caloric expenditure. It seems likely that the continually improving world standards in endurance activities are at least in part due to the increasing amount of energy expended in training by today's world class athletes. The optimal training frequency for a given athlete is a function of his/her current fitness level, the relative importance of aerobic function in the particular activity for which he/she is training, and individual tolerance for training stress. As a general rule, three sessions per week should be considered a minimum. Higher frequencies of training are recommended in sports that rely heavily on cardiorespiratory fitness.

Duration. The average individual can obtain an acceptable level of cardiorespiratory fitness by participating in a primary aerobic activity for a duration of 20 to 30 minutes, three times per week. Beginners may need to start with intermittent exercise, (e.g., alternate walking and jogging), building gradually to 20 to 30 minutes of continuous activity. Endurance athletes, of course, may require far greater durations of exercise to attain full potential. For instance, marathon runners and swimmers often train for durations as great as two to three hours. However, for most team sports regular participation by athletes in continuous aerobic activity of one half hour duration will lead to the development of a cardiorespiratory fitness level that is consistent with championship caliber performances.

Intensity. Intensity of exercise may be quantified in several ways; perhaps most convenient is heart rate. Heart rate and rate of aerobic energy expenditure ($\dot{V}O_2$) are linearly related. Since maximal heart rate and $\dot{V}O_2$max are attained at the same exercise work load, the percentage of $\dot{V}O_2$max may be accurately estimated from the percentage of maximum heart rate attained during exercise (see Figure 22.2). A substantial volume of research has led to the conclusion that the threshold for generation of an aerobic training effect is found at approximately 60% of the $\dot{V}O_2$max (American College of Sports Medicine 1980). This corresponds to about 70% of the maximum heart rate.

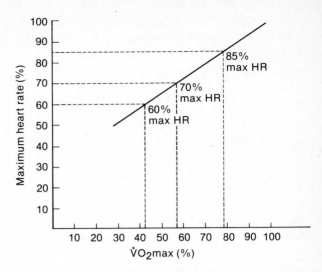

Figure 22.2 The relationship between percentage of $\dot{V}O_2$max and percentage of maximal heart rate is Linear and consistent for different persons. Therefore, percentage of $\dot{V}O_2$max can be accurately estimated from percentage of maximal heart rate.

One technique for estimating the heart rate that corresponds to the training threshold exercise intensity is provided by the following equation (Karvonen 1957):

$$THR = RHR + 0.6\,(MHR - RHR)$$

where

THR = Training Heart Rate (beats/min)
MHR = Maximum Heart Rate (beats/min)
RHR = Resting Heart Rate (beats/min)

The resting heart rate may be determined by counting the radial or carotid pulse while the individual is under resting conditions. Maximum heart rate can be estimated by the following equation:

$$MHR\ (beats/min) = 220 - age\ in\ years$$

It should be noted that the aforementioned technique designates a lower limit for training intensity. For trained individuals a somewhat higher intensity may be appropriate for sustained, continuous training. Very high-intensity training, at heart rates approaching maximum levels, is appropriate for some endurance athletes and for athletes striving to maximize both the maximal aerobic power and the anaerobic capacity.

Continuous Training

The most commonly utilized aerobic training technique involves continuous activity. With such activity the heart rate is increased to a predetermined level and maintained at that level for the duration of the training session. The guidelines presented in the previous section apply most directly to continuous training. The intensity of continuous activity may be varied from one training session to the next. The bulk of the training for endurance activities should consist of continuous activity of moderate intensity (70–80% MHR) and relatively long duration. This has been termed long slow distance (LSD) training. In addition, however, the endurance athlete will benefit from occasional bouts of higher intensity continuous training (85–90% MHR) of moderate duration. High-intensity continuous training may be particularly useful in increasing anaerobic threshold (Davis et al. 1979).

Interval Training

Interval training involves alternate periods of very intense work and periods of active recovery. Interval training is usually done in a controlled environment (e.g., a track or swimming pool) where the duration of work and recovery periods may be accurately timed. Interval training offers the benefit of allowing the athlete to perform, in total, a considerable volume of very high-intensity exercise in a single training session. For instance, an endurance swimmer might perform 20 repetitions of a 50-meter sprint with 30 seconds of recovery between each sprint; altogether the swimmer will

have covered 1000 meters at a very high intensity. Numerous approaches to interval training have been devised. While space does not allow description of each specific technique, it can be stated that all methods require that the following variables be designated in advance: duration and intensity of the work interval, duration and intensity of the recovery period, and the number of repetitions. Intensity of exercise can be designated in terms of heart rate. During the work interval, heart rate should increase to 75% or more of the maximum heart rate; during recovery it should fall to approximately 60% of the maximum heart rate. A detailed discussion of interval training has been provided by Fox and Mathews (1974).

Repetition training is a specialized form of interval training in which the work phase is near exhaustive and the recovery is almost complete. For instance, in a given repetition training session an 800-meter runner might perform two 600-meter runs at race pace with a full recovery intervening between the two.

Fartlek running involves a combination of techniques such that continuous, interval, and repetition training are utilized in a single session. The Swedish term *fartlek* means "speed play" and denotes that the various intensities of work are selected by the athlete on an unstructured basis. A typical fartlek running session might involve an hour of continuous running during which the athlete might run in random order several fast sprints, interval runs, and repetition runs. Since fartlek training can be conducted in an attractive environment (e.g., park or golf course), it represents a relatively enjoyable means for the athlete to participate in high-intensity exercise.

Adaptations to Endurance Training

Previously sedentary persons (beyond the age of puberty) who initiate an aerobic endurance training program as described in the preceding passages normally experience a 10 to

20% increase in maximal aerobic power. Even more profound improvements are frequently observed for anaerobic threshold that may increase as much as 100% (see Figure 22.3). Larger increases in $\dot{V}O_2$max and AT may occur with long-term training. The tangible results of these physiological adaptations are: (1) a marked increase in the absolute intensity of exercise that can be sustained for a extended period of time, (2) substantially reduced stress during performance of exercise at standard submaximal intensities, and (3) increased rate of recovery following vigorous exercise. These improvements in exercise tolerance and physical working capacity result from physiological adaptations in both the cardiorespiratory system and in the skeletal muscles that are trained.

The cardiorespiratory system adapts in such a way as to increase the system's oxygen transport capability (Scheuer and Tipton 1977). Table 22.2 lists the documented cardiorespiratory adaptations to endurance training. Of these

Table 22.2: Cardiorespiratory Adaptations to Aerobic Endurance Training

Maximal Exercise
  Increased stroke volume
  No change in heart rate
  Increased cardiac output
  Increased ventilation

Submaximal Exercise
  Increased stroke volume
  Decreased heart rate
  No change in cardiac output
  Decreased ventilation (at relatively high workloads)

adaptations the most important may be the increase in stroke volume of the heart. This increase in stroke volume is observed under all conditions: rest, submaximal exercise, and maximal exercise. During maximal exercise an increased stroke volume means that maximal cardiac output is also increased, since maximal heart rate is not substantially altered by training (remember, cardiac output = heart rate × stroke volume). This increase in maximal cardiac output is a major explanation for the increased $\dot{V}O_2$max that occurs with endurance training. Under conditions of rest and submaximal exercise heart rate decreases with endurance training, since the increased stroke volume allows a given cardiac output to be generated with fewer heart contractions per minute.

The skeletal muscle adaptations to endurance training complement those observed in the cardiorespiratory system. The muscle adaptations, listed in Table 22.3, enhance the oxidative metabolic capactiy of the trained tissues (Holloszy 1973). These adaptations allow the muscles to more effectively take up oxygen from the bloodstream and to utilize that oxygen in the aerobic metabolic process. This is particularly beneficial with high-intensity exercise that taxes the athlete's maximal aerobic power. Also, the muscles tend to become better adapted to performance of long duration, sub-

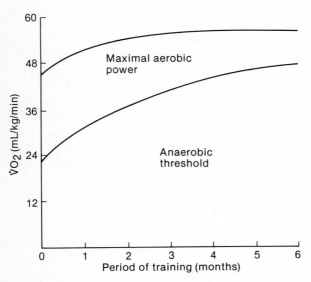

Figure 22.3 Aerobic endurance training typically increases maximal aerobic power ($\dot{V}O_2$max) by 10 to 20%. Anaerobic threshold may increase much more significantly.

Table 22.3: Skeletal Muscle Adaptations to Aerobic Endurance Training

Increased number and size of mitochondria
Increased activity of oxidative enzymes
Increased storage of glycogen and triglycerides
Increased myoglobin concentration
Increased capillarization
Decreased use of glycogen and increased use of fat during submaximal exercise

maximal exercise. With training the muscles develop an increased capacity for storage of the primary energy nutrients, glycogen (carbohydrate) and triglyceride (fat). Also, there is an enhanced potential for use of fat as an energy source and this adaptation tends to "spare" glycogen, which can be stored in rather limited amounts, even after training.

Flexibility
Principles of Flexibility Training

Relatively little controlled research has been directed toward identifying the optimal approaches to flexibility training. However, the extensive practical experience of athletes and coaches has identified several techniques that apparently are effective in increasing flexibility. All the methods for enhancement of flexibility involve stretching the muscles and other tissues that cross the joints.

A primary determinant of flexibility is muscle elasticity. Experience indicates that muscle elasticity is reduced following long periods of inactivity. Conversely, regular stretching of the muscles can apparently increase muscle elasticity. The aim of flexibility training is to maximize muscle elasticity (i.e., extensibility). "Flexibility exercises" accomplish this by stretching the muscles' connective tissues.

Ballistic Stretching

The most traditional approach to flexibility training is ballistic stretching. This procedure involves the application of force to a muscle so that it is rapidly and briefly stretched. Ballistic stretching often involves bouncing, jerky movements. Many of the common calisthenic activities, such as toe touches and trunk twists, are ballistic stretching exercises.

Ballistic stretching has been criticized on several grounds (deVries 1980). First, a rapid, forceful stretch is known to evoke the *stretch reflex*. This nervous reflex, which functions to protect a muscle from damage due to overstretching, causes a stretched muscle to contract. Contraction of a muscle is presumably counterproductive when the goal is to stretch it as completely as possible. Therefore, ballistic stretching may not allow for an optimal stretch of the muscles' connective tissues. Also, ballistic stretching may cause muscle soreness.

Nonetheless, it must be stated that no technique has been shown to be superior to ballistic stretching in terms of improving flexibility. Ballistic stretching may play a role in athletic fitness programs, but it should always be utilized carefully.

Static Stretching

Static stretching, long employed by yoga enthusiasts, has recently gained wide acceptance in athletic fitness programs. With static stretching the athlete assumes a position that applies a moderate stretch to a muscle group. The stretch is applied slowly and is maintained for ten seconds or more. It is important to note that the stretch should not be so extreme as to cause significant pain. Figure 22.4 demonstrates several common static stretching exercises.

Static stretching reportedly avoids some of the problems associated with ballistic stretching. A static stretch may evoke the *inverse myotatic reflex*, which after a brief delay causes a stretched muscle to relax and accommodate the stretched position. This relaxation should allow a more effective application of force to the muscle connective tissues. Experimental evidence suggests that static stretching is as effective (but

Figure 22.4 Static stretching exercises. (*A*) Standing toe touch. (*B*) Seated toe touch. (*C*) Calf stretch. (*D*) Overhead toe touch. From Fox, E. L., and Mathews, D. K. *Physiological Basis of Physical Education and Athletics.* 3rd ed. Philadelphia: Saunders College Publishing, 1982.

not more effective) than ballistic stretching in enhancing joint flexibility (deVries 1962). Also, deVries (1961) has shown that static stretching may help to prevent or relieve the delayed muscle soreness that may develop after vigorous exercise.

Passive Stretching

Passive stretching has been employed by physical therapists for many years to maintain joint flexibility in orthopedically handicapped and/or bedridden patients. In passive stretch-

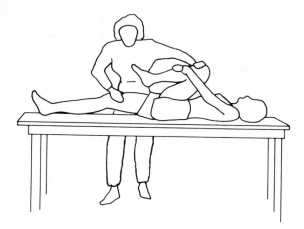

Figure 22.5 A passive stretch of the hamstring muscle group. The participant consciously relaxes the hamstring muscle group while the partner applies a force that stretches those muscles.

ing the participant consciously relaxes a muscle group while a partner (or therapist) applies a slow, static stretch to that muscle. This approach to stretching is being used with increasing frequency in the athletic setting. Figure 22.5 demonstrates a passive stretch of the hamstring muscle group.

An apparent benefit to passive stretching is its promotion of relaxation in the stretched muscle. This should allow the external force to be applied principally to the elastic component of the muscle. However, to date no studies have compared passive stretching to other techniques with regard to its long-term impact on joint flexibility in athletes.

Contraction-Relaxation Stretching

Contracting-relaxation stretching, also known as proprioceptive neuromuscular facilitation (PNF), attempts to take special advantage of the inverse myotatic reflex. The procedure involves performance of an active, forceful isometric contraction of a muscle, following which a partner applies a passive stretch to the same

muscle (see Figure 22.6). Theory suggests that this procedure promotes a full relaxation of the muscle during the stretching phase by powerfully stimulating the Golgi tendon organs during the contraction phase.

Experience indicates that the prior contraction of a muscle causes an acute increase in joint flexibility during a passive stretch. However, to our knowledge the long-term effects of contraction-relaxation stretching on flexibility in athletes has not been evaluated through controlled research. Nonetheless, this procedure is coming into common usage among athletes in certain sports (e.g., gymnastics, diving) and would seem to warrant further investigation by sports scientists.

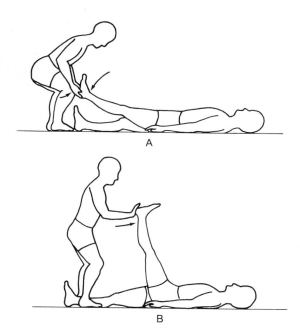

Figure 22.6 A contraction-relaxation stretch of the hamstring muscle group. (A) The participant performs a forceful isometric contraction of the hamstring musculature against a resistance provided by the partner. (B) The participant relaxes the hamstring musculature while the partner stretches that muscle group.

Body Composition
Principles of Modifying Body Composition

As was discussed in Chapters 18 and 21, body weight and body composition are determined by complex sets of genetic and behavioral factors. In an individual athlete body composition varies with long-term changes in caloric balance. Weight is gained when caloric intake chronically exceeds caloric expenditure; weight is lost when the reverse situation exists.

An athlete's body weight is largely a function of his/her overall stature (i.e., height) and body type. Both of these variables are determined principally by genetic factors. Therefore, behavioral traits such as dietary and exercise habits can modify body weight only within the limits imposed by inherited characteristics. Likewise, body composition (% fat) tends to vary only within the range established by the athlete's genetic endowment. Therefore, efforts to modify an athlete's body weight and body composition should be undertaken with the knowledge that in most cases massive changes are not biologically feasible.

Nonetheless, coaches do encounter many athletes in whom body weight and/or body composition are modifiable and whose performances would be enhanced by appropriate changes in these variables. In these cases, the goal should be to achieve the desired alteration in a manner that avoids negative side effects in terms of both health and athletic performance. Some athletes can benefit from an increased body weight; in other athletes a loss of fat is appropriate. In the following passages we describe safe and effective methods for achieving these body composition changes.

Fat Loss Techniques

Coaches often encounter athletes who feel that they should "lose weight." This belief is particularly prevalent in endurance activities but is common in many sports. Likewise, many coaches tend to feel, on the basis of intuition, that an athlete's performance would be enhanced if he/she "lost weight." The decision as to whether or not an athlete should lose weight should be based on an objective measure of body composition. Using the methods and standards presented in Chapter 21 the coach or trainer should measure the athlete's % fat. If the athlete's % fat exceeds the level associated with optimal performance in the specific sport, then a loss of weight would be appropriate. *Ideally, the loss of weight should be entirely fat. Seldom is a loss of lean weight desirable for either health or athletic performance.* After measuring the athlete's % fat and establishing a desired % fat goal, the following equation can be employed to compute the athlete's desired body weight:

$$\text{desired weight} = \frac{(100 - \text{initial \% fat}) \times \text{initial weight}}{100 - \text{desired \% fat}}$$

This equation assumes that the weight loss is achieved with no change in lean weight. This should be the goal, although it may not always be entirely possible. The likelihood of achieving this goal will be greatly enhanced if the fat loss is achieved through a program that: (1) includes vigorous exercise as a means of increasing caloric expenditure, and (2) avoids a severe restriction of caloric intake (McArdle et al. 1981).

A pound of body fat is equivalent to approximately 3500 kilocalories (kcal) of energy. Therefore, in order to lose a pound of fat an athlete must accumulate a caloric deficit of 3500 kcal. It is important to note that this deficit need not be accumulated over any particular period of time. In most cases fat loss programs are most effective when the loss of weight is achieved gradually. Most experts recommend that fat be lost at a rate not exceeding 1 to 2 lb per week. If we assume that the goal is a loss of 10 lb in ten weeks, the athlete would need to implement a program that causes a 3500-kcal deficit per week. This could be achieved by: (1) increasing caloric expenditure by 3500 kcal per week, (2) decreasing caloric intake by 3500 kcal per week, or (3) increasing caloric expenditure and decreasing caloric intake so that the net deficit is 3500 kcal per week.

The first option, which involves only an increase in caloric expenditures, can be achieved in athletes who are not already engaged in endurance training. However, this may require an increase in exercise training that is so great as to violate the principle of progression (see page 297). For example, an athlete expends approximately 100 kcal of energy for each mile of running. Therefore, to expend an extra 3500 kcal per week the athlete would need to increase his/her exercise activity by the equivalent of 35 miles of running per week. This may not be feasible for some athletes and may not be wise in others.

The second approach to fat loss involves a significant restriction of caloric intake. *This approach is seldom recommended in athletes.* Severe caloric restriction places the athlete at risk for development of nutritional deficiencies and may deprive the athlete of the food energy (particularly carbohydrate) needed to support vigorous training and competition. Also, it should be noted that severe caloric restriction is associated with a substantial loss of lean weight and this is usually undesirable in athletes.

In many cases, the optimal approach to fat loss in athletes involves combining an increased caloric expenditure with a moderate decrease in caloric intake (Zuti and Golding 1976). With athletes who initially have a normal caloric intake a moderate reduction in caloric intake (e.g., 200–300 kcal per day) can be achieved without compromising nutritional status. By increasing the caloric expenditure through additional exercise the athlete can insure that the weight lost will be almost entirely fat. The combination of increased exercise and

modest dietary restriction can generate a relatively rapid fat loss (e.g., 1 lb per week) without demanding that the athlete adopt a highly stressful behavior change.

Tables 22.4 and 22.5 provide information regarding the caloric value of common foods and forms of exercise. These data may be used by

Table 22.4: Caloric Values of Selected Food Items

	Kilocalories
Breads and Cereals	
White bread, 1 slice	64
Whole wheat bread, 1 slice	65
Corn muffin	180
Saltine cracker	14
Raisin bran, 1 cup	200
Wheat flakes, 1 cup	108
Cooked wheat cereal, 1 cup	128
Fruits and Vegetables	
Canned peaches, ½ cup	127
Applesauce, ½ cup	105
Frozen strawberries, ½ cup	140
Raw apple	75
Raw orange	64
Orange juice, 6 oz.	90
Canned green beans, ½ cup	23
Boiled potato	80
Raw carrot	20
Meat and Fish	
Broiled hamburger, 3 oz.	245
Pork chop, 3.5 oz.	260
Fried ocean perch	195
Shrimp, 3 oz.	100
Meat loaf, 2.7 oz.	240
Dairy Products	
Milk, whole, 1 cup	160
Milk, skim, 1 cup	90
Raw egg	75
Butter, 0.5 oz.	100
Margarine, 0.5 oz.	100
Cheddar cheese, 1 oz.	115
Pastries and Snacks	
Vanilla ice cream, 1 cup	275
Chocolate bar, 1 oz.	152
Peanuts, dry roasted, 1 oz.	170
Popcorn, 1 cup	39
Potato chips, 1 oz.	156
Chocolate chip cookie	50
Apple pie, 1 slice	180

Table 22.5: Caloric Equivalents of Selected Exercise Activities

Sport or Activity	Kilocalories Expended per Minute (kcal/min) of Activity
Climbing	10.7–13.2
Cycling 5.5 mph	4.5
9.4 mph	7.0
13.1 mph	11.1
Dancing	3.3–7.7
Football	8.9
Golf	5.0
Gymnastics	
Balancing	2.5
Abdominal exercises	3.0
Trunk bending	3.5
Arm swinging, hopping	6.5
Rowing 51 str/min	4.1
87 str/min	7.0
97 str/min	11.2
Running	
Short distance	13.3–16.6
Cross-country	10.6
Tennis	7.1
Skating (fast)	11.5
Skiing, moderate speed	10.8–15.9
Uphill, maximum speed	18.6
Squash	10.2
Swimming	
Breaststroke	11.0
Backstroke	11.5
Crawl (55 yd/min)	14.0
Wrestling	14.2

From The American Association for Health, Physical Education, and Recreation: *Nutrition for the Athlete.* Washington, D.C.: AAHPER Publications, 1971.

the coach in devising a fat loss program that is safe, effective, and customized for the individual athlete.

Weight Gain Techniques

In some sports optimal performance may demand that the athlete manifest a high body weight. Examples would be shot putters in track and field and linemen in football. Consequently, the coach may encounter athletes in whom performance would be enhanced by a gain in body weight. *In almost all cases a weight gain is most beneficial to performance if it comes in the form of lean weight.* Thus, the principal goal of weight gain regimens is to add lean muscle mass.

Athletes can gain lean weight by adopting programs that meet two fundamental criteria: (1) a positive caloric balance must be maintained (i.e., caloric intake exceeds caloric expenditure), and (2) a comprehensive resistive exercise program should be implemented. In athletes it is neither feasible nor advisable to attain a positive caloric balance by reducing caloric expenditure. Therefore, this criterion must be met by increasing caloric intake. Only a modest increase in caloric intake is needed and there is no requirement that a disproportionate amount of foods high in protein be ingested. However, the athlete should be certain that his/her diet contains an adequate portion of protein (i.e., 10–15% of total calories). The resistive exercise program should follow the procedures discussed earlier in this chapter for strength training programs. Since hypertrophy is specific to the muscles trained, resistance training should be performed with all the major muscles groups in the body.

Weight Loss Myths

Contemporary American society is burdened by several widely held misconceptions regarding methods for weight loss. Regretably, some of these myths have infiltrated certain athletic groups. Coaches should take steps to ensure that their athletes know the facts about modifying body composition. Specifically, the following three misconceptions should be laid to rest.

1. *Body fat can be lost through procedures that cause heavy sweating.* Sweating causes a transient reduction of body water and therefore a temporary decrease in body weight. Sweating *per se* does not decrease fat weight

nor does it permanently decrease body weight. Water lost through sweating is quickly replaced as fluid is ingested. Therefore, athletes should not attempt to modify body composition through procedures such as sauna baths, steam baths, or wearing of rubber/plastic suits during exercise. The latter practice is particularly dangerous because it markedly restricts evaporative heat loss and places the athlete at increased risk of heat illness. Rubber or plastic suits have no place in athletic conditioning programs.

2. *Body fat can be lost rapidly and permanently through severe restriction of caloric intake.* Many "crash diet" plans have been foisted upon the public in recent years. Most of these diet plans are based on the assumption that fat weight can be lost permanently by markedly reducing caloric intake for a brief period and then returning to a normal dietary pattern after the desired fat loss has been attained. Theoretically, this technique could be successful; however in actual practice it seldom results in a *permanent* weight loss. Crash diets cannot be maintained in the long term. Following crash dieting participants usually return to the same habits that caused the initial fat gain, and therefore the fat tends to return. Also, as noted previously, crash diets are unsound nutritionally and cause a substantial loss of lean weight. In the first few days of crash dieting the participant may experience a "dramatic" weight loss. *This early loss of weight is not primarily fat.* This reflects only the degradation of muscle and liver glycogen and the elimination of the water that is stored with the glycogen. With depletion of muscle glycogen the athlete may tend to feel very sluggish when exercising. Consequently, for many reasons, crash diets are not recommended for athletes.

3. *Fat can be lost from specific body areas ("spot reduction") by exercising the muscles in that region.* So-called "spot reduction" of fat cannot be achieved through any technique short of surgery. Exercise can bring about a loss of body fat. However, the fat that is metabolized in offsetting an increased caloric expenditure tends to be mobilized from all the adipose tissues around the body. Therefore, there is no advantage in exercising only the musculature in a specific part of the body. Of course, topically applied ointments, vibrators, and massage are useless procedures when it comes to losing body fat.

Special Problem: Weight Loss in Wrestlers

One of the most nagging problems in sports medicine concerns the use of extreme weight loss techniques by wrestlers who seek to "make weight." Wrestlers compete in weight classifications and normally are required to "weigh-in" a few hours prior to competition. An alarmingly common practice involves a combination of fluid deprivation and accelerated fluid loss during the 24 to 48 hours prior to competition. This procedure can cause a rapid and substantial weight loss, but it also is associated with reduced physical performance capacities (Ribisl 1974). In addition, in immature athletes there is considerable concern that repeated binges of dehydration and chronic maintenance of a very low % body fat may impair growth and development.

The issue of weight loss in wrestlers has been studied extensively by Dr. Charles Tipton and his colleagues at the University of Iowa (Tipton and Tcheng 1970). The findings of Tipton and others have led the American College of Sports Medicine to issue a position stand on the problem of weight loss in wrestlers, the key elements of which are presented in Table 22.6.

Designing Training Sessions
Sequencing of Training Techniques

Most athletic conditioning sessions should include several types of exercise, each selected to enhance a specific fitness component. In organizing individual conditioning sessions

Table 22.6: American College of Sports Medicine Position Stand on Weight Loss in Wrestlers

It is the position of the American College of Sports Medicine that the potential health hazards created by the procedures used to "make weight" by wrestlers can be eliminated if state and national organizations will:

1. Assess the body composition of each wrestler several weeks in advance of the competitive season. Individuals with a fat content less than five percent of their certified body weight should receive medical clearance before being allowed to compete.
2. Emphasize the fact that the daily caloric requirements of wrestlers should be obtained from a balanced diet and determined on the basis of age, body surface area, growth and physical activity levels. The minimal caloric needs of wrestlers in high schools and colleges will range from 1200 to 2400 Kcal/day; therefore, it is the responsibility of coaches, school officials, physicians and parents to discourage wrestlers from securing less than their minimal needs without prior medical approval.
3. Discourage the practice of fluid deprivation and dehydration. This can be accomplished by:
   a. Educating the coaches and wrestlers on the physiological consequences and medical complications that can occur as a result of these practices.
   b. Prohibiting the single or combined use of rubber suits, steam rooms, hot boxes, saunas, laxatives, and diuretics to "make weight."
   c. Scheduling weigh-ins just prior to competition.
   d. Scheduling more official weigh-ins between team matches.
4. Permit more participants/team to compete in those weight classes (119–145 pounds) which have the highest percentages of wrestlers certified for competition.
5. Standardize regulations concerning the eligibility rules at championship tournaments so that individuals can only participate in those weight classes in which they had the highest frequencies of matches throughout the season.
6. Encourage local and county organizations to systematically collect data on the hydration state of wrestlers and its relationship to growth and development.

coaches should take care to ensure that the various activities are sequenced in a complementary fashion. No single organizational pattern is best for all sports and there is no research evidence to indicate that a particular sequence provides optimal physiological benefits. Nonetheless, it is possible to provide some guidance on this issue.

In general, it seems appropriate to begin a conditioning session with a warm-up, the details of which are discussed in the following section. After warming-up the athlete should proceed to the exercise activity that develops the fitness component that is most critical to performance in his/her sport. For example, power/strength athletes (e.g., most team sports, weight events in track) should perform resistance exercise first, whereas endurance athletes should perform their endurance training first. Later in the session activities should be performed that address less critical fitness components.

Many coaches and athletes employ a so-called "hard-easy" pattern in the design of training programs (Bowerman 1974). This procedure involves alternating days of relatively intense, demanding training with days in which the training is much lighter. Physiologically this technique has considerable merit, since it increases the likelihood that the athlete will recover fully after vigorous training and thereby minimize the risk of overtraining. With the hard-easy pattern athletes can focus on the fitness component of primary concern on the "hard days" and train for the less critical fitness components on the "easy days." For example, middle distance swimmers might perform very demanding endurance swim training on Mondays, Wednesdays, and Fridays. On the alternate days they might swim for a shorter period of time and at lower intensity, thereby leaving adequate time and energy for strength and flexibility training activities.

Warm-up and Cool-down

Warm-up. Warm-up is a physiologically sound practice that has become a widely accepted feature of athletic conditioning programs and precompetition regimens. Warm-up entails performance of light to moderate intensity exercise prior to a higher intensity exercise bout. Warm-up exercise benefits performance largely because it increases the temperature of the active muscles (Bergh and Ekblom 1979). This increase in muscle temperature allows the muscle to contract and relax more quickly. Warm-up also facilitates a release of oxygen from hemoglobin and elevates the rate of oxygen consumption so that anaerobic energy demand is reduced at the onset of vigorous exercise (i.e., lower oxygen deficit). In addition, many athletic trainers feel that proper warm-up can reduce the risks of developing musculotendinous injury and muscle soreness. An effective warm-up can be obtained with ten to 15 minutes of moderate-intensity aerobic activity. For example, the athlete might jog at a pace that elevates the heart rate to approximately 60% of its maximum. This dose of activity is sufficient to elevate muscle temperature but should not cause fatigue. This aerobic exercise should be supplemented with a brief bout of flexibility exercises. Prior to a strength training session it may be appropriate to perform one submaximal set of each training exercise using a relatively low resistance. In skill dependent sports it is efficient to combine warm-up exercise with relevant skill practice. For example, the soccer player might warm-up by practicing dribbling and ball control skills while jogging continuously around the perimeter of the field.

Cool-down. As was discussed in Chapters 16 and 17 vigorous exercise markedly increases the rate of muscle metabolism and the levels of the cardiorespiratory functions. With cessation of exercise the metabolic rate and cardiorespiratory functions fall rapidly back toward their resting levels, despite the fact that a high concentration of lactic acid may still be present in the muscle and blood. Clearance of lactic acid and overall recovery can be facilitated by continuing to exercise at a moderate intensity (Belcastro and Bonen 1975). Also, simple logic suggests that there is merit in allowing the bodily functions to return gradually to resting levels

following heavy exercise. Therefore, it is recommended that athletes "cool-down" by engaging in ten to 15 minutes of light, aerobic exercise following a demanding training session of competition. It is recommended that the cool-down routine include a brief battery of static stretching exercises, since they may tend to prevent delayed muscle soreness.

Circuit Training

Circuit training is a form of exercise that involves performing a series of different exercises in rapid succession. Many forms of circuit training have been utilized successfully in various athletic settings. Circuits can be constructed using virtually all modes of exercise and can be designed to emphasize one or more of the major fitness components. For example, a circuit designed to develop muscular endurance and flexibility might consist of a sequence of five calisthenic muscular endurance exercises (e.g., push-ups, sit-ups) alternated with five static stretching exercises. Athletes might be instructed to spend two minutes at each "exercise station" and to recover for 30 seconds between stations.

Circuit Weight Training is an application of circuit training that is worthy of special mention. Circuit weight training, as typically used in athletic and adult fitness situations, involves performance of a series of isotonic or isokinetic resistance exercises. Usually, the resistances are established so that a relatively large number of repetitions (e.g., 30–40) can be performed at each station. The athlete exercises for approximately one minute at each station and recovers for 15 to 30 seconds between stations. This approach to circuit training has been promoted by certain commercial interests as exercise that can improve several fitness components. Specifically, it has been suggested that circuit weight training can simultaneously increase muscular strength, muscular endurance, and cardiorespiratory endurance. These claims appear to be somewhat overstated. Available research evidence indicates that circuit weight training does improve each of the aforementioned fitness components but does so less effectively than programs that utilize the specific guidelines presented earlier in this chapter (Gettman et al. 1978; Wilmore et al. 1978). For example, circuit weight training can increase cardiorespiratory endurance, measured as maximal aerobic power, but not to the degree attained with standard aerobic exercise training techniques. Nonetheless, circuit weight training may be useful when the goal is attainment of acceptable (though not optimal) levels of performance in several fitness components.

Summary

Athletic fitness can be best developed with conditioning programs that combine proper individual exercise techniques in a manner that is consistent with several established principles of training. These principles include overload, consistency, specificity, progression, individuality, initial training state, periodization, plateauing, and attention to stress.

The major components of athletic fitness can be enhanced as follows:

Muscular strength. Isotonic or isokinetic resistance exercise performed three days per week, three sets of five to six repetitions of each exercise with resistance established at the five- six-RM level.

Muscular endurance. Similar techniques as used for muscular strength but with resistance set at the ten-RM level.

Aerobic Power and Speed. Increase muscular strength in the relevant muscle groups and improve mechanical efficiency (skill) of specific power movements.

Anaerobic capacity. Regular high-intensity interval training with the work interval of one to two minutes duration and recovery intervals of five to ten minutes duration.

Cardiorespiratory endurance. Primary aerobic exercise performed at least three days per week for 30 minutes per session at an intensity demanding a heart rate of 70 to 85% of maximum.

Flexibility. Static, passive, and/or contraction-relaxation stretching exercises performed at least three days per week ten to 30 minutes per session.

Body Composition. Lose body fat by combining moderate restriction of caloric intake with increased caloric expenditure through aerobic exercise; add lean weight by moderately increasing caloric intake and implementing a comprehensive resistive exercise program.

References

Amercian College of Sports Medicine. *Guidelines for Graded Exercise Testing and Exercise Prescription,* 2nd ed. Philadelphia: Lea & Febiger, 1980.

Belcastro, A.N., and Bonen, A. Lactic acid removal rates during controlled and uncontrolled recovery exercise. *Journal of Applied Physiology,* 39:932–936, 1975.

Bergh, U., and Ekblom, B. Physical performance and peak aerobic power at different body temperatures. *Journal of Applied Physiology,* 46:885–889, 1979.

Bowerman, W.J. *Coaching Track and Field.* Boston: Houghton Mifflin Co., 1974.

Clarke, D.H. Adaptations in strength and muscular endurance resulting from exercise. In *Exercise and Sport Sciences Reviews.* Vol. 1. Edited by J.H. Wilmore. New York: Academic Press, 1973.

Davis, J.A., Frank, M.H., Whipp, B.J., and Wasserman, J. Anaerobic threshold alterations caused by endurance training in middle-aged men. *Journal of Applied Physiology: Respiratory, Environmental and Exercise Physiology,* 46:1039–1046, 1979.

deVries, H.A. Electromyographic observation of the effects of static stretching upon muscular distress. *Research Quarterly,* 32:468–79, 1961.

deVries, H.A. Evaluation of static stretching procedures for improvement of flexibility. *Research Quarterly,* 12:381–89, 1962.

deVries, H.A. *Physiology of Exercise for Physical Education and Athletics.* 3rd ed. Dubuque, Iowa: William C. Brown Co., 1980.

Dintiman, G.B. Effects of various training programs on running speed. *Research Quarterly,* 35:456–463, 1964.

Fox, E.L., and Mathews, D.K. *Interval Training-Conditioning for Sports and General Fitness.* Philadelphia: W.B. Saunders Co., 1974.

Fox, E.L., McKenzie, D., and Cohen, K. Specificity of training: metabolic and circulatory responses. *Medicine and Science in Sports*, 7:83, 1975.

Gettman, L.R., Ayres, J.J., Pollock, M.L., and Jackson, A. The effect of circuit weight training on strength, cardiorespiratory function, and body composition of adult men. *Medicine and Science in Sports*, 10:171–176, 1978.

Goldberg, A., Etlinger, J., Goldspink, D., and Jablecki, C. Mechanism of work-induced hypertrophy of skeletal muscle. *Medicine and Science in Sports*, 7:185–198, 1975.

Gollnick, P., Armstrong, R., Saubert, C., Pickl, K., and Saltin, B. Enzyme activity and fiber composition in skeletal muscle of untrained and trained men. *Journal of Applied Physiology*, 33:312–319, 1972.

Hay, J.F. *The Biomechanics of Sports Techniques*. 2nd ed. Englewood Cliffs, New Jersey: Prentice-Hall, Inc., 1978.

Holloszy, J.O. Biochemical adaptations to exercise: Aerobic metabolism. In *Exercise and Sport Sciences Reviews*. Vol. 1. Edited by J.H. Wilmore. New York: Academic Press, 1973.

Karvonen, M., Kentala, E., and Mustala, O. The effects of training on heart rate. A longitudinal study. *Amer. Med. Exper. Biol. Fenn.* 35:307–315, 1957.

Luttgens, K., and Wells, K.F. *Kinesiology*. 7th ed. Philadelphia: Saunders College Publishing, 1982.

McArdle, W.D., Katch, F.I., and Katch, V.L. *Exercise Physiology: Energy, Nutrition and Human Performance*. Philadelphia: Lea & Febiger, 1981.

Mueller, E.A., and Rohmert, W. Die geschwindigkeit der muskelkraft zunahne vei isometrischen training. *Int. Z. Angew. Physiol.* 19:403–419, 1963.

O'Shea, J.P. *Scientific Principles and Methods of Strength Fitness*. 2nd ed. Reading, Massachusetts: Addison-Wesley Publishing Co., Inc., 1979.

Pate, R.R., Hughes, D., Chandler, J.V., and Ratliffe, L. Effects of arm training on retention of training effects derived from leg training. *Medicine and Science in Sports*, 10:71–74, 1978.

Pollock, M.L. How much exercise is enough? *Physician and Sportsmedicine*, 6:50–60, 1978.

Ribisl, P. When wrestlers shed pounds quickly. *Physician and Sportsmedicine*, 2(7):30–35, 1974.

Scheuer, J., and Tipton, C. M. Cardiovascular adaptions to training. *Annual Review of Physiology*, 39:221–251, 1977.

Selye, H. *The Stress of Life*. New York: McGraw-Hill Book Company, 1956.

Tipton, C. and Tcheng, T.K. Iowa wrestling study. *JAMA*, 214:1269–1274, 1970.

Wilmore, J.H., Parr, R.B., Girandola, R.N. et al. Physiological alterations consequent to circuit weight training. *Medicine and Science in Sports*, 10:79–84, 1978.

Zuti, W.B., and Golding, L.A. Comparing diet and exercise as weight reduction tools. *Physician and Sportsmedicine*, 4:49, 1976.

Recommended Reading

Anderson, B. *Stretching*. Bolinas, California: Shelter Publications, 1980.

Berger, R.A. *Applied Exercise Physiology*. Philadelphia: Lea & Febiger, 1982.

Burke, E.J. (Ed.). *Toward an Understanding of Human Performance*. 2nd ed. Ithaca, New York: Mouvement Publications, 1980.

Daniels, J., Fitts, R., and Sheehan, G. *Conditioning for Distance Running*. New York: John Wiley and Sons, 1978.

Lamb, D.R. *Physiology of Exercise, Responses and Adaptations*. New York: Macmillan Publishing Co., Inc., 1978.

Pate, R.R. Principles of training. In *The Injured Athlete*. Edited by D. Kulund. Philadelphia: J.B. Lippincott Co., 1982.

Shephard, R.J. *Endurance Fitness*. 2nd ed. Toronto: University of Toronto Press, 1977.

Wilmore, J.H. *Training for Sport and Activity*. 2nd ed. Boston: Allyn and Bacon, Inc., 1982.

Credit: University of Virginia Sports Information.

Training for Special Athletic Groups

23

At one time organized athletic competition was almost exclusively the domain of healthy, young adult males. That time is now past. In recent years we have witnessed a rapid and dramatic extension of opportunities for sports participation into all segments of society. The manifestations of this trend are many. Athletic programs for females have grown at a remarkable rate at all competitive levels. Youth sports programs have become highly organized and in some cases fiercely competitive. Sports programs for middle-aged and older adults have become commonplace. Most communities now offer athletic activities for physically and mentally handicapped persons. Truly, the world of sports has undergone an explosive expansion.

As the opportunities for sports participation have grown, so too has the demand for coaching services. Public schools, which at one time employed coaches only for high school boys, now routinely hire persons to work with girls' teams and with handicapped athletes. Community-based recreation specialists may well be called upon to direct youth sports programs and to lead athletic activities for senior citizens. Consequently, coaches must be prepared to design training programs that are appropriate for various distinct populations.

The general principles discussed in previous chapters of this book apply to athletes whether they be female or male, handicapped or able bodied, or old or young. However, the various athletic subgroups do have certain, specific characteristics that impact on athletic performance and that may affect responses to exercise training. It is essential that coaches understand and appreciate these unique traits. This chapter emphasizes the physiological factors that affect the sports participation of four special groups: females, young children, senior citizens, and the impaired or handicapped.

The Female Athlete

Only rarely in athletics do males and females compete directly against one another.

Sex-based segregation of sports programs is a tradition in athletics at essentially all competitive levels and in virtually all countries of the world. Undoubtedly, this tradition developed for a number of reasons, not all of which would be considered noble by present-day standards. The principal reason that the sexes continue to be segregated in sports today is that in most activities the performance standards for females and males are clearly different.

In most sports in which direct comparisons are possible the performance levels of males exceed those of females. These performance differences may in part reflect societal attitudes that traditionally have led a greater percentage of males than females to pursue competitive athletics. As the cultural barriers to sports participation have been removed, the performance levels of females have improved markedly. For example, between 1973 and 1983 the world's best marathon run for women improved from 2 hours 46 minutes to 2 hours 22 minutes. Over the same period the record for men improved only 20 seconds—from 2:08:33 to 2:08:13. The experience of women marathon runners has been repeated in many sporting activities. As more women have pursued serious training and competition, performance standards have improved dramatically.

Despite the dramatic increases in athletic participation by women, a performance difference between males and females has tended to persist. This suggests that at least part of the sex difference in athletic performance is related to genetically determined biological factors. Recent research in exercise physiology has tended to reinforce the conclusion that sex differences in certain fundamental anatomical and physiological variables explain many of the male-female differences in athletic performance.

Physiological Characteristics of Female Athletes

In most ways females respond to exercise in the same manner as do males. However, the sexes do differ in certain exercise-related anatomical and physiological factors. In terms of athletic performance, the most important physiological sex differences are in the areas of body size, body composition, and cardiovascular function.

Body Size and Muscular Strength. After about the age of 13 years males tend to be taller and heavier than females. At maturity the average male is 5 inches taller and 30 to 40 pounds heavier than the average female (Wilmore 1982). These differences in body size provide males with an obvious advantage in certain sports in which performance is directly related to height (e.g., basketball) and/or body mass (e.g., weight events in track and field). The greater weight of males is associated with a greater muscle mass, and consequently males tend to be stronger than females. Wilmore (1982) has reported that composite strength scores are 30 to 40% greater in males than in females. However, much of this difference is due to the female's markedly lower upper body strength. Leg strength tends to be nearly the same in females as males. Sex differences in strength are apparently due entirely to differences in the quantity not quality of muscle. Of course, strength is a key determinant of performance in all sports that involve application of force to external objects (e.g., contact sports, softball, discus throw). Strength is also a key determinant of anaerobic power (see Chapter 21). This difference in body weight and muscle mass probably explains much of the sex difference in performance in power-related sports activities.

Body Composition. During puberty sex-specific hormone functions cause males to develop an expanded muscle mass, whereas females tend to add adipose tissue. In young adults % body fat averages about 25% in females and 15% in males. This difference is due to the females' greater absolute fat weight and lower absolute lean weight. The sex difference in body composition is observed in athletes as well as nonathletes. While athletes of both sexes tend to be leaner than the sedentary population, female athletes are usually observed to be fatter than comparably trained males (Wells and Plowman 1983). Thus, the sex difference in body composition is apparently due, at least in part, to true sex-linked genetic factors.

The sex differences in body composition probably explain much of the male's margin of superiority in many athletic activities. In any activity that involves moving the body weight excessive fat tissue negatively affects performance. Fat tissue constitutes a mass that must be moved, and it therefore adds to the energy that must be expended during exercise. In whole-body power movements, such as jumping and sprinting, performance is related to the ratio between leg strength and total body weight. Excess fat tends to decrease this ratio and, therefore, negatively affects anaerobic power (expressed relative to body weight).

The same basic principle applies to endurance activities in which performance is highly related to $\dot{V}O_2max$, expressed relative to body weight (mL/kg/min). Fat contributes to the weight that must be moved during endurance exercise but does not contribute to the athlete's ability to consume oxygen. It has been noted that $\dot{V}O_2max$ values, *expressed relative to lean weight*, are nearly the same in highly trained males and females. However, this observation is of little significance in activities in which athletes are called upon to move their entire body weight. It does suggest that the performance of females should more closely approach those of males in supported-weight endurance activities such as cycling and swimming than in weight-bearing activities like running.

Cardiovascular Function. As was discussed in Chapters 17 and 21, performance of aerobic endurance activities is limited primarily by the oxygen transport capacity of the cardiovascular system. Available evidence suggests that the average female's potential for oxygen transport is lower than the average male's. Females manifest a lower blood hemoglobin concentration than males and they also tend to have a smaller heart even when heart size is expressed relative to body weight. A lower hemoglobin concentration is associated with a lower oxygen-carrying capacity in the blood and a smaller heart is associated with a smaller maximal stroke volume and maximal cardiac output.

Owing to her lower oxygen transport capability and greater % body fat, the female tends to demonstrate a weight-relative $\dot{V}O_2max$ value that is lower than that of her male counterpart. In nonathletic adults this difference in weight-relative $\dot{V}O_2max$ is about 20%. The difference is a bit narrower in highly trained athletes. For example, in world class endurance athletes (i.e., runners, cyclists, swimmers) $\dot{V}O_2max$ approximates 70 mL/kg/min in females and 80 mL/kg/min in males (Saltin and Astrand 1967).

Menstruation and Exercise

Menstruation and Athletic Performance. Between the ages of menarche (11–15 years) and menopause (40–55 years) the average female passes through a menstrual cycle every 28 days. The menstrual cycle is controlled by a series of hormones produced by the hypothalamus of the brain, the pituitary gland, and the ovaries. Each menstrual cycle is associated with the maturation of an ovum, the extrusion of that ovum from the ovary, and the preparation of the uterine wall for implantation of a fertilized ovum. If fertilization does not occur, the heavily vascularized lining of the uterus is sloughed off and menstrual bleeding occurs.

At one time it was generally assumed that a female athlete's potential for exercise performance was impaired during the menstrual period. However, several controlled studies and many anecdotal reports have led to a substantial qualification of this belief. Research has indicated that the physiological responses to exercise during the phases of the menstrual cycle vary considerably in different females. Available evidence suggests that most females should be able to train and compete normally throughout the menstrual cycle. However, some women experience fluid retention and abdominal cramps during the premenstrual and menstrual flow phases of the cycle. These athletes may require a reduced or modified training regimen during that time. If female athletes do not experience such difficulties, they should be encouraged to participate fully in athletic activities.

Athletic Amenorrhea

In recent years sports medicine specialists have expressed increasing concern about apparently high rates of secondary amenorrhea in certain athletic groups. This condition, which has been labeled "athletic amenorrhea," is characterized by the absence of menstruation in an athlete who has experienced menarche. Amenorrhea is usually associated with anovulation (i.e., failure of the ovary to release an ovum); consequently most amenorrheic athletes are infertile. Several studies have reported greater than normal incidences of amenorrhea in athletic groups such as distance runners, gymnasts, and ballet dancers (Dale et al. 1979; Feicht et al. 1978; Frish et al. 1980).

The causes of secondary amenorrhea in athletes are not well understood. It has been suggested that the condition may be triggered by a reduction in % fat (Frish and McArthur 1974); however, this hypothesis has not been supported by all the relevant studies. Wakat and coworkers (1982) observed normal reproductive hormonal functions in several amenorrheic distance runners, suggesting that the dysfunction was above the level of the hypothalamus in the brain. It is possible that secondary amenorrhea may be a response to the high levels of physical and psychological stress associated with athletic training and competition.

Whatever its cause, athletic amenorrhea is apparently a reversible condition that can be eliminated by a reduction in exercise load. Available evidence suggests that amenorrheic athletes who had normal menstrual cycles prior to initiation of heavy training tend to revert to normal menstrual patterns after cessation of heavy training.

Pregnancy and Exercise

Surveys of former highly competitive female athletes indicate that: (1) participation in sports has no long-term effect on fertility, and (2) athletes tend to have normal pregnancies and childbirth experiences. Concerns that athletic competition and vigorous exercise may injure the reproductive organs of females have no apparent basis in fact. The weight and size of the fetus will not allow most female athletes to continue serious training and competition beyond the first few months of a pregnancy. However, athletes and other active women should be encouraged to maintain a regular, moderate exercise program well into a pregnancy. Of course, this recommendation assumes that the supervising physician has not noted any specific contraindication to exercise.

The physiological and anatomical changes associated with the latter stages of pregnancy usually preclude successful participation in competitive athletics. However, many women have returned to competition after a pregnancy and have achieved personal best performances. Pregnancy need not signal the end of an athlete's career.

Training Responses in Females. With few exceptions females and males show similar physiological adaptations to exercise training. As a general rule, females and males who are exposed to the same training programs respond with comparable percentage increases in fitness levels. Of course, for most fitness components average males start from a higher level than average females. For example, available evidence suggests that females and males experience comparable increases in maximal aerobic power with aerobic endurance training (Massicotte et al. 1979).

Females also demonstrate substantial increases in strength with resistance exercise training (Wilmore 1974). However, in contrast to males, females tend to gain strength without developing a bulky musculature. This suggests that in females strength increases principally through nervous system adaptations rather than via muscular hypertrophy (see Chapter 22). Therefore, most females can participate in strength training without fear of experiencing a "masculinizing effect." The typical female's low level of the hormone testosterone probably explains this sex difference in the hypertrophic response of muscle to resistance training.

The Young Athlete

Sports programs for young children have been commonplace for many years. In the past most of these programs were conducted in a relatively low key manner and were focused principally on a few team activities such as baseball and basketball. However, in recent years many youth sports programs have become highly organized and fraught with competitive pressure. There has been a substantial expansion of organized programs in individual sports such as swimming, gymnastics, and track and field. At the same time contact team sports like ice hockey and football have experienced substantial growth. Most medical authorities would agree that children should be given every opportunity to participate in vigorous exercise. However, many exercise physiologists and sports medicine specialists have expressed concern about certain aspects of many youth sports programs. A detailed discussion of the impact of human development on athletic skill performance was presented in Chapter 13. This section addresses several of the physiological aspects of athletic participation in children.

Growth, Development, and Sports Performance

With few exceptions children are unable to match the athletic feats of adults. This is because the process of physical maturation is ac- companied by numerous physiological and anatomical changes that, taken *in toto*, have the effect of increasing the individual's capacity for vigorous exercise. A youngster's passage to physical maturity is usually conceptualized as involving two concurrent processes. These processes are known as *growth* and *development*. Growth refers strictly to an increase in body size. The term development, in this context, is defined as age-related changes in physiological functions that are independent of those explained by growth.

Effects of Growth and Development on Exercise Performance. The increase in body size that occurs during childhood is associated with increases in several exercise-related physiological functions. For example, increased height is associated with increases in the length of the body's long bones. Longer bones constitute longer "lever arms" (see Chapter 12) and greater mechanical advantage in the performance of many sports skills. As body weight increases so too does muscle mass. Since muscular strength is directly proportional to the cross-sectional area of the muscle, strength and strength-dependent athletic performances tend to increase progressively throughout the growth process.

Performance of endurance exercise improves as a result of both growth and developmental changes. Increased muscle mass and increased size of the cardiovascular and respiratory organs increases the child's capacity for consumption of oxygen. A developmental increase in blood hemoglobin concentration also contributes to the child's gradual increase in maximal aerobic power. This increase in $\dot{V}O_2$max is most notable when expressed simply as liters of oxygen consumed per minute. Little change in $\dot{V}O_2$max, expressed relative to body weight, is observed during childhood. Nonetheless, the child's ability to perform weight-bearing endurance exercise (e.g., running) does gradually improve. This improvement is apparently due principally to increases in overall work efficiency (i.e., reduced oxygen cost of activity) resulting from increased mechanical efficiency (Daniels and Oldridge 1971).

As a child's nervous system matures his/her coordination and motor control improve. These changes result in gradual increases in skill level and in the rate at which new athletic skills can be mastered. A complete discussion of the developmental influences on motor skill acquisition was presented in Chapter 13.

Effects of Exercise on Growth and Development. The impact of exercise on growth and development is not well understood. Extreme forms of weight-bearing exercise may cause early termination of bone growth and reduced height. However, the bulk of the evidence suggests that normal physical training has no effect on height (Malina 1979).

Some evidence suggests that prolonged strenuous training during childhood may positively affect development of body composition, bone mineralization, muscle size, and cardiorespiratory function (Malina 1979). However, the scientific support for these conclusions is skimpy. The scientific literature is severely lacking in longitudinal observations of the relationships between growth and development and physical activity in children. At the present time the fairest conclusions are that: (1) at least moderate amounts of exercise are needed to stimulate normal growth and development, (2) prolonged exposure to physical training may positively influence development of certain physiological systems, and (3) long-term participation in very extreme forms of physical exercise may negatively affect growth and development of the skeleton.

In some sports it has become common practice for athletes to begin heavy training at quite a young age. For example, youth programs in swimming, gymnastics, and tennis have become very intense and highly competitive. In these sports young athletes occasionally have achieved very high levels of competitive success (e.g., Olympic medals, national championships). This circumstance is much more common among females than males because of the earlier maturation of females and on account of the increased body fatness that accompanies puberty in females. At the present time there is no scientific evidence to suggest that this sort of early involvement in highly competitive sports carries a negative physiological effect. Nonetheless, coaches of athletes who achieve early success should be particularly sensitive to their physical and psychological needs.

In the vast majority of sports there is no apparent advantage to early specialization and heavy training. As was discussed in Chapter 13, too early specialization may have a negative impact on general development of fundamental movement patterns. Though our scientific knowledge is incomplete, experience suggests that the highest competitive levels are most frequently attained by athletes who initiate systematic physical training in adolescence or early adulthood.

Training the Young Athlete

Trainability. Research has shown that children are physiologically responsive to exercise training. However, for several reasons they may not be as responsive as young adults. Most young children naturally seem to lead lives that by adult standards are quite active. Therefore, in order to stimulate a training response with children it is usually necessary to apply a greater amount of exercise than with sedentary adults.

Also, training responsiveness may vary with a youngster's stage of development. Postpubescent adolescents are apparently more physiologically responsive to training than prepubescent children. It has been theorized that children who are experiencing rapid growth and development may be adapting physiologically at a peak rate. The added stimulus of moderate exercise training at this time may be relatively inconsequential. After the stage of puberty has been completed and the youngster's hormonal status has become more like that of an adult, responses to training tend to be of greater magnitude.

Precautions in Training Young Athletes. As a general rule, children are able to participate in vigorous exercise training with little risk to health. Nonetheless, sports medicine specialists have advised that certain precautions be taken in conducting sports and exercise programs for children. Most of the concern derives from the fact that the child's skeleton is immature and undergoing rapid growth. During this period the skeleton is vulnerable to injuries that if not properly diagnosed and treated can cause permanent damage.

The long bones of the body grow through the deposition of calcified bone tissue at specialized structures called epiphyses. These cartilaginous plates are located near each extremity of a long bone (see Chapter 10 and Figure 10.3). Since the epiphyseal plates are not calcified, they are structurally less stable than the rest of the bone. Consequently, these plates are prone to slippage and fracture. Epiphyses may be damaged by traumatic injury or by repetitive applications of force through a tendon that inserts nearby.

Epiphyseal injuries do not occur in a large percentage of young athletes. Nonetheless, such injuries can be precipitated by numerous types of athletic participation (Larson and McMahon 1966). For example, gymnasts who contact the ground in a straight-legged position can damage the epiphyses at the proximal end of the tibia. Pitchers in baseball have been known to damage an epiphysis at the distal end of the humerus. Epiphyseal fractures may occur with traumatic injuries in various sports such as football, ice hockey, and many others. Some concern has been expressed regarding the possibility that repetitive activity like distance running may negatively affect bone growth in the lower extremity. However, to date this suggestion has not been substantiated by scientific investigation.

Epiphyseal injuries appear to be the only unique health risk associated with athletic activity in children. Youngsters may experience the same traumatic injuries that occur in older adults. Likewise, as with older groups, a small percentage of children may have cardiovascular, respiratory, metabolic, or orthopedic impairments that limit their athletic participation. However, there is no evidence to suggest that vigorous exercise training causes cardiovascular, respiratory, metabolic, or nonepiphyseal orthopedic illnesses. To the contrary, most experts agree that regular exercise beneficially affects child growth and development.

Training Methods. Relatively few controlled exercise training studies have employed children as subjects. Consequently, our knowledge of the optimal training methods for children is rather incomplete. Available evidence suggests that, in general, the guidelines described in Chapters 21 and 22 can be safely and effectively applied to young athletes. However, scientific information and prevailing opinion in sports medicine suggest that the following recommendations should be heeded when training young athletes:

1. High resistance strength training should be approached with caution in children. Owing to the risk of epiphyseal injuries, most experts recommend that resistance training be pursued using relatively light weights and a relatively large number of repetitions (e.g., 15–20). Also, it should be recognized that training-stimulated strength gains are likely to be greater in older, more mature youngsters than in prepubescent children. Therefore, in young children strength training should be used sparingly and with limited expectations.

2. The more extreme forms of endurance training and competition should be avoided in children. Specifically, it seems unwise for immature youngsters to pursue extremely long-duration activities such as full marathon runs (American Academy of Pediatrics 1982). However, physiologically less stressful forms of endurance exercise seem entirely appropriate for most children.

3. Growing children should be discouraged

from adopting extreme measures to control or modify body weight and/or body composition. Specifically, low calorie diets and dehydration techniques should not be utilized by young athletes. Such practices are nutritionally unsound and may disrupt normal growth and developmental processes.

4. Competitions in certain sports should be organized in such a manner as to prevent excessive participation by individual athletes. Since some repetitive activities, such as pitching in baseball, can apparently cause epiphyseal injuries, rules should be instituted to restrict an individual's time of participation. For example, young baseball pitchers might be limited to three innings of pitching per game.

5. Great care should be taken in organizing contact sports programs for children. Rules should be instituted to minimize the risk of injury and these rules should be rigidly enforced. Properly fitted and mechanically sound protective equipment should be employed. In prepubescent children, contact sports should be modified to eliminate or markedly reduce forceful physical contact. For example, flag football might be substituted for tackle football.

6. Many sports medicine authorities believe that the physical well-being of young athletes is most likely to be threatened in sports programs that involve a high level of psychological stress. Of particular concern is parental pressure. In the absence of excessive pressure, children are unlikely to harm themselves in an athletic training situation. Consequently, efforts should be made to educate parents and other adults regarding the potential risks and benefits of sports participation for children. Youngsters may benefit from the discipline involved in athletic conditioning and from a modest level of competitive stress. But there is little to gain and much to lose when overzealous adults pressure young children to train and compete in an excessively stressful environment. *Youth*

sports should always be conducted with the young athlete's long-term well-being as the first priority.

The Older Athlete

The number of middle-aged and elderly athletes has grown markedly in recent years. Among professional athletes careers have been extended by lucrative financial rewards. The ranks of the older amateur athletes have swollen, in part, as a result of a reduced work week and proportionally increased leisure time. Highly competitive age group competitions are now common in tennis, swimming, track and field, road racing, cross-country skiing, and a vast array of team sports. This increased sports participation by older persons has raised numerous questions regarding the effects of aging on athletic performance and concerning the appropriate methods for training senior athletes. In this section, we endeavor to answer some of these questions.

Aging and Exercise Performance

Aging is associated with numerous changes in physiological functioning. In general, after the age of 30 most physiological systems manifest a gradual decline in functional capacity. Many of these systems directly affect exercise performance, and consequently most components of fitness and motor performance tend to decline with advancing age.

Skeletal Muscle Function. Through most of adulthood muscular strength decreases very slowly. After age 50 the rate of decline is increased, but even at age 60 muscular strength is maintained at 80 to 90% of its maximum value observed between the ages of 20 and 30 (Montoye and Lamphiear 1977). The age-related decline in muscular strength probably reflects both disuse and a true aging phenomenon. Animal studies have shown that aging is associated with a gradual decrease in the number of metabolically active muscle cells.

Cardiorespiratory Function. Heart function tends to decline steadily with advancing age. Maximal heart rate decreases approximately one beat per minute per year and may be estimated from the following equation:

maximum heart rate (beats/min)
$$= 220 - \text{age (years)}$$

Both resting and maximal exercise cardiac output decreases at the rate of about 1% per year. Thus, at age 60 maximal cardiac output equals about 75% of the value observed in 30 year olds. Also, vascular adaptations to changes in blood pressure are slower in older persons than in their younger counterparts.

Pulmonary function at rest and exercise declines with aging. This is due largely to a decrease in compliance of the thoracic wall. During exercise pulmonary diffusing capacity and efficiency of ventilation are reduced in older persons. Therefore, as compared with younger persons the elderly ventilate at a higher level at any given submaximal exercise work load.

Body Composition. Aging is associated with increases in body weight and absolute fat weight. Lean weight gradually decreases. Therefore, % body fat gradually increases with advancing age. As was discussed in Chapter 21, a high % fat adversely affects athletic performance in weight-bearing activities.

The loss of lean weight is principally due to losses of muscle tissue. While the decrease in lean weight may be partly reflective of a true aging phenomenon, increases in fat weight and total body weight would not seem to be biologically inevitable. Such changes are probably related to the decline in habitual physical activity that is associated with aging in contemporary American culture.

Physical Working Capacity. Maximal metabolic powers and capacities decrease with advancing age. Most clearly documented is the decline in maximal aerobic power ($\dot{V}O_2$max), which decreases by about 50% between the ages of 25 and 75 years (Hodgson and Buskirk 1977). This is apparently due to reduction in both the cardiorespiratory functional capacity and the oxidative capacity of skeletal muscle tissue.

Anaerobic power and capacity manifest age-related decreases. However, the causes of these declines are not well documented. Presumably, they are related to decreases in lean muscle mass and decreased muscle enzyme activities.

Characteristics of Older Athletes

There is no question that athletic performance and physical working capacity (PWC) tend to decline with advancing age. However, there is uncertainty regarding the extent to which these decreases in functional capacity reflect true aging phenomena. It is possible that an age-related decrease in PWC could be due in large part to reduction in habitual physical activity.

Cross-sectional and longitudinal studies of senior athletes and other regular exercisers indicate clearly that high levels of physical performance can be maintained well into older age. Studies of older athletes have consistently shown that these persons manifest physical fitness levels that match or exceed those of sedentary persons who are several decades younger. For example, Heath and coworkers (1981) observed a mean $\dot{V}O_2$max in excess of 58 mL/kg/min in male masters endurance athletes (mean ages = 59 years). Long-term follow-up studies of regular exercisers suggests that PWC declines in active persons but does so at a slower rate than in sedentary persons (Kasch and Wallace 1976).

Experience indicates that in most sports the highest levels of performance can be maintained well into the fourth decade of life. This seems particularly true in long-duration, endurance activities and in sports that rely principally on mastery of complex motor skills (e.g., golf, bowling, baseball). Even in power-dependent activities, such as football and basketball, many professional athletes are now extending their careers beyond age 40. Available physiological data suggest that this should be entirely possible for most athletes.

Training the Older Athlete

In designing conditioning programs for older athletes the principles discussed in Chapters 21 and 22 should be employed. Available research indicates clearly that older persons are physiologically trainable (Benestad 1965; deVries 1970). Indeed, they tend to manifest improvements in performance that are, percentagewise, about the same as observed with younger persons. Of course, the initial baseline for the elderly tends to be relatively low. Consequently, the absolute amount of improvement and final performance levels are lower in the elderly than in younger persons. Also, the training-induced rates of change in physical performance may be reduced in the elderly.

As was discussed in Chapter 21, training programs should focus on the fitness needs of the individual athlete and the physical demands of the particular sport. In applying this principle to senior athletes, the coach should recognize that older persons often have somewhat unique fitness requirements. In particular, older athletes should pay attention to maintenance of flexibility. With advancing age the body's connective tissues tend to lose extensibility. Consequently, the muscles become less flexible and joint range of motion is reduced. Such losses of flexibility negatively affect performance in many sports (see Chapter 21) and may place the older athlete at increased risk for musculotendinous injury. Thus, as athletes age their conditioning programs should dedicate increased effort to maintenance of good joint flexibility.

Precautions for the Older Athlete

In working with senior athletes coaches should bear in mind that advanced age is a risk factor for several health problems. Old age, in itself, is not a reason for persons to avoid or limit participation in vigorous exercise. However, several diseases and physiological impairments that may limit exercise tolerance are common in older persons.

Of particular concern are the cardiovascular diseases such as coronary heart disease (CHD). Old age is a principal risk factor for CHD. Since vigorous exercise may be dangerous for persons with advanced CHD, coaches should ensure that senior athletes are carefully screened for cardiovascular health status. A physician's clearance for participation in vigorous exercise should be obtained for previously sedentary persons over age 50. A graded exercise stress test, administered by properly trained personnel, is a particularly useful procedure for older persons who are beginning exercise programs. Regardless of the screening procedures employed, older persons should build very gradually into an exercise training program.

With advancing age, bone mineral content tends to decrease. This predisposes older persons to osteoporosis and bone fractures. Available research indicates that regular exercise helps to maintain the bone mineral content in older persons. Nonetheless, it seems wise to recommend that persons over age 60 avoid contact sports and other athletic activities that may cause traumatic injuries of the skeleton.

Finally, some evidence indicates that older persons are less tolerant of heat stress than younger persons. This suggests that senior athletes should take particular care to acclimatize themselves fully before competing in hot and/or humid conditions and to adhere to the other recommendations made in Chapter 19.

Impaired or Handicapped Athletes

Coaches often encounter individuals who because of physical or mental conditions are restricted in their ability to participate in athletics. Generally, these individuals may be categorized as *impaired* or *handicapped,* based on the nature of the modifications that must be made in the sports activity to allow the individual to successfully participate.

An *impaired athlete* is one who because of some organic or functional condition is limited in participating in some sports-related activities. The impaired performer can often be integrated into selected sports with slight modifications.

A *handicapped athlete*, however, is restricted from participation in the regular athletic program. Often, safety conditions preclude participation of both handicapped and nondisabled persons in the same athletic event. However, the handicapped performer can participate in sport-related activities that have been appropriately modified.

Coaches are frequently placed in the position of deciding whether or not a child can participate in a sport with his/her nonhandicapped peers. This decision should be made only after thorough investigation of the child's condition, consultation with medical personnel, and discussion with the child and his/her parents. Often, this decision is made more difficult because of the lack of specially adapted sports programs. This may leave the regular program as the only alternative. Successful integration of an impaired or handicapped athlete into the regular athletic program depends on factors such as the physical demands of the sport, level of competition, nature and extent of the organic or functional condition, and the child's emotional and psychological stability.

Impaired and handicapped children tend to mirror their nonhandicapped peers in their need for involvement in sports and competition. Historically, impaired and handicapped individuals have been denied participation in regular athletic programs by uninformed individuals. In many cases only very limited access to programs and facilities have been provided. These exclusions often were not based on any specific reason but rather on the assumption that impaired and handicapped persons cannot safely or successfully participate in sports.

These discriminatory practices have resulted in federal and state legislation that provides for equal opportunities for handicapped children to participate in programs that are similar to those provided to nonhandicapped children.

Legislative Mandates

Federal legislation ensures that impaired and handicapped individuals not be discriminated against in educational and recreational programming. Specifically, two comprehensive laws, PL 94-142, the Education For All Handicapped Children Act of 1975, and Section 504 of the Rehabilitation Act of 1973 (PL 93-112) ensure the rights of handicapped individuals. These laws have significantly influenced educational and recreational programs and encouraged a more humanistic treatment of the handicapped.

Section 504 of the Rehabilitation Act clearly indicates that handicapped individuals may not be excluded from participation or denied the benefits of any program offered to nonhandicapped children. This legislation further mandates that an impaired individual may not be denied access to regular athletic programs unless the condition significantly affects performance or places the participants at risk. If it is determined that the individual should not participate, then a substantially equal opportunity must be offered. Handicapped individuals who should not participate in regular sports programs but who could benefit from a modified or special program are entitled to such opportunities.

PL 94-142, the Education For All Handicapped Children Act, requires that equal educational opportunities be provided to all children. This includes participation in intramural and interscholastic activities. This legislation further requires that the programming be provided in the *least restrictive environment*. The law indicates that, to the maximum extent possible, all handicapped children should be allowed to participate with their nonhandicapped peers. No longer should the handicapped child automatically be placed in a special program. Such placement should occur only after a thorough assessment of the child's ability to safely and successfully participate in the regular program.

Although both of these federal laws affect only programs receiving federal assistance (primarily public schools and recreation programs), the moral implications influence athletic programming at all levels. The decision to deny the impaired or handicapped child the right to participate in an athletic program is one that must be carefully considered. Frequently, the individual who cannot participate in one sport because of an impairment can be directed to another activity in which different physical and mental demands will allow him/her to participate safely and successfully.

Integrating the Impaired Athlete into the Regular Athletic Program

The impaired athlete should be provided the opportunity to participate in the regular athletic program whenever possible. Frequently, this can be readily accomplished without substantial modifications to the activity. Usually, impaired athletes can be integrated more easily into individual sports than into team sports.

Traditionally, coaches have tended to limit the athletic participation of impaired persons because of concern over their physical safety. Although safety is a valid consideration, coaches should resist the tendency to be overly protective. Extreme precautions are often unneeded.

A great many disabled persons have successfully participated in a very wide range of sports. Archery, snow skiing, wrestling, and gymnastics are only a few of the activities in which impaired athletes have safely and successfully participated. In working with impaired athletes the coach should focus on the individual's abilities rather than his/her disabilities.

In most instances an impaired individual can and should be successfully integrated into the regular athletic program. A thorough knowledge of the athlete's impairment and medical history and a careful review of the individual's athletic ability allows the coach to properly assess the potential for successful integration into regular sports programs.

Specialized Athletic Programs for the Handicapped

In many instances a handicapping condition is so significant as to restrict an individual's participation in the regular athletic program. Handicapped athletes have the alternative of changing to a sport that requires different physical demands or to participate in specialized athletic programs modified to allow safe and successful competition. Handicapped athletics should be assisted in realistically evaluating their limitations and in selecting appropriate athletic alternatives.

In recent years, numerous organizations have been founded to provide sports opportunities for various handicapped populations (see Table 23.1). A popular program is the Special Olympics, sponsored by the Joseph P. Kennedy, Jr. Foundation, which provides mentally retarded persons with positive athletic experiences. Similarly, the United States Association of Blind Athletes (USABA), National BEEP Baseball Association (NBBA), National Wheelchair Basketball Association (NWBA), National Wheelchair Athletic Association (NWAA), and National Association of Sports for Cerebral Palsy (NASCP) have developed extensive programs for handicapped athletes. Each organization has developed a set of rules and guidelines to govern its sports competition. A challenging task faced by many of these groups is implementation of classification systems based on the extent of the athlete's handicap. This method of ability grouping enables participants to compete on an equitable basis by matching them against athletes who have a similar level of disability.

Although these programs are found throughout the United States, some handicapped athletes may not have direct access to them. Often, financial and other limitations restrict full im-

Table 23.1: Organizations for Handicapped Athletes

American Athletic Association of the Deaf, Inc.
2835 Hilliard Road
Richmond, Virginia 23228

American Blind Bowling Association
150 North Bellaire Avenue
Louisville, Kentucky 40206

American Wheelchair Bowling Association
2424 North Federal Highway
Suite 109
Boynton Beach, Florida 33435

Braille Sports Foundation
730 Hennepin Avenue, S.
Suite 301
Minneapolis, Minnesota 55403

Canadian Amputee Sports Association
18 Hale Drive
Georgetown, Ontario
Canada L7G4C2

Canadian Wheelchair Sports Association
333 River Road
Ottawa, Ontario
Canada K1L8B9

International Sports Organization for the Disabled
Stoke Mandeville Sports Stadium
Harvey Road
Aylesbury, Bucks
England

National Association of Sports for Cerebral Palsy
United CP Associates, Inc.
66 East 34th Street
New York, New York 10016

National Handicapped Sports and Recreation
4105 East Florida Avenue
Denver, Colorado 80222

National Wheelchair Athletic Association
40–24 62nd Street
Woodside, New York, 11377

National Wheelchair Basketball Association
110 Seaton Building
University of Kentucky
Lexington, Kentucky 40506

National Wheelchair Marathon
369 Elliott Street
Newton Upper Falls, Maryland 02164

National Wheelchair Softball Association
P.O. Box 737
Sioux Falls, South Dakota 57101

Ontario Wheelchair Sport Association
585 Tretheway Drive
Toronto, Ontario
Canada M6M 4B8

Special Olympics
Joseph P. Kennedy, Jr. Foundation
1701 K Street, N.W.
Washington, D.C.

Sports 'n Spokes
5201 North 19th Avenue
Suite 108
Phoenix, Arizona 85015

Telephone Pioneers of America
BEEP Ball Information
195 Broadway
New York, New York 10007

United States Association of Blind Athletes
55 West California Avenue
Beach Haven Park, New Jersey 08008

Wheelchair Sports Foundation
40–24 62nd Street
Woodside, New York 11377

plementation of these special athletic opportunities. In such instances the handicapped athlete's only alternative is to participate in an individualized sports activity within his/her limitation. Coaches have a responsibility to provide these individuals with as much support and guidance as possible.

Summary

Participation in competitive sports is now common in all segments of American society. Certain subgroups manifest physiological traits that alter their exercise tolerance and sports performance. Females, as compared with males, demonstrate lower levels of muscular strength, anaerobic power, and maximal aerobic power. These differences are due largely to sex-linked variations in body size, body composition, and cardiovascular function. In young athletes aging is associated with gradual increases in most aspects of exercise performance. These increases derive from increases in body size (i.e., growth) and from maturational changes (i.e., development). In older persons, aging brings reductions in exercise tolerance. However, older persons are physiologically responsive to training and senior athletes often demonstrate functional capacities that exceed those of younger, sedentary persons. Many sporting opportunities are now available to the impaired and the handicapped. In working with such athletes coaches should carefully assess the nature of each individual's impairment or handicap. Impaired or handicapped athletes should be provided with opportunities for sports participation that develop their full athletic potential.

References

American Academy of Pediatrics. Risks in long distance running for children. *News and Comment*, 33(6):11, 1982.

Benestad, A.M. Trainability of old men. *Acta Medica Scandinavica*, 178:321–327, 1965.

Dale, E., Gerlach, D.M., Martin, D.E., and Alexander, C.R. Physical fitness profiles and reproductive physiology of the female distance runners. *Physician and Sportsmedicine*, 7:83–95, 1979.

Daniels, J., and Oldridge, N. Changes in oxygen consumption in young boys during growth and running training. *Medicine and Science in Sports*, 3:161–165, 1971.

deVries, H.A. Physiological effects of an exercise training regimen upon men ages 52–88. *Journal of Gerontology*, 25:325–336, 1970.

Feicht, C.B., Johnson, T.S., Martin, B.J., Sparks, K.E., and Wagner, W.W. Secondary amenorrhea in athletes. *Lancet*, 2:1145–1146, 1978.

Frish, R.E., and McArthur, J.W. Menstrual cycles: Fatness as a determinant of minimum weight for height necessary for their maintenance or onset. *Science*, 185:949–951, 1974.

Frish, R.E., Wyshak, G., and Vincent, L. Delayed menarche and amenorrhea in ballet dancers. *New England Journal of Medicine*, 303:17–19, 1980.

Heath, G.W., Hagberg, J.M., Ehsami, A.A., and Holloszy, J.O. A physiological comparison of young and older endurance athletes. *Journal of Applied Physiology*, 51:634–640, 1981.

Hodgson, J.L., and Buskirk, E.R. Physical fitness and age: With emphasis on cardiovascular function in the elderly. *Journal of the American Geriatric Society*, 25:385–392, 1977.

Kasch, F.W., and Wallace, J.P. Physiological variables during 10 years of endurance training. *Medicine and Science in Sports*, 8:5–8, 1976.

Larson, R.C., and McMahan, R.O. The epiphyses and the childhood athlete. *JAMA*, 196:607–612, 1966.

Malina, R.M. The effects of exercise on specific tissues, dimensions, and functions during growth. *Studies in Physical Anthropology*, 5:21–52, 1979.

Massicotte, D.R., Avon, G., and Carrineau, G. Comparative effects of aerobic training on men and women. *J. Sports Medicine*, 19(1):23–32, 1979.

Montoye, H.J., and Lamphiear, D.E. Grip and arm strength in males and females, Age 10 to 69. *Research Quarterly*, 48:109–120, 1977.

Saltin, B., and Astrand, P.O. Maximal oxygen uptake in athletes. *Journal of Applied Physiology*, 23:353–358, 1967.

Wakat, D.K., Sweeney, K.A., and Rogol, A.D. Reproductive system function in women cross-country runners. *Medicine and Science in Sports*, 14:263–269, 1982.

Wells, C.L., and Plowman, S.A. Sexual differences in athletic performance: Biological or behavioral? *Physician and Sportsmedicine*, 11(8):52–63, 1983.

Wilmore, J.H. Alterations in strength, body composition and anthropometric measurements consequent to a 10-week weight training program. *Medicine and Science in Sports*, 6:133–138, 1974.

Wilmore, J.H. *Training for Sport and Physical Activity*. 2nd ed. Boston: Allyn and Bacon, Inc., 1982.

Recommended Readings

Albinson, J.G., and Andrew, G.M. (Eds.). *Child in Sport and Physical Activity*. Baltimore: University Park Press, 1976.

deVries, H.A. *Physiology of Exercise for Physical Education and Athletics*. 3rd ed. Dubuque, Iowa: William C. Brown Publishers, 1980.

Drinkwater, B.L. Physiological responses of women to exercise. In *Exercise and Sport Sciences Reviews*. Vol. I. Edited by J.H. Wilmore. New York: Academic Press, 1973.

Kalakian, L.H., and Eichstaedt, C.B. *Developmental/Adapted Physical Education: Making Ability Count.* Minneapolis: Burgess Publishing Co., 1982.

Seaman, J.A., and DePauw, K.P. *The New Adapted Physical Education: A Developmental Approach.* Palo Alto, California: Mayfield Publishing Co., 1982.

Shephard, R.J. *Physical Activity and Aging.* London: Croom Helm Ltd., 1978.

Sherrill, C. *Adapted Physical Education and Recreation: A Multidisciplinary Approach.* Dubuque, Iowa: William C. Brown Publishers, 1981.

Thomas, J.R. *Youth Sports Guide for Coaches and Parents.* Washington, D.C.: AAHPER Publications, 1977.

Note: Page numbers in *italics* indicate illustrations; those followed by (t) indicate tables.

Index